CATHOLIC SOCIAL THOUGHT:
TWILIGHT OR RENAISSANCE?

BIBLIOTHECA EPHEMERIDUM THEOLOGICARUM LOVANIENSIUM

CLVII

CATHOLIC SOCIAL THOUGHT
TWILIGHT OR RENAISSANCE?

EDITED BY

J.S. BOSWELL, F.P. McHUGH,
AND J. VERSTRAETEN

1425

LEUVEN
UNIVERSITY PRESS

UITGEVERIJ PEETERS
LEUVEN

2000

ISBN 90 5867 103 8 (Leuven University Press)
D/2001/1869/10
ISBN 90-429-0973-0 (Peeters Leuven)
ISBN 2-87723-549-1 (Peeters France)
D/2000/0602/179

Library of Congress Cataloging-in-Publication Data

Catholic social thought: twilight or renaissance? / edited by J.S. Boswell,
F.P. McHugh, and J. Verstraeten.
    p.cm -- (Bibliotheca Ephemeridum theologicarum Lovaniensium; 157)
English and French.
Based on a seminar held Apr. 11-14, 1999 in Cambridge, England.
Includes bibliographical references and index.
ISBN 2877235491
    1. Sociology, Christian (Catholic)--Congresses. 2. Christian ethics--Catho-
lic authors--Congresses. I. Boswell, Jonathan. II. McHugh, Francis P. III. Ver-
straeten, Johan. IV. Series.

BX1753.C383 2001
261.8'088'22--dc21   00-050211

Leuven University Press / Presses Universitaires de Louvain
Universitaire Pers Leuven
Blijde-Inkomststraat 5, B-3000 Leuven (Belgium)

© 2000 – Peeters, Bondgenotenlaan 153, B-3000 Leuven (Belgium)

PREFACE

The tasks of organising and pulling together the proceedings of an expert seminar on Catholic social thought are obviously complex and would not have been achieved without a lot of support and co-operation from many institutions and individuals.

First of all, the editors of this volume would like to acknowledge the indispensable help received from the staff of the Von Hügel Institute, particularly Dr Bernadette O'Keeffe, from the Master and Fellows of St Edmund's College, University of Cambridge, and from the Centre for Catholic Social Thought, Faculty of Theology, Katholieke Universiteit Leuven. Crucial financial assistance came from two sources, to which we are deeply indebted: the Porticus Foundation acted as intermediary in finding funds to support both the seminar in April 1999, from which this book has grown, and the preparation of the book itself, while the Tablet Trust funded a John Fisher Scholarship in Catholic Social Thought, held by Jonathan Boswell during 1998-99, largely related to the project. Also crucial was the issue of final publication. We were delighted that the book was accepted for inclusion in the *Bibliotheca Ephemeridum Theologicarum Lovaniensium* and would like to express our thanks to the general editor of the BETL series and to the publishers, Leuven University Press and Peeters, for their advice and efficient production.

The initial work was undertaken by a core team of Jonathan Boswell, Frank McHugh and Johan Verstraeten working in both Leuven and Cambridge, the scenes of some previous collaborative efforts going back several years. Together, we worked to identify potential contributors in a number of European countries. Selective reviews of many hundreds of relevant published sources were carried out, covering literature in six languages, and involving work in libraries in both universities, as well as in Paris. This phase of the work also included invaluable contributions by Ingeborg Gabriel of the University of Vienna, who helped over German sources and some general ideas for which we were most grateful. To a large extent, our efforts were complementary. Thus, Johan Verstraeten chaired the early "brain-storming" sessions which shaped our agenda, Jonathan Boswell prepared an outline paper as a background for the April 1999 seminar, and Frank McHugh largely organised this event.

A seminar was held in Cambridge, in 1999, April 11-14, under the title *Whose Ethics? Which Priorities? Catholic Social Thought in Transition*. Papers were contributed by seventeen participants, and these were subsequently developed to form nearly all the essay contributions to this volume. Details of the contributors are given in an appendix. We would like to thank them warmly for the huge amount of thought and hard work they put in. We are very grateful to John Coleman who, although he was not directly involved in the initial project, provides a careful evaluation of most of the strands in the book. Though not contributing directly to this collection, many participants in the seminar have added important influences through their contributions to discussion: Zenon Bankowski, Paul Dembinski, Irene Freudenschuss-Reichl, Henri Gagey, Robert Keen, Kees Klop, John Milbank, Matthias Nebel, Michael Naughton, James Sweeney and the late Rev Philip Bloy. To all of these we are grateful for their co-operation and support. We would also like to thank Charles Lynch and Philip Bonn for their help in organising and managing the day-to-day business of the seminar.

Chain reactions followed from the seminar, which proved as challenging and encouraging an experience for ourselves as for the other participants. A task force was set up by Johan Verstraeten, including Simona Beretta, Julie Clague, Linda Hogan and Walter Lesch, as well as the three editors, with the aim of carrying forward the project in several ways additional to the book, and with an eye to the longer-term. The onerous task of knitting together the disparate papers presented at the seminar was initiated in Leuven. Detailed textual editing of the papers, including correction, revision, consultation with authors and indexing was carried out in Cambridge, including much helpful advice and assistance on computer aspects from Yevgeny Khmel. Special tribute is due to Godelieve Ginneberge for her work both in the initial standardisation process, and in later formatting and standardising of footnotes and much final nuancing and adjustment for publication. Her skill, patience and assiduity at various stages have been invaluable.

In the case of some French contributors a decision was made, with their agreement, to simplify things by publishing their texts in their own language. This, we trust, should add to the European flavour of the collection.

Finally, the book owes much to the historic, artistic and scholarly contexts of our two universities. Both Leuven and Cambridge have proved stimulating backgrounds for our teamwork and co-operation, including many congenial discussions. More importantly, they have been seedbeds for the reflection, debate and larger network of friendships out of which this collection has grown, and which we hope will make a wider contribution, in the future, to the aims and commitments we share.

Jonathan BOSWELL
Frank MCHUGH
Johan VERSTRAETEN

CONTENTS

THE LAST 100 YEARS: TWO INTERPRETATIONS

SOURCES AND STRUCTURES

ENGAGEMENT WITH SECULAR DEBATE

INTRODUCTION

Neither in the current bubbling debate on political theory nor in the heated exchange of ideas on national and international politics does Catholic social thought make an effective entry on the public stage in our day. Externally, it is all too often ignored even by the "people of good will" appealed to in the papal encyclical *Centesimus annus*. Inside the Catholic Church it is more frequently neglected than vigorously adopted or put into action. Even among interested parties, it labours under a certain crisis of identity. On a wider canvas it finds itself in a vortex of challenges posed by liberal individualism and crude capitalism, by widespread social injustice and division in contemporary society, and by dominant currents of thought which, while sympathetic in some ways to Christian values, do not seem to want or need the sacred, the spiritual or the ecclesial.

The present volume contains eighteen essays by (mostly European) Catholic intellectuals, drawing on approaches ranging from public theology and social ethics, through political philosophy, political economy, history and sociology, to thinking about policy. The initiative behind the book came in the wake of a conference on official Catholic social teaching which had, typically of its *genre*, so focussed on the latter as virtually to ignore the *non*-official thinking which has also played a vital part in the tradition. By contrast, a keynote of our initiative was, and is, *"more than encyclicals"*. In order to consult other experts in the field and, at the same time, to break through the barrier of ignorance about Catholic social thought ("CathST") in each others' countries, a network of key academic personnel in Catholic social thought and social ethics was identified in most of the EU countries and questioned for their reaction to a position paper setting out the causes, nature and implications of the neglect of non-official Catholic social thought.

This led, after a year's preparatory work, to the seminar held in Cambridge in April 1999, entitled *Whose Ethics? Which Priorities? Catholic Social Thought in Transition*, the original *locus* for these essays. Those involved have sought to get away from a tradition of works on CathST which limit themselves to exposition, exegesis or discussion of the social encyclicals of the popes from Leo XIII's *Rerum novarum* to John Paul II's *Centesimus annus*, or the corpus of what is usually called Catholic social teaching ("CST"). Our cues are taken from parallel and long-standing but relatively neglected traditions of Catholic non-official social thinking, involving both groups and individuals: the traditions of von Ketteler, Scheler, Dehon, Sturzo, Maritain, Mounier, Lebret, Charles Plater, Leo O'Hea, John Ryan, John Courtney Murray, Dorothy Day, of the Christian trade unions and social circles, and, in more recent times, of the liberation and political theologians, and many others. Catholic non-official social thinking, hereafter labelled as "CNOST", frequently acted in the past as precursor, stimulator and developer of the official teaching. It still has an ability to connect with social, political and economic specifics in ways which go beyond the proper ambit of the social teaching. Indeed, a revival of CNOST, in the view of the contributors, is essential both for an effective Catholic intellectual presence in contemporary public debate and for a vigorous contribution by Catholics and the Church to remedying modern social problems.

Although some of the essayists imply unease about the seeming narrowness of an exclusive concentration on *Catholic* social thought, in defence of this singular perspective it must be said that it is not adopted in any un-ecumenical spirit but in the interests of a deepening of a tradition which does possess some critical mass both historically and conceptually, and which, it is hoped, may thus be made available to others in a richer form. More general approaches often end up with a sharing of abstract, under-explored generalities.

The essays converge in criticising or distancing themselves from a number of past excesses and mistakes in CathST, both official and non-official: notably a frequent rigidity or pseudo-precision, over-confident or triumphalist claims to provide "solutions", a rule-book rather than a guide-book approach. They do not accept a widespread limitation of CathST to the *magisterium* of the Church or the official social declarations of the Popes and Councils (while according to these, of course, the appropriate close attention and respect). The assumption is that the drive and inspiration which comes from the Church's official social teaching, essential and vital as it is, particularly in proclaiming over-arching values and guidelines, needs to be complemented and carried forward by thinking which is able to adapt to varying geographical and cultural contexts, to take greater risks (including political risks), to offer alternative approaches to policy or prescriptions for social, political and economic improvement, and hence, often, to be prepared to be controversial among Catholics as well as in the world outside.

These essays represent such exercises in CNOST. They all show commitment to Catholic belief and Christian values, and go on to engage with the social, political and economic implications for the pursuit of social justice. They also reflect a lot of direct experience of academic disciplines, currents of opinion and movements of social action outside as well as inside the Catholic Church. There is a marked orientation towards what may be called "middle-level social thinking"; that is, thinking in the large and complex areas which lie between, on the one hand, broad values and principles and values, and, on the other, concrete action and decisions. Typically, such middle-level thinking means using a) models of society, politics or the economy; b) theories of history and of social, political and economic relationships; c) empirical observation and analysis; and d) thinking about policy and "improvement". All of these will be found here in various mixtures, along with pervasive, underlying influences from philosophy, social ethics and theology. Many of the essays use leading contemporary thinkers on the borders of Christian social thought or, more likely, "outside the camp" altogether, as interlocutors: such as A. MacIntyre, J. Rawls, A. Sen, M. Walzer, J. Habermas, P. Ricœur. The essays follow a certain progression. Allowing for frequent overlaps, there is a broad movement of the book from basic questions about identity (what *is* CathST?), through relationships with contemporary social thought, to more concrete projects for social action and reconstruction.

The book starts with two interpretations of the development of official Catholic social thought in modern times. Jean-Yves CALVEZ, a veteran leading authority on the subject, offers something of an intellectual biography, a personal narrative of continuities and changes, and his own responses to them, including not only inspiration but also a persistent unease throughout as to challenges unmet. Calvez's contribution needs to be read alongside his recent book *Les silences de la doctrine sociale catholique*[1]. Next, in a stimulating interpretation which evokes disagreements in later essays, Staf HELLEMANS draws on sociological and political categories in order to argue for a particular historical theory of the development of Catholic social teaching from the 19th century onwards, one which suggests radical or quantum transformations – from a largely time-limited type of CST reflecting an "ultramontane mass Catholicism" linked with "modernity", through upheavals mainly linked with the Second Vatican Council, to a still incomplete "post-modern" mutation.

While such interpretations stress discontinuities, particularly since the 1960s, others put more emphasis on foundations and characteristics of

---

1. J.-Y. CALVEZ, *Les silences de la doctrine sociale catholique* (Débattre), Paris, Les Éditions de l'Atelier, 1999.

basic, perennial social ideas and values in CathST. What place, if any, is there for a restated Aristotelian-Thomist related concept of "natural law"? Given the pervasive foundations of Catholic social thought in doctrine, scripture and sacrament, what emphasis should be placed on a hermeneutics of biblical sources or on core doctrines as direct inspiration for social ideas and values? What role has been, or should be, played by CNOST, affecting not only rational discussion but also imagination, *praxis* and policy? Above all, wherein lies any *distinctiveness* in CathST vis-à-vis contemporary secular thought about politics, economy, society? Does the "difference" arise only in the area of religious validation, spiritual motivation or "additional reasons" for values or pursuits shared with others? Is Catholic social thought also substantively different *qua* social thought, whether in terms of distinctive concepts, its own interpretation of familiar concepts, or some special prioritisation of these?

A second group of essays is largely addressed to such "foundational" issues. Frank McHUGH anatomises a wide range of contemporary tendencies in moral philosophy and social ethics: he argues that an important tradition, "natural law", or an ethical wisdom based on human nature and human reason, has suffered from much deformation over long periods and once again needs more serious attention than it has latterly received, but in a freer and non-mechanistic sense, perhaps less contentiously titled as "common social wisdom". Johan VERSTRAETEN presents a broad framework for understanding CathST as an historically embodied social tradition which involves not only rational thought, including critical dialogue with other such traditions, but also (decisively) both reflection and *praxis* in a continuous relationship of hermeneutic interpretation and inspiration with Gospel narrative, poetry and metaphor, challenging to constant deepening renewal. Walter LESCH repudiates what he sees as pretentious or divisive claims of privileged access to social truths in "classic", historical Catholic social thought. Drawing on theoretical debates and the experiences of many younger intellectuals in Germany since the 1960s, he advocates a Christian effort for justice and for co-operation with secular thought which would, taking a cue from "discourse ethics", draw on a universally accessible set of rules for fair and rational discussion. Taking a different line, Jonathan BOSWELL finds in CathST something of a distinctive, perennial but still *under*-stated inner structure or "pattern", which tends to reflect core doctrines and experiences. He identifies this as a triad of inter-related social values of power-sharing, justice for the poor and solidarity, with solidarity as pivot and organising principle, which he sees as having radical (devolutionist, egalitarian and, above all, sociability-enabling) implications for policy.

In the third section the focus is on how the existing corpus of CathST relates, in whole or part, to some significant currents of contemporary thought. Chantal DELSOL finds a wide, painful distance between a perennial Christian anthropology of responsibility, sociality and fallibility, within a spiritual *telos* for the human person, and most of contemporary secularism. Her vision is of a ceaseless quest for socio-political checks and balances amidst inescapable tensions and disappointments. Julie CLAGUE examines a range of controversies on "human rights" vis-à-vis CathST, concluding in favour of an appropriately qualified inclusion of this concept. Alois BUCH takes up the issue of communication of a CathST now all too often esoteric or misunderstood, both internally and externally. He urges much wider forms of openness and ecumenicity, seeing these as not inimical to parallel efforts at greater depth also in other churches and faiths. In two further essays the dominations exercised by economism, marketism, utilitarianism and individualism come under searching scrutiny. Stefano ZAMAGNI probes, sweepingly and sharply, the inconsistencies and excesses of orthodox economic ideology, and its anthropological, ethical and empirical reductionism. Bernard PERRET targets the related crudities of conventional models of "wealth creation" and measurement. Both these essays, though, do find some more hopeful potentials in contemporary political economy, respectively for reciprocity and relational values in the "civil economy" of co-operative and social enterprises, and for wider social indicators and concepts of "social capital" or well-being which lie closer to ideas of full human flourishing or "the common good".

Certain guiding threads run through these and other essays: namely, 1) Christian anthropology (the freedom and dignity of the human person, the social and communitarian aspects of human nature) as implying co-operation with some parts of contemporary secular thinking, confrontation with others; 2) the "peak notion of solidarity" in various forms, as "community" or "relationality", or in lesser ways as "civic spirit", "interdependence", "culture of giving", "reciprocity", "communion of goods", key aspects of "social capital"; 3) "subsidiarity" in terms of "civil society", "power-sharing" or "intermediate associations"; and 4) "justice" and "option for the poor". But although these may be good guiding principles, they still need a lot of working through and connecting, by way of middle-level thinking, to ideas for policy. The contributions in this book do no more than point to some possible ways forward.

In the final set of essays, focussing on more concrete issues of *praxis* and structural reform, five levels of action are touched on – health and social care, Third World development, reform of international finance, co-operative enterprise, and inclusion of the poorest sections of society – with the institutions in question ranging from the specifically Catholic, through the ecumenical, to the would-be multilateral and global. Here are essays by Linda HOGAN on a relatively new Irish Catholic agency for international aid and development, *Trocaire*; and by Alain THOMASSET, who raises critical questions on the identity and mission of Catholic institutions for health and welfare in France. Jef VAN GERWEN and Simona BERETTA contribute essays on international finance, in the former case elaborating detailed proposals, in the form of finance ethics, for bringing greater order and justice into financial markets and the system world-wide. Simona Beretta adds some further theological and ethical insights on the regulation of unruly finance. Luigino BRUNI eloquently describes the experience of the "Economy of Communion" which has developed over recent years under the aegis of the Focolare movement, in Italy and elsewhere. Finally, in a revisitation of the "preferential option for the poor", Donal DORR finds Church practices and attitudes still critically and tragically deficient. Both for Christians and in terms of general political action, he advocates more radical methods of "being with" and "listening to" the socially deprived and marginalised.

In a concluding essay, John A. COLEMAN provides a careful evaluation of most of the strands in the book, one reflecting an exceptional scholarly knowledge of worldwide social Catholicism, the more useful because Coleman was not directly involved in the initial project. His synthesis on the history and character of CathST counters some polarising arguments in earlier essays, putting the case not for a reduction or "reinvention" but for "retrieval" *plus* development. He adds some stimulating reflections on a social Catholic voice within a pluralistic, largely secular society. Here some notes sound on "liberalism" which may seem odd to many European ears (likewise an expression of sympathy with European Christian democracy even up to the 80s). An additional benefit from this essay, however, lies precisely in its "transatlantic response" to our largely European perspectives, focussing on some parallel as well as dissimilar currents, in the American context, relative to our common cause.

Where, then, do these essays stand in relation to the great political debates of our day? Starting with Calvez and continuing in many others, albeit with important nuances, one resounding negative stands out.

There is a clear rejection of an apparently hegemonic form of present-day capitalism, characterised as individualistic, market-imperialist, consumerist, and grossly unequal. But there is no harking back to another historically influential model, even though this was much espoused by Catholic social forces in the post-war decades, and beloved by older-style Christian democrats. That was a "middle way" composed of market regulation and "social partnership", *plus* coalitionism or political "centrism". While this model is not necessarily completely *passé* or unrealistic, it finds no resounding defence in this book. Nor will readers find tendencies towards "revivalism" of such successive historical blueprints of CathST as corporatist "vocational order", or Chestertonian distributism, or "Catholic workerism" à la JOC or Dorothy Day, or a Christian political party – as distinct, of course, from the more enduring value inspirations that lay behind such projects.

There is an obvious distance from "third way" thinking if this is interpreted as a political strategy to woo the "middle majority" or as a mere "public/private" eclecticism, or as a faceless, sweeping, "modernisation". That, after all, is something not so different in practice from the older "middle way" or even, perhaps, not so principled. On the other hand, things start to get warmer when the "third way" moves towards a rhetoric of "community" or "solidarity", "responsibility", as well as rights, "devolution", "civil society", and "social inclusion". But only on condition that key ideas of such perennial centrality for CathST, indeed so historically indebted to Christian sources, advance beyond mere rhetoric to take on flesh and blood. Those who seek more specific follow-up of these values should find much pertinent material here. So should "communitarians" dissatisfied with the too-abstract slant of most "communitarian" writers of recent years. For the themes of civil economy and co-operative enterprise, of social indicators and social capital, of political "voices" for the marginalised, of an insertion of relational values into the economy *ab initio* (in other words, not just as redistribution *post facto* to wealth creation but as intrinsic to economic creativity), these are nothing if not fertile ground for forward thinking policy, even if their specifics remain unclear.

A fair number of contributions indicate a desire for a more radical macro-orientation, beyond the usual categories. No unitary paradigm nor yet a comprehensive prospectus, partly because it is obvious that many key policy issues are not addressed (for example, environment and ecology, gender and family, migration, crime, electoral systems). Readers will nonetheless note some would-be mould-breaking sets of proposals: for a redistribution towards, and forms of inclusion of, the very poor and excluded, going well beyond current practice or even aspiration; for top-to-bottom reform of unjust and chaotic financial systems, extending to a new global financial order; and for the facilitation of basic human socia-bility and inter-group contact as a cardinal priority for public policy on employment, environmental, technological and social issues (a "politics of time" as well as of "place" and of "forums"). The likely implications of all this would be radical indeed, including a significant reduction in business power both politically and culturally and not only in high rates of taxation and "active government", but also bigger transfers of power from the nation state both "down" and "up", and much flying in the face of populism or crudely majoritarian democracy. Again, not all our contributors would agree – but then, that is the way with CNOST.

Finally, a further word on a critical question in this book, namely the "distinctiveness" of Catholic social thought *qua* social thought. A large majority of the essays take the view that this body of thought does have special or distinctive features *qua* social thought, an interpretation for which the term "substantivist" may be useful. However three broad approaches to such a "substantivist" view can be identified. Each of these is consistent with the varying political orientations just mentioned, and all three imply major tasks for CNOST.

A first approach, only occasionally reflected in this book, is to find in the values and principles of CathST a high degree of self-sufficiency, thus putting the main emphasis on their recovery, sustenance and pro-jection. Here the rules of engagement with secular thought are fairly tightly drawn. The implications for policy are viewed as relatively clear. The primary task is seen as educational, indeed the approach might be described as substantivist-pedagogic in style or form. A second approach, while also viewing the principles and values as persistent as well as clear and central, sees a need for strenuous rethinking as to their application or adaptation. Such rethinking is to apply to relationships with secular thought, whether of rapport, coalition or opposition; also to the issue of what sort of "institutional carriers", to use Coleman's term, may be appropriate in contemporary contexts, and not least to theories of improvement or ideas for public policy. Most of the essays reflect this sort of adaptive or expansive substantivism, often because of the specific tasks they tackle in these respects.

However, the agenda opened up by this book goes further. There is a need to re-explore the values and principles themselves, and particularly their continuous stimulation from religious beliefs and practices. This implies a re-rooted, deepened approach to distinctiveness, one which is constantly reconnecting with theology and faith. Neither pedagogy nor of a basically unequal capacity or strength. At the same time, development, even economic and social, is intimately connected by him with vocation, a distinctively religious concept. With Paul VI, also, the movement to give a more theological content to social doctrine continues.

Just at this time there emerged a different Catholic view of society, "the theology of liberation", of South American provenance and, it is fair to say, of a more revolutionary content, a development by the end of the 1960s. This rejected traditional social doctrine and judged "development" as a way of condoning and maintaining unjust structures. What is required is to eliminate unjust structures. The unjust structures being international, inextricably tied to dependency on rich central economies, must be loosened from this dependency. Traditional social doctrine is too moderate: it is "social" and tries to avoid being political, whereas it is essential to be political. And at this time the political chord was being sounded by Johann-Baptist Metz, whose political theology was having a strong influence on theologies of liberation.

This was not a period for quiet, peaceful assimilation of the social doctrine of the Church. Even Paul VI had seemed to retreat from a universal social doctrine in his letter *Octogesima advenies*, to Cardinal Roy, in 1971. I would dare to say, in spite of Vatican II and the important teachings of Paul VI on development, that Catholic social teaching did not take the necessary step forward. The liberal alternative to it was making advances at the same time, aided by Mrs Thatcher and Mr Reagan, and together with the radical liberationist views inside the Church made for an attack on two fronts. In some parts of the world, less affected by the winds from South America, for instance in Africa, the situation was more peaceful. The word was still "development" and all the advice given by the Church, Paul VI in particular, was welcome, helping people in thinking about their problems. The same still applies to Asia. Later on the theology of liberation style would also spread to other countries, especially to India and Sri Lanka.

In this time of tension a new pontiff had been elected. From Poland, he has been a teacher of the Church's social doctrine. He had experienced Catholic social doctrine as a strong leverage in a country where there is not much theology spread among the people but where faith and Church practice are widespread, and Marxism disliked. He could not be convinced of the wisdom of abandoning the Church's traditional social teaching as the theologians of liberation propose, especially with a view to introducing in its place elements of Marxist doctrine or method. At the same time he was in a sense close to the theologians of liberation, in his stress on the evangelical source of Christian views on society.

John Paul II quickly took up the fight on behalf of human rights, especially freedom of conscience and religion, and also of association (for the workers under the authoritarian structures of Communist industry). He raised "solidarity" as a Catholic banner. But in Latin America he called for a return to the "Social Doctrine" of the Church, during his early appearance at Puebla in 1979: he signalled his opposition to class struggle and all violent means of transformation. His idea of transformation is through the pressure of association. (This, I must say, never quite becomes a programme so that in this respect Pope John Paul's approach appears rather negative.)

As change begins to take hold in Eastern Europe, even before the outright collapse of Communism, the Pope begins to deal with the problem of economic systems. In *Laborem exercens* (1981) he advocates a socialisation that would be fully respectful of the "subjectivity of society", not like Communist socialisation which crushes that subjectivity. In *Sollicitudo rei socialis* (1987) his emphasis on and praise of economic initiative appeared to go further than in any previous official document of the Church. During the same period there arrives on the scene the pretentious challenge of neo-liberalism, presenting itself as the only reasonable economic form of organisation, even to the point of neglecting social demands. The Pope will have the courage to listen and change his language and to speak rather positively of modern economic enterprise, of the market, of profit itself, even in a sense of capitalism, making distinctions between an acceptable one and another which has to be rejected. But he has the courage, also, to draw out all the limitations, dangers and injustices that may go with that kind of economy.

It depends how you read it, but *Centesimus annus* (1991) can be seen as a formidable indictment of what is happening in the world economy of today. But a word of caution is called for. I shall not enter into detail about this now, but only mention that the Pope had at times a feeling after the encyclical that his thinking was used dishonestly by some, reading only some sentences and ignoring others, in order to defend the status quo of economic policies. This explains some later reactions, even outbursts of the Pope: to a newspaper, for example, to which he said: "It had some good aspects after all, that Communism"; or to businessmen whom he met in Mexico, rejecting the poverty of economic science, which is only part of the truth, when the reality of poverty and injustice is the other; or in 1997 at a meeting of the Pontifical Academy of Social Sciences where he strongly criticised competition without rules, and lax current practices.

Can I claim now that it is well received? The resistance of the old pontiff to popular, optimistic, naive views is impressive. He wants to keep us awake, as is acknowledged by quite a few people. The teaching proper, with its foundations, with its nuances, is unfortunately not widely known. Of the major authoritative statements of the Church's social teaching even educated people hardly read more than two or three sentences reported by the newspapers. There is a very serious problem of the diffusion of the social teaching of the Church; and Catholic non-official social thought is not much known either. Simple presentations are not available. Thinking that some *mea culpa* is at hand, I wish that we, scholars or something of the kind, would complain about the way the Church's documents are written. But then, we ourselves do not write good books, available, accessible, modern, especially for ordinary people.

I think it is clear that we live, particularly after *Centesimus annus*, in a time of uncertainty in relation to the social teaching of the Church. The Pope has said that capitalism without a firm framework which puts economic freedom at the service of integral human freedom for all, is unacceptable. He has not given a view, though, either in *Centesimus annus* or more recently, as to how far such a firm framework is actually yet in place. In his 1997 speech to the Pontifical Academy of Social Sciences, he tends to say that such a context is not in place, but that speech remains a minor document. Pius XI spoke in clearer terms in *Quadragesimo anno* in 1931, but this is long forgotten.

THE SILENCES OF CATHOLIC SOCIAL THOUGHT

I published in 1989 a book *L'économie, l'homme, la société*, coming back to the subject after a long absence (I was away from the academic scene for about 15 years). In this I brought up to date, after the years of the Council, my first book *Church and Economic Society*. The presentation was the same and the chapter headings unchanged. More recently, I wrote two shorter books, one *Développement, emploi, paix* (1989), the other *L'Église devant le libéralisme économique* (1994). In the process of writing the latter, and taking into account the whole history of the Church's relationship to economic liberalism, I began to feel that my own approach had not been sufficiently radical.

In fact, I have come to think that there are some silences or near-silences in the present social teaching of the Church, over issues that will have to be faced up to. Some of these silences or near-silences are to be found in the area of politics: how to deal with a right of man on which there is no consensus? Or what is the precise relationship of democracy to truth or truths? Others are to be found in the field of economics. A basic question arises first over unemployment. Should the Church declare support for work-sharing with shared income, particularly in relation to short-term unemployment? Should it indicate support for speedy transfer towards jobs in services, especially person-to-person services, where traditional industrial employment is clearly in decline due to technological change? Is it enough simply to say that unemployment is an evil, that it is destructive of family and, more generally, of the social bond? Here I observe a "silence", the topic having been hardly touched upon after the encyclical on work in 1981.

Second, the whole field of new financial operations, or the new context for global financial operations, has changed drastically. Just to give one example of the many related instabilities and injustices, there exists today the possibility of destroying enterprises and human communities of work, without advance notice, just through the buying and selling of shares, with little or no knowledge of the real situation on the ground, and, let me repeat, without notice. There is a virtual "silence" of the church in this whole area, (though the Pontifical Council for Justice and Peace sponsored a small booklet on the subject by my two French friends, de Villeroy and de Salins).

Third, as I hinted before, the Church will have to come back to the problem of unequal capitalism. By this I mean, not capitalism as such, not the economic system, but the situations where capital is or has come under the control of few persons, whereas the great majority of other persons are capable of bringing to the economic process only their labour. Capital, as we know, is powerful, accumulative, can afford to wait, is not personal in the sense that its owner or controller does not depend on it in a narrow way. Work, on the other hand, is personal in many senses of the term, many people depending on it almost completely. Work is also ephemeral; if it is not "used" today, nothing of it is left tomorrow. This can be remedied through forms of insurance, through association too, but only partly so. It has become clear, from the experience of two centuries or more, that such situations of inequality in the distribution and control of capital produce tensions or social divisions. Most people remain dependent and lack the opportunity to influence or take part in these processes which are so important for their lives.

The Church has criticised capitalism with an adjective "primitive" capitalism, where work is treated as a commodity and capital is turned into an obsessive pursuit of profit. What must come under judgement, however, is the very structure of unequal capitalism. Means must be sought to control capital so that it will be more equally distributed. Perhaps measures can be used to equalise the starting conditions for all, or to revert periodically in some systematic way to a degree of equality. It seems impossible to keep silent in such an important area. John Paul has touched on it only indirectly, stressing the dangers in the existing system which marginalises so many people and where only a few succeed in entering the educated and prosperous system while the vast majority remain on the side of the road, without participation, even without hope. This is a situation which will have to be addressed more seriously by humankind. There is no reason to think that the economy, like all things human, cannot be reformed or remodelled for the good of humankind, though this may be doubted by many today. Christianity, after all, insists that man is a creator, made in the image of the Creator of all things.

Finally, I think, big questions arise over the definition of the social teaching of the Church. John Paul II has tended to relate this to theology, specifically to moral theology. Others including myself would put the principal stress on evangelical sources, not pure philosophy or natural law. But the social teaching of the Church, as John Paul II has himself demonstrated, cannot refrain from practical judgements, practical conclusions and recommendations. In this field the bishops also have a part to play in their own capacity to lead the people of God. You are not a bishop only when you preach the Gospel. For example, the bishops of England and Wales insisted in their 1996 statement that the Church should not be timid in making recommendations in the area of the economy as well as in that of politics. There is also the important role of non-official thought in complementing and carrying forward the official social teaching, an aspect of my own experience referred to several times above, which is all too often overlooked and which forms a leading preoccupation of the essays which follow. A certain clarification of the nature of the social teaching of the Church is thus still pending, a subject addressed in a small book which I recently completed on "the silences" of present official teaching. The way forward, I am convinced, will have to pay attention to relative roles. It will also have to balance the need for changing applications and what is, for all Christians, a constant exigency or fixed point, namely the return to the Gospel.

Centre Sèvres   Jean-Yves CALVEZ
Paris

IS THERE A FUTURE FOR CATHOLIC SOCIAL TEACHING AFTER THE WANING OF ULTRAMONTANE MASS CATHOLICISM?

The publication in 1891 of the encyclical *Rerum novarum* is generally considered as the first and still most impressive official milestone of what is commonly called Catholic social teaching or doctrine[1]. Its development in the past century is no mere coincidence. My view is that classical social doctrine is the product of a specific form of modernity and, still more, of a specific form of Catholicism, an ultramontane mass Catholicism which flourished from about 1850 to 1960. After 1960 this form of Catholicism slid into a major crisis. As a consequence the classical social doctrine lost its durability. Will Catholic social doctrine and thinking, like the ultramontane form in which it emerged, disappear or linger on at the margin? Or will it, along with Catholicism in general, take on a new, viable form? That, I believe, is the issue at stake.

Although not a specialist, I will in this chapter attempt to provide a "historical-sociological perspective on Catholic social teaching". In the first part, I explore the rise and the undeniable vitality of Catholic social doctrine before 1960. The second part outlines briefly my interpretation of the major reasons for the crisis of the classical doctrine after 1960. The attempts at renewal are traced in the third part. I conclude with a speculative scenario.

I. ULTRAMONTANE MASS CATHOLICISM AS SEED-BED OF THE CLASSICAL CATHOLIC SOCIAL DOCTRINE

In their well-known *Église et société économique*, Calvez and Perrin rightly portray Catholic social doctrine as "an historical answer to an historical problem"[2]. The social encyclical *Rerum novarum*, issued by

---

1. Salemink and Dorr give fine historical overviews: T. SALEMINK, *Katholieke kritiek op het kapitalisme 1891-1991. Honderd jaar debat over vrije markt en verzorgingsstaat*, Amersfoort-Leuven, Acco, 1991 and D. DORR, *Option for the Poor. A Hundred Years of Vatican Social Teaching*, Maryknoll, NY, Orbis Books, 1992.
    2. J.-Y. CALVEZ, & J. PERRIN, *Église et société économique. L'enseignement social des Papes de Léon XIII à Pie XII (1878-1958)*, Paris, Aubier, 1959, p. 22.

Leo XIII in 1891, sought to present the Catholic answer to a concrete problem, namely the "social question" in a context of "wild" capitalism. The encyclical letter triggered a huge response, and that not only in Catholic circles. Jean Jaurès called it "a socialist manifesto". The ultramontane Catholic Georges Goyau designated it as "the social dogma of the church". Cardinal Lecot summarised the encyclical under the title "catechism on social matters". Leroy-Beaulieu, an author of liberal-catholic posture, wrote: "Rome has spoken: the Church has henceforth a social doctrine"[3]. Indeed, it is fair to say that there was, before 1891, no Catholic social doctrine, in the sense of an ecclesiastically systematised, approved and propagated set of principles and statements on social and economic matters. Before that date these matters were, of course, extensively and controversially discussed by Catholics, but *Rerum novarum* gave them the eagerly awaited Roman frame of reference, a frame that was further developed in the course of the 20th century, in particular with the publication of the encyclical *Quadragesimo anno* in 1931 by Pius XI.

Interpreted in this way, responding to the social question with Catholic doctrine seems almost an obvious thing to have done. The lack of a comparable doctrine on the Protestant side, however, hints at deeper reasons. Explaining the formation of Catholic social doctrine is not possible without turning to the inner dynamics of pre-1960 Catholicism. My argument is that it is essential to understand that it was a new form of Catholicism, ultramontane mass Catholicism, that generated Catholic social doctrine. Classical Catholic social doctrine was linked in the most intimate way to ultramontane mass Catholicism. It presupposed a high degree of centralisation; it exemplified the ultramontane desire for doctrine; it was an element in the *reconquista* strategy of the church. It also constituted the frame of reference for the large Catholic social organisations which constituted the Catholic subculture.

1. *"Rome has spoken"*

Classical Catholic social doctrine is first and foremost a papal doctrine, forged and proclaimed by the popes themselves in encyclical letters. It is not disputed that a broad discussion was raging behind the scenes and that many specialists, particularly between 1930 and 1960, devoted themselves to this agenda. Yet without doubt, the centre of gravity lay in Rome. The encyclicals *Rerum novarum* and *Quadragesimo*

---

3. Citations from J.-M. MAYEUR, *Catholicisme social et démocratie chrétienne. Principes romains, expériences françaises* (Histoire), Paris, Cerf, 1986, pp. 60-65.

anno largely instituted the doctrine. Leo XIII and his successors were apparently capable of issuing statements over a wide range of controversial topics and of declaring them binding for all the faithful. How this doctrine was to be translated into practice, and the extent to which the statements were binding, became hotly debated topics. The importance attached to the interpretations of the encyclicals shows clearly the centrality of the papal doctrine and the extent of centralisation in the Church. The context of modernity made such a high degree of centralisation possible.

It is true that a policy of centralisation had been pursued by Rome for centuries. For evidence of this claim one could go back even to the first centuries of Christianity[4]. Still, it is important to realise that the decisive drive towards centralisation was effected only in the 19th century[5]. In the 18th century, sixteen of the 26 German bishops refused to proclaim in their dioceses the papal condemnation of Febronius's Episcopal book of 1763[6]. A century later, all bishops submitted to the dogma of papal infallibility of 1870, although it had been fiercely contested at Vatican Council I[7].

The unprecedented centralisation of the church by Rome after 1800 was a predisposing condition for the emergence of Catholic social doctrine. From a distant, relatively unknown figure without much influence on the local churches, the pope became in the 19th century an all-powerful and intensely active leader intervening, if necessary, in the church affairs of even remote regions. It soon became a habit – encouraged by Rome! – of parties in dispute to invoke Rome in the hope of a Roman decision in their favour. And so, in the years after 1880, the pressure mounted on Rome from diverse sides to issue a solemn statement on the worker question. The local churches were becoming far more oriented towards Rome, that is, "ultramontane". At the same time, Rome became able to transfer its messages down to the rank and file with an unprecedented intensity. Like Rome, the dioceses were centralised. The priests received a much improved education. The rank and file were regularly mobilised, under supervision of the clergy, and better instructed in matters of faith and morals.

---

4. See, for example, L. LAEYENDECKER, *Om de beheersing van het charisma. Heil en macht in de R.K. Kerk*, Amsterdam, Koninklijke Nederlandse Academie voor Wetenschappen, 1993.

5. R. AUBERT, *De kerk van de crisis van 1848 tot Vaticanum II* (Geschiedenis van de kerk, 10), Hilversum-Antwerpen, P. Brand, 1974, pp. 71-87.

6. L.J. ROGIER, *De kerk in het tijdperk van verlichting en revolutie* (Geschiedenis van de kerk, 7), Hilversum-Antwerpen, P. Brand, 1974, p. 103.

7. AUBERT, *De kerk van de crisis* (n. 5), p. 84.

The encyclical *Rerum novarum* is a case in point. It demonstrates to what extent the Church had been rebuilt after the revolutionary era into a new, hierarchical mass organisation that could lead Catholics all over the world from its centre. Decreed in Latin, the encyclical was soon, in whole or in part, translated into numerous languages Its content was widely distributed in the form of tracts and books. Pastoral letters of the bishops supported the popularisation of the encyclical. Conferences and meetings were held throughout the Catholic world. In the Catholic labour movement commemoration of the encyclical became a yearly ritual. Overall, Catholics raised pope and encyclical to a mythical level, proclaiming Leo XIII "Pope of the workers" and hailing *Rerum novarum* as the *magna carta* (*QA* 39).

2. *A Desire for Doctrine*

The label "doctrine" indicates that Catholic social teaching was not meant as an amalgam of scattered declarations without coherence or profound implications. The aim was to establish a systematic set of authoritative instructions. As a technical term, the label "Catholic social doctrine" spread during the inter-war period. During the pontificate of Pius XII it was used frequently and emphatically[8].

It can be safely claimed that already Leo XIII wanted to set out in *Rerum novarum* a systematic scheme of principles. His aims are clearly stated in the introductory paragraphs of his encyclical: "Therefore, venerable brethren, as on former occasions...we... have issued letters on political power, on human liberty, on the Christian constitution of the State, and on similar subjects, so now we have thought it useful to speak on the condition of labour ... in order that there may be no mistake as to the principles which truth and justice dictate for its settlement" (*RN* 1)[9]. Even today John Paul II has stated in his recent social encyclicals *Sollicitudo rei socialis* (1987) and *Centesimus annus* (1991) that Catholic social teaching is a rich "doctrinal corpus" (*SRS* 1) and that it "is an essential part of the Christian message" (*CA* 5). This profound desire to formulate the Catholic response to social problems in terms of a Church doctrine which is binding for all the faithful is related intimately to ultramontane Catholicism.

---

8. CALVEZ & PERRIN, *Église et société économique* (n. 2), pp. 17-20.
9. All citations of the social encyclicals will be drawn from D.J. O'BRIEN & T.A. SHANNON (eds.), *Catholic Social Thought. The Documentary Heritage*, Maryknoll, NY, Orbis Books, 1992.

Given my lack of knowledge of historical theology, it is with some hesitation that I present a sketchy historical outline of this desire for doctrine in the 19th and 20th centuries. It is true that the early Church councils elaborated and defined some of the basic dogmas of Christianity. The ecumenical councils of the 4th and the 5th centuries are, in formulating the Trinitarian and Christological doctrines, of central importance here. But by the end of the Patristic period (usually dated to the eighth century) there was a sense that the basic doctrines were in place. Throughout the Middle Ages, the Church left the development of theology more or less to the university theologians and was more concerned with spreading spirituality and establishing moral and disciplinary control over the faithful. On the doctrinal front, efforts were mostly limited to the demarcation from heresies which were regarded as dangerous. Even the Council of Trent was more directed towards the demarcation from Protestantism and towards organisational and pastoral measures. It is only with the slow rise of modernity after 1500 that Catholic theology, challenged by Protestantism and by the Enlightenment, came to be seen as an instrument of the Church with the task of codifying the content in a set of positive, controllable statements. Fundamental theology became dogmatic theology. The drive towards systematisation and doctrine was further enhanced by the rise of modern science and modern philosophy – e.g. Leibniz, Hegel, and in the 19th century by the dominance of neo-Thomism[10].

The increasing dogmatisation of theology went hand in hand with the increasing prominence of the pope. Dogmatic theology became a Roman matter. With the transformation of the Church into a hierarchical mass organisation, Rome and the Pope finally had the means to inculcate their opinions throughout the Church. To outline the basic tenets on an issue encyclicals became favourite devices. Gregory XVI and Pius IX had done the groundwork. Beginning with *Aeterni Patris,* the encyclical by which he imposed Thomism on Catholic education, Leo XIII used this ideological means extensively to foster an all-embracing teaching, covering all aspects of life in modernity. No pope before or after him issued so many encyclical letters. During a pontificate of 25 years, no less than 86 encyclicals were proclaimed[11], that is, more than 3 per year. It was an important component of the overall "Leonine strategy", the rolling back

---

10. F.-X. KAUFMANN, *Theologie in soziologischer Sicht,* Freiburg, Herder, 1973, pp. 78-92.
11. J.T. ELLIS, *From the Enlightment to the Present. Papal Policy Seen through the Encyclicals,* in *Catholic Historical Review* 69 (1983), no. 1, 51-58, esp. 54.

of secular modernity with the means made available by modernity[12]. The dogmatisation of issues and its publication in the form of encyclicals became a centrepiece of papal ideological politics. As Leo XIII had taken the lead through previous encyclicals on topics such as politics and freemasonry, with *Rerum novarum* he now turned to social issues. Until Vatican Council II, his successors would continue this strategy and this use of encyclicals.

3. *Instaurare Omnia in Christo*

As early as 1885, Leo XIII had hinted that he wished to make a major pronouncement on the social question[13]. The publication of *Rerum novarum* thus did not come as a complete surprise. Nevertheless, the willingness of so many Catholics to accept the declarations of the pope on such a delicate and controversial issue cannot but strike us today. The more so because the social question, at first sight, seemed to lie miles away from the more obviously religious matters with which the Church was usually concerned. Finally, in a Church that adored tradition an encyclical on the social question was thematically unprecedented. How can this obvious and self-assured "intrusion" into non-religious spheres of life be explained?

The motto of the ultramontane Catholics of the 19th and 20th centuries was *Instaurare omnia in Christo* ("To restore all things in Christ") – to reconstruct the whole order of modern society along Christian lines. With a sense of mission and triumphalism, the Catholic Church called for a rechristianisation of modernity. She claimed for herself the right and duty to intervene in all matters of life, profane as well as religious. In so doing, the Church continued an old fundamental conviction. In the Middle Ages a protracted investiture struggle between the Holy Roman emperor and the Roman pontiff had been waged. After 1800 the Church attacked modern secular currents, and modernity in general as the new Antichrist. In order to roll back this "lethal" threat, the Church wanted to give guidance, then, to all sectors of life, from education through politics to social and economic issues, to the dismay of her adversaries who advocated a complete separation of religion and politics. So Leo XIII proclaimed self-consciously: "We approach the subject with confidence, and in the exercise of the rights which belong

---

12. B. MacSweeney, *Roman Catholicism. The Search for Relevance*, Oxford, Blackwell, 1980, pp. 61-91; E. Poulat, *Église contre bourgeoisie. Introduction au devenir du catholicisme actuel* (Religion et sociétés), Castermann, Tournai, 1977

13. Mayeur, *Catholicisme social et démocratie chrétienne* (n. 3), p. 50, no. 15.

to us" (*RN* 13). Forty years later, referring to Leo XIII, Pius XI wrote that "it is our right and our duty to deal authoritatively with social and economic problems" (*QA* 41).

So far I have emphasised the continuity in the totalising world view of the Church. But it would be wrong to overlook the different way in which this remarkable totalising capacity of the Church was brought into practice. First of all, it was no longer a struggle fought between nobility and clergy. Instead, the whole mass of the population was called into action. The social encyclicals called on all Catholics to restore the Christian order through Catholic action. In this respect it is significant that both Leo XIII and Pius XI spoke extensively and positively of the benefits of (Catholic) associations, those eminently modern institutions. That the two encyclicals were so well received by the rank and file within the Church and gave such a strong impulse to the development of Catholic associations and organisations shows the profound modernisation of Catholicism after 1800[14].

In the second place, the context of modernity brought the Church into a completely new situation. The pre-modern Church had been able to play a leading role because she had taken, besides her religious role, care of formal education, charity, science and local administration and because she was closely intertwined with the world of politics. The increasing institutional differentiation after 1800 – the differentiation of science, education, social care from religion, and the widening separation from politics and economics – made religion a more purely religious matter. One would expect then – and the proponents of a secular modernity did expect it – that the Church would withdraw into this "purely" religious heart of the matter. But actually, that didn't happen. Strengthened by its transformation into a mass organisation, the Church, and more particularly the popes, set themselves up as the leaders and true guides of the world. At least in the Catholic communities, this posture succeeded remarkably well. And where these communities had a dominant position, as in Austria and Belgium around 1900, the Church was even able to regain the leading cultural position in society.

To give guidance and to control the Catholics, in particular the wide ranging network of Catholic organisations in all spheres of life, thus became a matter of paramount importance for the Church. Its leading position, and in the end its objective of restoring the Catholic order of society, was at stake. As we have seen, the proclamations of encyclical

14. S. HELLEMANS, *Religieuze modernisering*, Utrecht, Katholieke Theologische Universiteit, 1997.

letters, in order to outline the main principles that should guide the Catholics and their many organisations, was a prime instrument in this strategy. This applies especially to the social sphere. Here the unity of Catholics, deemed necessary as a precondition for the *reconquista* of modernity, was seriously threatened. It was also in this field that the biggest mass organisations of ultramontane mass Catholicism were generated.

4. *Symbiotic Relation With the Catholic Labour Movement*

So we come to the last distinctive ultramontane characteristic, which was strongly related to the genesis and the flowering of classical Catholic social doctrine: the growth of Catholic mass social organisations. Usually separated by class – as organisations of industrial workers, peasants, middle classes and employer – they rose within the Catholic community after 1850 and more especially after 1900. With membership in many cases going well over the hundred thousand, they became a significant feature of Catholic life. Hence the imperative of timely Church supervision and presence. In most countries the class factor introduced tensions among the leaders of these organisations. The leaders of these organisations – including their chaplains, nicknamed in Germany "the cardinals" (*Verbandskardinäle*) – were even more powerful than many a diocesan bishop. Moreover, in the eyes of the Church, the temptation of the secular world to which membership and leaders of organisations were exposed had to be checked with equally strong religious incentives. Catholic social doctrine provided an overall ideological frame for this strongly felt imperative of Church supervision. It assigned to these huge organisations a legitimised position as an important component of the Catholic world, under the authority of the Church. This was to be an outstanding achievement of classical social doctrine.

In particular, the Catholic labour movement maintained a close, even symbiotic relation with classical social doctrine[15]. For a long time, the presence of the movement within the Church was viewed with unease. *Rerum novarum* gave the Catholic labour movement a much needed papal legitimisation with the well known addition, inserted at the last minute by the Pope himself, that associations could be formed by "workmen alone" (*RN* 36). In the young and fragile Catholic labour movement, *Rerum novarum* was soon seen as a baptismal certificate.

15. P. PASTURE, *Histoire du syndicalisme chrétien international. La difficile recherche d'une troisième voie* (Chemins de la mémoire), Paris, L'Harmattan, 1999. Chapter 1 gives an international overview.

Recent historical research may have falsified this thesis and may characterise it as an example of "invented tradition"[16]. But even if it is true that "*Rerum novarum* was only one crystallising moment in the development of the Christian labour movement"[17], the invented tradition demonstrates nevertheless the importance the labour movement attached to *Rerum novarum* and to Catholic social doctrine in general. Catholic social doctrine remained in fact so basic for the workings of the Catholic labour movement that A. Brys, the dean of the ACW in Belgium – a country with a very strong Catholic labour movement – could still state in the 1950's that the Catholic labour movement was the "instrument for the realisation of Catholic social doctrine"[18]. Moreover, it is clear that the papal guidelines concerning private property, the principle of subsidiarity, the theory of justice and the moral duty of class co-operation, strongly influenced the world view and actions of the movement.

Following the pre-eminent position of the Church in these Catholic organisations – the organisations within the Catholic world – it was almost inevitable that the Church hierarchy would give paramount attention to social issues. Any other response would have been puzzling.

II. THE END OF CLASSICAL SOCIAL DOCTRINE AFTER 1960

Ultramontane mass Catholicism, the religious formation within which the classical Catholic social doctrine had emerged and prospered, slid into a deep crisis after 1960. Given the intimate connection, it is no wonder that Catholic social doctrine would also be seriously affected. It would be criticised as a conservative ideology, moralist instead of emancipatory[19]. In the Catholic world, and more particularly in the Catholic labour movement, it lost its hold as a frame of reference[20]. The question then becomes whether Catholic social teaching can retain its vitality outside its context of origin. Can it still direct people and eventually mobilise them or will it, with the decline of ultramontane mass Catholicism,

---

16. E. HOBSBAWM & T. RANGER (eds.), *The Invention of Tradition* (Past and Present Publications), Cambridge, Cambridge University Press, 1983.

17. E. GERARD (ed.), *De christelijke arbeidersbeweging in België* (KADOC-Studies, 11), 2 vol., Leuven, Universitaire Pers, 1991, p. 16.

18. P. PASTURE, *Kerk, politiek en sociale actie. De unieke positie van de christelijke arbeidersbeweging in België* (HIVA-reeks, 14), Leuven, Garant, 1992, p. 208.

19. M.-D. CHENU, *La "doctrine sociale" de l'Église comme idéologie* (Essais), Paris, Cerf, 1979.

20. P. PASTURE, *Het A.C.V. en de katholieke sociale leer. Hoe hemel en aarde verzoenen?*, in *De Gids op Maatschappelijk Gebied* 82 (1991), no. 5, 447-465.

become outdated, like many other aspects of pre-Vatican II Catholicism, such as the role given to the Feast of Christ the King in the late 1920s and 1930s? In the preceding section I argued that Catholic social doctrine is the historic-specific product of an historic-specific form of Catholicism. My next step is to explore the ferment within post-1960 Catholicism with particular attention to the consequence for Catholic social teaching.

1. *A New Era in Modernity*

The preface to the study of the changes within Catholicism is the more general change within the wider society. Modernity as a societal formation after 1960 entered a new era characterised by generalised mass consumption, secularisation, individualisation and dissolution of class cultures, changes which had a direct impact on the status of Catholic social doctrine. Indeed, its impact before 1960 was also partly due to the prominence over a number of decades of one major issue, the social question. From the last quarter of the 19th century until well after the Second World War, the social question was widely considered to constitute the central contentious issue of modern society. This long-lasting emphasis did heighten the sense of continuity, so beloved by the Church. This all changed quickly after 1960. The social question, which had for a long time been seen as the Achilles heel of modernity, receded or changed in form.

The labour-capital polarity remained of course an important source of conflict. But on the one hand, new social problems which could not be properly reduced to the old social question (like the new poverty and social exclusion, stress and alienation, mass migration, violence, global-isation), made themselves felt. And on the other hand, tendencies and problems which undermined the centrality of the class conflict came to the fore: the de-industrialisation and tertiarisation of the economy, the individualisation process, new quests like feminism and ecology. The social question was no longer considered to be the root question around which all other problems gravitated.

Also, the way in which CST sought to deal with the social question had become outdated. With its combination of religious-moral guidance and corporatist organisation, Catholic social doctrine presented itself for a long time as the orderly "third way" between liberal capitalism and state socialism[21]. In the meantime, a socially corrected market economy,

---

21. J. VERSTRAETEN, *De sociale leer van de katholieke kerk en de 'derde weg'*, in L. BOUCKAERT & G. BOUCKAERT (eds.), *Metafysiek en engagement. Een personalistische visie op gemeenschap en economie*, Leuven, Acco, 1992, pp. 51-63.

blunting the sharp edges of the social question, had been established in the West. Although many issues remain unsolved and new ones have arisen, few people think nowadays that the key to their solution is to be found in religious guidance or a corporatist order. It is therefore acknowledged that Catholic social doctrine has thus both lost its central problem and the plausibility of its solutions.

2. *From Ultramontane Mass Catholicism to a Pluralist Catholicism*

It is my contention that the new era in which modernity was making its appearance in the sixties brought also a fundamental transformation of Catholicism. Ultramontane mass Catholicism collapsed and in consequence, as I see it, Catholic social doctrine suffered a severe setback. The Catholic Church has remained highly centralised after 1960. At the same time it is true that papal declarations have lost the impact they once had on the consciousness and behaviour of Catholics. In retrospect, the encyclical *Humanae vitae* (1968) can be seen as a watershed. Before this encyclicals were welcomed with reverence, sometimes with sheer enthusiasm, as was still the case with *Populorum progressio* (1967). Thereafter a negligent or even hostile attitude developed. The most recent social encyclicals have been met by a remarkable silence. Three major social encyclicals of John Paul II – *Laborem exercens* (1981), *Sollicitudo rei socialis* (1987) and *Centesimus annus* (1991) – caused much excitement within the wider Church and society. They were reported in the newspapers. Some ritual attention was given to them in the remaining Catholic social movements[22]. But they did not have the impact within or outside the Church, of the encyclicals of 1891 or 1931. The loss of impact of the papal declarations on social issues is not an isolated fact, nor, indeed, unconnected to moral doctrine on family and sexual behaviour, which held sway before the late 1960s but is now little observed either. More generally, the stimulating strength of Rome, once the source of universalisation throughout the whole Church of initiatives like the Sacred Heart devotion, frequent communion (see the decrees of Pius X) or Catholic action, has faded away. Rome can still dispose its old organisational apparatus to discipline theologians, but nonetheless it has introduced organisational changes both of a positive kind (the creation of new structures incorporating some lay voice) and negative

---

22. J. VERSTRAETEN, *'Sollicitudo Rei Socialis' en de christelijke sociale bewegingen in Vlaanderen*, in J. BULCKENS & P. COOREMAN (eds.), *Kerkelijk leven in Vlaanderen anno 2000. Opstellen voor Jan Kerkhofs* (Niké-reeks. Didachè), Leuven, Acco, 1989, pp. 189-195.

(like dismantling older structures such as the Congregation of the Faith). But these are self-protective measures. Far more significant is the fact that Rome is no longer able effectively to promote and propel world-wide devotional and religious activities as it routinely used to do prior to 1960. The loss of strength of the Church's centre is not due to a lack of dynamism on the part of the Popes or to misguided policy, but rather to the fact that a whole historical formation, namely, a hierarchy-driven mass Catholicism has come to an end. A pluralist Catholicism which looks less to Rome appears to have taken its place, one inhabited by individualised Catholics who, living in high modernity, keep distance from all organisations, including the Church.

The first target of Catholic social doctrine, the world of the Catholic social organisations, has also changed fundamentally. In a number of countries like the Netherlands and Germany they have nearly disappeared. In some other countries, like for instance Belgium, powerful movements are still active[23]. The movements in these last cases, however, have become thoroughly emancipated from ecclesiastical supervision and are no longer looking to Catholic social doctrine for guidance[24]. Even in its former strongholds, Catholic social doctrine has since the sixties become discredited and has thus lost its privileged operational base.

Finally, the broader theoretical frame of Catholic social doctrine, neo-Thomism and natural law doctrine, has come under harsh criticism and is almost removed from the theological scene. A new theological paradigm, equally shared, has not yet emerged. It can no longer be assumed that one will emerge. Indeed, an ecclesiastically-favoured style of theology, neo-Thomism, was also a characteristic feature of ultramontane mass Catholicism[25]. Now, instead of one dominant theory, many theological currents of a wide variety compete. Since Rome can no longer draw on one dominant theological language game, the possibility of developing a doctrine which aspires to stand above the quarrelling parties has become seriously questioned. Even the increased use of the Bible in papal documents and allocutions, evident since the Second Vatican Council, because it is subject to different interpretations is not yet a secure framework.

23. P. PASTURE, *Diverging Paths: The Development of Catholic Labour Organisations in France, the Netherlands and Belgium since 1944*, in *Revue d'histoire ecclésiastique* 88 (1994), no. 1, 54-90.
24. PASTURE, *Kerk, politiek en sociale actie* (n. 18), describes in detail the evolution in Belgium.
25. P. THIBAULT, *Savoir et pouvoir. Philosophie thomiste et politique cléricale au XIXe siècle* (Histoire et sociologie de la culture, 2), Québec, Les Presses de l'Université Laval, 1972.

III. CATHOLIC SOCIAL TEACHING AFTER 1960

The force of this argument about the strong links between Catholic social teaching and ultramontane Catholicism might suggest that there is no option but for the former to die with the disappearance of the latter. The soil of Catholic social teaching's flourishing became infertile after the 1960s and the most that could be expected is that it would linger on at the margins. Social phenomena, though, which are anchored deeply in a social environment, do not disappear just like that. To meet changing conditions, all sorts of adaptation strategies are tried. These transformational strategies can succeed or fail. When we apply this view to Catholic social teaching, what transformational strategies have been tried out in the last decades? Have these strategies been able to give new life to Catholic social teaching?

1. *New Themes*

In classical social doctrine and in modern society before 1960, the social question was considered crucial. After 1960, new themes come to the fore in the new era of modernity: Third World development, participation, disarmament and global world order, ecology and feminism, living in a mass consumer society. This agenda is also addressed by the Church, though selectively in the light of its understanding of its own role. To issues which are sensitive to the Church, like participation and feminism, the hierarchy does not pay much attention. When it does, as with the participation issue which became unavoidable sometime in the late sixties, the Church took great care not to widen intra-church criticism. On the other side, the Church is eager to take up international issues like world peace and world development. *Mater et Magistra* (1961) quickly took up the themes in the so-called "first development decade", followed by *Pacem in terris* (1963) and *Populorum progressio* (1967). Later they were extensively up-dated in *Sollicitudo rei socialis* (1987)[26]. The presence of a well-developed classical Catholic social doctrine eased the transition to international issues such as international social justice, "option for the poor". Moreover, through the rapid internal decolonisation of the Church and the sheer demographic weight of the Third World churches, the Church quickly evolved in the sixties from a Western, Italian-based institution to a genuine world Church. The multinational Second Vatican Council was important in this respect.

---

26. J. VERSTRAETEN, *Sollicitudo Rei Socialis. Een nieuwe stap in de ontwikkeling van de sociale leer van de Kerk*, Leuven, Acco, 1988.

The Catholic Church, while introducing new themes, was also anxious to emphasise continuity with the past. The new themes are throughout presented as legitimate extensions of the old subjects. So, to give an example, *Populorum progressio* (1967), before engaging with the topic of world-wide development, states: "Today the principal fact that we must all recognise is that the social question has become world-wide" (*PP* 3). Continuity is stressed through the many references to the previous social encyclicals, especially to *Rerum novarum*. A tradition has moreover been built up since *Quadragesimo anno* (1931) to refer in the title and/or the year of publication to the great encyclical of Leo XIII. So *Mater et Magistra* appears in 1961, the apostolic constitution *Octogesima adveniens* in 1971, *Laborem exercens* in 1981, and *Centesimus annus* in 1991. An exception took place with *Populorum progressio* (1967), a document issued in the wake of *Gaudium et spes* (1965), the pastoral constitution of the Second Vatican Council (see esp. Part II, Ch. 5). In order to stress the continuity with *Populorum progressio*, *Sollicitudo rei socialis* (1987) was even predated – the murder attempt on the Pope had delayed its publication. The eagerness to stress continuity illustrates a typical characteristic of Catholic discourse: innovation, especially doctrinal innovation, is suspect and has to be legitimised by rooting it firmly in tradition. "In effect", writes John Paul II in *Sollicitudo rei socialis*, "continuity and renewal are a proof of the perennial value of the teaching of the Church" (*SRS* 3). Since the Vatican II Council the term favoured is "living tradition".

In this way, a wide variety of new themes are smuggled in, after 1960, under the old labels "Catholic social doctrine" or "Catholic social teaching". Even far-reaching modifications are adopted with little reference to earlier rejection, as was the case with human rights, particularly the right of freedom of conscience and freedom of religion. In the same way, the once prominent option of the so-called "third way" between capitalism and socialism, has been implicitly given up[27]. An explicit break with the past was actually announced only once. With the harsh critics of the sixties in mind, Paul VI in *Octogesima adveniens* (1971) came near to detaching himself from the classical form and title of Catholic social doctrine. Papal social teaching is minimised here as a source of inspiration (*OA* 1). Further on it is said: "It is up to the Christian communities... to discern the options and commitments which are called for". In so doing, they can, though, "draw principles of reflection, norms of judgement and directives for action from the social teaching of

---

27. VERSTRAETEN, *De sociale leer van de katholieke kerk en de 'derde weg'* (n. 21).

the Church" (*OA* 4). This turn towards decentralisation and autonomy –
it is significant that the document was issued as an apostolic constitution
and not as an encyclical – was reversed under John Paul II, who again
stresses the doctrinal character of the tradition of social teaching since
Leo XIII, while dwelling on the new themes that were introduced after
1960. On the whole, however, his encyclicals are not innovative.

2. *New Actors and Styles*

Although there was a good deal of tension and debate within the
Catholic Church on social issues before and after the great social
encyclicals, classical social doctrine overwhelmingly focussed around
the papal writings, beginning with Leo XIII. Given Vatican strategy at
the time of Leo XIII, social teaching was an expression of ultramontane
mass Catholicism. But this situation changed in a major way after Vatican II. *Populorum progressio* (1967) still profited from the *élan* of the
Council. It was a refreshing and enthusiastic plea for Third World
development and a chief contribution from the Church in fostering
"integral development". It was to be the last social encyclical to elicit
much enthusiasm. It succeeded in giving a strong impetus to Third
World interests among the churches in the West as well as in the non-
Western world. But after that, the initiating or at least generating
strength of Rome seemed to evaporate. It is significant that in this
respect the project of the re-evangelisation of the Western world, so
beloved of John Paul II, failed to take off. Correspondingly, the social
encyclicals of John Paul II have failed to draw much attention outside
the world of specialists[28].

On the other hand, the decline of Rome's authority since the late sixties made room for new actors. Following the liberalisation movement
of the sixties, and the upgrading of the role of the bishops and Bishops'
conferences by the Vatican Council, local churches often had more room
for manoeuvre. Sometimes, initiatives were spreading laterally through
the world-wide Church even in spite of strong suspicions in Rome, as in
the case of liberation theology and the basic communities movement.
This trend towards more autonomy was stimulated by the growing presence of lay Catholics on Church commissions and standing committees,
who brought secular and professional expertise to bear on issues of the
day made and their influence particularly felt in the realm of Catholic
social teaching and action.

---

28. See VERSTRAETEN, *'Sollicitudo Rei Socialis' en de christelijke sociale bewegingen
in Vlaanderen* (n. 22) on local responses to *Sollicitudo rei socialis*.

Before 1960 most pastoral letters on social issues by bishops or by Bishops' conferences simply reiterated and popularised papal teaching[29]. But after the 60s the second tier of hierarchical authority moved to greater self-confidence. In all loyalty to the Pope, bishops and conferences of bishops acted more frequently on their own initiative, taking up issues which are barely dealt with by Rome and treating them in a self-conscious, creative way[30]. Moreover, some of these pastoral letters have received world-wide attention. The letter of the US conference of bishops on *The Challenge of Peace* became a model for similar letters in the European countries[31]. *Economic Justice for All* of 1986, again a letter from the US bishops, equally made the tour of the world[32], and the 1996 Statement by the Catholic Bishops' Conference of England & Wales, *The Common Good and the Catholic Church's Social Teaching,* received also widespread publicity.

More independent initiatives on social thought and issues have also been developing on non-official levels. Before 1960 Catholic intellectuals had to think and act within the narrow limits set by papal teaching on social issues, but since then many theologians, ethicists and social scientists have been adopting an autonomous and more critical role. The present collection contains many references to such work since the 1960s, and the conference in Cambridge which led to this book, inspired by a desire to explore and re-dynamise Catholic non-official social thought, also represents an effort at imaginative middle-level thinking complementary to the official social teaching. I want to stress that overall, one can see these and other post-1960 phenomena as symbolising a move from situations of domination and subservience towards relative positions in a debate. The task of "re-imagining Catholicism"[33] is no longer exclusively centred on popes: it is possible to see it taken up by bishops and lay people as well.

At the same time there has been a significant change in the style and ambition of official social teaching itself. The subtitle of *Quadragesimo anno* proclaimed the older theme: "On Reconstructing the Social Order

---

29. See the documentation by the UNION INTERNATIONALE D'ÉTUDES SOCIALES, *La hiérarchie catholique devant le problème social*, Paris, Spes, 1931.

30. For Belgium, see K. DOBBELAERE, *Over het publieke spreken van de Rooms Katholieke Kerk in een geseculariseerd België*, in *Onze Alma Mater* 53 (1999), no. 2, 204-232.

31. E. HERR, *Sauver la paix. Qu'en dit l'Église?* (Chrétiens aujourd'hui. N.S., 5), Namur, Culture et vérité, 1991, pp. 81-130.

32. Both letters are reprinted in O'BRIEN & SHANNON, *Catholic Social Thought* (n. 9).

33. E. KENNEDY, *Re-Imagining American Catholicism. The American Bishops and their Pastoral Letters*, New York, 1985.

and Perfecting It in Comformity with the Precepts of the Gospel". Building on the "unchanging and unchangeable" (*QA* 19) principles, deriving from divine Revelation and natural law, the pathways in the social realm leading to the re-christianisation of modern society, were outlined: strict observance of Catholic morals on the individual level, co-operation between workers and employers on the meso-level, a cor-- poratist organisation of the economy on the macro-level. Catholic social doctrine was the only orderly and safe "third way" between capitalism and socialism. In the eyes of Pius XI, the doctrine was the only antidote "to preserve the human family from dire havoc (*ab immani prorsus exitio*)" (*QA* 144).

After 1960 this *reconquista* approach was given up. The struggle for the retrieval of a natural, Christian order, which had been disrupted by modernity, gave way to a vision of evangelical testimony and commitment in this world. The deductive reasoning from the heights of natural law and Christian philosophy gave way before evangelical values, biblical references, the search for "the signs of the time" and the pressing appeal of the ideal of the Kingdom of God. Doctrinal statements receded before the appeal to values "to all men of good will", a clause regularly added since *Pacem in terris* (1963). The new style has been maintained in the social encyclicals of John Paul II, even if he continues to stress their doctrinal aspect.

IV. CONCLUSION AND CHALLENGES AHEAD

After 1960 the Popes continue to publish social encyclicals and documents. The speed of publication is remarkably higher then before. In these documents they repeatedly refer, always in a respectful manner, to their predecessors, so that at first glance changes seem to have only minor importance. I have tried to show in this chapter that this appearance of continuity is a false one. It is a typical Roman ecclesiastical style used to legitimate her statements and positions. The appearance of continuity is in part also due to the fact that Catholic social teaching is mostly analysed only at a conceptual level, as a stream of documents. What surprises me in is the eagerness with which many thoughtful commentators are ready to go along with this claim of continuity. Even an author like Dorr (1992) depicts Catholic social teaching, in his deservedly famous book, as a "coherent and organic tradition"[34], undergoing after

---

34. DORR, *Option for the Poor* (n. 1), p. 352.

1960 "one major change of direction"[35], reflecting the changing of sides
on the part of the church from being a natural ally of the established
forces of society to an "option for the poor".

In my opinion, the changes are much more profound. The whole functioning of Catholic social teaching, conceptually and in practice, has
changed seriously since 1960:
a shift from a highly focussed and specific issue of class conflict to a
heterogeneous collection of issues, loosely united by a humanist-reli-
gious perspective;
a move from a tight theological straitjacket towards speaking in many
tongues, with an appeal to basic values and to commitment in the modern world replacing the previous deductive outlining of an alternative
Christian order;
a retreat of top-down discourse in favour of a broad range of semi-
autonomous discourses involving multiple actors, the Roman voice more
as *primus inter pares*;
a tendency of the Catholic sub-culture and especially the Catholic social
movements to disappear or detach themselves from the Church, resulting
in a reduction of the impact of Catholic social teaching on the ground;
a marked decline in ultramontane mass Catholicism, with the Church as
a hierarchical mass organisation, and hence in the previous operational
base of Catholic social teaching.

Yet I wish to add immediately that this doesn't imply the end of
Catholic social teaching and thinking. From the side of society, also
from non-Catholics, there is still a demand for the Church to make public statements on burning contemporary issues. Moreover, it should be
acknowledged that the Church after 1960, in contrast with the 19th century, has not hesitated to address swiftly many new issues of present-day
society. This is in part almost certainly due to the presence of the modern tradition of classical social teaching. This made the Church sensitive
to social problems and to their structural base (see the concept of "structural sin" in *Sollicitudo rei socialis*). Furthermore, the basic documents
of Catholic social teaching – of course *Rerum novarum* but also *Gaudium
et spes* and *Populorum progressio* – continue to inspire and to serve as
models for present-day interventions and declarations of Catholics. So,
at first sight, there are many reasons not to fear a quick and complete
passing away of Catholic social teaching and thinking. The centenary
tradition, which forces the Church to face the structural social problems
of modern society, is still being continued, although it is now set at a

35. *Ibid.*, p. 379.

lower pitch and is advancing in scattered battle order and in a more undogmatic way, reflecting changes in the wider Church.

A final comment. In my opinion, important though the modifications in themes, actors and styles may be, these are not sufficient for Catholic social thinking to remain vital. Given the profound changes after 1960, the advent of a new era in modernity and in Catholicism, more far-reaching transformations seem necessary. First, lack of intellectual quality is surely a threat to the future of Catholic social thinking. People have a right to expect rigorous answers to real questions, Shallow thinking can be countered only by more international and interdisciplinary co-operation between social scientists and theologians, to include significant Third World countries and interests, and to encompass the perspective of an impending world-wide modernity, with its many concomitant problems. Global Catholicism is geographically and institutionally well suited to tackle the major challenges ahead (like mass migration and multiculturalism) from such a perspective. Second, Rome has not fully acknowledged or accepted the moves towards greater pluralism, participation and semi-autonomy outlined above, and it lacks a clear view on its own position in the new constellation. I believe Rome could yet remain a prime force in the social field provided it can move forward in these ways. For example, given the scattered contributions which are being made all over the world, Rome is still best suited to act as promoter and co-ordinator of world-wide discussions, and to synthesise them into major documents.

A final challenge is even more vital, though I see no simple answer to it. Since Catholics, let alone the population at large, can no longer be considered to constitute "auxiliary troops", the question now is how to draw attention to Catholic social teaching in a semi-secularised world, how to move people into action, how to mobilise good intentions. A certain solidity of Catholic social teaching is essential. The existence of models, institutions and groups that give us a glimpse of what can be done is important. The organisation of a permanent discussion, consultation and co-operation process on social issues will also contribute to the profile of Catholic social teaching. As Hengsbach, re-phrasing MacLuhan, stated: "The process is the message"[36]. Above all, daring to mobilise people at crucial moments in the face of real problems will be essential. Catholic mobilisation of the rank and file was a major strength

---

36. F. HENGSBACH, *Der Prozeß ist die Botschaft. Zur Pluralit?t der Subjekte kirchlicher Soziallehre*, in M. HEIMBACH-STEINS, A. LIENKAMP & J. WIEMEYER (eds.), *Brennpunkt Sozialethik. Theorien, Aufgaben, Methoden*, Freiburg, Herder, 1995, pp. 69-85.

in the past. But today the Church is hesitant to mobilise Catholics on social matters, as the ambivalent attitude to the peace issue in the eighties has shown. But if Catholic social teaching wants to have an impact, it will have to search for issues and occasions where it can mobilise to make its voice heard on behalf of its social vision. If not, its social declarations will be met, like the social encyclicals of John Paul II, with friendly disregard.

Catholic Theological University   Staf HELLEMANS[37]
Utrecht

37. The author thanks Frank McHugh, Patrick Pasture and Johan Verstraeten for their comments on an earlier draft and for the many bibliographical references they gave.

SOURCES AND STRUCTURES

MUDDLE OR MIDDLE-LEVEL?
A PLACE FOR NATURAL LAW
IN CATHOLIC SOCIAL THOUGHT

If the present social situation is to be controlled by Christian principles, thoughts will be necessary which have not yet been thought, and which will correspond to this new situation as older forms met the need of the social situation in earlier ages. These ideas will have to be evolved out of the inner impulse of Christian thought, and out of its vital expression at the present time, and not exclusively out of the New Testament[1].

PREMODERN – MODERN – POSTMODERN PARADIGM IN ETHICS

The current dominant project in moral and political philosophy is a pincer movement, squeezing ethical modernity's standard options of deontology, consequentialism, emotivism and contractarianism. Four standard options are denominated here to cover its most significant expressions, but the label "ethical modernity" embraces the theories of all those thinkers from the Enlightenment onwards who undertook the challenge of constructing a "science of morality". The project is fore-grounded in title and text from Spinoza's *Ethica ordine geometrica demonstrata* (1677) through to Sidgwick's *The Methods of Ethics* (1874)[2]. The ethical modernists divide into two groups. First, there are the thinkers, harbouring a limited conception of human nature and its *telos,* who built their moral science on one half of human experience, the calculative half, estimating morality and ethics in terms of self-preservation or the pursuit of pleasure. This group would include Hume, Hobbes, Grotius, Bentham and Mill and their utilitarian descendants in

---

1. E. TROELTSCH, *The Social Teaching of the Christian Churches*, Chicago, IL, University of Chicago Press, 1981, pp. 1012-1013.
2. "I have thought that the predominance in the minds of moralists of a desire to edify has impeded the real progress of ethical science: and that this would be benefited by an application to it of the same disinterested curiosity to which we chiefly owe the great discoveries of science": H. SIDGWICK, *The Methods of Ethics,* London, MacMillan, 1874, p. vi. An interesting discussion of religious, moral and aesthetic consequences of modernism can be found in R. SCRUTON, *An Intelligent Person's Guide to Modern Culture,* London, Duckworth, 1998, ch. 7. A recent work which touches on these themes in connection with the discussion of modernity is D. LACHTERMAN, *The Ethics of Geometry. A Genealogy of Modernity*, New York, NY, Routledge, 1989.

both philosophy and political economy. Hobbes may stand as the figurehead of the group, since he pre-eminently shifted moral thinking from
theoria to *techne,* using geometric deduction as the paradigm for reason
and leading a long march into a disenchanted world. The second group,
with Kant as its figurehead, grounded ethics in pure reason. The two
groups diverged in their epistemologies, but were united in being foundationalist in the sense that they projected ethics as a search for basic principles from which intermediate axioms could be deduced, rules formu-
lated and observable transitions made to the solution of particular cases[3].

ETHICAL MODERNITY

It is on this system of ethical modernity that the pincer movement has
shut. Until recently the debate was conducted between and within the
different schools of ethical modernity, but radical critiques of all their
theories are now proposed by one wing of the pincer movement, which
is pre-modern, and the other, which is post-modern. The former invokes
Aristotelian themes of virtue and the latter post-Nietzschean criticisms of
nihilism. The literature runs from Habermas to MacIntyre[4]. Following
Elizabeth Anscombe's earlier criticisms of rule-based ethics[5], MacIntyre,
according full recognition to the contingent aspects of human living, has
argued for a moral philosophy which is concerned with personal worth
and virtue rather than with methods for probing the rightness or wrong-
ness of particular acts[6]. Habermas analyses Nietzsche's dissolution of the

3. It is some indication of the achievement and durability of ethical modernity that it
provided until recently the standard syllabus in moral and political philosophy in British
universities. The typical syllabus for the degree in Politics, Philosophy and Economics at
the University of Oxford covered Descartes, Hobbes, Hume, Locke, Kant, Sidgwick, the
Oxford Idealists, Green, Bosanquet, G.E. Moore and Bradley. In his latest book John
Gray closes down the possibility of returning, a la MacIntyre, to a premodern tradition on
the grounds that it also is foundationalist. He writes: "There can, in my view, be no
rolling back the central project of modernity, which is the Enlightenment project, with all
its consequences in terms of disenchantment and ultimate groundlessness. The modernist
project of Enlightenment though it broke with premodern, classical and medieval, thought
at many points, was also continuous with it in its universalism and its foundationalist and
representationalist rationalism": J. GRAY, *Enlightenment's Wake: Politics and Culture at
the Close of the Modern Age,* London, Routledge, 1995, p. 152. My essay makes an
attempt to rescue medieval ethical theory from this closure.
    4. J. HABERMAS, *Knowledge and Human Interests,* London, Heinemann Books, 1972;
A. MACINTYRE, *After Virtue,* London, Duckworth, 1984.
    5. G.E.M. ANSCOMBE, *Modern Moral Philosophy,* in *Philosophy* 33 (1958) 1-19.
    6. J. HALDANE, *Thomism and the Future of Catholic Philosophy,* in *New Blackfriars*
80 (1999), no. 938, 158-171.

category of human nature and his nihilistic conclusions and proposes a critical theory of human behaviour and society (which he presents as a theory of knowledge and practical philosophy, and now, in his most recent book, in terms of "responses to the significant others"), emerging from human communication and community discourse and issuing in norms that are unconditionally binding[7]. The position of Wittgenstein is different, but radical in its own way. As part of his claim that the meaning and value of the world are inexpressible he argues that the ethical also is inexpressible, and "hence there can be no ethical propositions"[8].

Modern Natural Law as Part of Ethical Modernity

This fashionable critique of ethical modernity may be applied, with justification, to natural law theory, which also became foundationalist, a matter of method and rule-based, and thus open to many of the criticisms which are put forward by virtue ethics against ethical modernity. While Hume, Hobbes and the whole calculative school of moral and political philosophy were repudiating natural law and natural rights as "palaces built on sand and mud" (Descartes) or as "nonsense upon stilts" (Bentham), natural law thinkers borrowed from the intellectual fashions of the day, emphasising the self-contained systematic nature of their ethical theory and even stressing, in a way similar to civil law, the necessity of promulgation as an essential element. Jaffa lays at Aquinas's door the responsibility for the direction which natural law thinking took and he claims that Thomas treated natural law "as a kind of geometric system", and that even if he did not work out "a Euclidean system of natural law", one could infer such a system from his

---

7. Habermas, *Knowledge and Human Interests* (n. 4), p. 290. It is interesting to note how Habermas's approach to moral thinking has influenced German scholars concerned with moral philosophy, ethics and moral theology. For example, Helmut Peukert has confronted the inadequacy of ethics in face of the challenges of our age: H. PEUKERT, *Fundamental Theology and Communicative Practice as the Ethics of Universal Solidarity*, in *The Conrad Grebel Review* 3 (1985), no. 1, 41-65. See also H.-J. HÖHN, *Vernunft, Glaube, Politik. Reflexionsstufen einer christlichen Sozialethik* (Abhandlungen zur Sozialethik, 30), Paderborn, Schöningh, 1990. In relation to middle-level thinking on Catholic social thought, one obvious way forward is to encourage the exchange of ideas which is taking place at this seminar. The preparation of the seminar has demonstrated how, coming from different countries, we know of little of each other's literatures. A next step is to extend this exchange of ideas to other cultures, faiths and religions.

8. L. WITTGENSTEIN, *Tractatus Logico-Philosophicus*, 6.4312, London, Edinburgh University Press, p. 185.

writings[9]. There is some evidence, particularly in relation to Thomas's position on private property, that a calculative tendency had crept into his natural law thinking (a criticism of Aquinas put forward by John Colet and Erasmus at the end of the Middle Ages), and even if it is a questionable criticism of Aquinas himself, the reproach had certainly become deserved by the time of the "high Thomists" of the seventeenth century, neo-scholastics and of the "manualists" from 1880-1960[10]. The impression made on Thomistic thinking by this epistemological shift is recognised by Hans Küng in these words:

> It is easy to see how the triumphs of mathematics and of the experimental exact sciences connected with it, and thus finally also the Cartesian demand for rational method and mathematic and geometric clarity, certainty, evidence – and the Cartesian spirit of the age as a whole – influenced Thomistic theology and philosophy to no small degree...[11]

In late-nineteenth century's official and extensive development of Catholic social teaching or "Christian philosophy" (as Leo XIII preferred to call it in *Rerum novarum,* paras. 16 & 21), a clear underlying theme is to be found presenting a source of ethical wisdom and knowledge, deduced from "natural law", which exists apart from the explicit revelation of God in Jesus Christ, and which provides an ethical rule for all humankind because of a shared human nature. As in all Catholic moral theology, so also in official Catholic social teaching there are two different sources of ethical knowledge and wisdom: revelation and natural law. But in official Catholic social teaching, perhaps even more so than in other areas of moral thinking, there was a tendency to overstress the philosophical aspect.

It is nevertheless an exaggeration to represent this teaching as if it were exclusively derived from natural law, and neglectful of its biblical foundations, as became a fashionable criticism in the 1960s and 1970s. In defence of *Rerum novarum* it must be said, as Thomas Gilby claimed for

9. H. JAFFA, *Thomism and Aristotelianism. A Study of the Commentary by Thomas Aquinas on the Nicomachean Ethics,* Westport, CT, Greenwood Press, 1979, p. 176 and p. 223, note 23.

10. The manualists are those writers of courses in Thomistic ethics and theology who responded to the directives of Pope Leo XIII's encyclical *Aeterni Patris* (1879) for the education of seminarians. See J.A. GALLAGHER, *Time Past and Time Future. An Historical Study of Catholic Moral Theology,* New York, NY, Paulist, 1990; V. MACNAMARA, *Faith and Ethics. Recent Roman Catholicism,* Dublin, Gill & MacMillan, 1985. In connection with Catholic social teaching, interesting points on this topic are made by B. MACSWEENEY, *Roman Catholicism. The Search for Relevance,* Oxford, Blackwell, 1980.

11. H. KÜNG, *Does God Exist?,* London, William Collins Sons Ltd., 1980, pp. 22-29.

Aquinas's ethical teaching in the *Summa,* that it "is integrated in *sacra doctrina,* the teaching of the Gospel revelation, and its full import can be appreciated only when it is read as a living part of this organic whole"[12]. This tension between the claims of the two sources appears, for example, in paragraph 21 of *Rerum novarum,* (referred to above), where the Italian text (which was the basis for the Latin one) uses the term "evangelical law" instead of "Christian teaching"; and at the end of that same paragraph it reads "contained in the Gospel" instead of "which Christian philosophy teaches". Leo, who was an eminent Latin scholar, may be read as declaring his own philosophical preference in the final Latin text. However, although it is true that in its most guarded expression Catholic social teaching preserved a balance between reason and revelation as its twin sources of ethical knowledge, nonetheless papal social teaching continued to favour a moral philosophy methodology until as late as John XXIII's *Mater et Magistra* (1961) and *Pacem in terris* (1963); and after a shift of methodological emphasis at the Second Vatican Council, it has made a reappearance in the style of thinking of Pope John Paul II.

The monolithic cast of pre-Vatican II Catholic social teaching, with its emphasis on rational method, clarity and certainty, appropriated as the instrument of hierarchical authority, conferred a high profile on the corpus of teaching. In an unexpected way this magisterial style of teaching was re-enforced by increased cross-fertilisation with the social sciences. As early as 1920, Pope Benedict XV recommended close attention to social science, a line of development reiterated by Pius XI in the 1930s and elaborated by Paul VI in the 1970s, particularly in *Octogesima adveniens.* When positivist methodology took hold, particularly of sociology in the 1960s and 1970s, Catholic social teaching *eo ipso* became more objectivist. Whereas at first social sciences were seen as harsh critics of the abstract and a-historical metaphysics of Catholic social teaching and as a relativist corrective of the static and universalist social ethics deduced from natural law, later on they strengthened the "expertise" of Catholic social thought and added to the *nil sine episcopo* mentality of the *magisterium*[13]. As John Milbank has argued in a more

---

12. T. GILBY, O.P., *Principles of Morality* (Summa Theologiae, 18), Oxford, New Blackfriars, p. xxi.

13. These themes are extensively set out in F.P. MCHUGH, *The Social Role of the Roman Catholic Church in England, 1958-1982,* Cambridge University, Unpublished thesis, 1982. The wider debate is extensively discussed in D. MAUGENEST, *Le discours social de l'Église catholique de Léon XIII à Jean-Paul II* (Église et société), Paris, Centurion, 1985, ²1994. The significance of the debate is precisely identified in J.-Y. CALVEZ, *Les silences de la doctrine sociale catholique,* Paris, Les Éditions de l'Atelier, 1999, chapters 1 and 7.

general context, while post-Nietzschean social theorists grew suspicious of secular rationality, modern theologians worked ingenuously under constraint of a respect for the secular social disciplines, and this gave an increased confidence to bishops in their social pronouncements.

The tenacity of hierarchical control over social teaching in the Catholic Church in England remained unchallenged until the 1970s. In the wake of Vatican II reconstruction, the experience of the laity on organised Church committees, where they began to find a certain autonomous voice in ethics and theology, unmasked this formalist style of thinking and encouraged a fashionable rejection of natural law thinking. Until that time, certainty had reigned: the manualists insisted that the first principles of natural law (although I can find only one in Ia IIae, art. 94: "Good is to be done and sought after, and evil avoided" – all others are derived from this one) are knowable by every sane adult. Absolutism held: the principles were valid at all times and in every place (*Quod semper, quod ubique, quod ab omnibus*). They could be applied in every case to decide intrinsically good and evil acts (and there were many of them, for instance, duelling); and universalism (in an Aristotelian model) was selective: women's voices were not heard in social thinking, and Christian social teaching was European and Roman Catholic.

The coherent and self-sustaining nature of natural law social theory, part of the "seamless robe" of seminary Catholic theology in the 1950s and imbued with new strength in the writings of Jacques Maritain, an "open" and non-manualist Thomist who retained a natural law approach, though not in the one-sided distortion and rationalistic cast of the seventeenth century and subsequent manualists, formed my own introduction to Catholic social teaching. It seemed to contend with the problematic of social ethics, which is tension between the moral demands of principles and the seeming-autonomy of social realities. The presentation of CST in the 1940s and 1950s as "Catholic Sociology" provided something of a synthesis of ethics and social science, and the writings of the Christendom Group, coming from a Church of England provenance, offered support for this approach. An impressive proponent of this style of Christian social thinking (and someone who influenced my ideas at that time) was J.V. Langmead Casserley. Another much respected public voice was that of Archbishop Temple. My doctrinal orthodoxy was confirmed by my studies at Plater College, the Catholic Workers' College, Oxford and by my association with the Catholic Social Guild, though the study of economics and sociology (then in its positivist phase) introduced intimations of relativity into my thought structures. Any failure of nerve in the wake of Vatican II, however, was allayed by John Courtney Murray's *The Eternal Return of Natural Law*[14].

A Repudiation of Modern Natural Law

Modern natural law, a compound of Greek speculation, Roman Catholic manualist theology and idealism, has been subjected successively to attacks by writers: some from the legal profession, others moral philosophers, and, more recently, Catholic theologians, who, in my view, have not thought firmly about the theory or even taken the trouble to explore the exact nature of the claims made by natural law theory. John Finnis numbers among the legal writers: Kelsen, Ross, Hart, Raz, Wolfgang Friedman and Julius Stone[15]. Approaching the subject from a different angle, many in the Protestant tradition have rejected the idea of a source for ethical wisdom based on human nature and human reason. For this reason Karl Barth opposed both natural theology and natural law as well as the ontology on which they were based. Influenced by the change in methodology introduced by the Second Vatican Council, many writers on Catholic social teaching dismissed natural law too readily and paraded a rather bland view that there had been a shift away from natural law towards a more Gospel-based and faith-based approach. If this means, only, that there has been a shift away from ethics as a method and as rule-based, and from a formalist understanding of the term "Catholic social doctrine", then it was a welcome development, as was also the theological move towards a more Gospel-centred social thinking. But if it means (as it frequently has) that the shift implies the loss of a structure of thought which preserves a continuing and useful place for natural law in Catholic social thinking, and as it happens, can provide for modern virtue theory an intellectual underpinning which it seems to lack, then the development must be regretted[16].

14. J.C. Murray, *We Hold These Truths. Catholic Reflections on the American Proposition*, New York, NY, Sheed and Ward, 1961; J. Maritain, *Man and the State*, Chicago, IL, University of Chicago Press, 1951, pp. 108-114; J.W. Evans & L.R. Ward (eds.), *The Social and Political Philosophy of Jacques Maritain*, London, Bles, 1956; W. Temple, *Christianity and the Social Order*, Reading, Shepheard-Walwyn Ltd, 1976; A.M. Suggate, *William Temple and Christian Social Ethics Today*, Edinburgh, Clark, 1987; J.V. Langmead Casserley, *Morals and Man in the Social Sciences*, London, Longmans, Green, 1951.

15. J. Finnis, *Natural Law and Natural Rights* (Clarendon Law Series), Oxford, Clarendon Press, 1980.

16. This viewpoint is set out with great clarity and cogency in a classic critical review of John Finnis's book by B. Renton, *Finnis on Natural Law*, in *The Kingston Law Review* (1981), April, no. II/1, 30-68, to which I am much indebted.

Virtue Ethics

As an alternative to all rule-based ethical thinking, modern virtue ethics, derived from Aristotelian thinking, but uncoupled from his teleological biology and, *eo ipso,* from Aristotle's precise understanding of "nature", has become a first choice among academics. Cordner claims that "virtue ethics is prominent, if not pre-eminent, in contemporary moral philosophy"[17]; and Cottingham says of the theory that its revival "seems to be one of the most promising recent developments in philosophical ethics"[18]. Although virtue ethics has been confined, for the most part, to the reconstruction of moral theory, it has begun to influence political thought[19] and has been applied recently to business and finance ethics[20].

As with Aristotle and Aquinas, the latter of whom receives too little attention in the literature[21], modern virtue ethics focuses on the agent rather than on individual acts, on character rather than a system of general rules, on the perfection of the human soul rather than specific moral events, on human flourishing rather than calculative self-interest[22]. The attraction of this approach to ethics is appreciated even by some utilitarians, who, in yet another attempt to overcome the difficulties of calculating consequences as a method of making moral judgements, have moved from act – to rule – utilitarianism and now on to "character-utilitarianism"[23].

17. C. Cordner, *Aristotelian Virtue and Its Limitations*, in *Philosophy* 69 (1994), no. 269, 291-316, esp. 291.

18. J. Cottingham, *Religion, Virtue and Ethical Culture*, in *Philosophy* 69 (1994), no. 268, 163-180, esp. 177.

19. A. MacIntyre, *Whose Justice? Which Rationality?*, London, Duckworth, 1988.

20. E. Sternberg, *Just Business. Business Ethics in Action*, U.K., Little, Brown & Company, 1994; R.C. Solomon, *Corporate Roles, Personal Virtues. An Aristotelian Approach*, in D. Statman (ed.), *Virtue Ethics. A Critical Reader*, Edinburgh, Edinburgh University, 1997; J. Dobson, *Finance Ethics. The Rationality of Virtue*, New York, NY, Lanham, 1998.

21. In the 16 chapters of Statman's book, *Virtue Ethics* (n. 20), there are only 2 references to Aquinas and 1 to natural law.

22. It may be of some interest in making connections, which are often fruitful in "middle-level thinking", that contemporary natural law thinkers share with virtue ethics thinkers a preoccupation with the notion of "human flourishing". Statmans' book has 11 references in the index to "flourishing", as well as others to *eudaimonia;* and both Finnis and G. Grisez & R. Shaw, *Beyond the New Morality. The Responsibilities of Freedom*, Notre Dame, IN, University of Notre Dame Press, 1974, develop, respectively, "forms of good" and "purposes" leading to "human flourishing".

23. Statman, *Virtue Ethics* (n. 20), p. 7; G.-X. Santos, *Does Aristotle Have a Virtue Ethics?*, in Statman, *Virtue Ethics* (n. 20), pp. 260-285.

The Force and Failure of Virtue Ethics

Modern Catholic natural law both in its tight form, which held sway until the late 1950s, and in a weaker form which still creeps through much official and non-official Catholic social teaching and thinking, is vulnerable to many criticisms which apply to all forms of ethical modernity. For example, the rejection of a method and rule-based approach and the restoration to ethics of virtue and internal human worth should attract Catholic social thinkers, since, correspondingly, documents of Church social teaching, almost as if to make sure that what was being presented was not simply read as some kind of political manifesto, always end with references to virtue and theological themes[24]. The notion of "human flourishing", which is common to both natural law and virtue ethics, should encourage middle-level thinking about the nature of social ethics, and in so far as this is a retrieval of a dimension of orthodox Thomism it is *ipso facto* a retrieval of an aspect of virtue ethics which may be used as interlocutor of natural law, as Aristotelian pre-modernism is used as interlocutor of ethical modernity.

But to agree to submit modern natural law to certain corrections put forward by virtue ethics, or, indeed, the wider critique proposed by pre-modern or post-modern options, is not to be taken as a denial that resources exist in classical natural law theory which justify the task of giving natural law, in some form, an enduring place in Catholic social thought. Indeed, a retrieval of this kind may serve a similar purpose in strengthening virtue theory, which may itself be viewed as requiring a natural law foundation. One basic comment on modern virtue theory is that it needs to preserve Aquinas's dignified conception of the human *telos* and the virtues which make it known and attainable.

What virtue ethics seems not to do (and what any alternative paradigm in moral philosophy and ethics must attempt) is to demonstrate the inseparability of the concerns of modern philosophy and postmodern philosophy with sociological theory and political economy, and to include in this a construal of them all in relation to their ethical and religious thrust. For example, since the subjective turn which social theory took with Weber, human action has been a focus of sociological concern for writers such as Isaiah Berlin, A.R. Louch, Richard Bernstein and the whole school of ethnomethodologists[25]. Berlin and Louch have stressed

24. See, for example, *Rerum novarum,* par. 45.
25. A.R. Louch, *Explanation and Human Action* (Campus, 17), Berkeley, CA, University of California Press, 1969; R.J. Bernstein, *The Restructuring of Social and Political Theory*, Oxford, Blackwell, 1976.

the nature of human action as a moral concept; and Giddens, with his theory of structuration has unified theories of human action and structural theory. The complex relation of human-action-as-moral to political action, and to social structures, has important implications for virtue theory (noted by Pope John Paul II in his discussion of "structural sin" in *Sollicitudo rei socialis*), but their impact seems not to be appreciated by virtue ethics writers, with a resultant inability to develop a social ethic and to specify modalities for dealing with public policy. What is at issue here is a disagreement with MacIntyre's claim that the pre-modern virtue-centred ethics cannot accommodate modern systematic politics, whether liberal, conservative, radical or socialist.

Natural law, equally, must appreciate the implications of these developments in social theory, but it is a hopeful sign that indictments of the theory of natural law and attempts at reconstruction may end up renewing the tradition in the attempt to overcome it. MacIntyre's "tradition-constituted enquiry" may be used with a more forceful meaning: in order, that is, to argue that the element of truth-seeking and the pursuit of good (the objectives, respectively, of the speculative and practical reason in Thomistic philosophy) hold a privileged place in Catholic social thought. This is not to argue absolutism, universalism or inflexibility, since there is good reason to accept that there is agreement by both Aristotle and Aquinas that moral principles are true only for the most part *(ut in pluribus)* and not without exception. The principle of *epikeia (benigna interpretatio legis ubi deficit lex propter universale)* is not just an external escape-route from hard moral choices, but is intrinsic to the system of Catholic moral thought.

At this stage my proposal is a modest one: that the long-reflected element of moral philosophy in Catholic social thought, with natural law as theoretically central to it, is a persistent and distinctive one. What is needed now is not the abandonment of this central element, but the development of middle-level thinking to make informed connections between natural law, political economy and public issues, taking us beyond the legitimate aims of virtue theory and the usefulness of narrative. The restoration of natural law as a distinctive element in Catholic social thinking is part of the recovery of the Catholic tradition. It is not a fiction, but part of the Catholic myth, an element of our imagination and sympathy. Such a development would be timely in relation to the "theological turn" in sociology, which is bringing out convergences in recent thinking on politics and economics which until recently were considered closed by a critique of religion on which, claimed Marx, all criticism is founded. Milbank rather than MacIntyre is the fertile source on these themes, although it is not necessary to accept Milbank's synthesis of denigration (of everything, that is, except theology). What Milbank argues, however, cannot be dismissed lightly. As part of that synthesis (and this is a serious challenge to an even reconstructed natural law approach and equally to virtue ethics) he writes:

> In a sense, indeed, I am not concerned to provide an 'ethics' (and doubt even the desirability of doing so) but rather to describe a supra-ethical religious affirmation which recasts the ethical field in terms of religious hope; we may think of the good as infinitely realisable harmony if we believe that reality can finally receive such an imprint. This faith sustains ethical hope, but it also overthrows every 'morality'; every description in terms of such and such an inviolable law, uniquely valuable virtue or exemplary politics[26].

In a setting that is an "ecclesiology of life" rather than one of churches as moral critics of the state, John Milbank aims to dispose of nihilism with dogmatics. But the split between Caesar and God has not appeared in this form in history nor in the history of ideas (think of Hegel, Weber and Troeltsch), and one begins to ask in what sense his project has purchase on the realities of social life, and if such a strategy is likely to penetrate the reality of contemporary economic and political life? This is a serious question for Catholic social thinkers, since it has to be acknowledged that the corpus of official Catholic social teaching, as embodied in the encyclicals, in spite of its contemporary high profile, has not so far shown great penetrative potential. The recovery of the tradition must go beyond the standard exegesis of encyclicals to include the streams of thinking which constitute "Catholic non-official social thinking", as described by Jonathan Boswell in his essay in this collection.

The tenuous linkage of virtue theory to sociological theory not only produces a weak analysis of our contemporary ethical crisis but also seems not to assist the development of a social ethic. It is a-political and lacks a critique of institutions, with the result that it is not poised to challenge the present state of the world or its development on the edge of a new millennium. By not recognising any continuity between modernity – both theoretical comprehension and institutions – and its own enterprise, virtue ethics neither deals with the issues of authority and domination nor with the predicament of the modern state and society. It

---

26. J. MILBANK, *Enclaves, or Where is the Church?*, in *New Blackfriars* 73 (1992), no. 861, 341-352.

neglects, too, the subject of religions, church and state, which Milbank
exposes as central to the dilemma of secular reason. The discussion
seems fixed in academic terms and not inhabiting at all the world of
institutions which Catholic non-official social thinking must address.
The issue here is the challenge to any ethics (and Milbank and virtue
ethics are being used as interlocutors of natural law) to be able to provide a structural as well as a personal ethic.

The sociology of the question is proposed by Giddens in his claim that
the features of society which post-modernists most want to explain
(social fragmentation, the end of foundationalist knowledge and the
uncontrollable pace of social change) are already explicable under the
name of "modernity" or, more accurately, "high modernity". Giddens,
concentrating on the institutional side, describes modernity by four social
formations: capitalism, industrialism, surveillance (the gathering and use
of information) and military power[27].

Along with the inherent reflexivity of knowledge made possible in
modern society by information technology, these constitute "high-
modernity", and any attempt to supersede modernity must deal with
this reality. From the side of contemporary secular institutional thinking
there is evidence of a new awareness of and interest in ethical considerations. For example, the recent World Bank document, *The World
Development Report on Poverty,* has an unusual vocabulary: empowerment, opportunity, voice and participation, vulnerability and safety nets,
global forces and the poor. Harking back to the quotation at the beginning of this paper, any viable social ethic must relate the inner impulse
of Christian thought to congenial secular apprehensions of the moral
dimension of the new situation. Peukert and other writers influenced by
Habermas have appreciated the challenge in this form; and if there is a
place for natural law, it also must be able to confront this challenge.
This collection is an initiative in setting an agenda for Catholic non-
official social thinking: it is beginning with an attempt to think from
within the Catholic tradition. This is only a first step: the dialogue with
other churches, faiths, religious traditions and other continents must follow.

27. A. GIDDENS, *The Class Structure of Advanced Societies*, London, Hutchinson,
1978; ID., *The Constitution of Society. Outline of the Theory of Structuration*, Cam-
bridge, Polity Press, 1984; ID., *The Third Way. The Renewal of Social Democracy*,
Cambridge, Polity Press, 1998; G. ARRIGHI, *The Long Twentieth Century. Money,
Power and the Origins of our Times,* London, Verso, 1994; J. O'NEILL, *The Market.
Ethics, Knowledge and Politics* (Economics as Social Theory), London, Routledge and
Kegan, 1998.

The Place of Natural Law

My examination of the incompleteness of virtue ethics presented in this paper may seem to give the theory an attention it does not merit, but the aim has been, first, to use virtue ethics as an interlocutor to clarify questions which a contemporary formulation of natural law must deal with; and, second, to indicate ways in which modern natural law itself became part of "ethical modernity", thereby making it a participant in the muddle that is contemporary ethical and political thinking. Influenced by systemic considerations, neo-Thomists and manualists listed the following claims as descriptive of natural law:

that ethical norms can be derived from facts;
that what natural law recognises as self-evident must be recognised as self-evident by all;
that the first principles of natural law are inferred from speculative principles, or from facts, or from metaphysical propositions about human nature, or about the nature of good and evil, or from teleological conceptions of human nature;
that natural law presupposes the existence and will of God;
that natural functions and faculties must not be deflected from their natural ends (the "perverted faculty" argument).

Apart from the sense of unreality which such language and concepts evoke, it is worth indicating some of the muddle in this kind of approach to natural law. First, it is not clear what the "is/ought" debate means or whether it means anything at all, as extensive literature has demonstrated. What is true is that all moral apprehensions (not "propositions", which is a verbal mode) can be derived only from the world of facts, for there is nowhere else to go. They are not logically deduced or inferred since logical inference is not, anyhow, our customary path to truth. The extensive literature in philosophy and Catholic theology since Vatican II has covered the muddled nature of much thinking on natural law, although what has happened, it is being claimed here, is that the baby has been thrown out with the bath-water.

Not that these debates are anything new. Natural law as "right reason", of unvarying, universal and everlasting application, soon created difficulties for those theologians who incorporated it, from Greek, Roman and Stoic sources, into their theology. It became necessary, for example, to adjudicate the claims of faith and reason, or to decide that they were co-extensive or at least mutually supportive. The more influence ascribed to natural law, the less the need for moral theology, which was quite unacceptable to Scotists and nominalists. Theologians never quite arrived at satisfactory answers to the problems of reconciling "natural justice" with the theology of original sin, or unvarying prescriptions with cultural variations in mores and legislation. There is still a prolific literature on these dilemmas[28].

THE DISTINCTIVENESS OF NATURAL LAW

There are two themes which bring out the contrast between Aquinas's treatment of natural law ethics and those pre-modern and post-modern alternatives (especially virtue ethics) which have been counter-opposed to ethical modernity. The first is the nature of practical knowledge. The second is the relation of history to ethical reflection and practice.

Central to Aquinas's discussion of natural law in Ia-IIae, Q. 94, art 2 is the distinction he makes between speculative reason (whose object is truth) and practical reason (which directs the doing of a task). Both of these are "self-evident principles" *(per se nota)*. A self-evident principle, as understood by Thomas, is what we would now call "analytic proposition", that is one that does not deliver any new knowledge but unfolds for us the same statement in additional words. Aquinas points out that the statement "man is rational" is not self-evident in the same way as "the whole is greater than the part", and it seems that his theory of knowledge includes apprehensions as intuited from experience. "Good", as the task which the practical reason directs as to be done, is intuited in this way, or, as Aquinas put it, there are "things to which man has a natural inclination" and "which are naturally apprehended as human goods". Reason naturally apprehends four such goods: the preservation of human life, the sexual drive and nurture of children, a desire to know the truth, to live in society.

Two points are worth underlining: first, this approach to natural law distinguishes it from deduction and ethical casuistry; and second, there is clearly a structural and societal dimension to this ethic. Thus, the implications of practical knowledge readily lead to social ethics and even to politics.

---

28. F. MOBBS, *Is Natural Law Part of Revelation? – The Answer of the Manualists, Germain Grisez and Timothy O'Connell*. The early and medieval aspects of this question are well discussed and documented in J. VINER, J. MELITZ & D. WINCH (eds.), *Religious Thought and Economic Society. Four chapters of an Unfinished Work*, Durham, NC, Duke University Press, 1978, esp. pp. 118-121. In connection with Catholic social thinking, Jean-Yves Calvez perceptively identifies Pope John Paul II's restoration of the term "social doctrine" and the use of natural law from the time of the Puebla conference as a way of preserving the distinctiveness of Catholic social teaching: CALVEZ, *Les silences de la doctrine social catholique* (n. 13), pp. 19-30. My thought in this section has been greatly influenced by Renton's article *Finnis on Natural Law* referred to above (n. 16).

Aquinas, like Aristotle, realised, however, that it is impossible to devise guiding ethical principles for particular cases and he adapted the Greek philosopher's *phronesis (prudentia,* in Aquinas) as the means-end judgement directed towards the ultimate end. In Book V of *The Nichomachean Ethics,* Aristotle defines "practical wisdom" as "a disposition of grasping truth, involving reason, concerned with action about what is good or bad for the human being". The important role which *prudentia* is called upon to play is to be a bridge between knowledge and virtue, and between general principles and guidance on particular actions. As mentioned earlier, even when all these measures are in place, it still remains the case that ethical principles are true only for the most part. There remains the fundamental question whether any principle or method is adequate for identifying particular goods in specific cases. What is being claimed here, as a strength of natural law, is that the determination of the ethical life is a complex matter calling for attention to detail and one with a certain "elective affinity" (to use Weber's phrase) to thinking about policy.

Looked at from another angle, Aquinas's ethics is not a self-contained system independent of his theology or his metaphysics. For example, his philosophical distinction between *facere* and *agere* may be put to good account in discussing his approach to creation and sustainability; and by incorporating prudence, charity and *praxis* into its method Aquinas's ethics provides a larger role for creative thinking than has been hitherto accorded to natural law taken in isolation from its ontological context. Thinking back to the reference to Thomas Gilby earlier in this chapter, what is being suggested here is that Catholic social thought in a Thomistic style is not purely philosophical, but is disposed to theological expression and even to political implications: it is for other papers to develop these themes. In addition to a fruitful theology of creation, Thomas's discussion of the *verbum mentis* and his double meaning for *logos,* might deliver an aesthetic which would enrich theology. It may even be that new readings of these elements would make a place for John Milbank's challenging claim, which must be considered by middle-level thinkers if Catholic social thought is to be revised:

> ...Christians are moroi not phronomoi (not prudent, not ethical) and only phronimoi in Christ according to an economy in which loss turns out to be gain (I Cor. IV:10). Fools, because they give themselves away, and not for a cause, not to a city, not to a place, only as links in a continuous non-teleological chain of givings-away[29].

29. MILBANK, *Enclaves* (n. 26), p. 345.

THE VIRTUE OF JUSTICE

Aquinas's theory of natural law cannot be taken in isolation from his discussion of the virtues, which includes natural virtues, infused virtues, prudence and charity. Amongst these, justice holds a privileged position, connected to the fourth natural good mentioned above: to live in society. He takes his lead from Aristotle, who taught that "all men mean by justice that kind of state or character which makes people disposed to do what is just", so that "justice is first in the mind and will of people before it emerges in acts". In its most general form, "justice is complete virtue in its fullest sense... because he who possesses it can exercise his virtue not only in himself but also towards his neighbour". It follows that "justice in this sense is not part of virtue but virtue entire"[30].

Aquinas explains that each virtue, fidelity, generosity, kindliness, cheerfulness, truthfulness, courage, has a content of its own, but as directed to the common good each virtue is justice. Aquinas calls this "general" justice. Because of this, all human actions must be "other-regarding". Following Aristotle, Aquinas distinguishes general justice into "commutative" (exchange) and "distributive" justice. The former covers the justice of exchanging thing for thing, and is arithmetic. But distributive justice is different. It demands discrimination, and the determination of the obligations of distributive justice turns upon people's place in the community. As Aquinas puts it:

> Whereas in commutative justice the equalisation which justice requires is that of things to things, in distributive justice it is according to the proportionality of things to persons... the exercise of distributive justice involves taking into consideration such qualities of people as give them a title or qualification in virtue of the things that go to make up their situation[31].

Distributive justice is more about giving than making claims on others and is a matter of individual responsibility as well as of the governors of the state. It is not simply the case (as Cajetan claimed and later commentators have followed) that in society "exchange justice orients the parts to one another, while distributive justice orients the whole to the parts"[32]. Distributive justice as explained by Aquinas may be claimed

---

30. ARISTOTLE, *Nichomachean Ethics,* trs. D. ROSS, Bk. V,1; 1129a01130a, Oxford, University Press.

31. THOMAS AQUINAS, *Summa Theologiae,* IIa-IIae, Q. 58, art. 5 & 6.

32. CAJETAN, *Commentaria in Secundum Secundae Thomae de Aquino.* This view is repeated in the Preface to Vol. 37 of the Blackfriars edition of *Summa Theologiae,* p. xv.

as fulfilling the personal and corporate role which is being staked out by some political theorists and experts in Catholic social thought for solidarity. In fact, my own view would be that distributive justice is the moral theory foundation of solidarity (in a sense they are the same concept), though I would wish to recognise modern political realities which have given solidarity a wider meaning and relevance and a degree of applicability in contemporary conditions. There is no desire to make natural law omni-competent, but only to emphasise its moral foundations which are fertile for reconstructing modern social ethics. In case it may thought that I am unmindful of Thomas Gilby's deference to the place of theology referred to above, it needs to be added here that however strong may be the grounding in natural law as defended in this essay (and to be further explored), a current of inspiration and meaning for these values and concepts from scripture, doctrine and sacrament, in diverse and ever-renewed ways, will have a life of its own (as Boswell and Verstraeten rightly emphasise) and within a tradition of *duplex ordo* finding ample room for both.

Understood as a proportionate distribution of duties, resources, privileges and obligations in society, distributive justice and the notions of "solidarity", "subsidiarity", and "a preferential option for the poor", as basic features of sound Catholic social thought, are intimately connected, and, indeed, cannot be understood independently of each other. "The dignity of human nature" and "the common good" are guiding visions for Catholic social thought and action. The other four are principles bringing the vision, through middle-level thinking, into connection with the realities of social life and a range of policy questions.

THE RELEVANCE OF HISTORY

The charge that natural law methodology implies an a-historical conception of human existence and experience and that it rests on a static view of human nature has been levelled by both philosophers and theologians. Thus Crowe has written that "natural law is vitiated by a basic failure to take account of the fact that man's nature is affected by his existence, that history is present in the kind of being man is". From a theological perspective Gründel refers to "...the abstract metaphysical nature of man which is the basis of natural law" and contrasts this static view of natural law with that of the Bible, whose "moral directives are oriented to men in the concrete and have the character of a 'situated ethics'"[33]. It is possible to present an extended defence of the historicity (in the sense of conditions of time and place playing an indispensable role in the concrete process of self-making and self-development of human beings) of natural law theory, but that can be read in Armand Maurer's *St Thomas and Historicity*[34].

As was made clear above, in Aquinas human knowledge, as apprehended from "facts", is experiential and historical. This indeed is a point on which he is explicit, when he writes that "since our intellect is not eternal, the truth of propositions which we form is not eternal either, but had a beginning at some point in time"[35]. Even his concept of human nature seems "history-friendly" in the way he discusses its changeableness: unlike divine nature, human nature is changeable. Accordingly, those things that pertain to natural justice can vary according to the variations of one's station in life and the requirements of the human condition[36].

Even in his development of what appears to be an abstract discussion of the notion of "being", Aquinas observes a sense of history and a theory of improvement. In the Preface to the *Commentary on the Ethics,* he stresses the creative role of human reason in moral, political and technical activities. Reason, he writes, "produces an order in the very act of reflection"[37]. In the style of MacIntyre, what is being advocated here is a pre-modern use of Aquinas's philosophy and theology to provide a fuller context for the notion of natural law as an element in his ethics. The rejection of an incomplete understanding of (modern) natural law, and a retrieval of Aquinas's more subtle notions is well-expressed by Milbank:

> For Aquinas natural law had meant transcendental equity and therefore precisely that which conjoined the particular instance of justice to the divine and eternal in the surpassing of all mere regularity of convention. But now, for modernity, natural law transcribes the sealed-off totality of nature, where eternal nature consists in the most invariable of rules[38].

The conjunction of particular instances to the divine and eternal in a properly understood theory of natural law, as well as surpassing rules

33. M.B. CROWE, *The Changing Profile of Natural Law*, The Hague, Nijhoff, 1977, p. 270; J. GRÜNDEL, *Natural Law*, in K. RAHNER (ed), *Encyclopedia of Theology. A Concise Sacramentum Mundi*, London, Burns Oates, 1975, pp. 1017-1023.
34. A. MAURER, *St Thomas and Historicity* (The Aquinas Lectures, 43), Milwaukee, WI, Marquette University Press, 1979.
35. THOMAS AQUINAS, *Summa Theologiae,* I, Q. 6 ad 4.
36. *Supplement to Summa Theologiae*, 41,1.
37. THOMAS AQUINAS, *Commentary on the Ethics,* Preface, nn. 1-4
38. J. MILBANK, *Theology and Social Theory*, Oxford, Blackwell, 1990, p. 10.

and regularity, may also provide the foundations for the priority which must be given to "solidarity" in Catholic social thinking. In a remarkable article written almost a quarter of a century ago, Christian Lenhardt, stimulated by a "theological" tone in the writings of some members of the German critical school, proposed a re-reading of Marxism and socialist theory in terms of "anamnestic solidarity"[39]. The thesis presented by Lenhardt required a teleological perspective in Marxism and a revision of the idea of dependence on the universalistic nature of its economic propositions. But teleology in Marxism would not be a simplistic utopian prospective (any more than it is in natural law), but, rather, a thought pattern of continuity which gave a role to "memory" and allowed a place for the dead ("the enslaved predecessors") as connected to the present generation (struggling for emancipation) and for the generation of emancipated successors. Solidarity in socialist theory would then be anamnestic, commemorative.

This line of thought is not novel in Catholic social theory, since *anamnesis* is enshrined in the vocabulary of Catholic theology and worship, and J.-B. Metz has explicated the importance of memory in respect of social theology[40]. The more subtle understanding of natural law proposed here would be open to parallel development and may sustain a social ethics of solidarity more easily than socialist theory can. In dealing with the important notion of solidarity in CathST, imaginative connections of this kind must be made and models suggested. Looking at a different philosophical tradition, Alasdair MacIntyre (especially in *Whose Justice? Which Rationality?*) has attempted to show the close association between Liberalism as a philosophy of economic life and the claim that "there is no alternative" to market forces. The ideology of individualism is thus presented, paradoxically, as a quite special kind of "solidarity". This opinion was supported by a number of well-known commentators on Catholic social teaching (Michael Novak, and Richard Neuhaus among them) in their claim that Pope John Paul's 1991 encyclical, *Centesimus annus,* accepted the proven superiority of

39. C. LENHARDT, *Anamnestic Solidarity: the Proletariat and its 'Manes',* in *Telos* (1975) 133-154.

40. See *Catechism of the Catholic Church,* London, Geoffrey Chapman, 1994, section 1103; K. RAHNER, *Theological Investigations.* 19: *Faith and Ministry*, London, Darton, Longman &Todd, 1983, pp. 150-151: The meaning of worship is that "people celebrate in a temporal sequence the anamnesis (memory) of events that have occurred once for all in salvation history"; In the *New Catholic Encyclopedia,* '*anamnesis*' is set in the context of the experience of fellowship, and it is claimed that remembrance is inseparably linked with action: *New Catholic Encyclopedia.* 1: *A to Azt*, New York, NY, McGraw-Hill Book Company, 1967, pp. 475-476.

capitalism. Fukuyama has celebrated the same victory of liberalism; and this philosophy has taken hold of contemporary British political and economic life, albeit with some qualifying checks and balances. Natural law theory as explored here would furnish social ethics with concepts of solidarity and distributive justice wholly critical of such a view.

To recover the conception of natural law as transcendental equity and to make this an element in the development of Catholic social thinking is consonant with the aims of this collection, one of which, perhaps the most important, is to explore what is distinctive in Catholic social thought by contrast with secular approaches to morality. The aim is not to restore natural law in a monolithic cast as the sole foundation for Catholic social doctrine. A recognition of the importance of pluralism engendered by years of teaching social sciences; the acknowledgement that after Hegel it makes no sense to adopt an a-historical approach; the appreciation of the significance of the economic foundations of so much human activity learned while teaching courses in Marxism and Christianity; the potential of political theology first appreciated in 1977 when I reviewed J.-B. Metz's *Faith in History and Society*, followed later by the probing analysis provided by Peukert – all these inspired me to a critical review of social ethics and of CST in its earlier natural law form; but an attempt to overcome it has only succeeded in renewing it. And the answer to the question, "What difference does CathST based on a natural law approach make?" is that its essential elements – justice, solidarity, subsidiarity and an option for the poor – facilitate debate with our post-modern contemporaries, who are preoccupied with the same questions.

"A ROSE BY ANY OTHER NAME..."

If, as Troeltsch suggested, we are to think thoughts that have not been thought before, it should be considered whether the very name "natural law", like a whisper from an ancient past, carrying encrustations (law, nature, absolutes, universals) which it cannot shake off, impedes the possibility of placing the theory at the service of Catholic social thought[41]. Yet if such an enterprise is to be, and seen to be, a "tradition-constituted-enquiry", another name for natural law will need to incorporate essential elements of the long-reflected theory.

41. For an analysis of problems relating to any attempt to retrieve the ancient tradition, see P. SIMPSON, *Contemporary Virtue Ethics and Aristotle*, in *Review of Metaphysics* 45 (1992), no. 3, 503-524.

While this paper has defended a place for natural law in CathST, albeit with a modified understanding of some of its basic notions such as "reason" and "revelation", there has also been an emphasis on other distinctive socio-political ideas and terminology: justice, common good, community, solidarity, subsidiarity, *prudentia*. Perhaps what is needed is a search for an alternative nomenclature to "natural law", one that would preserve basic notions and, at the same time, capture the sociological overtones. One suggestion is "Common Social Wisdom" (CSW). This term has the advantage of preserving MacIntyre's idea that the reconstruction of any ethics must be a tradition-based-enquiry. It must not be thought of in any way as a "lowest common denominator". Each word in the term captures essential elements of the Catholic tradition of social thought. The word "common" has references, at once, to the shared nature, dignity and *telos* of persons and to the involvement of each and every person in the creation of ethical life. The word would include echoes of "the common good" and it signifies the aspect of the "vulgar" (that is, "of the people") vision of social thinking. A parallel can be found in the use of the term "common sense" in the so-called Scottish Tradition of economics which emphasises a popular foundation for economic thought as an alternative to the abstractions and high knowledge of "the scholastic headpieces", as Thomas Reid, the founder of the Scottish School of political economy, called them[42]. In this form, the word "common" retains something of the universalisable aspect of Catholic social thinking, appealed to, often, in the encyclicals in the claim that this teaching is for all people.

The word "social", as well as indicating the more obvious claim that this part of ethical teaching has socio-political objectives, recalls the "person-in-society" foundation of Catholic social thought and, along with the overtones of "common", identifies the communitarian nature of this corpus of thought and teaching. This understanding of the tradition of Catholic communitarianism emphasises that the person is socially embedded, that community is a person-enhancing collectivity, that social

---

42. T. REID, *An Inquiry into the Human Mind on the Principles of Common Sense*, Edinburgh, printed for A. Millar, London, and A. Kincaid and J. Bell, Edinburgh, 1764: "In this unequal contest betwixt Common Sense and Philosophy, the latter will always come off both with dishonour and loss... But, on the other hand, Philosophy has no other root but the principles of Common Sense; it grows out of them, and draws its nourishment from them". p. 7; T. REID, *Essay on the Intellectual Powers of Man*, Edinburgh, printed for John Bell, and G. G. J. & J. Robinson, London, 1785; M.A. LUTZ, *Economics for the Common Good*, London, Routledge, 1999; R.F. CRESPO, *La Economia como Ciencia Moral: nuevas perspectivas de la teoria economica*, Buenos Aires, Universitas SRL, 1997.

life is radically complementary and participatory. "Common social wis-dom" rejects liberalism, with its privacy of "a life to be led from the inside", with major implications for Catholic social thought on the mar-ket and the creation of wealth.

The word "wisdom", with its echoes of *phronesis* in Aristotle and *prudentia* in Aquinas, refers to the virtues without which the dignified *telos* of human beings cannot be reached[43]. The very name "wisdom" carries biblical overtones and may make this approach open to narrative theology. It emphasises the character of the person rather than individual acts, and implies that morality is not produced mechanistically by appli-cation of rule-based theory. Thus understood, the term Common Social Wisdom describes not an "approach" (in the sense of a methodological tool) but, rather, a "tradition" which encourages rigour of thought, the importance of common human experience, the motivating force of theo-logical imagination and the *praxis* of ecclesial communities[44]. Rather than simply drop the term "natural law", as *Gaudium et spes* did, the suggestion is that it should be replaced by a term more fully recognising the profound change in the *attitude* of the Catholic Church to its social teaching, which the Second Vatican Council was attempting to express.

CONCLUSION

Using virtue ethics as an interlocutor, a number of weaknesses have been identified in neo-Thomist and manualist formulations of natural law ethics. They may be classified, in common with the weaknesses of ethi-cal modernity, as foundationalist, governed by method, and rule-based.

---

43. In connection with the role of virtue and prudence, Pierpaolo Donati, in a recent monograph, has discussed the relation of charity to prudence, which he then sets in a well-constructed sociological framework to study the issue of welfare provision. It is a subtle development of the interplay of social theory and social ethics: P. DONATI, *Pensiero sociale cristiano e societa post-moderna*, Roma, A.V.E., 1997, pp. 113-125.

44. One useful task for middle-level thinking, in connection with ethics and social theory, would be to compare the way in which current discussions of "common sense economics" make a systemic place for ethics in economic theory and "common social wisdom" in Catholic social thought creates a bridge to ethics in economic and financial enterprise. This might help to develop a theory of improvement (which is singularly lack-ing) in business and finance ethics, and to help these currently emerging disciplines to develop a social ethic capable of dealing with macro issues. There is a growing literature on common sense in economic theory, beginning with P. WICKSTEED, *The Alphabet of Economic Science. Elements of the Theory of Value or Worth*, New York, NY, Kelly & Miller, 1889/1995; and documented extensively in a recent thesis: F.V. COMIM, *Common Sense Economics. Essays on the Role of Common Sense in the History of Economic Thought*, Cambridge, University of Cambridge, October 1998. Unpublished.

Using classical Thomism as an interlocutor of these later styles of calculative natural law, I claim that it is possible to reconstruct natural law ethics, articulated in connection with its ontological suppositions, as a reflexive and rich ethics that encourages human flourishing, uncovers a place for creativity and offers a structural dimension which gives it purchase on the social realities of a globalised world. Thomism itself emerges as the best form of virtue theory.

Von Hügel Institute, St Edmund's College   Francis P. McHugh
University of Cambridge

RE-THINKING CATHOLIC SOCIAL THOUGHT AS TRADITION

I. A CLASSIC CRITIQUE OF THE OFFICIAL DEFINITION

Catholic social thought is more than "a doctrinal corpus" of texts issued by the magisterium of the Roman pontiffs and beginning with the encyclical *Rerum novarum* of Leo XIII.

The definition of Catholic social thought exclusively as "doctrine" is problematic because, among other reasons, it has caused historical misunderstandings. At the time of the papacy of Pius XI, when *Quadragesimo anno* was issued (1931), "doctrine" was used to refer to a third way model between Marxist collectivism and liberal individualism. In that context "social doctrine" was interpreted as a fundamental "unchanged and unchangeable" theoretical framework based on natural law and revelation. This has led to a confusion between the "unchangeable" formal principles belonging to the *duplex ordo* of natural law and divine revelation[1], and a historically contingent political and social "third way" theory which was legitimated as its contemporary expression. When a time-bound theory becomes legitimated on the basis of unchangeable principles a historical and contextual critique of this theory becomes impossible and easily leads to ideological misuse[2]. This was particularly the case when authoritarian regimes adopted the Catholic third way as an official or semi-official doctrine[3]. There is of course another possible picture of *Quadragesimo anno* than that of a rigid doctrine leading to ideological misuse. But even when distinctions are made between the nuances of the text and its historical functioning or misuse, the ideological misuse remained a historical fact. This prompted the Second Vatican Council to adopt a different approach which *Gaudium et spes* has labeled as "scrutinising the signs of the time and interpreting them in the light of the Gospel".

---

1. For the meaning of the *duplex ordo* see U. NOTHELLE-WILDFEUER, *Duplex ordo cognitionis. Zur systematischen Grundlegung einer katholischen Soziallehre im Anspruch von Philosophie und Theologie* (Abhandlungen zur Sozialethik, 31), Paderborn, Schöningh, 1991.
2. Cf. M.-D. CHENU, *La "doctrine sociale" de l'Église comme idéologie* (Essais), Paris, Cerf, 1979.
3. The critical remark with regard to Pius XI and his attitude towards Fascism is given by O. VON NELL-BREUNING, *The Drafting of Quadragesimo Anno*, in C.E. CURRAN & R.A. MCCORMICK (eds.), *Official Catholic Social Teaching* (Readings in Moral Theology, 5), New York, NY, Paulist, 1986, pp. 60-68.

The tradition of Catholic social teaching presented by Pope John Paul II shows an awareness of the need to avoid the risk of ideological distortion. In contrast with the practice of Paul VI the present Pope has re-appropriated the concept of "doctrine" to describe the corpus of official social teaching, but he clearly warns against an identification with past interpretations. His clear view is that "the Church's doctrine is not a third way between liberal capitalism and Marxist collectivism, nor even an alternative to other solutions less radically opposed to one another: rather, it constitutes a category on its own. Nor is it an ideology, but rather an accurate formulation of the results of a careful reflection on the complex realities of human existence, in society and in the international order, in the light of faith and of the Church's tradition". Its main aim is to interpret these realities, judging their conformity with or divergence from the lines of Gospel teaching on man and his vocation. It is a normative critique, a theology and a guide to Christian behaviour[4].

Moreover, if we look in detail at what John Paul II means when he uses the concept of "doctrine", it becomes evident that he has something else in mind than merely a return to the classic deductions from the *duplex ordo*. His method is based more on a theological anthropology than on natural law. For him, the heart of the matter is a theological foundation of the dignity of the human person, which was in the beginning mainly Christocentric *(Redemptor hominis)*. John Paul II has stated explicitly that social "doctrine" is a branch of theology:

> ...the Church's social doctrine with its concern for man, its interest in him and in the way he conducts himself in the world belongs to the field of theology and particularly of moral theology (*CA* 55).

Moreover, John Paul II's shows a steady inclination to connect this type of "doctrine" to a theology of a witness-church:

> Today, more than ever, the Church is aware that her social message will gain credibility more immediately from the witness of actions than as a result of its internal logic and consistency (*CA* 55).

Doctrine and a radical, even heroic moral *praxis* are strongly connected with each other. In *Veritatis splendor* he goes so far as to plead for a radical and general ethic of martyrdom. To his statement that "through the moral life faith becomes confession, it becomes witness", he adds that its best expression is "the supreme witness of martyrdom" (*VS* 89). And although he acknowledges that martyrdom is a special

---

4. Important texts are *Centesimus annus*, 3; 53-59 and *Sollicitudo rei socialis*, 41.

calling, he does not hesitate to say that "there is a consistent witness which all Christians must daily be ready to make, even at the cost of suffering and great sacrifice" (*VS* 93). This option for a witness church (which is, in the Troeltschian sense, a "sectarian" option) marks a departure from the more conciliatory approach of his predecessors. This shift raises the question whether "doctrine" is a defensible term to describe CST and whether "ethics" is at all an adequate rubric for this study. Would it not be more accurate to speak of "social theology"?

Secondly, the limitation of Catholic social thought to the texts of the *magisterium* is by no means uncontested or uncontestable within the Church, and has not always been the view of either scholars or activists in the field of the Church's social mission. If nothing else, a glance at the quantity of letters from Bishops' conferences in different countries on the economy and development and contemporary social issues is enough to persuade us that even the scope of official teaching is wider[5]. Taking into consideration the variety of situations in the world, Paul VI already acknowledged that it had become impossible for the Church "to utter a unified message and to put forward a solution which has universal validity" *(Octogesima adveniens* 4). The alternative is not only to validate the contribution of the Bishops' conferences but also of local church communities. Paul VI went on to say that it is "up to the Christian communities to analyze with objectivity the situation which is proper to their own country" and "with the help of Holy Spirit, in communion with the bishops who hold responsibility and in dialogue with other Christian brethren and all people of good will, to discern the options and commitments which are called for in order to bring about the social, political and economic changes seen in many cases to be urgently needed" (*OA* 4).

This judgement, which urgently needs to be re-activated, opens up new possibilities for non-official Catholic social thought at grass-roots and local levels and for the development of CathST, as integrally related to new insights in official social teaching. It is a matter of regret, however, that Paul VI does not clarify the methodological implications of this vision for the definition of Catholic social teaching as tradition, but that, presumably, is precisely the role of CathST.

Last but not least, it is important to put into perspective the use of *Rerum novarum* as the absolute point of departure for papal social teaching. Recent historical research has sufficiently demonstrated that even

---

5. R. BERTHOUZOZ, R. PAPINI e.a. (eds.), *Économie et développement. Répertoire des documents épiscopaux des cinq continents (1891-1991)* (Études d'éthique chrétienne, 69), Fribourg, Éd. universitaires, 1997.

when one recognizes the symbolic meaning of *Rerum novarum,* even its radical edge, and taking into account the fact that many contemporary scholars do not rate highly the social thought of most encyclicals from the pre-Leonine period, especially because of their anti-modern attitude, we should not be put off from claiming that encyclicals from the pre-Leonine period do contain socially relevant force. One can find in pre-*RN* texts important matters such as a critique of Enlightenment claims concerning society and individuality and on usury and the use of money. According to M.J. Schuck, it can be claimed that at least since 1740 there is a "pope's communitarian understanding of the self and society"[6].

So far I have suggested three arguments for going beyond a narrow definition of Catholic social teaching, even when this is widened to take in the new ecclesiological insights of Paul VI and John Paul II. But even then, this part of Church teaching insufficiently acknowledges the role of non-official thought. I can illustrate this from a document of the Congregation for Catholic Education which distinguishes between "two elements": "the official social doctrine of the Church and the various positions of schools of thought which have systematically explained, developed and ordered the social thinking contained in papal documents"[7]. The distinction is welcome, but the document nowhere offers a theoretical framework to integrate these two levels. Moreover it has too narrow a view of what might be the contribution of non-official Catholic social thinking since it leaves no room for anything other than the "explanation, development and ordering" of papal teaching.

One of the best descriptions of the complexity of Catholic social thought is offered by H. Büchele, who distinguishes four elements: social pronouncements of popes, council and colleges of bishops; social pronouncements of local or regional churches represented by bishops conferences; the level of scientific and academic discourse (known in Germany as *Christliche Gesellschaftslehre*) [The second reflection in liberation theology could be interpreted as belonging to this level]; and the interpretative level of groups which refer to CST in order to clarify their commitment and formulate socio-political statements and positions.

Büchele considers levels 1 and 2 as "official church social teaching" and levels 3 and 4 as the "tradition of its interpretation"[8]. The distinction

---

6. M.J. SCHUCK, *That They Be One. The Social Teaching of the Papal Encyclicals, 1740-1989,* Washington, DC, Georgetown University Press, 1991.

7. *Guidelines for Teaching the Church's Social Doctrine in Forming Priests. 30 December 1988,* in *The Pope Speaks* 34 (1989), no. 4, 293-342.

8. H. BÜCHELE, *Christlicher Glaube und politische Vernunft. Fur eine Neukonzeption der katholischen Soziallehre* (Soziale Brennpunkte, 12), Wien, Europa Verlag, 1987, p. 14.

though useful remains unsatisfactory because it gives the impression that there is a separation between papal teaching and the tradition of inter-pretation, whereas they are both part of the same tradition of reflection and practice. Moreover, even Büchele underestimates the role of grass-roots praxis and reflection and does not bring it into a relation with aca-demic reflection in the process of a search for new perspectives.

II. CATHOLICISM AS SOCIAL TRADITION

"Each of us contributes more to the common good when we dare to undertake a journey into our own particularity ... than when we attempt to homogenize all differences in favor of some lowest common denomi-nator"[9]. This statement by David Tracy provides a starting point for my view that all theories of justice and social ethics are inescapably tied to particular traditions of thought and social practice. Rational inquiry and every type of social *praxis* is (at least in the first instance) tradition-con-stituted and tradition constitutive[10]. Or, to put in the words of Ricœur: "none of us finds himself placed in the radical position of creating the ethical world *ex nihilo*"[11].

This does not mean that we can dispense with generally accepted rules of justice and basic principles for the organization of the *polis*. We still need a non-arbitrary moral foundation, and from this point of view the claims of the natural law tradition still have something to offer (see McHugh's essay in this collection). But the paradox is that the classic answer given by the Catholic Church in terms of a universal natural law, human rights or arguments based on human dignity is, in the post-mod-ern context, now viewed as no more than one opinion from a particular tradition. On the other hand, a plurality of particular traditions does not mean that they cannot offer arguments or interpretations which might be recognised and accepted by others as rational. As a reasonable tradition the Catholic social tradition of reflection can at least contribute to an overlapping consensus (in this sense the tradition of discourse ethics remains a challenge). But while acknowledging the need for general rational principles and argument, I take sides with Michael Walzer's

9. D. TRACY, *Defending the Public Character of Theology*, in *The Christian Century* 98 (1981), 350-356, esp. 353.

10. A. MACINTYRE has developed this insight most clearly in *Whose Justice? Which Rationality?*, Notre Dame, IN, Notre Dame University Press, 1988.

11. P. RICŒUR, *Ethics and Culture: Habermas and Gadamer in Dialogue*, in *Philosophy Today* 17 (1973) 153-165, esp. 159.

view that general principles acquire their substantial meaning in the context of particular traditions of reflection. There are first of all "thick" interpretations, and then what we consider to be generalized "thin" principles or interpretations, which are principles whose meaning can never totally be abstracted from the context of meaning determined by the particular traditions from which the thin concepts are derived[12].

I also agree with Michael Walzer that, before one can speak adequately about social goods, their distribution and the political, economical and cultural spheres in which this distribution takes place, and even before one can work out an ethical theory about such distribution, one needs to understand the meaning of these goods. In my view, this understanding can differ not only according to the different spheres to which these goods belong, but also by reason of the particular shared understandings of a tradition or a people. The Catholic social tradition can be interpreted as a tradition which comprises a particular set of shared understandings about the human person, social goods and their distributive arrangements. This particular understanding is grounded in a living relation to the constitutive narratives provided by the Bible, integrated in a theoretical framework which makes it possible for the Catholic understanding to remain open to rational explanation and public debate. A distinctive "cultural" feature is its connection to sacramental and liturgical practices (which will receive more detailed attention when I deal with "memorializing celebrations").

Being a living narrative and reflective tradition, Catholic social thought can thus be described as "an historically extended, socially embodied argument"[13]. It is what J.P. Wils has described as an interpretation *in actu*[14]. It is a continuous learning process of interpretation and re-interpretation of the meaning of the human person as a social being and of the shared understandings within the Catholic community (both in the synchronic and diachronic meaning) about social, economic and political goods and their distribution. This is not to deny that there is continuity in the validity, relevance and affirmation of its vision of the person and the common good, and of its basic principles such as human dignity, subsidiarity, solidarity and justice; but the real point is that we need to distinguish between the formal affirmation of vision and principles and

_____

12. Cf. M. WALZER, *Thick and Thin. Moral Argument at Home and Abroad* (Loyola lecture series in political analysis), Notre Dame, IN, Notre Dame University Press, 1994.
13. A. MACINTYRE, *After Virtue. A Study in Moral Theory*, London, Duckworth, 1985, p. 222.
14. Cf. J.P. WILS, *Traditie en globalisering* (F.J.J Buytendijklezing), Nijmegen, Nijmegen University Press, 1998, p. 13.

the evolution of their meaning which is subject to change through process of continuous reinterpretation.

Consequently, Catholic social tradition is not something static. It has nothing to do with "conservative antiquarianism". As a living tradition it goes beyond fidelity to the past and opens out to the future. It makes possible "a grasp of those future possibilities which the past has made available to the present"[15]. As such, it cannot be equated with a sclerotic fossilisation or accumulation of cliches[16]. In a form of conformist repetition it simply could not remain as a living tradition[17]. It would, instead, become a damaging tradition, characterized by a decline of capacity to express changing realities and, in this case, "bent under the load of their sacralized use", its words would become "mortified"[18].

If a vibrant CathSt is to continue and develop, two aspects of tradition are important as we search for a renewed approach: the connection between traditions of inquiry and communities, on the one hand, and the necessity of meeting epistemological crises, on the other.

1. *Tradition and Context*

A tradition is always connected with a community. We become a community by inheriting and interpreting our place within a tradition, by sharing meanings or interpretations of social realities and their normative frameworks. According to MacIntyre, moreover, each tradition, as intellectual inquiry, is necessarily connected with a mode of social and moral life. Intellectual inquiry is not a theoretical world apart from the life of communities, but an integral part of that life and of the forms of that life as they are embodied in social and political institutions. It makes no sense to speak of a tradition in abstraction from community structures which legitimate it, nurture it, and function as the locus for its ongoing commitment.

This is central to our present discussion: we cannot conceive of a Catholic tradition of reflection and *praxis* as an abstract theoretical framework which would stand on its own, apart from a particular community or communities with their historical "modes of social and moral life". This implies that, when the historical social context of a tradition changes, when the Catholic community with its ethos changes, this has immediate implications for the tradition itself. Take, for example, the

---

15. *Ibid.*, p. 223.
16. *Ibid.*
17. P. VAN TONGEREN, *Ethics, Tradition and Hermeneutics*, in *Ethical Perspectives* 3 (1996) 175-183, esp. 180.
18. G. STEINER, *After Babel*, as quoted in WILS, *Traditie en globalisering* (n. 14), p. 13.

pre-Vatican II form of CST. Historically it was connected with a specific form of community life such as ultra-montanist social Catholicism or Catholic labor movements. The disappearance of the one or the secular-ization of the other has deprived classic CST of its original historical subject and context of meaning. Consequently, it cannot survive without both a fundamental reinterpretation of its theoretical content and the dis-covery or creation of a new bearer of that tradition. In other words, when the social context in which Catholic social tradition concretizes itself becomes radically different from the past, when the classic forms of Catholic social movements disappear or become secularized, CST would become meaningless if it refused to adapt and reinterpret its original form and content. There is, moreover, the problem that the referent com-munity, which is no longer a clearly defined group but a variety of dif-ferent social contexts on a global scale. In this respect *Octogesima adveniens* is right in its claim that a classic universal doctrine, with a common message and solution for all different social contexts, is highly problematic.

Catholic social thought, as a tradition of reflection and *praxis*, cannot be articulated in a way which would deny the diversity of modes of social and moral life in different contexts, unless one is prepared to say that one single Catholic community culture for the whole world is still possible. In other words, if we want to understand how Catholic social thought can become concrete and meaningful in the world of today, we cannot ignore the sociological background questions which are put for-ward by Staf Hellemans in his contribution in this collection. But neither can we afford to ignore the challenges of globalisation.

2. *Tradition and an Epistemological Crisis*

When we consider Catholic social tradition as practical interpretation, this will inevitably create epistemological challenges and crises. It raises new questions, problems, challenging interpretations and new internal and external tensions. In this regard I agree with MacIntyre that "at any point it may happen to any tradition that by its own standards of progress it ceases to make progress, it can become sterile, there can be conflicts over rival answers to key questions which can no longer be settled ratio-nally", and even the methods of inquiry can become so inadequate, that a systematic breakdown of inquiry becomes a real threat[19].

First of all there is the challenge of internal conflicts which are a con-sequence of the ongoing discussion, or even tension, between different

19. MACINTYRE, *Whose Justice? Which Rationality* (n. 10), pp. 361-362.

attempts to interpret meaning. Such conflict can be avoided, of course, by imposing from above one single interpretation (as appears in chapter 2 of *Veritatis splendor*); or it is possible that one interpretation or school can become intellectually so superior during a certain period that it is spontaneously recognised as the best expression of the tradition (cf. neo-Thomism). But in both cases, the dominant interpretations may end up too narrow to deal with new questions arising during the process of historical development of the tradition. It can happen that the interpretation which is in the ascendancy imposes itself so strongly that important intra-tradition sources of meaning or earlier historical expressions of the tradition become marginalised or forgotten.

An active tradition can retain its significance only if it succeeds in continuing its relevant and marginalised dimensions which are meaningful in light of the realities of its time. When a tradition becomes too much alienated from its living or neglected sources, or separated from its narrative roots, it is unavoidably attenuated. A symptom of this might be, for example, a change in vocabulary which narrows the possibilities for interpretation. In her detailed study of the vocabulary of *RN*, Francoise Monfrin, demonstrates that the use of classic and scholastic Latin and the abandoning of the original patristic language has sometimes led to a change of the original meaning of texts, especially in passages about poverty and charity, where loyalty to the original language would have been more in conformity with radical socialist interpretations[20]. The fear felt by the authors of *RN* for socialist ideas was probably so great that it hindered a correct reading of the patristic tradition. More respect for the original patristic universe of discourse and its vocabulary could have resulted in a more critical text.

Another example of neglect of an important dimension of Catholic social thought relates to its foundational anthropology which has become particularly important since the epistemological shift from natural law to more personalist arguments in *Mater et Magistra*. One of the most original contributions in this regard is the theological foundation of the anthropology set out by John Paul II, although in the beginning of his pontificate his theology had a certain exclusivity by reason of his emphasis on its Christocentric dimension. According to him, the mystery of

---

20. F. MONFRIN, *Pauvreté et richesse. Le lexique latin de l'encyclique: inspiration classique ou inspiration patristique*, in CNRS. GRECO N. 2, *Rerum novarum*. Écriture, contenu et réception d'une encyclique. Actes du colloque international organisé par l'École française de Rome et le Greco n. 2 du CNRS (Rome, 18-20 avril, 1991) (Collection de l'École française de Rome, 232), Rome, École française de Rome, 1997, pp. 133-186.

man can be understood adequately only in light of the mystery of Christ. John Paul II has balanced this Christocentric approach by a more Trinitarian theology in *Sollicitudo rei socialis*. The difference between a Christocentric and Trinitarian anthropology confronts us with the question of the limits of the Western theological tradition. Would a better integration of the theology of the Greek patristic period and of Eastern churches not deepen and enrich the anthropological basis?

Catholic social thought, then, is confronted not only with internal tensions but also as discourse that claims to be relevant for society with external tension. In order to respond to these constraints two elements need to be considered: its relation with social sciences and its relation with other traditions. The first of these can be dealt with briefly since that question is sufficiently clarified elsewhere[21]. The problem in the Catholic world is somewhat different from Milbank's construal of a great weakness in social theology. It is not so much that there is too much dependence on social sciences (as Milbank contends), but that their role is, in fact, minimised. At least there is an ambivalence or a tension between formally praising social sciences for their contribution to a better understanding of the human and societal situation and fundamentally under-valuing them.

More attention is given to criticizing the danger of ideology in social sciences than to taking into account their research results or their justified criticisms. In spite of its improved sensitivity to cultural questions, *Octogesima adveniens* is not without blame in this regard. Even in that document there is a tendency to put the social sciences into a kind of secondary and ancillary role. This is particularly the case in *CA* when John Paul II declares that "The human sciences and philosophy are helpful for interpreting man's central place within society and for enabling him to understand himself better as a social being. However, man's true identity is only revealed to him through faith". The lack of qualification to his later statement that "the church receives 'the meaning of man' from divine revelation" runs the risk of claiming too much (*CA* 54-55). There must be a question whether or not this overestimation of theological knowledge has not been one of the reasons why there is so little input from social sciences in recent encyclicals? Is *Centesimus annus* not problematic in this regard? Did the authors sufficiently take into

---

21. I will put aside the question whether a dialogue with the social sciences is still possible after Milbank's massive attack against a theology which refuses to affirm itself as a radical alternative social science in opposition to the secular social sciences which are presumed to be based on an ontology of violence, cf. J. MILBANK, *Theology and Social Theory. Beyond Secular Reason,* Oxford, Blackwell, 1990.

account the ideas and arguments which eminent economists and social scientists presented during a seminar organized by the Pontifical Commission for Justice and Peace and other gatherings of experts in preparation of the centenary of *Rerum novarum*[22]?

The second constraint, extensively described by MacIntyre in *Whose Justice? Which Rationality?* is the clarification of the relation with competing or even incommensurable traditions. That other traditions are in competition is not difficult to understand, but whether meanings can be shared and interpretations made bridgeable are not questions for easy resolution. On these difficulties MacIntyre holds the position that there is always the possibility of learning to understand the other incommensurable point of view from within in an imaginative way. One can come to inhabit an alien or incommensurable tradition of reflection and, in so doing, recognize how significant features of one's own tradition, to which one has been blind, can be discovered and characterized from that other culture's point of view. For MacIntyre the example par excellence is the incorporation by Aquinas of Aristotelian theories into the Christian theological tradition. It would be a mistake, however, to treat this as simply a model to be repeated. The worst solution for CathST today would be to become a sort of self-referential or time-bound static Thomism, which would, in fact, be against the spirit of Thomas Aquinas himself[23]. It is one thing to defend the continuity of the tradition and to remain loyal to its basic inspiration and its concern for a non-arbitrary foundation of moral norms, and another simply to re-appropriate a framework in its history-bound totality. We have to avoid, as Maritain pointed out, both "univocity", which is a strict repeating of the expressions of the past, and "equivocity", which is introducing new thoughts without any connection to the historical tradition. Maritain's solution, which he called "analogy", was to start from the same fundamental basic pre-suppositions out of which one constructs a vision which gives relevance in a new context and historical situation.

The aim here is, at once, to warn that CST is often in danger of repeating Thomistic teaching in a fundamentalist style, and to recommend that CathSt should preserve the tradition but remain open to new

22. See PONTIFICAL COUNCIL FOR JUSTICE AND PEACE, *Social and Ethical Aspects of Economics. A Colloquium in the Vatican*, Citta del Vaticano, Pontificia Commissio Justitia et Pax, 1992.

23. This in no way contradicts my personal appreciation of Thomas Aquinas whose thinking is often much richer and nuanced than that of some of his interpreters (cf. my study: *Thomas van Aquino en de theorie van de rechtvaardige oorlog* (Cahiers van het Centrum voor vredesonderzoek, 2), Leuven, 1984.

insights and new forms, some of which will come from other traditions and from secular thought, even if at first they seem incommensurable. In a complex global and pluralist world with new problems, new social challenges and radically new technological contexts, a permanent critical dialogue with different theories and tradition is a necessity. CathST must be looked at as tradition-constituted but enrichable by narrative and *praxis*.

III. CATHOLIC SOCIAL TRADITION AS NARRATIVE TRADITION

Until now I have relied heavily on MacIntyre's theory in an attempt to understand better the nature of CathST as a tradition of inquiry, but it is time to draw attention to an important aspect missing from his approach.

I am not suggesting that MacIntyre does not understand the narrative basis of a tradition. A careful reading reveals that he does appreciate it, but only in so far as it plays a role at a first stage in a linear historical development; namely a stage in which the beliefs, utterances, texts and persons taken to be authoritative are deferred to unquestioningly: "Every such form of inquiry begins in and starts from some conditions of pure historical contingency, from the beliefs, institutions, and practices of some particular community which constitute a given. With such a community authority will have been conferred upon certain texts and certain voices" (p. 354). For MacIntyre it is only in the first period, when all these elements remain unquestioned, that the narratives have their place. For a tradition, development means going beyond that stage towards a second period in which inadequacies have been identified but not yet remedied, and a third in which response to those inadequacies has resulted in a set of re-formulations and re-evaluations as well as new formulations and evaluations, designed to remedy inadequacies and overcome limitations (p. 355). Although MacIntyre suggests that, once the final stage has been reached the new conceptual and theoretical structures must exhibit a fundamental continuity with the "shared beliefs" that preceded this stage, he nevertheless seems not to understand how the original narrative basis continues to influence the tradition.

In my opinion, such a point of view easily leads to misunderstanding of CathST. At the risk of over-simplification, the following picture seems implicit in MacIntyre's theory: first, there is the stage of the simple belief in biblical narratives, followed by the first theological development leading to a kind of Augustinian theology. When this approach was faced by an epistemological crisis, Aquinas introduced a definitive solution by integrating Aristotelianism. MacIntyre's account of the Thomistic tradition in *Three Rival Versions* and his enthusiasm for *Veritatis splendor* exhibit his intellectual respect for the sense of finality in Aquinas's solution. What is forgotten in this theory, however, is that, in order to remain a living tradition, the rational tradition, in this case Thomas's, needs to be continuously challenged by the reading and re-reading of the biblical texts. In the hermeneutic relation between a community acting and living in a contingent historical context and the text of the Bible with its universe of meaning, new insights and new practices can be generated which can radicalise and renew the given tradition of reflection. This perspective of the hermeneutic relation to the biblical narratives appears in the already mentioned method of Vatican II (*GS* 4) which consists of "scrutinising the signs of the times and interpreting them in the light of the Gospel". It leads to serious misunderstandings when the Gospel is reduced, as is often the case, to a fundamentalist citing of supportive quotations for stated principles. Judging in "the light of the Gospel" requires an appreciation of its narrative and metaphorical forms.

My claim at this point is that the relation between foundational narratives and the development of the tradition itself is a central concern for the development of CathST. Against MacIntyre, and inspired by Ricœur, I take the position that a Catholic social tradition of reflection and *praxis*, an essential dimension of CathST, not only needs inspiration from other traditions of interpretation and inquiry, but from a living relation to the text of the Bible. MacIntyre seems to have underestimated this. Through their poetic dimension the biblical narratives open a world of meaning and a hermeneutic horizon which makes it possible to enrich the established meanings, to criticize perverted meanings and to break open the limited hermeneutic horizon of our time, marked by an iron cage of bureaucratic, technocratic, managerial and instrumental rationality. The poetic dimension also helps us to understand that semantic and practical innovation (a new and more meaningful understanding of reality leading to new *praxis*) does not only come from theoretical insights, nor merely from an analysis of a changing historical context but also comes from a living and hermeneutical relation between a community of readers and the world of the biblical text. Those who read from the perspective of their historical context and are conscious that they refer to a specific world of meaning know that the texts cannot be reduced entirely to the input of meaning by the original authors. Precisely in the living hermeneutical relation between the readers and the world of the text,

new insights are born (semantic innovation) which are not simply like
new objective knowledge which is not otherwise available (that would
in moral matters contradict the reflective capacity of human beings and
underestimate the role of human reason). It is more a matter of new or
rediscovered perspectives and of a growing discernment about what
God wants His people to do in new historical contexts (which implies
that analysis and hermeneutics cannot be neglected in the task of overcoming fundamentalism). A living relation to biblical narratives contributes to a growing "social discernment" and in this sense to practical
innovation[24].

1. Re-imagining Society by Root-Metaphors and Narratives

When we try to understand how the biblical narratives allow us to re-
imagine our social reality – which is not the same as introducing new
utopias or ideologies – we have to consider among other aspects the role
of root-metaphors. Metaphors are vehicles of transcendence and freedom.
Their imagery awakens human energies, generates a world of meaning
and opens new vistas of human possibilities. Metaphors make a deeper
understanding of reality possible by producing an emotional shock "by
an intentional misuse of language", an impertinent addition to "normal"
understandings, or, to put it in the words of Ricœur, by a "kinship where
ordinary vision does not perceive any relationship" or by a "new predicative pertinence ... a pertinence within impertinence"[25].

They are based on a calculated error which brings together things that
do not go together and, by means of this apparent misunderstanding,
cause a new, hitherto unnoticed, relation of meaning to spring up between
the terms that previous systems of classification had ignored or not
allowed"[26]. The person confronted with a living metaphor has to pay
attention when "strange" juxtapositions of words take place[27].

For Ricœur one detail merits special attention: the word "predicative". For him the predicative pertinence does not function at the

24. The most inspiring book we have read about the poetry of the Bible is A. THOMAS-
SET, *Paul Ricœur. Une poétique de la morale: aux fondements d'une éthique herméneutique et narrative dans une perspective chrétienne* (BETL, 124), Leuven, University
Press, 1996.
25. P. RICŒUR, *The Function of Fiction in Shaping Reality*, in M.J. VALDEZ (ed.),
A Ricœur Reader. Reflection and Imagination, New York, Harvester/Wheatsheaf, 1991,
pp. 125 and 127.
26. P. RICŒUR, *Interpretation Theory. Discourse and the Surplus of Meaning*, Fort
Worth, TX, Texas Christian University Press, 1976, p. 51.
27. E.R. MACCORMAC, *Metaphor and Myth in Science and Religion*, Durham, NC,
Duke University Press, 1976, p. 74.

denominational level of words but on the level of predication, thus, in a broader context of sentence or text. This leads him to focus especially on the metaphoric function of the biblical narratives, especially the parables. Their employment, together with the eccentric elements, create a metaphoric tension between everyday life and the extravagant world of the narrative. Most important, however, is "semantic innovation"[28]. Metaphoric utterance is a creative mode of knowledge that offers new information. Metaphors not only express what people experience but also suggest possible new meanings and new perspectives on reality. They are a combination of dimensions: *epiphor* and *diaphor*. "An *epiphor* is a metaphor that achieves its meaning by expressing experience that is analogous to that of the hearer. ... Her response is, "Yes, that is precisely the way I feel"; or, "Yes, that is a way of looking at things that I have never considered before but I am sure it is right". A *diaphor,* on the other hand, is a metaphor that suggests possible meanings rather than expressing them, and which are confirmed by the hearers. It remains suggestive rather than expressive of experience and, when interpreted, literally always produces absurdity"[29]. All metaphors are composed of these two dimensions. There are no pure *epiphors,* otherwise they become pure analogies that do not suggest anything more than they say. There are also no pure *diaphors;* as without its expressive element, no one could resonate with such metaphor.

What is true of metaphors is also true of "root-metaphors". A root-metaphor is the most basic assumption about the nature of the world, society or experience: "the function of the root-metaphor is to suggest a primary way of looking at things or experience and this way of looking at things assists us in building categories or in creating art forms that will express this insight. Our very notions of what is true and what is meaningful rest upon our underlying assumptions about the nature of reality. Without such apprehensions about the nature of the world, knowledge would be impossible, for we would have no way of organizing our perceptions into a coherent whole"[30]. A shift in metaphors alerts us to the necessity of changing our perceptions of life and world.

According to Ricœur, one of the most important aspects of root-metaphors is that in the context of a tradition they can persist through time, and this because they can invoke a whole network of meanings and metaphors. Persistence, however, does not imply a static conception of

28. P. RICŒUR, *Word, Polysemy, Metaphor,* in VALDEZ, *A Ricœur Reader* (n. 25), p. 79.
29. MACCORMAC, *Metaphor and Myth* (n. 27), pp. 84-85.
30. *Ibid.,* pp. 94-95.

reality. Through metaphors and art, the world we live in is not only formed but can also be transformed. In the transformation process the root-metaphors open new horizons, they bring forth new possibilities for our interpreting the world we live in. It makes a difference, for example, whether we think of society from the perspective of an organic metaphor or from the perspective of a mechanical one; it makes a difference whether we talk of society as an aggregate of individuals (as in the concept of "collective individualism") and try to calculate their self-interest, whereby a (mechanistic) invisible hand leads to the realization of the greatest good for the greatest number, or when we refer to a society based on solidarity and an invisible handshake. In this sense the biblical understanding of society in terms of covenant or of the mystical body breaks through the individualistic frameworks of modernity and helps us to understand social reality in a qualitatively different way.

I think it would be enlightening to examine how the traditional texts of Catholic social teaching not only function as rational texts about principles and theories; but also as texts referring to powerful, biblically inspired root-metaphors which mould our pre-reflective understanding of social reality. It would also be interesting to explore to what extent principles and theories are connected and vitalized through the fundamental hermeneutic perspectives opened by these root metaphors. When we take, for example, an encyclical such as *On Social Concern*, many of these metaphors seem to play a central role, such as "structures of sin", evil "mechanisms", property under "social mortgage", the "health" of a political community, financial and social "mechanisms", the neighbour as living "image of God "the Father", the "brotherhood" of all in Christ, "communio" as the "soul" of the Church and vocation as a "sacrament". Have we not underestimated the metaphoric power of the social encyclicals? Are not these metaphors, with their impact on our presuppositions, at least as important as the theoretical explanations?

2. *Some Concrete Implications for Catholic Social Thought*

When we accept that many of our classic "Catholic" principles are more than philosophically pure, and that their meaning is influenced by root-metaphors from the world of the Bible, it becomes necessary to consider how biblical metaphors (or metaphoric texts and narratives) lead to a richer understanding of social reality, while also enriching the meaning of the classic principles of Catholic social teaching. Take, for example, the concept of solidarity, which, according to Cardinal Ratzinger, is, together with subsidiarity, the most important expression of the social implications of human dignity. "Solidarity" may be described in ontological terms, as the solidarists do, or in sociological terms as the product of socialisation, increase of interdependence at all levels (*MM* 59-62; *GS* 23-32), or as ethical response to the situation (*SRS passim*). In CathST, however, its significance goes beyond these meanings and beyond the popular usage it has acquired in contemporary popular political discourse, to signify an attitude which finds its image in the common fatherhood of God and the brotherhood of all in Christ – a solidarity which finds its concrete expression in bearing radical witness to our love of our neighbour, so that it make us ready for sacrifice, even the ultimate one, to lay down one's life for one's brethren. This type of "warm" solidarity is not a substitute for political forms of solidarity, but brings in a radicalisation and dynamism which go beyond every attempt to base solidarity on some form of enlightened self-interest.

It is worth exploring further how precisely the metaphoric and narrative aspects in Catholic social teaching have contributed to the creation of social movements. In moral theology it has become almost a commonplace that the Bible does not in the first place provide us with new moral insights and norms, that it does not provide us with "an adequate determination of what is morally right". The Bible is exhortative rather than "normative". As parenetic texts, the biblical narratives should be judged primarily in terms of their influence on the reader rather than in terms of being a manual of morality[31].

Biblical stories also challenge and disturb, however, and they cannot be told or heard without an awareness that a response is called for[32]. Karen Lebacqz refers in this context to the role of the remembrance of the stories in memorializing celebration (which brings us back to the role of the community). "If the story is not told, justice will die ... This means that worship and preaching the re-enactment of the story in memorializing celebration – are integral to justice, they keep alive the story that grounds the identity of the community in its history of justice and injustice"[33]. But how does the use of biblical metaphors and stories function in Catholic social thought? What shapes the attitudes of Catholics: the theoretical framework of Catholic social teaching or the remembrance of the stories though community life and worshipping? Is this active remembering not more fundamental than the knowledge of the

31. Cf. B. SCHULLER, *The Debate on the Specific Character of Christian Ethics. Some Remarks*, in C.E. CURRAN & R.A. MCCORMICK (eds.), *The Distinctiveness of Christian Ethics* (Readings in Moral Theology, 2), New York, NY, Paulist, 1980, pp. 207-233.

32. D.B. FORRESTER, *Beliefs, Values and Policies. Conviction Politics in a Secular Age*, Oxford, Clarendon, 1989, p. 28.

33. K. LEBACQZ, as quoted in FORRESTER, *Beliefs, Values and Policies* (n. 32), p. 29.

theoretical expressions of it in official Catholic social teaching? If so, what are the methodological consequences for its further development?

3. *Semantic Vigilance*

As I have already pointed out, when a community approaches the world of the biblical texts from its own historical context and experience, which is characterised by a narrowing of the hermeneutic horizon and perversion of memory, it is possible that, in this relation between reading, community and text, there is a semantic and practical innovation. But that leads also to semantic vigilance. Through its appropriation of the biblical narratives, the Catholic community can rediscover forgotten perspectives which make us in a special way critical towards what seems to be self-evident. One of these perspectives is the scandal of the Cross. According to Claus Demmer, a deeper understanding of the meaning of life that starts from the acceptance of the scandal of the Cross, can lead to a better understanding of the human person and his or her universal nature "under the conditions of a kenotic existence". It would be interesting to work out what this kenotic existence could mean for the understanding of human dignity, social action, thinking about justice and the redistribution of wealth. It could be said, for example, that the Cross leads to an understanding of social reality and historic achievements from the perspective of the victims of history; it makes it possible to acknowledge that society bears the face of its victims. The preferential option for the poor can be understood from this perspective. The Cross also opens our eyes to the tragedies of history. It warns against all manner of aesthetic minimization of suffering and ideological misuses and against a too optimist linear interpretation of history. It urges us to pay attention to the depths of human suffering to which our societies can descend. The dangerous memory of the Cross finally urges the churches to fight against the misuses of memory and ideological deformations of reality. It shapes a prophetic company of critics who remain vigilant with respect to meanings which risk being perverted by the logic of the market or technology.

IV. Conclusion

In order to understand the relation between official Catholic social teaching and CathST, we need to clarify what Catholicism means as a social tradition of reflection and *praxis* (CSTrad). This tradition can be conceived of as a complex interaction between a rational tradition

(including a critical dialogue with other such traditions) and the semantic and practical innovation facilitated by the reading and interpretation
of biblical narratives. Only from this perspective on the Catholic social
tradition as a broader tradition of *praxis* and reflection can Catholicism
become a source of inspiration for discussions about the economic,
social and political problems of our time.

Catholic University Leuven   Johan VERSTRAETEN

TOWARDS AN ETHICS OF RECONSTRUCTION
AND MEDIATION: CHRISTIAN SOCIAL ETHICS
IN DIALOGUE WITH DISCOURSE ETHICS

I. INTRODUCTION

It is in no way my intention that this paper should open up a completely new chapter in the development of Christian ethics and its social dimension. This would not only be over-ambitious because of the long and complex history of the Church's social teaching; it would also be insensitive not to acknowledge the immense work that has already been done in theology, philosophy and social sciences in order to understand and to support the Christian commitment to justice, peace and solidarity as a matter of clear and determined action. Such an engagement cannot be just a neutral analysis of what is going on in the society. We are already formed by our history, our memberships, options and desires which we have to interpret in the light of concrete challenges and in the horizon of fundamental convictions. If my remarks sound sceptical concerning the plausibility of a theology-based social doctrine and its implications, this caution is not meant to be a retreat from responsibility and solidarity with those who invest a lot in a Christian presence in a secular context. I just want to show that while this active and responsible presence may have particular sources of profound motivation, it has no privileged access to some arcane knowledge that could not be shared by other people. In this sense I am prepared to run the risk of a certain self-secularisation in order to establish a dialogue with non-believers at the level of a minimum of shared convictions and philosophical reason[1].

The Problematic of Catholic Social Thought

Catholic social thought (CathST) has been buried and revitalised several times and for many different reasons in recent decades, so I will not be the first who dares to speak in a short time-span about a tradition which has flourished for more than one century – with roots going back much further. Anyway it remains an interesting task for historians to

---

1. See J.A. VAN DER VEN, *Contemporary Christian Theology in a Secularized Society*, in *Bulletin ET* 9 (1998), no. 2, 199-219, for a more differentiated introduction to the topic of secularization.

reconstruct the building and to explore various transformations of this particular doctrine, thus opening up an important chapter in the sociology of religion[2]. But I wonder whether this genuine theory with its specific references for insiders to Catholicism remains a vital part of research and teaching in theological ethics, at least as far as I can survey these activities which exist on a world-wide scale. I look on myself as someone working in the area of ethics (both philosophical and theological[3]) with a special interest in social, economic and political issues. But I would never view myself as a privileged representative of one doctrine to the exclusion of all other possibilities in past and current debate. The project, which I prefer to call "Christian social ethics"[4] (because I am convinced that the question of the *Christian* identity has to be asked) is open to a variety of methods and interdisciplinary contacts and would only suffer from being restricted to the eternal interpretation of papal encyclicals. I am glad to know that this is a caricature of CathST. But sometimes I observe a kind of nostalgia which I try to understand – very often without success. It is much easier to pay tribute to the merits of a tradition when you are not expected or even urged to admire it entirely, like the composition of a wonderful symphony. I have to admit right at the beginning that my idea of social ethics is much more like a dish of mixed ingredients, or, to stick to the musical metaphor, like an assembly of voices without a conductor. There are even cries, loud cries, desperate voices. A social thinking that is "beautiful" is a contradiction in itself.

Let me give one depressing example. At this very moment in April 1999, Europe is at war. Do we have or do we want to say anything about

---

2. K. GABRIEL, *Gesellschaft im Umbruch – Wandel des Religiösen*, in H.-J. HÖHN (ed.), *Krise der Immanenz. Religion an den Grenzen der Moderne* (Philosophie der Gegenwart), Frankfurt am Main, Fischer, 1996, pp. 31-49.

3. This status is not always very comfortable because you are suspected of being an impossible hybrid.

4. Cf. also N. BRIESKORN & J. MÜLLER, *Gerechtigkeit und soziale Ordnung*. FS Walter Kerber, Freiburg im Breisgau, Herder, 1996; F. FURGER & M. HEIMBACH-STEINS (eds.) *Perspektiven christlicher Sozialethik. Hundert Jahre nach Rerum novarum*, Münster, Regensberg, 1991; T. HAUSMANNINGER (ed.), *Christliche Sozialethik zwischen Moderne und Postmoderne*, Paderborn, Schöningh, 1994; M. HEIMBACH-STEINS, A. LIENKAMP, & J. WIEMEYER (eds.), *Brennpunkt Sozialethik. Theorien, Aufgaben, Methoden*. FS Franz Furger, Freiburg, Herder, 1995; F. HENGSBACH, B. EMUNDS, & M. MÖHRING-HESSE (eds.), *Jenseits Katholischer Soziallehre. Neue Entwürfe christlicher Gesellschaftsethik*, Düsseldorf, Patmos, 1993; H.-J. HÖHN (ed.), *Christliche Sozialethik interdisziplinär*, Paderborn, Schöningh, 1997; D. MIETH (ed.) *Christliche Sozialethik im Anspruch der Zukunft. Tübinger Beiträge zur Katholischen Soziallehre* (Studien zur theologischen Ethik, 41), Freiburg, Universitätsverlag, 1992; J. MÜLLER & W. KERBER (eds.), *Soziales Denken in einer zerrissenen Welt. Anstöße der Katholischen Soziallehre in Europa* (Quaestiones disputatae, 136), Freiburg im Breisgau, Herder, 1991.

this situation? Would some of us like to repeat (not without some satisfaction) the old theory of the just war? I must say that I don't have any
answers to these most irritating questions. What irritates me more is the
silence of most European intellectuals, including Christians. It is alarming because we could read the current events as the capitulation of moral
rationality in many respects. To what extent must theology and ethics be
affected by this experience of evil?

I used to read the corpus of texts belonging to the social teaching of
the Catholic Church (CST) as a series of documents inviting a close
study of the Church's ambivalent attitude towards modernity and of its
growing sensitivity to the different forms of injustice and suffering[5]. I
cannot celebrate the beginning of CST at the end of the 19th century
without thinking of the authoritarian anti-modernism of most of its
founding fathers. Marie-Dominique Chenu's little book on the church's
social doctrine as an *ideology*[6] should still be read and discussed by students of Christian social ethics because it shows clearly the changing
theological influences on the texts presented by the magisterium. Apart
from its contents, CST can be considered as an exceptional example of
early mass communication. It is an unusual thing that somebody wants
to reach the whole world with his message concerning the social, economic and political system. As a logical consequence the texts are now
quickly available in the leading media system of our time, the Internet,
where they share the destiny of so many other messages that will no
longer attract our attention because they disappear in a flood of signs.

Most newspapers, radio and TV stations mention the publication of a
new encyclical as a special event. But there seems to be no real need for
such a text – neither outside nor inside the community of Catholics. As
far as I see CathST has not at all profited from what we call the "boom"
of ethics during the last twenty years. On the contrary, as a theory with
a rather conservative design it is rarely taken into consideration in the
discussions of topics of "applied ethics". In order to put it in a provoca-
tive way: could it be that CathST gives answers to questions that only
few people ask? At a rather general level it contains a lot of solemn declarations which it is difficult to contradict. Serious ethical reflections are
only generated in situations of conflict where opposite claims have to be
considered – not in order to find a consensus at any price, but in order to

5. See the famous collection of papers in C.E. CURRAN & R.A. McCORMICK (eds.),
Official Catholic Social Teaching (Readings in Moral Theology, 5), New York, NY,
Paulist, 1986.
6. M.-D. CHENU, *La "doctrine sociale" de l'Église comme idéologie* (Essais), Paris,
Cerf, 1979.

get into the logic of the different points of view in a moral universe now without a central perspective[7]. That is the moment when mediators have to intervene: searching for agreement, reconciliation, fair and acceptable solutions. Of course there may be situations in which human life cannot be defended without the legitimate use of force. Once again: social ethics is not about an idyllic utopia for aesthetes.

II. THE TRANSFORMATION OF CATHOLIC SOCIAL TEACHING

I have hesitated a little before deciding to present my view of a venerable tradition as the personal story of learning and teaching. Some aspects may be simply the expression of my limited understanding of a complicated history. On the other hand, this presentation tries to give a faithful report of many discussions in which I took part in the '70s at the University of Münster. It is the experience of more than twenty years that leads me and many others to a friendly but clear dissociation from the classical form of CST and to the discovery of Christian social ethics "beyond CST"[8]. The scientific reasons for this distance are combined with a number of personal impressions and encounters.

1. Farewell to "Classical" Doctrine

For many of those born in the '50s and '60s, Catholic social teaching within German faculties of Catholic theology seemed to be the affair of elderly men in dark suits with good contacts to the German association of employers and little interest in the real challenges of inequality and injustice on the national and international level, afraid of everything that could be connected with socialism and far from the contemporary debates in philosophy and social sciences. I remember that it was relatively easy to be successful in the examinations because it was sufficient to read conservative newspapers for some days in order to acquaint oneself with the examiner's world view and his favourite topics. In many faculties CathST belonged (and still belongs) to the department of practical theology and was thus dissociated from the intellectual ambitions of systematic theology, particularly moral theology (from which CathST as

---

7. M. HUNYADI, *La vertu du conflit. Pour une morale de la médiation* (Humanités), Paris, Cerf, 1995.
8. HENGSBACH, EMUNDS, & MÖHRING-HESSE, *Jenseits Katholischer Soziallehre* (n. 4); W. LESCH & A. BONDOLFI (eds.), *Theologische Ethik im Diskurs. Eine Einführung* (UTB für Wissenschaft, 1806), Tübingen, Francke, 1995.

an academic discipline derived). I am personally indebted to moral theology and moral philosophy for most of the intellectual frameworks which I bring to social ethics in a Christian context, and I would even say that the strict division of labour between moral theology and social ethics does not make sense any more. What about the important ethical issues of bio-medicine and bio-technology? Do they belong only to the field of moral theology? Of course not. In most practical questions we have to deal today with aspects of justice *and* of a "good life"[9], of social structures *and* of individual responsibility. They are interwoven and can only be separated for analytical reasons.

If CST and CathST were not attractive to young students because of their strange paternalistic style and the burden of natural law, the same characteristics began to change rapidly in moral theology during the '70s. It was a time of lively discussions about what is specifically Christian in ethics and about autonomy. The academic and strategic aim was a greater independence of moral theology from the *magisterium*'s control and the open dialogue with secular reason. By the way, all this happened on the basis of some kind of Thomistic rationalism and not at all in discontinuity with tradition. Looking back to these developments we might say that moral theology came a little closer to the standards of CathST with its preference for norms and values that are recognised by all men and women of good will, not only Catholics.

The shift towards the paradigm of the autonomy of moral reason perpetuates the tendency strengthened by the Second Vatican Council where *Gaudium et spes* can be read as the common reference point for moral theology and social ethics. Christian ethics has become intellectually habitable by those who do not accept the simple deduction of norms from eternal principles and who refuse the authoritarian way of defining what is meant by "Catholic identity". Moral theology and CathST can now meet on the ground of human rights discourse and are more and more accepted as reasonable partners in ethical deliberations in pluralistic societies.

The concrete practice of this engagement in the public debate differs from one European country to the other. I am convinced that the mutual information about these different styles is one of many good reasons for a closer European co-operation. As a member of various ethical study groups in Switzerland I had never been asked before whether I was a Catholic or Prostestant, a theologian or a philosopher. I was invited to

9. J. HABERMAS, *Erläuterungen zur Diskursethik* (Suhrkamp Taschenbücher Wissenschaft, 975), Frankfurt am Main, Suhrkamp, 1991.

participate as an ethicist. In France things seem to be rather different because the members of the National Advisory Committee for Ethics are supposed to represent "spiritual families" and cannot expect to improve their image as independent specialists for ethical issues. But I am not sure whether we should really be interested in presenting ourselves primarily as such family members or as experts who have acquired skills in ethical argumentation. Provided we adopt this position of secular humanism, the question of an ethicist's Christian identity remains of course unanswered. If we refuse the option in order to profit cynically from an academic position in theology this question has to be treated in the interest of intellectual honesty[10].

Whereas moral theology is more and more characterised by the separation between rational argumentation and religious motivation, social ethics (close to CST and also dominant in a lot unofficial grassroots movements) is getting more and more biblical and theological whether we like it or not. If we prefer to regard theological ethics as an integral whole (and I like to do so for the sake of consistency), we cannot be satisfied with the lack of interest in the relationship between theological and philosophical ethics which is one of the key questions of modernity in the context of systematic theology[11]. In a certain way we are now living the experience made by biblical scholars one hundred years before us when the interpretation of biblical texts became a matter of philological and historical expertise that has nothing to do with faith. We have to organise our research in the hermeneutical triangle of the biblical narrative, the doctrine of Christian community and the claims of secular reason[12]. Otherwise we are not safe from the dangers of fundamentalism.

2. From Political Theology to Social Ethics

About twenty years ago a lot of German students of my generation found what we had been looking for in the programme of political theology. Johann-Baptist Metz published his *Faith in History and Society*

10. Even if I do not agree with him on most points it is thanks to people like John Milbank that we have to deal with this challenge of theological identity, J. MILBANK, *Theology and Social Theory. Beyond Secular Reason* (Signposts in Theology), Oxford, Blackwell, 1990.

11. C. THEOBALD, *Glauben im* modus conversationis. *Zum Ansatz einer theologischen Theorie der Moderne*, in E. ARENS (ed.), *Kommunikatives Handeln und christlicher Glaube. Ein theologischer Diskurs mit Jürgen Habermas*, Paderborn, Schöningh, 1997, pp. 33-70.

12. A. ANZENBACHER, *Christliche Sozialethik. Einführung und Prinzipien*, München, Paderborn, 1998; W. KERBER, *Sozialethik* (Grundkurs Philosophie, 13), Stuttgart, Kohlhammer, 1998.

in 1977. It became one of the most important references for the early shaping of my identity as a student of theology even if I was a little bit embarrassed by Metz's dramatic rhetoric and his preference for the apocalyptic drama. Political theology and its even more important sister, the theology of liberation, have contributed a lot to the *aggiornamento* of Catholicism after Vatican II[13]. But for those theologians interested in philosophy it was not enough.

It was Helmut Peukert who helped us to make the next step with his work on epistemology and communicative action[14]. The book culminates in the impressive reconstruction of the ideal community of communication and the paradoxes of universal solidarity, drawing the line from the theory of action and the early roots of discourse ethics to the Jewish-Christian ideal of solidarity including the innocent victims of history. Unfortunately Peukert as a priest had to leave the faculty of theology after his marriage. Edmund Arens has managed to continue the ambitious project of a theology based on the paradigm of communicative action[15] with a privileged link between fundamental theology and social ethics[16].

3. *The German Background*

These are some of the influences that have accompanied my journey to Christian social ethics as a deontological, procedural, universalistic and cognitive type of theory in close contact with secular moral philosophy. You may have noticed that most of the references have a German academic provenance. It is not by accident that the route from political theology to a revised version of critical theory (the Frankfurt School) found an encouraging intellectual climate in the West German society after May 1968. The New Left of the '70s and political theology as a part of it cannot be understood without the traumatic memory of National Socialism and the deep mistrust entertained by all who do not see the necessity of legitimising their position by well-founded arguments. The simple reference to what is usual under given circumstances

13. See W. KROH, *Kirche im gesellschaftlichen Widerspruch. Zur Verständigung zwischen katholischer Soziallehre und politischer Theologie*, München, Kösel, 1982, on the relation between political theology and the tradition CST.

14. H. PEUKERT, *Wissenschaftstheorie – Handlungstheorie – Fundamentale Theologie. Analysen zu Ansatz und Status theologischer Theoriebildung*, Frankfurt am Main, Suhrkamp, 1978.

15. ARENS, *Kommunikatives Handeln und christlicher Glaube* (n. 11).

16. W. LESCH, *Theologische Ethik als Handlungstheorie*, in E. ARENS (ed.), *Gottesrede – Glaubenspraxis. Perspektiven theologischer Handlungstheorie*, Darmstadt, Wissenschaftliche Buchgesellschaft, 1994, pp. 89-109.

does not count. Richard Rorty may feel good in the tradition of American democracy and liberalism and point to the fact that he is just an American in order to explain why he has pragmatic reasons for certain ideas. A German citizen would not dare to adopt a similar attitude. At least Apel expressed how much he was outraged by a pragmatism of this kind[17].

The development of discourse ethics (in the tradition of Kantian moral philosophy) in the late '70s and the early '80s by Jürgen Habermas[18] and Karl-Otto Apel, which was a reaction to the destruction of moral conscience in Nazi Germany, represented an attempt to construct a solid foundation for legitimate norms acceptable even to those who did not share a common religion or any other world view. This theory of moral philosophy, in the two closely related versions shaped by Apel and Habermas, works on two levels. On the theoretical level it lays the foundations of a normative approach grounded in certain presuppositions of argumentation. Communicative rationality could not work without a number of validity claims such as our reciprocal recognition as equal persons in an infinite community of enquirers; and when we begin to engage in a discussion of a controversial question we already agree about the possibility of a consensus to be found by non-violent means. As regards the procedure for testing the validity of moral norms, this is similar to Kant's analysis of maxims in the context of a universal law that should be independent of personal visions of the good and happy life. But in contrast to Kantian ethics this universalising attitude is not only a matter of private conscience, but of communicative action in a universe of moral pluralism. Discourse ethics on its practical level tries to combine these particular points of disagreement and conflict with the open perspective of free discussion and negotiation where each person can present the most convincing arguments in favour of possible solutions, taking into account the interests of all parties concerned by enforcing a rule. By reconstructing the moral point of view, discourse ethics does not deduce any norms from a metaphysical principle. But it shows that it is reasonable to stick to the ideal of impartiality and justice. By participating in a practical discourse we agree with the fundamental norm of putting ourselves in the situation of the other. This can be interpreted as amounting to nothing other than a procedural and inter-subjective version of Kant's categorical imperative.

17. K.-O. APEL, *Diskurs und Verantwortung. Das Problem des Übergangs zur postkonventionellen Moral*, Frankfurt am Main, Suhrkamp, 1998.
18. J. HABERMAS, *Moralbewußtsein und kommunikatives Handeln* (Suhrkamp Taschenbücher Wissenschaft, 422), Frankfurt am Main, Suhrkamp, 1983.

In spite of the international attention given to discourse ethics I don't think that it has produced a coherent school. Philosophical theories which attach importance to foundational issues are less successful nowadays than those which are more relativistic. And in the framework of German society a theory of consensus and post-conventional moral reasoning has to face new challenges because of the transition of Eastern Europe, the end of the German Democratic Republic and the unification of the two German states in 1990. The idea of peaceful negotiations and the patient balancing of all interests that should be considered was much easier to realise under the condition of an economically healthy welfare state in the shadow of the Berlin wall. In view of the tensions, frustrations and uncertainties in the eastern parts of Germany it is impossible to teach ethics in the same way as in the security, wealth and neutrality of Switzerland. The growing clamour in the twentieth century for economic justice for all has to be carried forward, although it is not at all evident at the moment whether we will succeed. But our efforts will be crucial for the future of the traditional nation states and the unification of Europe. I now want to show to what extent a procedural theory of social ethics can contribute to the clarification of our concepts.

III. The Project of Modernity

The affinity between the Frankfurt approach to an ethics of communicative action and a new type of Christian social ethics[19] can be partly explained by the common interest in the "unfinished project of modernity" (Habermas) with all its promise of progress, peace, liberty and prosperity. We know that the opposite can become true as well ("dialectics of Enlightenment") so that there is no reason for a naive enthusiasm.

Modern societies have to cope with the *paradox of consensus*: they need a minimum of common values and at the same time they promote the process of structural differentiation and the individualisation of moral standards[20]. That is why moral judgements in the area of complex interaction have to be sociologically informed. If this is not the case we risk producing values and norms that will never be accepted by persons coming from different backgrounds. There is of course not only one version

19. See Habermas' critical answers to some theologians working with his theory, J. Habermas, *Texte und Kontexte* (Suhrkamp Taschenbücher Wissenschaft, 944), Frankfurt am Main, Suhrkamp, 1991, pp. 127-156.

20. G. Kruip, *Sozialethik als Verfahrensethik*, in H.-J. Höhn (ed.), *Christliche Sozialethik interdisziplinär*, Paderborn, Schöningh, 1997, pp. 41-58.

of the "story of modernity". With Michael Walzer we can distinguish at least three ways of generating norms under the conditions of a post-traditional society[21]. We find those who seriously believe that we just have to receive norms given by a higher human authority or by God ("path of illumination"). Others are convinced of finding acceptable and valid agreements again and again in the never ending effort of communicative action ("path of invention"). And a third group prefers to discuss, criticise and modify what is already going on in conflicts about moral issues ("path of interpretation"). According to this construction discourse ethics would belong to the second type of moral theory, although it includes as well some aspects of interpretation. But it is clearly linked to the idea of self-legislation of competent individuals (autonomy) and a corresponding need for the self-organisation of modern societies.

I think that we should pay attention to the postmodern critics of modern social theory and ask if the story of rational and communicative discourse only represents another narrative *grand récit* (in the sense of Lyotard) without being more plausible than any other doctrine. As far as I see the best answer to such a challenging relativism is to cultivate a high capability of reflecting norms within the hermeneutical circle of invention and interpretation. In this framework Catholic social thinking certainly has its role to play together with other projects searching for the common good. In Germany this hermeneutical construction is known as the "Böckenförde paradox"[22] so named after Ernst-Wolfgang Böckenförde, a lawyer and former judge of the Federal Constitutional Court. He has defended the thesis that modern secular states depend on normative resources and presuppositions which they cannot generate and guarantee themselves. Therefore they have a vital interest in encouraging and protecting the freedom of religion and the active participation of religious communities in the procedures of democratic deliberation.

IV. Outline of a New Paradigm of Christian Social Ethics

As a partner in a self-critically reflected project of modernity Christian ethics can help to establish a new relation between religion and politics.

---

21. M. WALZER, *Interpretation and Social Criticism* (The Tanner Lectures on Human Values, 1985), Cambridge, MA, Harvard University Press, 1987.
22. J.-B. METZ, *Religion und Politik auf dem Boden der Moderne. Versuch einer Neubestimmung*, in H.-J. HÖHN (ed.), *Krise der Immanenz. Religion an den Grenzen der Moderne* (Philosophie der Gegenwart), Frankfurt am Main, Fischer, 1996, pp. 265-279, esp. p. 270.

If religion can no longer be regarded as an anachronism and part of a private counter-world, we should nevertheless take care not to fall back into the patterns of pre-modern triumphalism. The new paradigm of social ethics with a Christian background is no radical revolution of former theories but a series of reasonable transformations.

1. *A Revised Version of CathST: "Political, not Metaphysical"*

According to Jürgen Habermas, ethics and social theory have to be conceived on the ground of post-metaphysical thinking because society is not an organic unity with one powerful centre but a structure of subsystems and competing interpretations. The appropriate theoretical approach to this reality is a combination of linguistic analysis and contractualism. With our speech acts we participate in the process of finding institutional arrangements that can be freely willed by everyone concerned. A similar idea of this dialogical structure of ethics has been presented in John Rawls' writings on political liberalism[23]. It is interesting to note that the main principles of his *Theory of Justice* (1971) had a remarkable impact on the American bishops' pastoral letter *Economic Justice for All* (1986). This shows that advanced forms of Christian social ethics and official teaching do not want to be limited to the repetition of communitarian values[24].

2. *The Turn to "Applied Ethics"*

It has often been observed that discourse ethics is mainly interested in foundational questions and has little to say in the debates on applied ethics. This is not true if we read the discourse paradigm as a two-level-theory, a theoretical and a practical part. The theoretical research deals with meta-ethics and normative philosophical ethics in order to show the pragmatic presuppositions of argumentation and the transcendental possibility of a universally normative validity. The practical part refers to the non-ideal actual world where there is no special status for the theorist. Moral philosophers and moral theologians find themselves on absolutely the same level with all the other people involved in the resolution of

23. J. RAWLS, *Justice as Fairness: Political not Metaphysical*, in S. AVINERI & A. DE-SHALIT (eds.), *Communitarianism and Individualism* (Oxford Readings in Politics and Government), Oxford, University Press, 1992, pp. 186-204.

24. See S. MULHALL & A. SWIFT, *Liberals and Communitarians*, Oxford, Blackwell, 1992, for a concise reconstruction of the philosophical debate. See also W. REESE-SCHÄFER, *Grenzgötter der Moral. Der neuere europäisch-amerikanische Diskurs zur politischen Ethik* (Suhrkamp Taschenbücher Wissenschaft, 1282), Frankfurt am Main, Suhrkamp, 1997.

concrete problems. If ethicists manage to help others to make their ideas clear and to find the reflective equilibrium of all the aspects that have to be taken into consideration this would already be a valuable service. In other words, the turn to applied ethics is no playground for visionaries and preachers but an opportunity to elaborate good arguments in an open process of deliberation[25].

3. *The case of the German Consultation (1994-1997)*

The new style of Catholic social thinking can be illustrated by a number of documents published by regional churches since the 1980s. I have already mentioned the American letter on economic justice (1986). The Austrian letter on social issues (1990) is a similar example. We have now reached a further dimension of democratisation by the enlargement of the community of inquiry so as to be a real ecumenical platform. This is not the place to have a closer look at the specificities of Protestant social ethics during its history. It is good news that in Germany Protestants and Catholics have succeeded in starting a joint venture of consultation and arriving at a result that is not without interest for all the members of the civil society. The text *For a Future in Solidarity and Justice* (1997) offers a synthesis of ecumenical aspects, of official and non-official traditions, of theology, philosophy and social sciences. Dealing with unemployment and the crisis of the welfare state, the politics of sustainability and also addressing the churches' entrepreneurial responsibility (with its educational, social and medical institutions the two churches are among the most important employers in Germany!) this document opens a new chapter in the history of Christian social ethics[26].

The process and the result correspond very well to the definition of the practical discourse: "Ideally, the outcome of discourse will be a rational consensus. However, any particular consensus as the product of a concrete, historically situated and hence limited community of communication is fallible. Hence in principle it must be open for revision. Consensus can be spurious in a number of ways. If the communicative rationality that was presumed to have been exercised in some specific consensus-oriented process can be shown to have been flawed, or if new arguments relevant to the contents of some particular consensus should emerge, discourse has to be taken up again. Discourse is thus an open-ended

---

25. J.-M. FERRY, *L'Éthique reconstructive* (Humanités), Paris, Cerf, 1996.
26. The same type of ecumenical project entitled *Which Future do we want to have?* is now in course of consultation in Switzerland.

project"[27]. If Catholic social thinking is prepared to accept this presupposition it has finally arrived in the intellectual landscape of modernity without selling its soul.

The participation in a democratic deliberation does not mean, surely, to give away one's own convictions. "Discourse ethics accounts for the social binding force of moral commitments only to the extent to which such commitments can be justified by appeal to universalisably good reasons. Moral commitments, of course, may and do rest on many other force-giving sources. And not every moral commitment is by the nature of its particular content addressed to everyone. ... The contention of discourse ethics is, rather, to spell out the cognitive kernel of morality: if morality has a rational core at all, then that core will have to manifest itself in the ideas that govern our procedures for discursively reaching consensus about the validity of prescriptive claims"[28].

V. TENTATIVE CONCLUSIONS

The final remarks here are some provisional answers to the central questions of our seminar. Who are the responsible actors of CathST? Which priorities should be set for the future of CathST? For an ethics relying methodologically on a philosophical theory of practical discourse the answer to the first question is quite clear. Even if the Church as an institution continues to promote a social doctrine of her own there is no privileged access to truth in matters of society, economy and politics. If CathST wants to be more than just another private ideology it has to take part in the process of democratic deliberation on the basis of empirical evidence. CathST has no lessons to teach when there are problems to be solved. This does not mean that the background of religious convictions and anthropological presuppositions does not matter. But they have to be articulated in a language that reaches those who are not convinced by religious faith. Anyway I don't see how we could maintain the distinctiveness of *Catholic* social ethics in demarcation from Protestant or other positions. As far as issues of social ethics are concerned we will have done enough if we are able to explain what is *Christian*.

With regard to the controversial theoretical difficulties I touched upon in my paper, the efforts in fundamental theoretical research should be

---

27. M. KETTNER, *Scientific Knowledge, Discourse Ethics, and Consensus Formation in the Public Domain*, in E.R. WINKLER & J.R. COOMBS (eds.), *Applied Ethics. A Reader*, Oxford, Blackwell, 1993, pp. 28-45, esp. p. 31.
28. *Ibid.*, p. 32.

given a high priority. Among the practical issues which are most challenging for contemporary Christian ethics those which centre around
human rights and the problem of exclusion have high priority, at the
national and international level. As Oswald von Nell-Breuning puts it:
we have "to bend capitalism" ("den Kapitalismus umbiegen"), accepting a market economy and at the same time taking counter-measures
against its destructive consequences. The fact that there are more and
more human beings treated as completely "superfluous" according to
the logic of economics cannot leave us indifferent. Using the philosophical means of modernity social thinking has to remain a critical observer
of the pathological effects of the global acceleration of all kinds of
mobility and efficiency[29].

Université Catholique de Louvain   Walter LESCH

---

29. A. HONNETH (ed.), *Pathologien des Sozialen. Die Aufgaben der Sozialphilosophie*
(Philosophie der Gegenwart, 12247), Frankfurt am Main, Fischer, 1994.

SOLIDARITY, JUSTICE AND POWER SHARING
PATTERNS AND POLICIES

I. INTRODUCTION

Thoughtful adherents of the values proclaimed in the official social teaching of the Catholic Church face daunting problems in contemporary society. Many of us experience a considerable unease. We feel that something, somehow, is not "working" or "getting through". There is pervasive neglect of official social teaching within the Catholic world, even by relevant academics, activists or commentators. There is much introversion and repetition even where the official teaching is taken seriously. In response to the Church's public standpoints a striking mismatch is evident between high aspirations and a low external profile[1].

To explain such problems it seems unsatisfactory to rely on blanket interpretations of a fallen world, or to relate the neglect to mass secularisation, media or ideological bias, or even to the manifest failures of Christians to practise their own precepts and to live out Gospel values, notably in relation to the poor[2]. But if satisfaction is not an option, neither is resignation. Surely something can be done to remedy this striking gap in the Catholic intellectual presence in contemporary debate? Surely some improvement is urgent and must be feasible in a society badly in need of reconstruction, where the values of human dignity, solidarity, social justice and subsidiarity are so gravely short-changed?

The "reception" of CST suffers to some extent from controversies over "authority" in other areas. A vigorous tradition of thought about society, politics and the economy becomes harder to sustain and popularise when so many regard as alien or out of touch the stances taken by the *magisterium* and papacy on the roles of women, on contraception[3],

---

1. The high aspirations are extensively set out in G. WEIGEL & R. ROYAL (eds.), *A Century of Catholic Social Thought. Essays on Rerum Novarum and Nine Other Key Documents*, Washington, DC, Ethics and Public Policy Center, 1991.

2. On the last issue, see C. ROYON, *Pas d'ecclésiologie sans les pauvres*, in C. ROYON & R. PHILIBERT, *Les Pauvres, un défi pour l'Église*, Les Éditions de l'Atelier, Paris, 1994, pp. 529-549.

3. The latter is suggested as a principal explanation in P.J. HENRIOT, E.P. DEL BERRI & M.J. SCHULTHEIS, *Catholic Social Teaching. Our Best Kept Secret*, Maryknoll, NY, Orbis Books, ²1988.

and on tightly centralised Church governance. But the tradition itself offers ambiguities and difficulties. For many of us it can be at once an indispensable focus, a mandate calling for faithful obedience, a beacon of inspiration, yet *also* a merely comfortable or convenient rhetoric, an abstract icon, a secure yet privatised anchorage which is kept well away from our (largely secularised) professional lives. Moreover, something of an "identity crisis" stems from a wide range of contemporary influences. How far is Catholic social thought universal and perennial? How far is it "distinctive"? Does it imply distinctive policy prescriptions in contemporary advanced societies?

My assumption in what follows is that "social thought" includes much that is relative and contingent, prone to ephemerality or misjudgement. It also encompasses ideas and values of perennial or universal relevance: basic concepts of human flourishing, virtue or *telos*; freedom, order, justice, state, civil society, exchange, coercion, co-operation etc; the "great ideas" of political philosophy and social ethics, and of political economy in its earlier, larger sense. An essentialist and universalist standpoint here will partly reflect personal factors. My childhood saw the great battles with Fascism, Nazism and Stalinist Communism, helping to trigger an early search for counter values grounded in absolutes. The linguistic-analytical-positivist excesses of Oxford philosophy in the 1950s evoked dismay. Perennial and foundational values were to be sought partly because of deep objections to "capitalism", individualism and orthodox economics, partly to validate a form of ethical social democracy as corrective[4]. All of this transpired before I became a Catholic, indeed it was not unrelated to a long pathway to conversion[5].

It is a familiar criticism that traditional Catholic social thought has often claimed too much for perennials and universals. Indeed, the tradition has not lacked examples of overstatement or triumphalism. But in

---

4. Wartime experiences were critical. I was also influenced by Fabian socialist antecedents, an Irish nanny's songs and stories of rebellion, and visits by refugees from Nazi Germany. Some of my family had sympathies with militant Marxism-Stalinism, which I strongly opposed. The post-war Labour government and its reforms in adversity seemed worthy of support. National Service and later experiences in industry and politics consolidated left-centre sympathies. Though intellectually bracing, the prevailing ethos of politics, philosophy and economics at Oxford came as an annoying anti-climax. Its cross-disciplinary character, however, did usefully discourage the idea of tightly specialised discipline boundaries in social thought.

5. My family were staunchly atheist or agnostic. Before leaving school, however, I was drawn towards high church Anglicanism, the Christian socialism of Richard Tawney, and, not least, the writings of Maritain, Mounier, Gilson and Chesterton, which helped to set me on a long road to conversion some fifteen years later.

the contemporary situation I do not think these are the principal dangers. Rather, I believe that Catholic social thought now mainly suffers from amnesia, under-statement or under-development both in the realm of perennials and universals, and in that of contingent thinking about policy, and that these two forms of weakness inter-relate.

This paper suggests, first, that a revitalisation of Catholic social thought requires *inter alia* a clear recognition of the role of its non-official, largely lay and experimental streams: both their historical contributions and their continued indispensability. Next comes a brief discussion of, and an affirmative answer to, the question of whether a distinctive identity and form is to be expected in Catholic social thought *qua* social thought. Third, I offer a possible way of thinking about such a form or "deep structure" at the level of perennial and universal ideas, one mainly influenced by forms of "Catholic experience and belief"; namely, a close inter-relatedness between core values of solidarity, power-sharing diversity and justice for the poor, with solidarity at the peak. Finally, I briefly provide some examples of what this distinctive value pattern might suggest by way of broad policy thinking in an advanced society.

II. RETRIEVING THE NON-OFFICIAL STREAMS

A first weakness of Catholic social thought in the contemporary context is a relegation of its non-official, non-ecclesiastical stream (henceforward abbreviated to "CNOST") to the margins, in terms of both historical understanding and continuing roles, as compared with the official teaching of the *magisterium* (Catholic social teaching or "CST").

At first sight the leading official formulations themselves do not make this inevitable. For they have described their own ambit very broadly. *Positively*, it is to provide "fundamental principles and general directions" (*QA* 11), "a set of principles for reflection, criteria for judgement, and directives for action" (*OA* 4), "an indispensable and ideal orientation" (*CA* 43). A recent definition goes wider: "a body of doctrine which is articulated in the Church, interprets events in the course of history, with the assistance of the Holy Spirit, in the light of what has been revealed by Jesus Christ", while the Catholic bishops of England and Wales describe official teaching as "a set of signposts, showing the way forward...a set of questions by which we can examine the way we live". Calvez and Perrin in their classic 1958 study fairly comment that, drawing on Revelation, philosophical terminology and reflection form the principal content[6]. Such formulas do not appear as obviously "monopolising". They are capable of varied interpretation and are not necessarily inconsistent with a wide interpretation of the role of CNOST.

The official texts have tended towards rather narrow characterisations, however, as to what they do not cover. It is "the practical side of these problems" (*QA* 41-43); "technical solutions" and "the proposal of economic and political systems or programmes" (*SRS* 41); "models" and "the confrontation of concrete problems in all the social, economic, political and cultural aspects as they interact" (*CA 43*). Sometimes a stigma is attached to what is avoided, as with Paul V1's contrast of (secular) "ideology" with (magisterial) "doctrine" (*OA* 26-29). In 1958 Calvez and Perrin would see the division as between "fundamentals" and "mutables", "the unchangeable" and "the institutional": more narrowly, they would characterise the excluded contents as "technique and application"[7]. "Application" is a term that has surfaced repeatedly, though without clarification.

As to the role of CNOST in areas uncovered by the *magisterium*, references are action-orientated or sparing as to the intellectual challenges. Thus the "ends" enjoined by the teaching "will be attained more certainly the greater the number of those ready to contribute their technical, professional and social competence" (*QA* 96). The "reduction" of social principles into practice lays on Catholics the rubric of "see, judge and act", meaning, respectively, "reviewing the concrete situation", "forming a judgement in the light of principles", and "deciding what can and should be done to implement them", where differences of opinion can arise "*even* among sincere Catholics" (*MM* 236 and 238, my italics). "It is up to the Christian communities to analyse with objectivity the situation...proper to their own country" (*OA* 4)[8]. Catholics should promote "the measures inspired by solidarity and preference for the poor", and be "witnesses and agents of peace and justice" (*SRS* 42, 47), and "The practical and experiential dimension of the teaching is to be found at the cross-roads where Christian life and conscience come into contact with

---

6. *Catechism of the Catholic Church*, Dublin, 1994, 517; CATHOLIC BISHOPS CONFERENCE OF ENGLAND AND WALES, *The Common Good and the Social Teaching of the Catholic Church*, Catholic Bishops of England and Wales, 1995; J.-Y. CALVEZ, & J. PERRIN, *Église et société économique. L'enseignement social des Papes de Léon XIII à Pie XII (1878-1958)*, Paris, Aubier, 1959, trans. by J.R. KIRWAN as *The Church and Social Justice. The Social Teaching of the Popes from Leo X111 to Pius X11, 1878-1958*, Chicago, IL, Henry Regnery Co., 1961.

7. CALVEZ & PERRIN, *Église et société économique* (n. 6), pp. 54-55, 57, 59.

8. A wider formulation, though a single country context raises difficulties, as do concepts of empirical "analysis" and "objectivity" (see below).

the real world" (*CA* 59). Overall, the thought of a complementary inter-action between the *magisterium* and other streams hardly features. The relationship with CNOST, whether as an historical fact or a desideratum, remains unclear.

To the limited extent that Catholic social thought is pursued it is the official teaching which almost totally fills the picture. This is clear in manuals, standard texts or published collections, in Catholic academic institutions, and in study groups or conferences for "people in the world". Not even internal critics are exempt. Catholic critics of papal social teaching – alleging dogmatism, deductivism or a-historicalism – often imply that the remedies lie essentially with the m*agisterium*. The changes they seek, it appears, are still expected to come from the centre or, in some variants, the national or regional episcopates, not from CNOST. A further factor is relevant. Particularly between the 1940s and the 1960s, through much of Western Europe, a variety of Christian (mainly Catholic) trade unions, professional bodies, action groups and political parties played important roles. For all their defects, these organ-isations tended to act as conduits, focuses and innovators in CNOST, and their subsequent marked retreat has contributed to its lower profile. Whether this gap is being adequately filled by new organisations in the areas of anti-poverty, justice, peace and overseas aid is not yet clear[9].

To someone whose entry to the tradition came from CNOST the situa-tion seems bizarre. I for one started with Maritain, Mounier's *Feu la Chrétienté*, Lebret's *Économie et Humanisme,* and parts of Peguy, Gilson, Chesterton, Berdyaev. Later inspiration came from Sturzo, Scheler, Ryan, Simone Weil, Sobrino. It was thus that I travelled towards *Rerum n*ovarum, *Quadragesimo anno, Mater et Magistra, Gaudium et spes* etc. The marginalisation of CNOST appears paradoxical for an insti-tution as historically embedded as the Catholic Church. Minute exegesis of official texts takes precedence over attention to grass roots oral tradi-tions, folkway cultures or interactions with *praxis*[10]. Many individuals who exercised influence at critical points, often behind the scenes and often precisely on papal statements, are neglected. The leading Catholic social thinkers are virtually forgotten except by small bands of (some-times antiquarian or esoteric) enthusiasts. While the tradition of including past thinkers in a live, continuing conversation still flourishes in political

9. See essays in this volume by Hogan, Thomasset and Bruni: *infra,* pp. 183, 191 and 239.

10. At the age of seventeen, I heard a young *militant* of the Catholic left in France describe his regular combination of reciting the Rosary with a "see, judge and act" rubric orientated towards social justice and *contre le capitalisme*. It made a strong impression.

philosophy and social ethics, in other traditions of social ideas, and not least in theology, it is curiously absent in modern Catholic social thought.

A retrieval of historical CNOST is needed not only in the interests of a full understanding of the tradition, but also to hold open its potential future role. However the official teaching develops, it is unlikely to be willing or able to cover the whole ground by itself. The *magisterium* could hardly address all the relevant tasks in applied theology, anthropology, political philosophy, political economy, let alone policy thinking. It would surely risk undue involvement if it tried, perhaps even compromising its more fundamental spiritual mission. It will still need CNOST to act as experimenter, developer, active partner. Doctrine, sacrament and scripture offer ever-rich potentials for illuminating the social world which it is the right and duty of all of us, laity as well as papacy and episcopate, to draw on. Major tensions will persist in and around social *praxis,* notably the duties and temptations of power, how far Christians should act unitedly in society as distinct from working with others, and a contrast between benign or stark views of the world or, as a comparison between Rahner and von Balthasar puts it, between two views of "human frustration", respectively as "incompletion" and "tragedy"[11] – all requiring thought by socially involved Christians who feel these tensions *within themselves.*

It is tempting to underestimate the complexity of the areas between broad principles on the one hand (typically the province of CST), and, on the other hand, "action" or "decision" (themselves liable to varied or subtle definition). A huge need arises for middle-level thinking relating to concepts, theories, historical trends, interpretations of social reality, ideas of improvement[12]. Such tasks have not been superseded by "modernity" or "social science", nor can they be avoided, in an odd conjunction of fideism and naive empiricism, by direct jumps to "reality" aided by faith. A temptation in Catholic circles as elsewhere is to over-estimate the ability of the human and social sciences to "provide knowledge" or clarify "the facts", let alone to "solve problems"[13].

---

11. R. WILLIAMS, *Balthasar and Rahner,* in J. RICHES (ed.), *The Analogy of Beauty. The Theology of Hans Urs von Balthasar,* Edinburgh, Clark, 1986, pp. 11-34, esp. p. 32.

12. I discuss a salient aspect of this historically in *Catholic Communitarianism and Advanced Economic Systems. Problems of Middle-level Thinking since 1891,* in P. FURLONG & D. CURTIS (eds.), *The Church Faces the Modern World. Rerum Novarum and Its Impact,* Hull, Earlsgate, 1994, pp. 49-69.

13. For example *une méthode inductive* in M.-D. CHENU, *La "doctrine sociale" de l'Église comme idéologie* (Essais), Paris, Cerf, 1979. And see C.E. CURRAN, *Directions in Catholic Social Ethics,* Notre Dame, IN, University of Notre Dame Press, 1985: "teaching begins with an empirical description of the contemporary reality... an analysis of the

Without effective middle-level thinking Catholic social thought is even at risk of covert and naive forms of dependence on secular ideologies. Engagement is still needed in normative political theory and political economy. It is not just that social reality necessarily has to be interpreted through mediating values. Those values themselves are inherently complex and need persistent exploration as to their meanings, interactions and prioritisation. Not least, there is the complex area of thinking about policy and strategy across a wide range of urgent contemporary problems, calling for political risk-taking which CST cannot tackle. In view of all this, can anyone seriously pretend that the future scope for CNOST should not be extremely large?

III. SEARCHING FOR PATTERNS

To retrieve the full corpus of Catholic social thinking is a precondition for investigating any distinctive content, pattern or form it may offer *qua* social thought. Yet serious doubts may be entertained as to whether such an enterprise is justifiable or desirable.

A first objection rests on past sins of commission and omission. It may be said that the tradition has too many skeletons in the cupboard, meet only for abandonment. There is much truth in this for no "retrieval" can avoid its share of a collective Catholic pain. There is indeed much to repent. Contrition is in order, not only celebration, in view of the elements of authoritarianism, racism or Fascism which appeared at various times: anti-semitism in various countries, *Action Française* and Vichy, Lueger, Maurras, Dollfuss, Petain and Salazar. On a different qualitative level perhaps, lurk the familiar defects of the post-1945 (originally largely Catholic-inspired) Christian democratic parties: their evaporation in some cases, their eventual loss of working class support, their increasing tendencies towards "power fatigue", political conservatism, secularisation, sometimes even corruption[14].

---

contemporary situation... all the necessary data from the applied sciences", pp. 17, 20 and 55. Traces of such positivistic over-estimations can also be found in some official texts.

14. For post-1945 Christian democracy, including some more positive features mentioned below, see R.E.M. IRVING, *The Christian Democratic Parties of Western Europe*, London, Royal Institute of International Affairs, 1979, and J.-M. MAYEUR, *Des partis catholiques a la démocratie chrétienne: XIXe-XXe siècles* (Collection U. Histoire contemporaine), Paris, Colin, 1980, and his *Catholicisme social et démocratie chrétienne: principes romains, expériences françaises* (Histoire), Paris, Cerf, 1986. See also M. EINAUDI & F. GOGUEL, *Christian Democracy in Italy and France* (Archon Books), Notre Dame, IN, University of Notre Dame Press, 1952, and M.P. FOGARTY, *Christian Democracy in Western Europe 1820-1953*, London, Routledge and Kegan, 1957.

Yet there is a good deal on the other side of the balance sheet. Christian trade unions struggled for worker participation, "democratic planning", a humanisation of work. Economic co-operation and mutuality were fostered by organisations for farmers, credit or banking, civic participation by movements like the JOC. The cause of anti-poverty became central for countless organisations and religious orders. In Western Europe after World War II Christian political influences played a major part in promoting Franco-German reconciliation and early moves towards the European Economic Community (EEC). Christian democrats worked alongside social democrats and liberals to exorcise Fascism and to hold at bay a militant, Soviet-dominated Communism. In Italy Christian democrats broadly saw off both the far right and the extreme left; in the Low Countries they were flywheels for advanced civic consensus and social welfare; in West Germany they fostered both political devolution and a "social market" economy not without some affinities with Catholic social thought. To see all this as part of a pattern with some continuing relevance is surely not unjustified.

Further doubts come mainly from outside the camp. There are criticisms of an inherent formlessness or insubstantiality in Catholic social thought: "a collection of positive and negative polemics... without constructive value"; "a rag-bag or hotch-potch"; "uncritical ecclecticism or an opportunist syncretism of unrelated parts"[15]. Again such strictures cannot be entirely discounted. Though they may reflect anti-Catholic bias or lack of knowledge, they are partly a reaction to the tradition's higgledy-piggledy development, its emergence in separate phases, often facing in different ways, successively engaging with industrial capitalism, classical political economy, Marxist Communism, right-wing totalitarianism, "technocracy", "New Right" individualism etc.; partly also a reaction to a high degree of sheer *complexity* particularly in CST. The varying foundational emphases in Doctrine, Scripture, Tradition, Natural Law: the ramified structure of texts, degrees of authority, processes of formulation and communication channels: the national and cultural variations: an appearance of fluidity, shifts and overlaps in defining core concepts – all this is genuinely baffling to insiders, let alone outside

---

15. Gramsci, cited in T. GODECHOT, *Le Parti Démocrate Chrétien Italien* (Bibliothèque constitutionnelle et de science politique, 7), Paris, LGDJ, 1964; G. POGGI in S.J. WOOLF (ed.), *The Rebirth of Italy*, London, Longmans, 1972; Alfred Diamant, cited in J.A. COLEMAN, *Development of Church Social Teaching,* in C.E. CURRAN & R.A. MCCORMICK (eds.), *Official Catholic Social Teaching* (Readings in Moral Theology, 5), New York, NY, Paulist, 1986, pp. 169-187, esp. p. 177.

enquirers[16]. Whether it should deter a search for *implicit* patterns is another matter.

The search for an underlying pattern will be mistrusted by those who define Catholic social thought (or social thought in general) as a piecemeal, *ad hoc* phenomenon, a series of reactions to particular problems. It will be distrusted by those suspicious of the *superbia* of claims to universal social truths derived from "natural law" or from Christian Revelation, and by those who see such claims as inimical to good relations with non-Christians and secularists, or to a wider "dialogue" or "discourse" which they believe should rely on more widely accepted values[17]. But these proposals for a stripping-down of Catholic social thought, while understandable as a reaction to past or present mistakes or exaggerations, surely constitute an *over*-reaction to them. They are unjustifiably reductionist, I think, both in underestimating a modified case for "natural law" and, more seriously, in constricting the scope for credal, experiential Christianity to generate social values or value patterns of a universal and perennial character, albeit perhaps in refined or restated forms, including, it should be added, some which also enjoin wider dialogue.

Further doubts come from tendencies I would label as "motivationalist". These discount the view that Catholic social thought may itself produce socio-political ideas or at least re-organise them, or that it can offer agendas for reconstruction of society, the economy, politics. Instead, the "motivationalists" exalt other sorts of claim, those relating to virtue or *praxis*. Their stress is on supportive reasoning, additional motivation and spiritual strength for social action: a view shared by all parts of the tradition, often stated in the closing sections of encyclicals, but here given almost exclusive emphasis. Thus, "Christians cannot pretend on behalf of their faith that they have their own ethical theory. They have specific reasons but no other arguments than anyone else can have for whatever they hold... The "Christian quality" or "surplus" depends on "the rationality of Christian argumentation, "a specific orientation", or "privileged points of attention"[18]. The stress on personal agency is shared with

16. If an enquiring, perhaps sympathetic secularist were to ask (a) why she should be interested in Catholic social thought? and (b) what mainly distinguishes it from secular social/political thought? what would be our anwers, say in 50 words or 300 words, and what variations would those answers reveal?

17. For a viewpoint of this character, see for example Walter Lesch's essay in this volume, pp. 51-60.

18. B.J. DE CLERCQ, *The Christian Profile of Christian Social Ethics*, in J.A. SELLING (ed.), *Personalist Morals. Essays in Honor of Professor Louis Janssens* (BETL, 83), Leuven, University Press, 1988, pp. 265-278. The same author quotes E. Schillebeeckx from the latter's *Jesus. An Experiment in Christology*, London, Collins, 1979: "Faith in God

two other tendencies: virtue ethics, with its stress on character and its linkages with the rejection of universalist/objectivist ethical theories[19], and "business ethics", with its focus on "better behaviour" by individuals or corporate organisations[20].

I would suggest these views neglect much that is vital or constitutive. Neither "a specific orientation" nor "privileged points of attention" make sense without recourse to content, including some persistent and universal content. Can one really dispense with intellectual effort over substantive social thought in fields occupied by social ethicists, political philosophers and political economists? For Christians, can this be a purely individualistic process? Can the Catholic social tradition have been wholly misguided in engaging collectively in these fields for so long, whatever the attendant mistakes or exaggerations? Not least serious, there is a risk of conservative bias in the "motivationalism" of virtue ethics, business ethics and the rest. Faced with the turbulent and deeply disturbing problems of international finance, for example, it will exude only pious platitudes. To avoid structural or systemic issues in society, politics and the economy slides too easily towards acceptance of the *status quo*. It neglects ideas of "structural sin" or pervasive injustice, as also efforts at improvement through collective agency, legislation, organised public pressure, parties or movements, and countervailing power.

Another viewpoint does propose a content-laden distinctiveness, but in a very limited way. Secular socio-political thought is bi-polarised into a series of opposite extremes: collectivism/ individualism, public/private, state/market, "socialism/capitalism". Catholic social thought is then cast in the doubly virtuous role of avoiding their excesses while combining their valid elements: a "middle", "central" or "third way"[21]. Historically popular among social Catholics, this label is a not unreasonable way of

revealed and personified in Christ enables Christians to resist, to withstand resignation, cynicism and scepticism, to persevere in their resistance because they have stronger reasons and specific motives".

19. The rejection of universalist/objectivist ethical theories such as Kantian deontology and utilitarianism, along with natural law, is of course a shared theme among modern Aristotelians and Wittgensteinians.

20. For a critique of "business ethics" for its individual and micro-agency bias, partly on empirical-historical grounds, see J. BOSWELL, *The Under-Development of 'Business Ethics'. An Historical Critique*, in *Ethical Perspectives* 4 (1997), no. 2, 105-115.

21. For example, "Either rapacious individualism offset by totalitarian regimes, or Catholicism" – Emile Keller in 1865, cited by P. MISNER, *Social Catholicism in Europe. From the Onset of Industrialisation to the First World War,* New York, Crossroad, 1991; Catholic social thinking as "neither capitalist nor socialist" but "search for the middle way" – COLEMAN, *Development of Church Social Teaching* (n. 15); or even "Le modèle rhénan, fils de la doctrine sociale des Églises Chrétiennes", in M. ALBERT, *La Semaine sociale européenne, 1997.*

describing much that emerged in the political economies of West Germany, Austria and the Low Countries (and Scandinavia) over long periods after 1945. Good economic records in terms of growth, employment and counter-inflation occurred within systems which combined markets and private enterprise with significant amounts of regulation, redistribution and social welfare. In fact, a "state/market" duality falls a long way short of delineating these "Rhenish model" systems which also invested heavily in "social co-operation". A key role was played by institutions for labour/employer rapprochement, income and price restraint, and mediation between socio-economic groups: something much closer to Catholic social thought and often encouraged by it[22]. But my main point here is that the phenomenon was, or is, both historically contingent and restricted to political economy. It hardly suggests a pattern at the heart of the social values proclaimed by Catholic thought.

I admit that a desire for "form" and "distinctiveness" in this area is likely to reflect personal proclivities. In my case these have included certain theological stimuli (de Lubac, Adam, von Balthasar, Kasper, Moltmann), together with an English Catholic minority context where "identity" has mattered a lot historically in face of surrounding greater forces, and an aesthetic streak in search of patterns, whether in religious belief, culture or social thought[23]. However, the most important consideration is not personal, but rather inferential from, or related to, the nature of Catholic Christianity. To put the point in a form which entertains counter-factual speculation, it seems unlikely that a long tradition of social thought would fail to reflect, at least to lesser degrees and implicitly, something of the shape discoverable in core Catholicism itself.

IV. Power Sharing Diversity, Justice for the Poor and Complex Solidarity as Pivot

Where, then, can such a pattern be found? In the first place, I suggest, not mainly in the broad concepts of human dignity and "common

---

22. For a conceptual and historical treatment here, see J. Boswell, *Community and the Economy. The Theory of Public Co-operation*, London, Routledge, 1990/1994.

23. H. de Lubac, *Catholicism. A Study of Doctrine in Relation to The Corporate Destiny of Mankind*, London, Burns Oates and Washbourne, 1950 and K. Adam, *The Spirit of Catholicism*, London, Sheed and Ward, 1954, conveyed for me a patterned shape, as does Von Balthasar's aesthetic approach. Post-Reformation Catholicism in England has been relatively free of entanglements with political, cultural or "establishment" power, and has included Irish working class influences. Its context has featured a doctrinally heterogeneous Anglicanism, vague forms of religiosity, and an increasingly widespread indifferentism. In relation to the thematics of this essay, an "aesthetic streak" would include analogies with architectural and musical forms.

good". These have tended to encircle the main corpus of Catholic social thought, forming in a sense a majestic prologue or precondition for it. A normative anthropology is proposed, a view of the *telos* and eternal destiny of the human person, and a first approximation to the purpose of human society. Here are assumptions or preconditions, forming an initial frame, a broad starting orientation for a tradition which has, however, attained considerably more specificity. For it should be obvious that Catholic social thought has penetrated much further into the values to be pursued in social, political and economic life, the substantive yardsticks of a "good society". And here three main sets of ideas have tended to occupy the central ground, for which the broadest of provisional labels are "justice", "subsidiarity" and "solidarity".

The tradition frequently gives these three comparable prominence[24]; their varying definitions feature repeatedly; there can be few standard expositions where they are not at the centre. Even where the main emphasis is put elsewhere, perhaps on the gateway concepts of "person" and "common good", ideas related to justice, subsidiarity and solidarity still tend to find their way into the script, if only to avoid undue abstraction, to remain true to their ubiquity in the tradition or to confront more directly the parallel secular traditions, where they have featured so much albeit in different forms (see below). Sometimes only one or two of the three receives top treatment: "solidarity and subsidiarity", "solidarity and justice" or just "solidarity" or "justice"[25]. But again, the other values in the triad seldom, if ever slip completely from view, tending rather to become qualifiers of the favoured component/s or constituents of its/their definition.

---

24. For a recent example see CATHOLIC BISHOPS CONFERENCE OF ENGLAND AND WALES, *The Common Good* (n. 6).

25. For (a) see for example J. HÖFFNER, *Fundamentals of Christian Sociology*, Westminster, MD, Newman Press, 1962. For (b) NATIONAL CONFERENCE OF CATHOLIC BISHOPS, *Economic Justice for All* (United States Catholic Conference Publications, 101), Washington, DC, United States Catholic Conference, 1986. Leading exemplars of (c) are Max Scheler, Luigi Sturzo, Heinrich Pesch and François Perroux, with reflections in the political ideas of Aldo Moro, *Scritti e Discorsi 1940-76*, and J. DELORS, *L'Unité d'un homme. Entretiens avec Dominique Wolton,* Paris, Jacob, 1994, and a recent formulation is P. DONATI, *Pensiero Sociale Cristiano e Societa Post-Moderna*, Rome, 1997. For (d), key figures were Francesco Nitti, John Ryan, Dorothy Day, Giorgio La Pira, with D. DORR, *Option for the Poor. A Hundred Years of Vatican Social Teaching*, Dublin, Gill and MacMillan, 1983, an invaluable guide, and leading formulations in P. FREIRE, *Pedagogy of the Oppressed*, New York, NY, Herder and Herder, 1970, G. GUTIERREZ, *A Theology of Liberation*, Maryknoll, NY, Orbis Books, 1986; C. BOFF & G. PIXLEY, *The Bible, the Church and the Poor* (Theology and Liberation Series), Maryknoll, NY, Orbis Books, 1989, and J. SOBRINO, *Christology at the Cross Roads. A Latin American Approach*, London, SCM, 1978.

All of which leads one to ask whether distinctiveness may rest precisely on such a co-prominence of solidarity, subsidiarity and justice. It may well be thought so, compared with the leading secular traditions, whose polarisations are all too familiar. Fixations on "liberty" among individualists, libertarians and the "New Right", and on its subtler "pluralist" variants among many liberals. Democratic socialist or "left centre" ethical agendas which focus almost exclusively on "equality" or "justice" alone, or "freedom" and "justice" together. Crude forms of "solidarity" and "equality" invoked by the "old left", a perverted "solidarity" by nationalists or Fascists. How appealing, then, to seize on a notion of Catholic social thought as somehow broader, more balanced or inclusive than any of these! But this surely does much less than justice to its developed content. The *meaning* of the relevant concepts in the tradition is not clarified. Key questions remain unanswered, notably *why* solidarity, subsidiarity and justice should go together, whether some sort of *priority* is to be found among them, and what is the nature of their *relationship*?

Let me now anticipate the broad contention that follows (space is lacking for a full formulation). I suggest that "distinctiveness" of identity and form *qua* social thought lies principally in a particular formation of the three leading social values, one where solidarity is at the peak and the other values are found to inter-penetrate and inter-relate in the light of solidarity. Further, I suggest that affinities are traceable between this formation and certain core characteristics of Catholic belief and practice.

The first point to be clear about is that whereas the dominant secular ideologies consign solidarity to exile or cinderella status, in Catholic social thought solidarity in various guises plays a crucial role. No less could be expected in view of its connectability with the evangelical and the supernatural. For though distinct from and less exalted than "love", it may open in the direction of love. I take "solidarity" to include many pale, crude approximations to love, or *vestigia Trinitatis*: relationships of community, sociability, conviviality, civility, *fraternité*, civic friendship, social consciousness, public spirit. Family, locality, workplace, bus queue, random encounter, are all testing grounds for solidarity. So, too, are civic life, politics, the supra-national spheres; also in lesser degrees, a national economy. Not only inter-personal relationships but also the important field of inter-group relations can be zones for its emergence. These features have been repeatedly celebrated in the encyclicals, and some Catholic social thinkers have explored them in some depth (Scheler,

Sturzo, Perroux)[26]. Let us call the resulting amalgam "complex solidarity".

It is important to realise that complex solidarity in Catholic social thought goes further than a first order descriptive acceptance of humanity as "socially constituted" (as stated almost tritely by some communitarian thinkers)[27]. Rather, it is to be a para-norm for personal life and society, through to eternity. It goes much wider than the "given", "tight", often parochial or conservative groupings of blood, place, memory, religion[28]. As for a reading of solidarity as simple homogeneity or identity, there lies perhaps the greatest travesty, for its essence is to be unity-in-diversity, difference not flattened but bridged or mutualised. Not that even solidarity is, or should be, an all-consuming concept. To interpret it to *include* justice and freedom, as distinct from being closely *related* to them, is arguably unhelpful. But at almost every turn solidarity in social Catholic terms imparts to these other values a distinctive character, to the extent that it is not too much to say that without it an understanding of the values of justice, human rights, freedom, subsidiarity etc. in Catholic social thought is impossible. Torn away from solidarity, a plausible similarity, perhaps even a superficial equivalence, may exist with understandings of the same terms in other traditions. Impelled and contoured by it, however, they take a quite different turn.

Take the Catholic social interpretations of "freedom", "power-sharing", "subsidiarity" and related ideas. They are emphatically not individualistic. The freedoms to which every person is entitled are to guarantee human dignity, to protect against slavery, above all to make room for growth *via* responsibilities and relationships. Indefinite "rights-ism" is off-bounds. Degrees of freedom are to attach also to associations or the varied forms of sociality needed for people's development. It was not for nothing that Christian movements worked hard to get this incorporated into some post-war European constitutions. Power is to be diffused, spreading out both *vertically* (from citizen, through locality or

26. See particularly M. SCHELER, *The Nature of Sympathy* (Rare Masterpieces of Philosophy and Science), London, Routledge and Kegan, 1954; and his monumental essay 'Christian love in the 20th century', in *On the Eternal in Man*, London, SCM Press, 1960; L. STURZO, *Essai de Sociologie* (Cahiers de la nouvelle journée, 32), Paris, Bloud et Gay, 1935; and F. PERROUX, *Communauté et société* (La communauté française: cahiers d'études communautaires, 1), Paris, PUF, 1942.

27. See for example M. SANDEL, *Liberalism and the Limits of Justice*, Cambridge, University Press, 1983.

28. I outline a wider idea of "complementary association" in J. BOSWELL, *Community and the Economy* (n. 22). For a parody of "given", inherited communitarianism, see S. LUKES, *The Curious Enlightenment of Professor Caritat. A Comedy of Ideas*, London, Verso, 1996, chapters 15-22.

region, to nation state, and supranationally), and *horizontally* (in terms of a plurality of political, cultural and economic forms). The term "subsidiarity" seeks to capture this idea of power-sharing, though it is usually applied too narrowly, only vertically or politically. Correspondingly any idea of "sovereignty", whether of nation state or any other temporal entity, is thoroughly misconceived[29]. Overall, these contentions make no concession to separate, unencumbered "selves", let alone to liberty as end-in-itself. Rather, they seek to nourish human and social diversity and complementarity. They see freedom, power-sharing and subsidiarity ultimately as preconditions for social unity-in-diversity or relational ends.

Ideas of "justice", "equality" and "option for the poor" are similarly affected. Justice is seen as demanding a less unequal division of resources, a calling to account of the rich and powerful, a raising-up of the poor. But criteria of solidarity-seeking at once intensify, qualify and widen these imperatives. Justice for the poor becomes more *urgent* since it is also a corollary of solidarity, in the sense that for some people to be left out or marginalised is offensive to community. It is *qualified* because justice alone is insufficient for community. Not least, justice for the poor is to be pursued in *wider* terms than resource redistribution, important though this is. Their self-organisation, representation and participation are also critical. This has radical implications in present day advanced societies where electoral systems fail the poor, where public indifference and a relatively comfortable "middle majority" shockingly discount the bottom quarter or *quart monde*[30], and where it is arguable that additional measures are needed to raise their civic profile and increase their political leverage.

V. FAITH AND EXPERIENCE AS DIRECT SOURCES

The pattern that emerges, then, is a combined pursuit of complex solidarity, power sharing and justice for the poor as highly interdependent values, with solidarity in the lead. This, I suggest, is not wholly surprising. For I think such a pattern can be shown to relate to many central features of Catholic faith and practice. Where else, it may be asked, would a central triad of values with solidarity in the lead come from?

29. J. MARITAIN, *Man and the State*, Chicago, IL, Chicago University Press, 1951, chap. 2.
30. J.K. GALBRAITH, *The Culture of Contentment*, Boston, MA, Houghton Mifflin, 1992.

Hardly, one suspects, from natural law or a body of universally accessible social values. While "natural law" may offer second-order validations of human dignity, common good, even of aspects of subsidiarity and justice, one thing it cannot do is to originate, let alone validate, a climactic principle of solidarity. For that a transcendental agency is needed, a specific manifestation of the divine. Not that Christian Revelation, with its super-elevation of love, triggers a determinate pathway to any formula for social reconstruction, whether the triad just suggested or any other. Nonetheless, a more modest claim is feasible, I think, to the effect that in practice Church doctrine and culture inculcate a habit of mind at least of aspiration to the triad, something which Catholic social thinking in turn is likely to reflect.

There are many ways in which Catholic beliefs and practices encourage ideas of diversity, equality and solidarity as correlates. The local parish or *communauté de base* is widely experienced as a solidaristic institution, a microcosm of unity-in-diversity, one with global connections, which institutionalises "alongsideness" and aspires to community. Catholics are bound to a central event, the Mass, as God's gift of Himself made equally to every person, binding diverse characters and gifts into One Body. In the Eucharist they see a Real Presence offered to all without qualification or distinction. There they see even base matter transformed, and a supreme Act of sacrificing relatingness repeatedly re-mediated and re-enacted. They also experience in the Communion of Saints a diversity of spiritual gifts where differences become complementarities, a treasury of merits and prayers to which all have equal access, and a further route to perfect community, including that between living and dead.

In the same context we cannot ignore what crucially differentiates credal Christianity (Orthodox, Protestant and Catholic) from both secularism and other world religions, namely the Trinitarian confession. Although the doctrine of the Trinity may suffer from much day-to-day neglect[31], its core status cannot fail to carry implications *inter alia* for social thought[32]. As supreme mystery derived from Revelation, all

31. Karl Rahner's sombre observation: "Despite their orthodox confession of the Trinity, Christians are, in their practical life, almost mere 'monotheists', so that 'the doctrine... leads its own respected life in the Church's liturgies but scarcely influences Christian self-consciousness": K. RAHNER, *The Trinity* (Mysterium salutis), London, Burns and Oates, 1970, p. 10 *et seq.*

32. For approaches to such a relationship, see J. MOLTMANN, *The Trinity and the Kingdom of God*, London, SCM Press, 1981, and *History and the Triune God. Contributions to Trinitarian Theology*, London, SCM Press, 1991, and L. BOFF, *Trinity and Society* (Liberation and Theology, 2), Tunbridge Wells, Burns and Oates, 1988. See also

human language remains abjectly pathetic in the face of it, only faintly analogical at best. All I can tentatively suggest here is that its nature super-elevates the values of diversity, equality and solidarity, and their reconciliation, as nothing else could. For it does nothing less than to read these into, and out of, the sublime. The Three Divine Persons, according to credal orthodoxy, are a) diversely distinct, b) absolutely equal, and c) perfectly loving and united both in their own eternal *perichoresis* and in the overflow of their love to humanity. Thus ideas of diversity, equality and mutual indwelling, and their unification, are exalted to the realm of absolute, infinite Deity, making their apotheosisation complete.

A useful social analogy for the Trinity arises in the sphere of choral music. Where unaccompanied voices sing in *polyphony* each voice part is at once equal to the others and interestingly distinctive, yet all blend unitedly and harmoniously together[33]. Those involved as participants may find this near-ecstatic. Intimation of eternal bliss it may be, further faint refraction of the Triune Deity, but by the same token not without relevance to social ideas. A yearning for these values to be both complete *and* reconciled seems implanted from the same Source. Unless a stark manichean dualism is introduced, the Trinitarian confession surely fosters and implies a desire for diversity, parity and love to be combined *even* in the temporal world.

Nor is such a desire mere wishful thinking, subject to provisos reflecting human fallenness and frailty. One is that only lesser approximations to the ideal values are available (see above). Another is that conflicts often arise in practice between pursuits of complex solidarity, pluralistic power sharing, and justice for the poor. For example, measures to increase social cohesion may involve more centralisation, while devolution may sacrifice some of the central power needed for redistribution to the poor. Yet a further proviso arises over the special elusiveness of the most important value, solidarity-in-diversity. This can never be engineered, let alone commandeered, and where finely approximated, it's hard to sustain. On every front therefore disappointments are likely. All that social action can do is to remove what appear to be the main obstacles, to tackle the seemingly worst impediments, at best to prepare the ground.

D.S. CUNNINGHAM, *These Three are One. The Practice of Trinitarian Theology* (Challenges of Contemporary Theology), Oxford, Blackwell, 1998, and M. VOLF, *The Trinity is Our Social Programme. The Doctrine of the Trinity and the Shape of Social Engagement*, in *Modern Theology* 14 (1998) 403-423.

33. Such a polyphonic structure is particularly characteristic of Renaissance and Counter-Reformation sacred music, notably that of Byrd, Guerrero, Palestrina, Tallis and Victoria.

At the same time, though, considerable interdependencies do also exist between the three pursuits. Thus, power-sharing diversity will fail the poor in key respects unless there is a redistribution of resources in their favour. Devolution presupposes a degree of underlying solidarity, sufficient at least to prevent the separate units from falling apart. Justice for the poor is more likely if the poor possess public visibility and some share in power, and if the more fortunate feel some solidaristic goodwill towards them. Again, solidarity-seeking risks a smothering conformism or coercion in the absence of power-sharing diversity. It will be radically incomplete, moreover, if justice for the poor is lacking or if there are gross disparities between individuals and classes.

To emphasise these interactions should be a special priority for Catholic social thought. Whereas at present their inter-relatedness tends to be merely implicit, it needs to be explicitly brought out: mere juxtaposition is not enough. Herein, I suggest, lies a unique contemporary obligation and opportunity. For who *else* can perform the task? No less is demanded by a situation where the dominant secular ideologies either neglect the core social values altogether under cover of technocratic economism or "modernisation", or where, more typically, they polarise among liberty and/or equality, with complex solidarity over and over again the victim, the exile, *il disparido*. Indeed, no other movement of thought has such strong grounds – both transcendental and practical – for asserting the combination.

VI. MAKING ROOM FOR SOCIAL INTERACTIONS

I conclude with a brief summary of a personal vision of where all this may lead in terms of policy thinking. What does the value pattern I have discussed imply for the sort of changes needed in advanced societies? It is customary to begin such an exercise with a number of disclaimers: that the concern is with broad directions of policy, not detailed blueprints; that such a vision is personal and subjective; that it makes no pretence of adequate coverage, let alone to a privileged relationship with Catholic social values. I would add a further attribute, hinting at controversy. To venture into this area is to take risks through experiment and abandonment of political detachment, precisely an important area for CNOST. In this sense it would not be difficult to find affiliations to a particular section of the tradition with long antecedents, one which may be termed "radical" or in some senses "left-wing".

From the viewpoint described above, two types of social cause require fervent support, each with a major following among contemporary secularists and others as well as Christians. One is political devolution; another is "anti-poverty", including radical redistribution. In both cases, though, extra urgencies, provisos and enlargements need to be stressed (see above) on the basis of Catholic social understandings of these concepts: political devolution not as crude pluralism, not as self-sufficient, but for relational, solidaristic ends, applied to social institutions as well, and combined with would-be unitive measures and some power transfers to supra-national levels; anti-poverty pursued with greater zeal as a corollary of community or solidarity and going well beyond resource redistribution, towards participation, inclusion and "voice".

However, the main point I want to emphasise in this context is different. The cause of complex solidarity goes much further than under-writing and conditioning these causes. It constitutes an objective in its own right, indeed a still higher one. It points to a further wide range of policies. While each of these policies may well have some proponents, they are hardly ever, if at all, viewed as related and interdependent, reflecting a coherent social philosophy. And their purpose, put simply, is to make room for diverse social interactions which are all too often stultified in complex, advanced societies.

A first theme here is one which secular social thinking of all types tends to neglect, that of *personal time*, its alienation or monopolisation. At present in advanced societies personal time is chronically maldistributed[34]. For many, perhaps most people, it is socially skewed or vitiated in different ways. Too much time at home with a tight nuclear family or dependants, or simply alone, or without a job. Too much time at work. Too much time spent in commuter travel, or in passive pursuits, or pressured away from recreation or sociality by commercialised Sundays. Against all this the solidarity principle asserts that personal time is a precious resource which we need for a balanced set of relationships, familial, local, occupational, recreational, including some contact with people outside our particular ethnic, cultural or other groups, and much farther afield. A wide range of measures should be advocated in this context: improved child care and domestic care services; local job creation; family-friendly employment policies; limitations on overtime; shifts from private to public transport; more active and relational uses of leisure time.

A second theme is *spatial*: to provide physical spaces and frameworks for diverse social interactions. Here again a multitude of obstacles stand

---

34. For a keynote recognition of this, see DELORS, *L'Unité d'un homme* (n. 25).

in the way. Not the least is the private car culture with the havoc this brings to neighbourhood unities, peace and tranquillity, pedestrian rights, human health and safety, and mutual civility. Not all these problems can be addressed directly or quickly. But human dignity and interaction demand a many-sided attack on the physical infrastructure, particularly of cities. The urban social humanism of Lewis Mumford is more relevant than ever[35]. New buildings on a human scale, curtailments of motorists' "rights" in city centres, public transit systems, extensive pedestrianisation, urban cafes and piazzas, public spaces: all would be part of such an attack.

A third theme is *institutions for social interaction.* In past phases Catholic social thought placed great emphasis on "intermediate organisations" in and around the economy (trade unions, guilds, tripartite bodies, *Mitbestimmung,* "vocational order" etc), and on *interclassismo,* multiclass political movements, and of course the Christian organisations themselves. Now the same broad objectives require additional or different approaches. People cannot be so easily "corporatised": the frameworks have to be more elastic, the gulfs to be bridged are more diverse. For example, new measures may be needed to foster forms of contact between the very old and the young; to promote forms of national civic service which can enlist young people to work on anti-poverty or environmental issues; to make territorial "twinning" arrangements with 2nd or 3rd world communities the norm for 1st world municipalities, not the exception. And along critical frontiers in society now marked by deep chasms new needs arise for forums or representative cross-sectional bodies, where different groups come into contact and discuss public issues[36].

Every major business or sectional organisation should have a forum attached to it, representing the various stakeholders. Certain highly powerful groups remain highly secreted and exempt from social exposure or public visibility: many financial institutions, the financial operations of MNEs, mass media proprietors, corporate lobbies. Single interest pressure groups compete adversarially for public attention and resources, immune from multilateral contacts or common good considerations. Forums are needed, not just regulation, to reduce such gulfs, opacities or secrecies, to help to bring the powerful to account for their actions, and

---

35. L. MUMFORD, *The Urban Prospect,* London, Secker and Warburg, 1968.

36. The attributes and roles of forums are discussed in my *Community and the Economy* (n. 22). I argue that their potentials for civil society and solidarity-seeking depend partly on some parallel structural conditions, of threshold continuity, organisational transparency and social monitoring, partly on a cultural ethos that accords high priority to dialogue *per se.*

to bring the too-separated groups together. They are equally needed to help to promote a higher visibility and public profile for the poorest groups in society. Some of these desiderata should be taken into account in debates on constitutional reform, which have become far too conventionally narrow[37]. For example, there may be a case for second or third chambers of parliaments to constitute national civic forums with such aims in view[38]. All of which means confronting head on an economistic, technocratic culture of impatience with "talking shops", one which discounts the processes of consensus-building, mediation, social mixing and mutual education which forums can help to promote.

This policy agenda is in a radical tradition of "structuralist" or "left-leaning" reformism[39]. It implies civic renewal and public services funded through adequate taxation. It is considerably at odds with the privatism, business supremacism and "low tax" civic apathy now all too characteristic of advanced Western societies. However, the policies are not paternalistic or *dirigiste*, still less utopian. Rather, the emphasis is on facilitation or the removal of obstacles to interaction, not guaranteeing it will result or be solidaristic in direction. A lot could still go wrong: for example, time freed from work may not be used familially or socially, even well contrived public spaces may be vandalised, cross-sectional forums may be messy and cantankerous. The purpose is to enlarge opportunities and potentials for the forms of community, sociability, civility or friendship on which our development as persons depend. At the same time there is enough here by way of fostering subsidiarity, diffused power or civil society to reflect those causes as well, along with greater justice for the poor. What is needed is the courage to project these values forward into integrated sets of policies.

I emphasise again that such constellations of prescriptions are both contingent and controversial. Some socially concerned Catholics may

37. For example, discussions on reform of the House of Lords in Britain have emphasised abolition of the hereditary principle and, more positively, ideas of nomination, or purely territorial forms of representation of the different nations or regions of the UK. Virtual absentees have been proposals for representation of social, generational and economic interests, for accountability of powerful groups presently outside civic society, and for a constitutional voice for the poorest groups in society.

38. This idea has long antecedents in the social Catholic tradition, including the enthusiasms of earlier corporatists such as La Tour du Pin, more sophisticated exponents, notably François Perroux, and an official emphasis on face-to-face forums generally, for which see R. CAMP, *The Papal Ideology of Social Reform. A Study in Historical Development 1878-1967*, Leiden, Brill, 1969. See also J. MARITAIN, *Man and the State* (n. 29), p. 214, where the idea takes an international form.

39. In many respects it goes wider and further than the "New Labour" project in the UK.

disagree with this particular package or take different approaches, as is necessary and desirable for CNOST. Proximately, they spring from middle-level thinking about contemporary trends and contexts, social, political and economic. A principal argument of this essay, however, is that a still longer chain of thought and reflection cannot dispense with distinctive patterns of social values, patterns which are essentially perennial and universal and which, in turn, can be found to reflect, in the main, aspirations springing from core religious beliefs and experiences. Without these largely faith-related patterns, I believe, the resources would not be available either to produce coherent policy prescriptions or to recognise and live with their vulnerability, let alone to act on them.

Von Hügel Institute, St Edmund's College,   Jonathan BOSWELL
University of Cambridge

ENGAGEMENT WITH SECULAR DEBATE

ACTUALITÉ DE LA PENSÉE SOCIALE CATHOLIQUE
DANS LES SOCIÉTÉS INDIVIDUALISTES
CONTEMPORAINES

Comme on sait, la pensée catholique sociale a connu son vrai développement à la fin du 19ième siècle, dans un contexte historique précis. Elle s'est construite non pas pour apporter des réponses à la place des politiques, mais pour rappeler des principes dont les politiques devraient tenir compte dans des sociétés qui se disent de culture chrétienne.

La pensée catholique sociale a connu divers déboires au cours du siécle écoulé, déboires dûs à la personnalité de certains de ses défénseurs, et à sa récupération par des courants extrêmes. Aucun des papes qui, depuis Léon XIII, s'appliquent à son élaboration, ne laisse percer des préférences pour une politique ou un système. Mais La Tour du Pin, que d'ailleurs Léon XIII avait cru socialiste, est un monarchiste nostalgique du Moyen-Age, en réalité le maître du jeune Maurras. Au début de ce siècle, sa pensée, passant par Maurras et par Massis, vient tenter de s'appliquer dans le Portugal de Salazar. Le courant corporatiste a de beaux jours devant lui jusqu'a la seconde guerre, même si les papes n'ont jamais jugé souhaitable un retour aux corporations. Pendant cette période, les courants corporatistes européens demeurent liés aux divers fascismes, que ce soit au Portugal, en Italie, en Slovaquie ou en Roumanie, pour ne citer que ces cas. Ainsi, ce courant demeure, depuis 1945, entaché d'une confusion dont il n'est pas innocent. Bien entendu, il convient de dissocier la pensée des Papes de ce que les penseurs et politiques en ont tiré. Mais si l'on évoque la possible actualité d'une pensée, il faut tenir compte tout d'abord de l'image, vraie ou fausse, qu'elle véhicule. La capacité d'influence d'une pensée tient beaucoup, surtout dans les sociétés spectaculaires de la modernité tardive, de sa capacité à se démarquer de ses scories historiques.

Par ailleurs, une pensée qui se proclame catholique se voue dès l'entrée à la suspicion, voire aux crachats, surtout dans un pays comme la France, mais pas seulement. La difficulté immense que nous avons eu à réactualiser l'idée de subsidiarité, pourtant essentielle à l'Europe qui vient, ne tenait pas seulement à la sophistication du concept et à sa sonorité disgracieuse, mais surtout, au fait qu'il s'agissait d'une idée catholique (énoncée pour la première fois au 19ième siècle par Monseigneur von Ketteler et par Léon XIII)[1].

Parler de l'actualité d'une pensée revient à analyser ses conditions d'accueil dans la société présente – précisément le problême de l'image –, et bien entendu, plus profondément, à se demander dans quelle mesure cette pensée est, ou est encore, opératoire, profitable, prometteuse, pour répondre aux problèmes qui se posent dans cette société historique particulière.

Si nous examinons la pensée sociale catholique, nous trouvons un corps de principes issus de la grande lignée allant d'Aristote à Maritain, fondé sur une anthropologie de la finitude, de la sociabilité, de l'autonomie et de la responsabilité. Ici l'homme est entaché du péché originel, c'est à dire que la frontière entre le bien et le mal passe au milieu de chacun d'entre nous. Les communautés de proximité sont essentielles au développement d'une vie digne, car l'individu ne se suffit pas entièrement, et ne trouve son véritable bonheur que dans la relation et la responsabilité. Ce qui suppose l'individu originellement endetté, porteur d'une dette de culture et d'éducation qu'il a charge de reconnaître sans pouvoir jamais la régler. La liberté de l'homme n'est donc jamais totale, mais toujours en situation. La définition du bien ne se trouve pas entièrement entre ses mains, puisqu'il existe des biens communs concentriques et emboîtés, depuis la société familiale jusqu'à la société civile, dont il dépend sans pouvoir les remettre en cause essentiellement, car ils sont fondés sur la certitude d'une «condition humaine».

Si nous regardons la société occidentale contemporaine, nous trouvons un individualisme grandissant et légitimé par le libre arbitre, une revanche des droits sur les responsabilités, une tendance avérée à privilégier le procédural au détriment du substantiel, par refus de diffuser aucune vérité principielle. L'individu de la modernité tardive est source de sa propre définition du bien, ayant justement remplacé le «bien» par les «valeurs» qui sont subjectives. Il est à la limite auto-fondé comme source de soi, et souverain, ou proclamé auto-suffisant. C'est dire que sa responsabilité vis à vis des autres, proches ou lointains, ne saurait provenir que de sa décision, et cesse lorsque cesse sa volonté. Le bien commun s'appelle ici intérêt général, ce qui indique clairement la différence,

---

1. L'idée de subsidiarité a été reprise au début des années 90 par les acteurs de la construction européenne, mais en dépit de discours, et de l'inscription dans les traités, elle n'a jamais été véritablement concrétisée dans les institutions européennes, sinon de façon jacobine, autrement dit, par dénaturation, cf. mon ouvrage *Le principe de subsidiarité* (Que sais-je, 2793), Paris, PUF, 1992, qui fait suite à *L'État subsidiaire* (Leviathan), Paris, PUF, 1992.

et découle de l'accord des membres de la société et non d'un quel-
quonque «ordre des choses» qui n'existe pas.

Au première vue, il n'existe entre la pensée sociale catholique et la
société occidentale contemporaine qu'un large fond de désaccord. En
France, la pensée dominante – qui n'est évidemment pas la pensée commune – laisse entendre, chaque fois que l'occasion lui en est donnée, la
distance entre l'une et l'autre. Elle explique cette distance par l'avancée
du progrès la pensée sociale aurait été élaborée pour d'autres époques,
pour des besoins et des modes de vie qui n'existent plus.

À dire vrai, la société d'aujourd'hui ignore ce courant de pensée, et
n'a pas envie de le connaître. Elle entretient vis à vis de lui des préjugés
tenaces. Faites dix heures de cours à des étudiants sur les premières lois
sociales en France à la fin du dernier siècle, expliquez-leur en détail que
les catholiques sociaux en sont à l'origine et non les courants socialistes
de l'époque: ils ne vous croiront pas. Ils vous soupçonneront vaguement
de fanatisme religieux, et oublieront aussitôt vos propos.

Faut-il donc considérer ce courant comme purement historique, et
voué aux circonstances qui l'ont fait naître? Je suis persuadée que non.
Car la pensée sociale ne s'attache à aucune époque précise. Elle ne
défend pas un système politique, économique ou social précis. Elle fus-
tige les excès de chaque époque et de chaque système. Ce qu'elle défend
positivement, c'est une anthropologie. Elle repose d'abord sur le postulat qu'une anthropologie existe. Ce postulat n'est pas partagé par la
société occidentale moderne, qui au contraire pense avoir conquis l'auto-
fondation individuelle, la primauté de l'existence sur l'essence, à la suite
des philosophies du soupçon et du lointain mais prophétique Pic de la
Mirandole.

C'est là, concernant la condition première sur laquelle repose cette
pensée, que l'incompréhension déja est totale. Ce n'est pas encore un
désaccord anthropologique: c'est un désaccord sur l'existence même
d'une anthropologie. Et pour prendre quelques exemples, cela se décline
ainsi: La pensée catholique pense que le petit d'homme est plus heureux
s'il grandit entouré de ses deux parents naturels, qui l'éduquent ensemble
dans un climat de sécurité et d'équilibre, lui apportant l'apprentissage de
la différence à travers l'expérience première de la différence des sexes.

La société contemporaine pense que si le petit d'homme ne peut gran-
dir seul, la structure familiale peut être réinventée selon les époques, et
prendre des formes très diverses, y compris celle d'un couple homosexuel élevant un enfant voulu pour la circonstance.

La pensée catholique pense, sur les traces d'Aristote (la propriété est
privée, son usage est à tous), que l'homme est trop égoïste pour entretenir

durablement la propriété publique sans en tirer profit pour lui-même, et que la propriété privée permet davantage le développement des biens nécessaires à la vie. Mais que l'homme n'est heureux que dans la solidarité sociale, et que les fruits de la propriété privée doivent être en partie redistribués à cette fin.

La société moderne a longtemps cru, et souvent croit encore, que le mal provient des institutions historiques, que des institutions bien repensées sauraient avoir raison de l'égoïsme humain, et que des structures collectivistes pourraient fonctionner grâce à l'abnégation de tous. Si la chute du communisme a porté un rude coup à cette espérance, dans nombre de nos pays (surtout catholiques) elle n'est pas pour autant éteinte, et la restauration du profit individuel s'organise dans une ambiance de NEP[2], c'est à dire à reculons et avec mauvaise conscience. La fin du socialisme peut donner lieu à un libéralisme exacerbé, et à la croyance, au contraire, que l'individu serait heureux dans la seule réussite égoïste. La société moderne se trouve actuellement en délicatesse avec des réalités humaines qu'elle redécouvre dans l'effroi: elle ne peut admettre d'avoir échoué à refaçonner l'homme selon ses volontés, mais n'a pas encore pu recommencer à élaborer une anthropologie, car elle récuse encore l'idée même d'une anthropologie (Icare).

La pensée catholique pense qu'un homme est plus heureux s'il se trouve en situation de réaliser par lui-même ce dont il est capable, plutôt que de tout recevoir d'en haut. L'histoire biblique de la création est significative à cet égard: Dieu laisse le monde inachevé.

La pensée catholique intègre la politique, avec ses conflits inhérents, dans la nature des sociétés, parce que l'homme est un être social ayant donc besoin d'être gouverné, mais aussi elle croit à la politique moderne comme débat entre projets de société, ce débat ayant vocation à rechercher l'amélioration constante des choses. Car elle voit l'homme comme une créature non-finie, apte à se parfaire toujours à travers l'expérience de ses erreurs.

La société contemporaine annonce la fin du politique, préfère facilement le consensus au débat, confond la politique et la gestion, et par déception des idéologies mortes, recule devant l'affirmation de projets nouveaux, et vit comme si la fin de l'histoire était déjà là.

La pensée sociale catholique est intemporelle, tant qu'il y aura des hommes. Elle énonce des principes fondamentaux qui correspondent aux

---

2. La Nouvelle Politique de Lénine, restauration partielle de l'économie de marché pour des raisons de pure nécessité, et dans l'attente de pouvoir revenir a l'économie ollectiviste.

besoins humains fondamentaux. Elle cherche le bonheur, qui s'accomplit dans le temps et dans l'espace (selon la responsabilité et au sein des petites sociétés). La société contemporaine ne croit pas à une condition humaine, elle ne croit donc pas à des besoins humains fondamentaux, et pour ces raisons elle cherche, davantage que le bonheur, le bien-être, qui se réalise solitairement et dans l'immédiat (l'urgence). Il y a donc une réelle contradiction entre la pensée sociale catholique et le moment contemporain.

Pourtant les rudes secousses qui ébranlent les postulats de la modernité sont en train de faire apparaître au sein de nos sociétés des interrogations déjà lourdes de sens. Nous sommes en train de revenir sur quelques postulats de la modernité triomphante. Le progrès comme avancée inéluctable vers le parfait, comme créance que le temps de l'histoire nous devrait, se trouve remis en doute et en cause. L'humanité ne pourra être refaçonnée par nos volontés. Nous ne pouvons changer l'homme. Nous apercevons avec effroi que le mal ne peut être éradiqué de la société[3].

Devant ces interrogations inquiètes, la doctrine sociale se trouve exactement «en phase» avec les tendances du temps. Autant elle se trouvait en contradiction avec l'époque au 19ième siècle, au moment du libéralisme économique triomphant, ou entre deux guerres, au moment de l'énorme vague de l'eugénisme et de la tentation raciste, autant elle correspond aujourd'hui à nombre d'ouvertures qui se profilent concernant l'avenir du monde. Citons quelques exemples d'idées ou de projets récents:

> la pensée du Nobel d'économie Amartya Sen, qui réclame la consolidation des autonomies (capabilités) comme préalable de l'assistance;
> les réflexions nombreuses sur l'allocation universelle, sur le revenu minimum d'activité, sur la légitimité ou non du *workfare state* remplaçant le *welfare state*: il s'agit là de répondre à l'inertie individuelle engendrée par la providence d'État, sans pour autant retomber dans une société de jungle économique;
> les courants récemment apparus qui se réclament du libéralisme social, rappelant clairement l'ordo-libéralisme d'entre-deux guerres, dans lequel la pensée sociale tenait une part non négligeable.

Nos sociétés ont compris que le collectivisme détruisait le monde commun et engendrait la pénurie générale. Elles savent aussi que l'impérialisme du marché ne suffit pas au bonheur des sociétés. Elles sont à la recherche d'un équilibre: c'est bien cet équilibre entre profit et solidarité, entre liberté et ordre, entre responsabilité et assistance, dont la pensée

---

3. Cf. mon ouvrage *Le souci contemporain*, Bruxelles, Complex, 1994.

sociale catholique prône la patiente et interminable quête. Lorsque les sociétés s'éloignent des tentations démiurgiques, lorsqu'elles saisissent que l'essentiel est de s'attacher au bonheur de l'homme présent, avec ses imperfections et ses déboires, et non à un homme futur ou abstrait, comme c'est le cas aujourd'hui, la pensée sociale catholique peut être une instance de sagesse apte à mettre en garde, relever les effets néfastes, désigner la perversion parfois cachée de certaines idéologies à l'œuvre dans les sociétés. Car elle ne prend jamais le parti d'aucun parti, et s'interesse seulement à définir les conditions du bonheur humain.

Il faudra cependant, si elle veut continuer à tenir ce rôle dans la société de la post-modernité, prendre garde à deux exigences:

Nos sociétés sont profondément méfiantes, voire irascibles, devant n'importe quelle institution qui voudrait apporter des réponses référencées à une doctrine. Aucun message ne convaincra s'il énonce des critères issus des livres saints ou de la pensée vaticane. Je crois que cela n'a pas d'importance. Car la pensée sociale se réfère, plus profondément, à la condition humaine, à la loi naturelle ou à ce que l'on peut appeler une «morale naturelle». Ce langage en revanche est audible par nos contemporains. Car dans nos sociétés qui rejettent désormais toute vérité universelle ou objective, le seul critère valable demeure l'expérience, et notamment l'expérience des catastrophes. Il s'agit pour les catholiques, non pas de reculer devant l'expression de leur message, mais de savoir exactement à quel niveau d'argument le développer. Je pense par exemple à l'influence grandissante de Tony Anatrella en France, dans le débat sur le PACS[4]: pour parler de l'homosexualité, il ne brandit pas la Bible, mais la psychanalyse, le discours finalement est le même, faut-il encore savoir comment se faire écouter.

Le problème actuel de nos sociétés n'est pas le libéralisme ni le socialisme, mais l'anthropologie: qui est un homme? Comment est-il heureux? Les débats devraient s'instaurer autour de cette question, puisque les idéologies de refaçonnement de l'homme se sont avéré impuissantes. Devant cette question anthropologique, nous n'avons plus comme enseignement que l'expérience malheureuse. La pensée sociale catholique peut donc contribuer à la réflexion. Mais elle devra faire l'effort d'accepter et de recueillir les nouveautés (ex. le travail: faudra-t-il revenir sur l'idée du travail chrétien, du travail occidental? Sa tentation congénitale demeure l'essentialisme, qui consiste à intégrer à la nature

---

4. Contrat permettant à un couple, hétérosexuel ou homosexuel, de bénéficier des avantages fiscaux du mariage, sans responsabilité vis à vis des enfants du conjoint qui devient répudiable à merci; loi votée par le parliament français in 1999.

humaine des modes d'être, comportements, qui relèvent des circonstances. Quand on se réclame de la «nature», il faut veiller à ne pas inclure dans la nature toutes les circonstances historiques. Distinguer l'essentiel de l'accessoire, distinguer ce qui doit résister au temps et ce qui peut être bouleversé, voilà la difficulté. Nous savons que s'il existe bien une «condition» humaine, celle-ci est métamorphique. L'humanité n'est ni figée ni finie. Et les transformations font partie de notre être. Cessant de jouer au démiurge, ayant pris conscience que nous ne pouvons pas faire de l'homme n'importe quoi, ne tombons pas pour autant dans un fatalisme.

Université de Marne-la-Vallée   Chantal DELSOL

"A DUBIOUS IDIOM AND RHETORIC":
HOW PROBLEMATIC IS THE LANGUAGE OF HUMAN RIGHTS
IN CATHOLIC SOCIAL THOUGHT?

I. INTRODUCTION

Alasdair MacIntyre's dismissal of human rights as "fictions" is well-known[1]. However, his criticisms came at a time when the Roman Catholic Church – particularly in the writings of John Paul II – has adopted the language of human rights as one of the key modes of discourse in its moral theorising and social and political writings. After a century of official hostility, human rights language is now fully incorporated into mainstream Catholic tradition, and the central role that has been allocated to it mirrors its wider importance as the common currency of social and political life. Thus, in 1979, John Paul II's Address to the United Nations described the Universal Declaration of Human Rights (1948) as "a milestone... on the path of the moral progress of humanity"[2]. One wonders whether the Roman Catholic Church could have embraced human rights so fully had the UN Declaration never been signed.

Do the Declarations and Conventions on human rights represent the high point of culture or the height of nonsense – even dangerous nonsense? Perhaps the triumphant note with which rights have been welcomed into Catholicism is misplaced and the corresponding theme tune should not be Handel's coronation anthem, "Zadok the Priest", but more appropriately Prokofiev's "Montagues and Capulets" suite in order to evoke the atmosphere of hot-headed claim and counter claim. Alasdair MacIntyre and Ernest Fortin argue that rights theories advance a distinctively modern view of the person-as-individual that is a corruption of and antithetical to the classical conception of the person-as-social fundamental to Christianity. For these writers, rights language is a product of Enlightenment *hubris*: a modern distortion of a noble antecedent.

Has Catholicism embraced the philosophical and anthropological presuppositions of the liberal theorists responsible for shaping modern

---

1. A. MACINTYRE, *After Virtue. A Study in Moral Theory*, London, Duckworth, ²1981, p. 70.
2. *AAS* 71 (1979) 1147-1148, par. 7.

understandings of rights and the individuals in receipt of them that it once so vehemently rejected? Or does Catholicism possess alternative resources with which to furnish justifications for rights other than those proposed by liberalism? Some Thomists have claimed to find the spirit of Thomas Aquinas in rights formulations, thereby anointing rights discourse and simultaneously revitalising the natural law tradition. These writers therefore judge human rights to be thoroughly compatible with Catholic social thought.

It is noteworthy that both the critics and advocates of rights presented here work from within a Catholic Aristotelian-Thomistic tradition and therefore share the same basic philosophical presuppositions about the social nature of the person pursuing common ends, but they read Thomas and his legacy in quite different ways. These diverse approaches inevitably invite consideration of the ways in which Thomas is read and his work held to be of relevance to contemporary questions.

Despite the ambiguous history of the doctrine of rights, the ongoing conceptual difficulties, and the putative dangers inherent in the continued use of rights language within Catholicism, my argument in this chapter will conclude that – provided they are supported by a sufficiently rich Christian anthropology – human rights can serve an important purpose in public discourse by providing a means by which the requirements of justice can be articulated to the modern world.

1. *Alasdair MacIntyre*

"The dominant and contemporary idiom and rhetoric of rights cannot serve genuinely rational purposes, and we ought not to conduct our moral and political arguments in terms derived from that idiom and rhetoric. In so saying, I formulate a position at odds not only with liberal proponents of the United Nations Declaration of Human Rights, but also with utterances of, for example, the National Conference of Catholic Bishops. My quarrel in this latter case is not, or not necessarily, with the substance of what the bishops have intended to assert on a variety of moral and political matters; but insofar as the form of their assertions has involved an appeal, or has appeared to involve an appeal, to a dubious idiom and rhetoric of rights, I believe that the bishops, quite inadvertently, may have injured their own case"[3].

MacIntyre presents us with a deeply pessimistic portrayal of both the function of rights and of the society that chooses to conduct its affairs by

---

3. A. MACINTYRE, *Community, Law, and the Idiom and Rhetoric of Rights*, in *Listening* 26 (1991) 96-110, esp. 96-97.

utilising this idiom. For MacIntyre, rights language operates as both tool and weapon for those seeking to protect their interests and assert their will in the basically hostile social environment which characterises post-Enlightenment modernity. Lack of trust and lack of any shared set of beliefs about the ultimate human good have rendered moral and political affairs increasingly contestable, so that appeals to a supposed rational standard to arbitrate between conflicting claims become phoney or futile. The dislocation of the concept of right from its classical locus, and its counterpart, the dislocation of the individual from society, occur together. Attempts to draw up universal lists of rights by particular historically and culturally situated persons are therefore doomed to failure. All that results is the creation of "rival catalogues" of competing claims, which in turn leads to yet further contestation.

MacIntyre's central difficulty is that rights are to be "characterised independently of any socially established framework of institutions and practices"[4]. A transmutation has occurred whereby *jus*, which in classical thought denotes a norm governing the relationships of individuals in community, has become a right possessed by individuals apart from social relationships. In other words, the historical emergence of the rights of man "was the culmination of a process in which what was originally a complex medieval account of God, nature, man and society had stage by stage been dismantled"[5].

What the Deists considered "a progressive liberation from superstitious entanglements" is, for MacIntyre, "a history of fragmentation and shipwreck"[6]. For, in jettisoning "appeals to the law of God", or "the character of nature theologically or metaphysically understood"[7], "claims about natural rights have lost their only possibility of derivation"[8].

This is crucial, for it is clear MacIntyre does not deny the possibility of re-anchoring rights within their original setting: "[F]rom the standpoint of a virtue ethics, rights would not primarily provide grounds for claims made by individuals against other individuals and groups. They would instead have to be conceived primarily as enabling provisions, whereby individuals could claim a due place within the life of some particular community, and the question of what rights individuals have or should have would be answerable only in terms of the answers to a prior

4. A. MACINTYRE, *Are There Any Natural Rights?*, Charles F. Adams Lecture, February 28, 1983, Bowdoin College, Brunswick, ME, p. 13.
5. *Ibid.*
6. *Ibid.*, p. 14.
7. *Ibid.*, p. 18.
8. *Ibid.*, p. 15.

set of questions about what sort of community this is, directed towards the achievement of what sort of common good, and inculcating what kinds of virtues"[9].

However, for MacIntyre, as a discourse carried on within a fragmented society, there can be no meaningful transposition of this Thomistic setting for rights to the wider society. It is therefore "seriously imprudent" to continue to "adopt the contemporary idiom and rhetoric of rights"[10]. To do so would expose the Church to two dangers: first, that in using the language of rights Christians, even unintentionally, come to accept the presuppositions of that vocabulary and, secondly, that points of controversy and difference will be emphasised in reaction thereby losing our perspective[11]. Rights also constitute a threat to Churches and other intermediate institutions such as schools and families, he claims, because characteristically rights are employed to challenge the *status quo*[12].

2. *Ernest Fortin*

Like MacIntyre, Ernest Fortin remains unconvinced of the wisdom of integrating the language of rights into Church statements, for rights-talk "takes its bearings, not from what human beings owe to their fellow human beings, but from what they can claim for themselves"[13]. Fortin believes that modern rights theory sits uncomfortably with and may be irreconcilable to the premodern, and largely Thomistic, Christian ethics based primarily on duty. The question, therefore, is the extent to which Catholic social thought has merely imported unreconstructed Enlightenment assumptions, thereby creating an unhappy juxtaposition of moral conceptions that are basically opposed: the modern alongside the premodern. For Fortin is convinced – as is MacIntyre – that the Enlightenment period heralded an entirely new era: "[W]ith the emergence of modern thought we come to a crossroad in the intellectual history of the West, one of those rare moments at which, through the agency of a handful of seminal thinkers, human consciousness underwent a radical

9. A. MacIntyre, *The Return to Virtue Ethics,* in R.E. Smith (ed.), *The Twenty-Fifth Anniversary of Vatican II. A Look Back and a Look Ahead,* Braintree, MA, Pope John XXIII Center, 1990, pp. 239-249, esp. 247-248.

10. MacIntyre, *Community, Law, and the Idiom* (n. 3), p. 106.

11. *Ibid.,* p. 109.

12. *Ibid.,* p. 105.

13. E. Fortin, *Human Rights, Virtue, and the Common Good. Untimely Meditations on Religion and Politics* (Collected Essays, 3), Lanham, MD, Rowman & Littlefield, 1996, p. 304.

transformation and the Western world was summoned to make a fundamental change in direction. Implied in this statement is the view that
modern thought is not a simple derivative of premodern thought but represents a decisive break with it, defines itself in opposition to it, and on
the level of its highest principles remains profoundly at odds with it"[14].

Fortin resists the conventional wisdom that modern thought is already
latent in premodern thought, without "hiatus or breach of continuity"[15].
This view tends to assess the modern period as a culmination and perfection of all that went before, with the thinly disguised premise of "the
ideology of progress"[16]. He implies these assumptions may underlie the
nonetheless "valiant attempts" of Thomists such as Maritain and Finnis
to integrate medieval natural law and modern rights[17].

The problem for Catholic social thought is that since its inception, the
Church has tried to incorporate both approaches into its official teaching,
and glossed over any apparent inconsistencies. Thus, Leo's explicitly
Thomistic *Rerum novarum* nonetheless appeals to the existence of invi-
olable natural rights, including a basically Lockean (non-Aquinian) conception of a right to private property. For Fortin, this strategy is deeply
problematic: "Thomas Aquinas, to refer... to the authority from whom
the encyclical purportedly draws the bulk of its theological inspiration,
either had never heard of [natural rights] or did not deem it necessary to
incorporate them into his scheme"[18]. Thus, Fortin argues, "... the problem with *Rerum novarum* is that it lives in two worlds between which it
cannot choose and which it is unable to harmonise completely"[19].

Fortin believes the same ambivalence has characterised Catholic
social teaching as a whole. It is seen, for example, in the "overwhelming emphasis" that the US Catholic Bishops place on human rights[20]:
"... the [U.S. Catholic] bishops may have confused some of their readers by using language that looks in two different directions at once: that
of rights or freedom on the one hand, and of virtue, character formation,
and the common good on the other. They would certainly be ill advised
to give up their vigorous defence of rights, especially since the pseudo-
morphic collapse of neo-Thomism in the wake of Vatican II has left
them without any alternative on which to fall back; but they have yet to

14. *Ibid.*, p. 192.
15. *Ibid.*, pp. 192-193.
16. *Ibid.*, p. 308.
17. *Ibid.*, p. 163.
18. *Ibid.*, p. 202.
19. *Ibid.*, p. 211.
20. *Ibid.*, p. 304.

tell us, or tell us more clearly, how the two ends are supposed to meet"[21].

Fortin believes that the U.S. Catholic Bishops have relied too heavily on the language of rights in their moral teaching on abortion, capital punishment, and warfare; while emphasis on the right to freedom of expression causes inevitable problems in cases where theologians dissent from magisterial teaching. In short, Fortin argues that the Catholic Bishops' teaching "combines traditional Christian doctrine with ideas that once were and may still be fundamentally antithetical to it; in short... it suffers from a latent bifocalism that puts it at odds with itself and thereby weakens it to a considerable extent"[22].

To assess some of these remarks, it is necessary to turn to some Thomists who have endeavoured to incorporate the language of rights into their natural law theories.

3. *Jacques Maritain*

Jacques Maritain (1882-1973) was just as vehemently opposed as MacIntyre and Fortin both to bourgeois liberalism and to what he terms as "the one-sided distortion and rationalistic petrifaction" of natural law that emerged in the seventeenth century[23]. Ironically, however, Maritain's revulsion at the horrors of Nazism and Communism led him to formulate ideas about the dignity of the human person, human freedom, human rights and democracy which were interpreted by critics as an accommodation to the post-Enlightenment philosophy he despised.

Maritain attempted a Thomistic defence of the doctrine of human rights as enshrined in the Universal Declaration. For Maritain, the philosophical foundation of the Rights of Man is natural law. As one of the philosophers invited to contribute to UNESCO's enquiry into the theoretical bases of human rights, Maritain was confronted with an apparent paradox: though UN member states were prepared to sign a declaration signalling basic agreement on a list of human rights, the signatories held different, even opposed philosophies of personhood and society. Maritain illustrated the problem by means of anecdote: "It is related that at one of the meetings of a UNESCO National Commission where human rights were being discussed, someone expressed astonishment that certain champions of violently opposed ideologies had agreed

21. *Ibid.*, p. 311.
22. *Ibid.*, p. 304.
23. J. MARITAIN, *On the Philosophy of Human Rights*, in UNESCO (ed.), *Human Rights. Comments and Interpretations*, London, Allan Wingate, 1949, pp. 72-77, esp. 73.

on a list of those rights. "Yes," they said, "we agree about the rights but on condition that no one asks us why". That 'why' is where the argument begins"[24].

How could nations with incompatible world-views and divergent rational justifications for human rights come to a genuine practical agreement on the specific content of a list of human rights? Not only was Maritain convinced that natural law grounds human rights, he had the temerity to suggest that only a natural law justification can adequately explain why consensus may exist on a moral position despite irresolvable disagreement on the underpinnings of that position. Maritain claimed to find support in Thomas for the view that the way in which the rational creature knows the natural law or the requirements of human flourishing is through "inclination" or "connaturality"[25]: "human reason does not discover the regulations of natural law in an abstract and theoretical manner, as a series of geometrical theorems... the very mode or manner in which human reason knows natural law is not rational knowledge, but knowledge through inclination"[26].

By this he meant that the natural or "unwritten" law – as he liked to call it – is known not in terms of formal principles or as a result of conceptual argument but because it pervades the creature. The practical knowledge required in order to do something (such as driving a car or playing a computer game), which becomes "second nature", is to be distinguished from the conscious and articulated theoretical knowledge of the activity required to teach another person the same practical skills. Those who participate in a certain sort of practice usually have different reasons for so doing, they may employ unique but effective techniques in pursuit of the practice, and they might give allegiance to rival schools of thought concerned with the theory of the activity; but they will all follow certain set rules or common procedures that make the pursuit intelligible.

Humankind's implicit knowledge of the natural law has given rise to patterns of social living by which humans inevitably conform to the law of their own nature. For this reason, we see a great deal of commonality in terms of similar practices and values. Yet because natural law is not rationally deduced but lived, we also witness considerable legitimate variation in particular rules and customs. Practical agreement among peoples on a list of human rights can come about because they share a

---

24. J. MARITAIN, *Introduction*, in UNESCO, *Human Rights* (n. 23), pp. 9-17, esp. 9.
25. Cf. *Summa Theologiae*, Ia, q. 1, a. 6; IIa-IIae 45.2.
26. J. MARITAIN, *Man and the State*, Washington, DC, Catholic University of America Press, 1951, p. 91.

sufficiently similar lived experience of what it means to be human, in light of which they have deduced some common standards of behaviour. Where MacIntyre sees irreducible difference in the historical evolution of humanity, Maritain sees common human nature.

Abstract rational reflection of the sort that seeks to provide justifications for human rights is a secondary activity. Whereas MacIntyre's preoccupation is precisely with the corrupted theoretical discourse of moral philosophy where the disagreements and rival truth claims are played out, for Maritain, these questions, while important to philosophers, need not trouble people who have reached the same conclusions: "these various [philosophical] systems, while disputing about the "why," prescribe in their practical conclusions rules of behaviour which appear on the whole as almost the same for any given period and culture"[27] Moral philosophy may be characterised by incessant quarrelling, but at least we are quarrelling about the same things!

Maritain's strategy of distinguishing between practical and theoretical knowledge allows him to account for some degree of shared morality despite cultural diversity. It also enables him to endorse the emergence of the philosophy of rights as part of the moral growth of humanity, whilst insulating this achievement from the philosophical errors of the Enlightenment and the disputes of rival moral theories: "Thus it is that in ancient and medieval times attention was paid, in natural law, to the obligations of man more than to his rights. The proper achievement – a great achievement indeed – of the 18th century has been to bring out in full light the rights of man as also required by natural law. That discovery was essentially due to a progress in moral and social experience, through which the root inclinations of human nature as regards the rights of the human person were set free, and consequently, knowledge through inclination with regard to them developed. But, according to a sad law of human knowledge, that great achievement was paid for by the ideological errors in the theoretical field"[28].

Maritain's effort has been dismissed by MacIntyre as "quixotic" for, according to MacIntyre: "in that theatre of the absurd, the United Nations, human rights are the idiom alike of the good, the bad and the ugly"[29]. Maritain's approach is certainly optimistic, but that optimism should be understood in the context of the wider post-war optimism that raised expectations of a community of nations. Convinced that rights

27. *Ibid.*, p. 80.
28. *Ibid.*, p. 94.
29. MacIntyre, *Are There Any Natural Rights?* (n. 4), p. 19.

philosophy need not be incompatible with nor antagonistic toward Christianity, Maritain wanted to reclaim human rights from their distorted past and restore them to their natural law origins so as to guarantee a richer anthropological vision than pure individualism allows, and in so doing demonstrate the perennial relevance of Thomism. And though Maritain was often naive in his optimism, he was blessed with the virtue of hope.

This said, Maritain was aware that rights language had serious flaws and he conceded that there would always be difficulty in establishing an order of values which could be agreed upon, since rights are not absolute but are limited in varying degrees[30]. Nevertheless, he believed rights could spell out some fundamental human values when they were seen as correlative with duties. The (natural) law that assigns our duties also assigns our rights[31].

That Maritain considered rights talk redeemable was undoubtedly in part inspired by Leo XIII's and Pius XI's prior incorporation of the language of natural rights into the social encyclicals such as *Rerum novarum* (1891) and *Quadragesimo Anno* (1931) after a century of Catholic hostility to natural rights. The influence of Maritain's Thomistic philosophy on subsequent Catholics (including Pope Paul VI) has been considerable and it continues to bear fruit within all strands of Catholic philosophy and theology including Catholic social thought.

4. *John Finnis*

If human rights constituted a central plank of Maritain's moral and political philosophy, the same is also true of John Finnis's natural law theory. For Finnis the "modern vocabulary and grammar of rights" is a particularly useful instrument in moral discourse: "[T]he modern usage of claims of right as the principal counter in political discourse should be recognised (despite its dubious seventeenth-century origins and its abuse by fanatics, adventurers, and self-interested persons from the eighteenth century until today) as a valuable addition to the received vocabulary of practical reasonableness (i.e. to the tradition of "natural law doctrine")"[32].

As in Maritain's scheme, the classical Thomistic conceptions of justice and the common good are retained. The language of rights is simply

---

30. MARITAIN, *Man and the State* (n. 26), p. 101.
31. *Ibid.*, p. 95.
32. J. FINNIS, *Natural Law and Natural Rights* (Clarendon Law Series), Oxford, Clarendon, 1980, p. 221.

a useful way of spelling out the requirements of justice and listing the various aspects of human flourishing which comprise the common good[33]: "[W]e realise what the modern "manifesto" conception of human rights amounts to. It is simply a way of sketching the outlines of the common good, the various aspects of individual well-being in community"[34].

Finnis, like Maritain, is reluctant to develop exhaustive lists of rights. However, he argues for what he prefers to call certain "absolute" rights derived from his list of basic human goods which he (controversially) argues it is always unreasonable to directly choose against. "Correlative to the exceptionless duties... are, therefore, exceptionless or absolute human claim-rights – most obviously, the right not to have one's life taken directly as a means to any further end; but also the right not to be positively lied to in any situation (e.g. teaching, preaching, research publication, news broadcasting) in which factual communication (as distinct from fiction, jest, or poetry) is reasonably expected; and the related right not to be condemned on knowingly false charges; and the right not to be deprived, or required to deprive oneself, of one's procreative capacity; and the right to be taken into respectful consideration in any assessment of what the common good requires"[35].

At this stage it becomes necessary to enquire whether such Thomistic rights theories as those identified with Maritain and Finnis are credible given the absence of the concept of natural rights in Thomas's writings. Finnis anticipates the question: "Though he never uses a term translatable as 'human rights', Aquinas clearly has the concept... Aquinas would have welcomed the flexibility of modern languages which invite us to articulate... forms of right-violation (in-iur-iae) common to all... as rights common to all: human rights"[36].

Whereas MacIntyre and Fortin consider duty and virtue to be the predominant themes in Thomas, Finnis explicitly denies this: "Aquinas' morality and politics is a matter of rights just as fundamentally as it is a matter of duties and of excellences of individual and communal character"[37].

Finnis's remark remains contentious. But the broader question remains: given that the modern concept of right was unknown and

33. *Ibid.*, pp. 198, 205 and 221.
34. *Ibid.*, p. 214.
35. *Ibid.*, p. 225.
36. J. FINNIS, *Aquinas. Moral, Political, and Legal Theory* (Founders of Modern Political and Social Thought), Oxford, Oxford University Press, 1998, pp. 136-137.
37. *Ibid.*, p. 138.

unknowable to Thomas, how can the term "Thomistic rights theory" make sense? The question, of course, implies some oxymoronic quality about the juxtaposition, and the glib answer would be that the issue is not whether rights can be located in Thomas, but whether one can find the spirit of Thomas in a rights theory. I believe that one can.

5. *Anthony J. Lisska*

Though he concedes that "Aquinas does not consider the concept of 'right' as such"[38], Anthony J. Lisska has recently followed Finnis in also suggesting "how a theory of human rights might be derived from Aquinas's account of natural law theory"[39]. The result is his own particular list of rights, "based upon the natural necessities determined by the human essence"[40]. Lisska extrapolates from Aquinas's treatment of the human inclinations or dispositions in the *Summa* to deduce what he believes to be corresponding rights to life, to bodily integrity, to knowledge of what is true, and to a just society[41]. That his account is somewhat forced is indicated by his translation of the inclination to have sensations and perceptions into a "right to bodily integrity", while resisting any similar reading of Thomas that might take the natural inclination to rear offspring as implying a corresponding but troublesome right to reproduce[42].

II. THE VERSATILITY OF THOMISM

What can we learn from these various Thomistic efforts to construct a viable Christian theory of human rights? Ironically, the theoretical differences these convinced Thomists exhibit seem to confirm Maritain's thesis all the more! If Maritain, Finnis and Lisska are to be believed, it looks as though Timothy Chappell's words are correct: "in political philosophy and in ethics, Thomism has not come to abolish the Enlightenment project, but to fulfil it"[43]. MacIntyre, however, would prefer to view Thomism's role as overcoming modernity, rather than being conformed

38. A.J. LISSKA, *Aquinas's Theory of Natural Law. An Analytic Reconstruction*, Oxford, Clarendon, 1997, p. 228.
39. *Ibid.*, p. 224.
40. *Ibid.*, p. 236.
41. Cf. *Summa Theologiae*, Ia-IIae, q. 94, a. 2.
42. LISSKA, *Aquinas's Theory of Natural Law* (n. 38), pp. 234-236.
43. T. CHAPPELL, *Response to John Haldane's 'Thomism and the Future of Catholic Philosophy'*, in *New Blackfriars* 80 (1999), no. 938, 172-174, esp. 174.

to it. In terms of the particular Thomistic constructions of rights theories mentioned here, what counts as distortion of Thomas: at what point or according to what method does interpretation lapse into licence?

Can Thomism court modernity without being deflowered (violated) or worse, denatured (changed in its nature)? The question forces consideration of how to distinguish between authentic development of a tradition over time and distortion of it. The solution is both elusive and complex and, for these reasons, it is also controverted. Clearly, one cannot invent a theory that bears no relation to the tradition and misleadingly stamp the "appellation Thomistique controlée" label onto it. Likewise, approaches that are overly-concerned to find a latent Thomistic justification for subsequent philosophical and linguistic innovation are also hazardous because of the tendencies to rely too heavily on one aspect of a greater part or to fall into the trap of linguistic distortion.

In terms of broad acceptability, does the language of human rights provide a means of enriching Christianity or of better articulating the content of commitment to the tradition (faith)? The very meaning of a living tradition is one that displays the sort of growth that, when considered retrospectively (and that is the only way a tradition can be considered), presents itself as an "unfolding". That is to say, changes in understanding or content that have taken place over time do not appear as random events, but as purposive; as a development and culmination of what has gone before. That a naive historicism can pervert this act of judgement is clear. The imperative to assimilate all that is new into a tradition can become irresistible if an over-arching narrative such as that of human progress in history is the interpretative key.

At least this much can be said: the inevitable organic growth of a tradition as rich as Thomism or Christianity – the sort of growth that allows that tradition to thrive – must be judged authentic to the extent that it enables its adherents to see further than their forebears, and to the extent that it furnishes them with a better self-understanding of that tradition. Christianity's success has stemmed from its openness to the wisdom of the "other" and from an ability to absorb this wisdom into its own scheme and make "theological sense" of it, while retaining its own identity and sense of continuity. This is how Maritain understood Thomism's ongoing conversation with the world: "[W]e are not concerned with an archaeological but a living Thomism... we must combat the prejudices of those who would... fail to understand its essentially progressive nature... By assimilating whatever truth is contained in these partial [philosophical] systems it will expand its own substance and deduce from it more and more penetrating shafts of light which will reveal the forces concealed in its truths"[44].

Nicholas Rescher speaks similarly of the ongoing development of the Thomistic tradition in light of its encounter with other philosophical traditions and its own ever-new engagement with the present: "Texts are historical fixities, their development ends with their production. But ideas, arguments and positions have a life of their own. They evolve over time and become reconfigured in the wake of the responses they evoke.... Philosophical doctrines and positions as such have a life of their own beyond the control of their inaugurators. They admit of refinement and development both in response to misunderstanding or criticism and in response to intellectual innovation on relevant issues. If they are not to be mere pieces of flotsam and jetsam of the past washed up on the shore of the present – inert driftwood and ready for decorative display – then they must be re-examined, refurbished and reworked to meet the needs and opportunities of changed conditions and altered circumstances"[45].

Thomism has thrived as a tradition because it has proved infinitely adaptable. Thus, Jean Porter can say: "Aquinas' permanent significance lies precisely in the fact that his thought contains the seeds of its own transcendence". His thought, she continues, "can be shown to be capable of addressing the tensions and problematics of the Christian tradition in our own time in a satisfactory way, albeit through expansion and development that will take us beyond the limits of Aquinas' own system (as he himself transcended both Aristotle and Augustine)"[46].

Christianity should consider the language of human rights as a direct descendent of natural law origins – though admittedly Thomas is a more distant relation than some in the family tree that traces the genealogy of rights. And, as in all families, there are a number of skeletons in the closet.

III. THE USEFULNESS OF THE LANGUAGE OF HUMAN RIGHTS

The writings of MacIntyre, Fortin and others have sensitised us to the abuses that can take place in appeals to human rights, to the philosophical muddles, individualist excesses and so on. However, David Fergusson

44. J. MARITAIN, *Preface to Metaphysics. Seven Lectures on Being*, London, Sheed and Ward, 1939, pp. 1-2 and 14.

45. N. RESCHER, *Response to John Haldane's 'Thomism and the Future of Catholic Philosophy'*, in *New Blackfriars* 80 (1999), no. 938, 192-202, esp. 200-201.

46. J. PORTER, *The Recovery of Virtue. The Relevance of Aquinas for Christian Ethics*, London, SPCK, 1994, pp. 172-173.

has recently examined the place of human rights discourse in Christianity and, whilst acknowledging its limitations and deficiencies, concluded: "The language of human rights is the only plausible candidate for a global moral language... To abandon it because of its inadequacies is to make the perfect the enemy of the good. The language of rights has an important function in articulating a moral consensus against some of the most flagrant abuses of our time"[47].

Of particular interest is Fergusson's reference to the human rights organisation Amnesty International in which members are united in a practical concern for and coordinated campaign to end "human rights abuses": "[Amnesty] draws support from a wide cross-section of populations, many of whom would use different thick [moral] discourses and many of whom would have difficulty articulating in any way the reason for their commitment to the principles of Amnesty. If it possible to recognise common moral ground in the absence of common moral theory, it ought to be possible for Christian theology to appropriate for specific tasks the language of human rights"[48]. He continues: "What is needed in Christian theology, therefore, is a theological explanation of why there might be common ground in the absence of common theory"[49]. I would suggest that Maritain's Thomistic theory of "knowledge by inclination" goes some way to addressing Ferguson's concern, in that it provides an explanation for the existence of moral agreement on human rights in the face of conceptual disagreement.

Human rights talk bridges the particularities of cultures and traditions. It shows signs of strain in the West from over-use but, fortunately for humanity, the construction as a whole shows no real sign of collapse. The short focus Enlightenment lens through which Alasdair MacIntyre has viewed Western liberalism has projected a distorted image of over-magnifying the modern malaise. The idea that earlier theorists were all individualistic and uninterested in the common good is not borne out by the historical evidence[50]. While no one disputes the existence of individualist excess, few judge liberalism to be a total failure. Indeed, most communitarian restructuring should be considered fine-tuning. I find myself in broad agreement with Jeffrey Stout's analysis: "The language

47. D. FERGUSSON, *Community, Liberalism and Christian Ethics* (New Studies in Christian Ethics, 13), Cambridge, Cambridge University Press, 1998, p. 168.

48. *Ibid.*, pp. 168-169.

49. *Ibid.*, p. 166.

50. B. TIERNEY, *The Idea of Natural Rights. Studies on Natural Rights, Natural Law, and Church Law 1150-1625* (Emory University Studies in Law and Religion, 5), Atlanta, GA, Scholars Press, 1997.

of human rights and respect for persons can be seen as a conceptual out-
growth of institutions and compromises pragmatically justified under
historical circumstances where a relatively thin conception of the good
is the most that people can secure rational agreement on. I support Mac-
Intyre's verdict on standard philosophical defences of this language. I
share his desire to rehabilitate talk about the virtues and the common
good. But I am less suspicious than he is of the language of rights and
respect itself. I am also less disposed to assume that talk about rights
and respect cannot live in harmony with talk about the virtues and the
good ... The judgements we share about the achievable good are ample
enough to justify our practice of ascribing rights"[51].

IV. HUMAN RIGHTS IN CATHOLIC SOCIAL THOUGHT

The incorporation into Catholicism of the language of rights forms
one part of the Church's complex engagement with modernity. It is no
accident that the language of rights enters Catholic social thought at the
same time as the nineteenth century Thomistic revival to which Leo XIII
lent such powerful support. In *Aeterni Patris* (1879) Leo had urged
Catholics to draw inspiration from the enduring value of St Thomas's
thought in order to meet the intellectual needs of the day. Thomism provided the context in which a reappraisal of Catholicism's relationship to
the modern world could occur. It, more than any other resources in the
tradition, could reduce the likelihood of a bumpy landing as Catholicism
began its descent from the timeless clouds of abstraction to land on the
terra firma of historical reality.

The period of Leo's papacy marks the point at which Catholicism
began re-assessing its attitude towards and place within the world.
Rerum novarum and subsequent social encyclicals engaged with and
offered responses to modern civil and political movements and new economic and social forces at large. They asserted an attitude of social concern rather than one of indifference to or detachment from the world.
The Gospel message was not simply to be pronounced to the world, but
lived within it. To be a Christian was to be involved in the deepest concerns of the whole human community. This enduring conviction unites
all Catholic social thinking and writing, both official and non-official, to
the present day, and motivates the social concern of Catholic activists,
practitioners and theoreticians.

51. J. STOUT, *Ethics After Babel. The Languages of Morals and Their Discontents*,
Cambridge, James Clarke & Co, 1988, pp. 225-256.

The Second Vatican Council cemented Catholicism's self-identity as a Church *in* the modern world, but it also became clear that Catholicism was, in David Hollenbach's words: "a transnational Church in a pluralistic world"[52]. Hollenbach draws an interesting parallel between the circumstances of the Roman Catholic Church at the time of Vatican II and that of the United Nations at the time of its foundation: "... they had a common concern with the problem of the unity of the human community and the task of finding norms and structures for world peace in the face of ideological pluralism and conflict ... in both assemblies the conflicts between Western and non-Western culture, and between rich nations and poor nations were conflicts *internal* to the two assemblies themselves. The need to find consensus on a normative basis for international justice and peace without suppressing the legitimate differences among regions and social systems led both bodies to a human-rights focus"[53].

Pope John XXIII's adoption in *Pacem in terris* of the rights already enumerated in the Universal Declaration, along with the Church's 1965 Declaration on Religious Freedom set out in *Dignitatis humanae,* established the central role that human rights were to play in Catholic social thought. Human rights serve an important transcultural and international purpose in expressing a set of universally applicable minimum standards for social living. At the same time, commitment to human rights has enabled Catholic social thought to reflect the legitimate pluralism that exists in the ordering of societies, via a sort of subsidiarity where individual nation states are left to determine how best to maximise human welfare within the bounds of respect for human rights. Previously, natural law had been invoked restrictively to emphasise the unchangeability of (a hierarchical) political order. This tended to encourage a Church too associated with maintaining the political *status quo*. Therefore, the incorporation of human rights into Catholic social thought has transformed the older Thomistic natural law model into one that can better account for the complexity and diversity that exists in modern social life. The sinusoidal progress of the Christian tradition is one in which new tributaries of thought can become fresh major currents.

Department of Theology and Religious Studies   Julie CLAGUE
Glasgow University

---

52. D. HOLLENBACH, *Justice, Peace and Human Rights. American Catholic Social Ethics in a Pluralistic World,* New York, NY, Crossroads, 1998, p. 88.
53. *Ibid.,* p. 91.

CATHOLIC SOCIAL THOUGHT IN TRANSITION
SOME REMARKS ON ITS FUTURE COMMUNICABILITY

INTRODUCTION

About three decades ago – shortly after the Second Vatican Council – among others the sociologist Peter L. Berger pointed out that transcendence had lost its impact on modern society with regard to both the general significance of religion in daily life and especially on the institutional impact of the major Christian Churches[1]. This process, which can be described as "an abdication of the supernatural", does not exclude some renewed search for the meaning of religion and even of Christian faith, both of which, in fact, have recently found new impetus in practical life as well as in the social sciences[2]. Both developments should be seen as complementary, and may be brought under the same paradigm of "autonomy" to describe both the loss and the rediscovery of religion. One side of the paradigm refers to the new euphoric trust in human freedom and its efficiency; and the other side, reflecting the counter-experience of radical failure, refers to the limits of that same freedom as it is interpreted in (post-)modern society and as it exemplifies itself in manipulative effects on public and private life, a dominance of anonymous complex structures, the low-effectiveness of personal involvement, helplessness in the face of seemingly omnipotent technology, damage to the natural environment, and such like[3].

No matter how attempts at appropriate interpretation of these changes are judged, the Church's teaching as well as theological reflection are surely influenced by them. Both Christian faith and theology have been, and still are, definitely affected by the loss of their former

---

1. P.L. BERGER, *Zur Dialektik von Religion und Gesellschaft. Elemente einer soziologischen Theorie,* Frankfurt am Main, Fischer, 1973, pp. 104v.

2. H.-J. HÖHN, *Gegen-Mythen. Religionsproduktive Tendenzen der Gegenwart* (Quaestiones disputatae, 154), Freiburg, Herder, 1994; the rediscovery of transcendence is already mentioned by P.L. BERGER, *A Rumor of Angels. Modern Society and the Rediscovery of the Supernatural,* Garden City, NY, Doubleday, 1969.

3. J. RÖMELT, *Vom Sinn moralischer Verantwortung. Zu den Grundlagen christlicher Ethik in komplexer Gesellschaft* (Handbuch der Moraltheologie, 1), Regensburg, Pustet, 1996, pp. 18v; ID., *Jenseits von Pragmatismus und Resignation. Perspektiven christlicher Verantwortung für Umwelt, Frieden und soziale Gerechtigkeit* (Handbuch der Moraltheologie, 3), Regensburg, Pustet, 1999, pp. 27v; for basic aspects see A.J. BUCH, *Libertà e vincolo del cristiano in politica,* in *Il Nuovo Areopago* 2 (1983) 90-105.

alleged self-plausibility. This applies, at a pastoral level, to Catholic moral and social teaching as well as to the academic disciplines of moral theology and Christian social ethics, which reflect the development of society as well as interpreting it from a Christian perspective. A lack of plausibility in moral and social teaching, particularly in respect of Catholic social teaching's lack of connection to implications for life and reality, points up a problem of their lack of communicability in pluralistic societies, leaving the churches with an uncertain voice in human matters. But in Catholic social thought (CathST), which is supposed to give the Catholic Church a purchase on social life and reality, such lack of plausibility is particularly weakening. The transparency, acceptance and effectiveness of Catholic social thought are all at issue in a social environment in which Christian belief now scarcely holds it own.

It is in this sociological context of the changing significance of religion and the role of churches that CathST may be portrayed as being in transition. Perhaps the first and most obvious manifestation of transition is in this area of communicability. The challenges, however, do not stop at the level of religious language and theological hermeneutics, important as these are. There are also serious challenges for the structure of religion and for the institutions of the churches. If "transition" is to be managed, both sets of problems, intellectual and structural, must be faced.

COMMUNICABILITY "AD EXTRA"

Among the major tasks of CathST, if we focus here specifically on the European and American scenes, are the interpretation of Christian social principles and their deployment on specific subjects in "applied ethics". The task would be difficult enough if standard methods needed to be applied to changes in conventional social formations, such as society, family, economy, employment; but, in an imaginative way, new perspectives need to be brought to bear on novel issues and their implications, which so far have scarcely been considered in Christian social ethics. These often bring forward new sociological data which end up constituting a new agenda for Catholic social thought and ethical reflection. For example, the economic, financial and ecological consequences of globalisation, and the implications of these for human identity, call for fresh ethical insights on creation and entail new understandings of individuality and solidarity in the interpretation of political and economic relations. The applicability of these principles in situations of increasing anonymity and to the complexity of decision-making structures and processes is a matter for careful middle-level thinking and a challenge to non-official Catholic social thinking (CNOST), as this is defined in basic position papers in this collection. Particular challenges, it should be added, remain for the development of social ethical criteria for dealing with global financial markets, not just so as to deal with the traditional application of theories of justice and of transparency and conflict-management, but looking to the fundamental principle of "sustainability" in its applications to ecology and the economy, to aspects of social institutions, such as education and health systems, the preservation of cultures, in dealing with resources of technology, research and bio-ethics.

These revolutionary developments constitute a challenge not just *for* Catholic social thought, but *to* Catholic social thought. Clearly there is a need for education in professional expertise and for dialogue and co-operation with experts if Catholic social thought is to make realistic assessments and applications. A network of competent exchanges has become imperative in order to provide professional and adequate advances in social ethical contributions to debate and which will operate to communicate these aspects among experts in their relevant fields. This makes Catholic social thought "application-effective". Given the complexity of the contents of many modern problems, some structured dialogue with relevant experts is an increasingly important requisite for the quality standard of Catholic social thought. Methodologically, it seems important to develop the sensitivity of moral theology and social ethics to the demands of modern society and to what may be looked for by way of theological reflection and comment. A further aspect of this openness would be the inclusion of various perspectives from other religions, faiths and secular sources. This twofold rehabilitation is part of the exercise of rendering CathST a more reliable and sound social ethics and applied ethics. The very exercise of strengthening both arms of the instrument will help to overcome the self-induced isolation which was noted at the beginning of this paper, and should open up the subject to a more effective future.

Orientation *ad extra,* then, does not mean simply inter-disciplinary academic dialogue with economics, other social sciences and relevant special disciplines, but counts in practical expertise and social experience as constitutive elements of social ethics. The aim should be not simply to take ethical standards and apply them in accordance with established practice, but to become a truly life-oriented, and hence, humane social thought. *Praxis* and theory are brought together.

Communicability "Ad Intra"

Nevertheless, any recovery of the tradition of CathST, extended so as to embrace aspects of the reality of faith and life, will integrate it into the message of the Church and its tradition. Changes in CathST must become part of the reality of faith and of the life of the Church. In principle, such responses are manifestations of the self-understanding of social thought. But the extent of the restructuring necessary for "CathST in transition" must include some awareness inside the Church of how to understand the complexity of issues and the sophistication of the working methods needed to deal with these. Thus, communicability *ad intra* is concerned with the relation of social thought, faith and church life in general; at a further stage, it relates to connections between Catholic social thought as a theological enterprise and official Catholic social teaching (CST) as well as to the specific practice of belief and life of the Church corporately and personally. Last but not least, a major task of concrete and creative Catholic social thought in transition is to communicate methods and results of its work also *within* the theological disciplines, in particular among experts in moral theology and social ethics. This is a particularly urgent task for CNOST. In the modern period, in addition to general theoretical questions relating to such matters as the validity of basic moral statements, there is a range of challenging issues, such as criteria of sustainability (regarding, for example, social security systems or protection of life in the bio-ethical sphere)[4]; or particular conclusions drawn from natural law and refined with certain historical hermeneutics[5]. The transition of Catholic social thought will not be open to a new future unless it courageously faces up to these new challenges and constitutes itself as communicating *ad intra*. Both challenges are essential for the self-understanding and for the identity of future Catholic social thought.

Relation between Internal and External Communicability

Without doubt, both perspectives of the communicability of "Catholic social thought in transition" are linked not only methodologically, but

---

4. Some examples for this are a different meaning of the principle *abusus non tollit usum* in the context of genetic methods and reproductive biology, the interpretation of *intrinsice malum* when considering historical hermeneutics, or a refined reflection of *cooperatio formalis* and *cooperatio materialis* in view of the efforts regarding the protection of the unborn etc.

5. E. SCHOCKENHOFF, *Naturrecht und Menschenwürde. Universale Ethik in einer geschichtlichen Welt* (Welt der Theologie), Mainz, Matthias-Grünewald, 1996.

also in respect of content. In fact, the relative ineffectiveness of recent Catholic social teaching *qua* social thought, as well as its limited impact on concrete decisions, are consequence of the weaknesses of the linkage. The Second Vatican Council explicitly emphasized, in a linked way, the idea of being Church in today's world[6]. It became increasingly clear over the second half of the twentieth century that there is a socio-political dimension to this "being Church in today's world" which connects the internal and external communicability of the annunciation of faith and theology and calls for Catholic social thought to be an integral part of the doctrine of life, as Pope John XXIII put it in paragraph 222 of *Mater et Magistra*.

Contrary to the somewhat strange opinion that Christian faith is opposed to secular commitment, the truth is, from a hermeneutic point of view, that Christian social ethics as well as the Church's social teaching were responses to the mentality and life of modernity, although their *extra* and *intra* communication was inside a specific and limited historical context. It is in this frame of mind that changes in the content and method of CathST are proposed, particularly as regards relations *ad extra*. CathST, thus adapted, will in its turn affect the character and style of official social doctrine. The natural place for listening and dialogue, both internal and external, is in connection with Catholic non-official social thinking, and then later relayed to CST. This will facilitate understanding of the social complexities to be faced and restrain CST from precipitous judgements. The relationship of CST and CathST is thus a fruitful one inside the integral mission of the Church.

AN ECUMENICAL DIMENSION FOR COMMUNICABILITY IN SOCIAL ETHICS

Any framework for social ethics in a modern pluralistic society, which recognizes the variety of moral traditions and theories in a context of profound value change[7], will, at least in a Christian context,

---

6. The community of the faithful "realizes that it is truly linked with mankind and its history by the deepest of bonds" (*Gaudium et spes*, 1). For the church it is therefore important to "recognize and understand the world in which we live, its expectations, its longings, and its often dramatic characteristics" (*GS* 4).

7. (With special reference to G. SCHULZE, *Die Erlebnisgesellschaft. Kultursoziologie der Gegenwart*, Frankfurt, Campus, 1992); H. BAIER, *Freiheit oder Sachzwang? Von der Vernunftethik zu Systemrationalität und Wertewandel*, in J. EISENBERG (ed.), *Die Freiheit des Menschen. Zur Frage von Verantwortung und Schuld*, Regensburg, 1998, pp. 60-81, esp. 69v – this view can also be interpreted as critical towards some results of the so-called "values study", cf. P. ESTER, L. HALMAN & R. DE MOOR (eds.), *The Individualizing Society. Value Change in Europe and North America* (European Values Studies), Tilburg, Tilburg University Press, 1993.

acknowledge the need for Catholic social thought to incorporate an improved ecumenical orientation. On the one hand, the search for Christian principles in basic sectors like the economy, financial markets, social institutions, technology and bio-ethics, to take a few examples, concerns all Christians individually as well as Christian churches and communities. In Europe, which is continually growing closer and linking East and West, there is a growing awareness of how important it is to include, for instance, the traditions and the outlook of eastern Christianity, and particularly of the Orthodox churches in discussions about mainline ethical questions. On the other hand, most people, especially in Europe and Northern America, are living in predominantly multi-cultural societies, in which there is not only the matter of ecumenical openness and co-operation among Christian churches to be considered, but also of an "enlarged ecumenism" in a dialogue with other faiths[8] in order to confront common problems and challenges to human development and social reconstruction. Christians, as has been said, can and should be "providers of visions"[9]. Catholic social ethics must widen its understanding of the conditions of communicability when trying to convey its message, especially in the large task of helping to inspire an understanding of a human structure for a globalised world – a contribution which is, at once, specifically Christian and a task to be shared with all people of good will[10]. Thus Catholic social ethics assumes its particular responsibility for the ecumenical communicability of its work and should try to include inter-religious, inter-cultural and inter-faith dialogue.

Finally and in summary: if Catholic social thought is to be effective in the face of the pivotal problems and questions posed by contemporary ethical imperatives it must remain internally and externally open-minded. Nothing less than this kind of effectiveness can facilitate the contribution which Christianity, from its perspective of eternity, brings to making life more humane. Recently, despite the limited impact of religious institutions on life in modernity, society seems to have become

8. Cf. A.J. BUCH, *Weltkirchliche Aspekte des Aufbruchs in die eine christliche Kirche. III. Ökumene und Ökonomie – Die Weltprobleme als ökumenische Herausforderung*, in *Ökumene. Aufbruch in die eine christliche Kirche* (Dokumentation '91), in *Hirschberg* 44 (1991), no. 7/8, 479-494, esp. 484-486.

9. To keep such a vision of the human being alive in a scientifically and technically oriented environment could mean e.g. constantly to emphasise that there is more to be taken into consideration in "dealing" with unborn life and the dying than a merely technical aspect.

10. This is especially necessary as there is need for a more and specifically Christian approach to social ethical thought due to the lack of significance of religion (see above).

more open-minded to reasonable and creative contributions from religion's social visions for the future, particularly as regards proposals from a Christian understanding of politics and economics. The appeal made here for a wider and ecumenical openness in Catholic social thought in no way suggests any restriction of its specifically Christian character. Neither does the attempt to broaden the range of analysis and conceptualisation of the technical side of the ethical enterprise impede the theological deepening of such social thought. On the contrary, all efforts which go into human strategies for coping with complex and often global problems, encouraged by openness and dialogue (in the way that co-operation in real life is), can only serve to emphasise the high profile of Christianity's attempted contribution as well as to deepen and enrich religious experience and theology. Such an open and, at the same time, profound approach is crucial for Catholic social thought, particularly in this phase of its transition. It offers Christian social ethics substantial opportunities for a renewed internal and external impact, including its implications for real life.

Clementia, Düsseldorf   Alois Joh. Buch

HUMANISING THE ECONOMY
ON THE RELATIONSHIP BETWEEN CATHOLIC SOCIAL THINKING AND ECONOMIC DISCOURSE

INTRODUCTION

We live in a time in which a growing number of social scientists, philosophers and theologians are discussing, with growing frequency, themes of common interest, advancing new avenues of research and proposing new grounds for debate. This renewed interest comes after several decades during which the two scientific areas, once quite close to each other, developed in substantial isolation from each other. It cannot be denied that for many scholars this separation remains unbridged. Many philosopher-theologians, on one side, and social scientists on the other, adhere to the view that to take under serious consideration the categories of thought employed in the other discipline is either lowering their professional status or, at best, irrelevant. Fortunately, more and more scholars, among those who show an interest in probing the temper of their research, find it useful and inspiring to try and overcome that separation.

It is precisely within such a framework – which resembles a sort of intellectual migration – that the question of the relationship between Catholic social thought (CathST) and economics as a scientific discourse can be dealt with. What kind of relationship does, in fact, exist between CathST and economics? What are the problems caused by closer collaboration between them? On the one hand, there are those who claim that CathST should act as a matrix within which economics takes shape as scientific discourse and draws strength for its theories. On the other hand, there is the position of those – nowadays the majority – who believe that all CathST can, or should offer the economist is a twofold support: to suggest selection criteria for prioritising economic problems and to provide guidelines for the practical utilisation of the results obtained by the economist. But in the actual process of the production of economic knowledge the horizon offered by official Catholic social teaching is next to irrelevant, indeed it is jealously kept apart. For example, CathST may suggest that searching into the unemployment question should be a priority in the economist's agenda; or it may advise on how to distribute fairly among its citizens the income produced in a country.

On the matter, however, of how one arrives at a specific theory of the labour market or how one is capable of explaining the level of income produced by a certain economy would be totally unconcerned with the value options stemming from CathST.

It seems to me that both positions are aporetic and therefore unacceptable, if on different grounds. The first one, because it would disclaim the autonomy of economic science. Yet, at least since *Gaudium et spes* such an autonomy has always been considered a value to be preserved, a principle recently reasserted in the encyclical letter *Fides et ratio* by John Paul II (One should not forget that from Aristotle down to the 18th century, economics was treated as a branch of practical philosophy without any independent status). The second position is unacceptable on more subtle grounds that need to be clarified.

Just at the time when, within economics, the well-known thesis of value-neutral study was asserting itself, a trend was gaining ground to consider knowledge produced by economic thinking as devoid of any normative or guiding function. Economic science – so the argument goes – does not accompany nor does it guide decision-makers' actions; rather, it observes and predicts human actions just as the physicist anticipates nature's motions. The acceptance of value judgements as marginal to scientific enquiry, allied to the persuasion that only this kind of rigorous method is rational, led to the adoption of the same scientific objectivity as an essential feature of economic reasoning. This is equivalent to saying that for an economist to be a scientist he cannot commit himself to judgements of value. Ends and dispositions are declared irrelevant to scientific reasoning, which has nothing to say about them; hence the spread of relativistic – not to say sceptical – attitudes among economists, even among those who declare themselves believers.

The uneasy position produced by this lack of a value framework is obvious to many modern scholars. This is especially true of those economists who are wont to question the scientific status of their own discipline, as is not unusual today. If we construe economics as one (certainly not the only) way to improve our understanding of the social world and to help improve certain social structures (for example, the welfare system), the economist cannot restrict his or her action range to matters of efficiency. Above all, he or she cannot ignore that the greater the range of important decisions to be made, the more urgent the need to clarify the criteria which underlie decision-making. "Even though he is aware of all this", writes Jonas, "the economic specialist still feels compelled to deny his science the status to supply those selection criteria, hence the authority to say 'yes' or 'no' to any proposed objective with the obvious exception of decisions merely concerning feasibility. Furthermore, if asked whether economic knowledge should be judge or a mere performer of its ends, the purist replies by choosing the latter. Such is the reply of scientific asceticism that he or she abides by in the name of economics' scientific purity"[1]. Yet we know today that values and scientific enquiry do not necessarily have to clash, as Pascal in modern times bravely maintained.

The extent to which this "scientific asceticism" is harming the comprehension of the problems of a post-industrial society and how far it is contributing to making CST a sort of pure ethical code of conduct is manifest to all. To me, CathST, in connection with CST, has a vital contribution to make to transdisciplinary methodology in the realm of social science by helping to define the hermeneutical horizon guiding a change of the categories of thought which are the basis of economic discourse.

Any attempt to restore within economic discourse the perspective of CathST is sure to be well received, at least not opposed, by the profession, more specifically by avowed non-believers, provided one can prove that such retrieval, while taking place in full compliance with the canons of scientific practice, will be of help in correcting some *aporias* and filling gaps in the discipline. In other words, one needs to be able to demonstrate that the introduction of Catholic social thinking categories into the developing process of economic thinking can widen, not restrict, the cognitive range of economic science, thus enabling it to firm up its grip on reality. My argument is that the best contribution that can nowadays be made for a re-conceptualisation of economic discourse lies in its capability to answer the following question: is it possible to humanise the economy and, if so, how can this be achieved? Given the present historical circumstance in which the only existing economic model is the market economy – neither command economy nor the celebrated mixed economy representing any longer credible alternatives – the question could also be rendered as: is it possible to devise a model of market capable of including all human beings and of every aspect of the fulfilment of the integral human person?

The pages that follow, presenting a twofold argument, should be read with the following two tasks always in view. First, to provide a critique of the claim that there is "one best way". It should be noted that this critique is all the more necessary in view of a tendency, observable today in economic practice, to derive a "unique policy" from that unique

---

1. H. JONAS, *From Ancient Faith to Technological Man*, Bologna, Il Mulino, 1991, p. 142 (translated by the author).

thought. The second task is to produce arguments in support of the model of a civil economy offering a viable alternative which humanises the market. The line of argument I am pursuing aims, on one hand, to avoid a utopian ideal above and beyond reality; and, on the other, a hopeless resignation that would ground all effort.

ON THE UNIQUE THOUGHT OF THE "ONE BEST WAY"

The fashionable "one best way" in economics is now put forward with such persuasiveness that it popularises the following representation of our market society[2]. The market is a contextualised institution resting on a clearly defined structure of accepted norms. It is obvious that legal norms cannot completely steer economic decisions, nor do they alone suffice to regulate entirely economic interaction. Within the existing framework of norms, culture and competition – "the two determining agencies in market economies", to use J.S. Mill's words[3], – will then answer the call. The specific significance of these two agencies is clearly not the same in the various historical phases: in traditional societies (pre-capitalistic ones) culture, viewed here as a body of social norms and conventions, is the driving agency; in modern societies competition is the driving force insofar as it progressively erodes those spheres of economic activity which rest upon social norms and conventions. An implication of such a vision is that in time the sphere of economic relations is going to be almost totally ruled by the forces of competition alone, which is tantamount to saying that the modern age, viewed as a phase in the cultural evolution process, inexorably tends to replace interpersonal relations with anonymous and impersonal market laws.

Of course, even advocates of the "one best way" have to admit that such a substitution will never be a total one. "Culture" can at no time be completely replaced by "competition" for the obvious reason that there will always be parts of economic activity in which the ruling principle of the exchange of equivalents is not going to apply. As we know, this is the principle behind familiar market transactions as they are described in economic textbooks. Even the most modern market society will include a sphere of economic relations which, whether or not they transit through the market, will be governed by social conventions and rules.

---

2. I have developed more extensively some of the points dealt with in the present paper in my essay *Valori e mercato*, in *Economia e Politica Industriale,* 101-102, 1999.

3. Quoted in E. SCHLICHT, *On Custom in the Economy*, Oxford, Clarendon Press, 1998, p. 23.

This is the sphere of activities making up the non-profit or third sector. It should be observed, however, that this is held to remain a residual sphere of relations with limited quantitative impact and in any case such that it should in no way impair the operational logic of competition: precisely, a third sector. So much so that serious problems arise as soon as non-profit activities exceed a determined dimension, thus leaving the niche within which they could enjoy full legitimacy. With regard to this, the situation of the USA is illuminating. In that country a subtle reaction has been going on for some years, aimed at delegitimising non-profit organisations. At the moment this action is pursued chiefly at the academic-scientific level (there are several working papers allegedly evidencing that the management by non-profit organisations of hospitals or welfare institutions is socially inefficient). One first sign at political level has, however, already been perceived: the Istook Amendment at the 104th USA Congress in November 1998 suggested the cancellation of all fiscal benefits accruing to some specific non-profit organisations (The bill presented by Republican Senator Istook eventually failed to pass by a few votes)[4].

This dichotomous portrayal of the reality of market societies generates a twofold disastrous consequence. From the viewpoint of the division of labour among disciplines, in the course of the last century, the separation has been crystallising between economics as the science which deals only with the sphere of economic facts and has *homo oeconomicus* as its specific mode of explanation, and sociology as the science dealing only with social facts, with *homo sociologicus* as its explanatory paradigm. The result thereof is that these disciplines, which should and could be complementary, ended up by each acquiring a specific identity precisely due to the assumption of such division.

The second, more significant consequence has been the emergence of a line of thinking which identifies the market as the ideal-typical place in which subjects are prompted to act "only" out of self-interest, whatever the latter may be – whether selfish or apparently unselfish. Indeed, in the wake of the theory of Gary Becker, co-founder of the Chicago School and Nobel Prize laureate for economics, altruism is nothing but disguised selfishness or at best enlightened egoism – exactly as in Nietzsche's lapidary and cynical statement "your neighbour praises the absence of selfishness because he benefits from it". Thus the conviction has been gaining strength that the only judgement of value the market

4. See L. SALAMON, *The Nonprofit Sector at a Crossroads. The Case of America*, in *Voluntas* (1999), 1.

can sustain is that of efficiency, conceived as the appraisal of the adequacy of means in view of the maximum (possible) achievement of the interests of the participants in the market game. It is easy to explain why this could happen. If the only motivation leading individuals to operate in the market is the pursuit of self-interest, it is obvious that the only possible assessment of market outcomes is whether or not the latter are the best in relation to the initially available resources. To entrust the market process with other ends, for example economic justice, is unthinkable. The market cannot, hence should not, be charged with such ends.

As the supporters themselves of this line of thinking admit, there are other values that the market as institution has to take into account, but they stand, as it were, at the beginning as basic conditions for the market to come into being and regularly operate. Think of values such as freedom, honesty and trust. One does, indeed, recognise that these values are necessary for an efficient market performance: in fact, it would not exist without freedom of enterprise or without freedom to enter exchange relations. Likewise, if economic agents do not meet their obligations, do not comply with the law in force, and, above all, if no close-knit network of trust relations is established, the market cannot operate. However, according to mainstream, economic thinking, all of this should be in existence before market operations begin. In any case, it is not the market's task to provide it; it is, rather, the task of the civil society and /or of the State.

Needless to say, the unique thought of the "one best way" is not even touched on by the doubt that results produced by the market process might eventually erode the core of values upon which it rests and without which any market economy would be extremely short-lived. If, for example, market outcomes do not comply with some standard of distributive justice, how can one assume that the values of honesty and trust will continue to support the market itself? St Augustine provides a cogent answer of extraordinary freshness when he writes "What is a community of citizens other than a multitude of people bound to one another by the tie of concord? In the State, what musicians call harmony is concord: civic concord cannot exist without justice" (*Civitas Dei,* 2, 21). Indeed, why should economic agents trust one another and meet their obligations if there is a perception or even full conviction that the outcome of the market process is plainly unjust?

What becomes of the interests or fate of those who, for one reason or another, fail to participate in the market game or are turned out of it as losers or because they lagged too far behind the winners? The answer which is provided is the State, an institution which is legitimised to intervene directly in the economic sphere each time this is necessary in order to cancel or to compensate socially disastrous consequences of the market functioning. In this way, however, the gap between the sphere of efficiency judgements and the sphere of value judgements widens instead of narrowing. In the first place, because this vision strengthens the belief that market is an allocative mechanism which can function *in vacuo,* regardless of the kind of society in which it is embedded, which means that the market is visualised as an ethically neutral mechanism whose results can be corrected by the State whenever they appear unacceptable by some standard of justice. In the second place, because it substantiates the idea that the market area coincides with the one in which only individual interests are protected, and the State area as the one in which collective interests are protected. Hence the well-known dichotomous social order that identifies the State as the forum of public interests (i.e., of solidarity) and the market as the forum of privatism (that is, as the arena in which only individual purposes are pursued). It is the "public", *viz.* the State that has to take care of solidarity by means of redistribution (the "rich" are taxed and the receipts are redistributed to the "poor"). The "private", i.e. the market, should take care of efficiency, *viz.* of the optimal production of wealth and of philanthropy or "charity" at the most.

THE INDEFENSIBLE THESIS OF THE "ONE BEST WAY"

What is unacceptable in this description of market societies, a description apparently so convincing and widespread in popular culture as to make it seem impregnable, almost a truth to be received without criticism?

In the first place, such a representation is misleading because law, culture and competition are not alternative instruments to solve the problems of social order, more specifically those connected with the co-ordination of economic decisions. These instruments are instead complementary, for the basic reason that, if market transactions rely upon social and legal norms prevailing at a given time, it is likewise true that the economic process itself tends to modify such norms. In other words, there is a substantial co-evolution between norms and economic behaviours. Therefore, the distinction between the paradigms of *homo oeconomicus* and of *homo sociologicus* is after all not so reliable as we were always made to believe. In fact, it is true that the more recent theory of evolutionary games has attempted to explain the outcomes of (social and legal) norms by viewing them as "routines" that are adopted since they appear as the winners, in competitive terms, in the solution of both co-ordination and bargaining problems. Along these lines, such theory has claimed to demonstrate that any social relation can be examined essentially as an exchange relation, and therefore the problem of a social theory would simply be reduced to a problem of exchange. It follows that what at a first glance may seem to be a "rule-following" behaviour, turns out to be a typical problem of rational choice in only slightly more complex contexts, which is tantamount to saying that every *homo sociologicus* ultimately harbours an ever-busy *homunculus oeconomicus*.

This instrumentalist conception of social and legal norms is unacceptable on two different grounds. On the one hand, it may account at most for co-ordination problems such as "why one travels on the right hand side of the street", but fails to explain why even in the complete absence of sanctions some people will conform to very demanding rules, or why there are people who donate anonymously or offer active services on a purely voluntary basis. On the other hand, although the instrumentalist conception of norms may be fine as long as we are investigating "how" one chooses, when it comes to explaining "why" one does, it is impossible to assume that values are just a datum. As adroitly pointed out by Becattini, in economic discourse there seems to be a predominance of studies assuming that "some of the most intrinsically human peculiarities of the economic agent such as his notions of justice, honour, loyalty and also his vaguest hopes and illusions [are] pre-economic data, or "accidental deviations from the rational norm" which reciprocally compensate within the vast body of data"[5].

Secondly, it is not true that maximum extension of the market area improves everybody's wellbeing. The aphorism according to which "a rising tide raises all boats" is not valid. As we know, this is the favourite metaphor of the recent liberal-individualistic formulation according to which the well-being of people, being a function of economic prosperity, is linked to the spread of market relations. The priority for political action should be to ensure all those conditions (fiscal, public administration, optimum allocation of property rights and so on) which foster a flourishing of markets. In that vision, the welfare state which redistributes wealth via taxation while keeping itself outside the wealth-producing mechanism, hampers economic growth, all the more so when it is greedy (causing major distorting effects in the market) and when its instruments are submitted to political uses, thus jeopardising normal democratic procedures. Hence the recommendation that the welfare system should take

5. G. BECATTINI, *Possibilità e limiti dell'economia di mercato*, in *Economia e Politica Industriale*, 101-102, 1999.

care solely of those whom the market contest leaves on the fringes of society. The others, those who manage to stay inside the virtuous circle of economic growth, will protect themselves through numerous solutions offered by private insurance schemes.

The weak point in this argument is to be found in the simple reason that the prerequisite of equal opportunities for all is one that has to apply throughout the life-span of citizens and not just *una tantum,* the moment they enter the economic arena. For all participants to enjoy actual conditions of freedom it is not sufficient to ensure equal opportunities at the start of the economic race. The market contest is indeed quite different from a sports contest. In the latter, the most gifted or capable wins the prize but this in no way confers upon him the possibility of, or bestows upon him, the right to start the next run from a vantage point: all, with no exception, compete under the same conditions, at any stage or tier of the game. Not so in market contests, where the winner of the first stage is quite often able to bend to his advantage, in an endogenous way, the rules of the game. (Economic history is rich in examples of this kind. We need but to recollect how monopolies and oligopolies developed in the course of time). Furthermore, the really alarming news about the "new economy" age – the economy of knowledge and information – is the appearance of a new kind of competition: "positional" competition as it was called by the late Fred Hirsch. The central feature of positional competition is the generation of "winner-take-all" outcomes, the so-called "superstar effect", as the American economist Shermin Rose called it. It is easy to see that in a context of positional competition equating across individuals initial opportunities is of little or no avail.

The results are there for everybody to see: never to the same extent as in the last two decades has one witnessed such a burgeoning of social inequalities, both horizontal (among different social groups) and vertical ones (among one subject and another), at the same time as the world's wealth has been growing at a pace never seen before. This is the great *aporia* of the present model of development: extraordinary economic growth (in the sense of sustained increases of wealth) and civil progress (in the sense of wider and wider spaces of freedom for people) are unable to keep the same pace[6]. It is therefore easy to understand why, under such circumstances, an increased affluence does not go hand in hand with greater public happiness. Indeed, limiting or even destroying the ability to partake in the economic game of those subjects who, for

6. See *The Assessment. The Twentieth Century Achievements, Failures, Lessons,* in *Oxford Review of Economic Policy* 15 (1999), no. 4.

some reason, are left on the market borders, while it adds nothing to the capabilities of the winners, produces a rationing of freedom which is always detrimental to happiness.

In the third place, it is not true that the market is an institution compatible only with the egocentric motivations of its agents. It is not true that market competition is generated "solely" by the self-interest of economic actors. This is not only factually untrue, as even casual observation will confirm, it is also theoretically reductive; and there is more to it. Ronald Coase's proposition according to which the market is a more than perfect substitute for Smithian benevolence, reaching farther than benevolence ever would, is on close scrutiny untenable. Briefly, the reason is the following. While acknowledging that in order to function the market implies the practice of benevolence and compliance with the code of commercial morality by all agents, Coase claims that market outcomes depend only on the self-centred interest of participants. Which is tantamount to saying that in order to exist and perform well, the market needs certain virtues to be practised by economic agents, but such practices have no bearing on the outcomes themselves of the market process because outcomes ignore those practices altogether: a patent paradox. Why ever should rational subjects practise virtues like benevolence or sympathy if the effects of market interaction were totally independent of such virtues? (One should remember that, unlike what happens with a scarce resource, the use of a virtue accumulates it, and vice versa).

It is true instead that, given certain conditions which I will elucidate in a moment, the market can become a means to strengthen the social bond, both by promoting wealth-distribution policies that make use of its mechanisms (instead of operating outside of it as is the case with redistribution carried out by the State), and by providing an economic space in which those values such as trust and solidarity upon whose existence the market itself depends, can be put into practice and therefore reproduced. In other words, there exists a variety of models of market societies, each compatible with one specific culture – seen as a body of values shared by agents. And it also means that the problem of the choice of the market model (or of the way leading to one specific market model) is as (maybe even more) interesting and noble for organised civil society as the search for efficiency conditions of a given market model, in its turn an expression of one "given" culture[7].

---

7. If I am right, this may be the ultimate meaning of the following passage by L. Einaudi: "Having believed for a long time that the task of the economist was not to state aims for the legislator, but to remind that, whatever the goal pursued by politics, the devices adopted should be sufficient and appropriate, I am today wondering whether

THE LIMITS OF THE LIBERAL-INDIVIDUALISTIC DOCTRINE OF RIGHTS

What explains the centrality within economic theory of the thesis of the "naturality and inevitability" of the "motivational supremacy" of what P. Wicksteed called non-tuistic self-interest, and therefore of the market as the forum of privatism? In order to answer, I must take up a position relating to the contemporary predominant version of liberal thought, the liberal-individualistic one. Liberalism is today the prevailing current in Western political and economic thought. Yet precisely this hegemonic position puts before liberal thought an unavoidable challenge, that of thoroughly clarifying the economic and social implications flowing from its individualistic version, according to which the conception of right can be seen as independent of the relations linking human beings to one another. By denying the cogency of the notion of common good and by visualising civil society simply as the sum of monad-individuals, this version proves incapable of accounting for the social character of rights, especially of those pertaining to the economic domain, and in so doing one cannot see how such version can be made compatible with Catholic social thought.

In fact, according to liberal-individualism, a right cannot be fully made use of unless the subject involved is capable of negotiating his own interests with other subjects. As neo-contractualistic literature clearly shows, a peculiarity of people participating from the very beginning, in the social covenant, is their ability to pursue their own interests by unrestricted negotiations. Now it is true that if contracting parties are somehow equal in their negotiating potential, the most efficient way for them to reach their goals is to be left free to negotiate with one another. But what about those who do not possess the same skills? As we know, the liberal-individualistic response is that they can be "represented", with their interests voiced by some gifted subject during the negotiating process that brings the social contract into being. An agent may be left out of the social contract if she lacks negotiating abilities or if no one accepts to represent her. This means that a subject is the holder of rights only as long as she is capable of pursuing her targets, directly or indirectly, as contracting party in some social pact.

I may finally conclude that, the economist should not sever his duty as a critic of means from that of stater of purposes, *that the study of aims is part of the science by the same extent* as *the study of means to which economists limit themselves*": Preface to C. BRESCIANI TURRONI & L. EINAUDI, *Introduction to Economic Policy*, Turin, 1942, pp. 15-16, italics added.

As G. Grant subtly observes, the majority obtains equality in the distribution of social benefits as a result of having agreed to a social pact; notwithstanding this, such equality "will exclude liberal justice from those who are too weak to enforce contracts – the imprisoned, the mentally unstable, the unborn, the aged, the defeated and sometimes even the morally unconforming"[8]. What I wish to stress here is that in spite of the due emphasis laid on the category of rights by the individualistic version of liberal thought, its bare rendering of what it means to be a person deprives the concept itself of any practical significance, at the same time as it removes any justification of the acknowledgement of the moral rights of people.

This difficulty survives even in the re-thinking of liberalism proposed by John Rawls in his celebrated 1971 work. As we know, Rawls argues that the constituents (those who choose the principle of justice in an original position and behind the veil of ignorance) are certainly rational, free and equal beings (here emerges the evident Kantian inspiration), yet they are rational only insofar as they are in a position to choose the principles of justice from behind the veil of ignorance and on the basis of self-interest. On close examination, the weakest side to the neo-contractualist theory is precisely its limited range of applicability. The persuasive force (in both moral and economic sense) of liberal-individualism is largely due to its affinities with the contract in the domain of positive right. In the latter context, the agreement between parties is evidence that what the parties consider to be their interest, represents the definition of what is just and – as long as one is prepared to accept the principle of the sovereignty of individual preferences – even of what is good. Undeniably, such an argument possesses very interesting peculiarities while exerting great intellectual appeal. On close examination, however, it will appear to be somewhat tenuous.

First of all, the contract traditionally governs relations of exchange of equivalents. Although the relevance of exchange relations, especially in an age, like ours, characterised by globalisation, can hardly be doubted, these do not exhaust the wide range of relations among subjects. One has but to think of pure conflict relations such as the ones related to problems of distributive justice; or of co-ordination relations, namely those from which social conventions and norms develop. The pretension to examine similar relations under the species of the contract would not only impair our comprehension of how a democratic social order can be

---

8. G. GRANT, *English-Speaking Justice,* Toronto, House of Anansi Press, 1985, pp. 83-84.

achieved, but it would also raise a moral question of great moment. In fact, if agreement among the parties were to be the fundamental criterion of what is just, or even good, not a few daily-life situations would completely escape moral control. As in the celebrated case of the prisoner's dilemma, we may well agree upon something considered evil by any moral theory other than the one that defines what is right or good in terms of what is susceptible of agreement.

A satisfactory theory of rights has to acknowledge the social quality of rights. The individualistic theory of rights that claims to assimilate the attribution of rights to the process by which individuals pursue their targets, is inadequate because its vision of the concept of person denies precisely what is essential to a person: interaction with others and the relationship to others as a value *per se*. Market co-ordination of given individual preferences is seen as an essentially value-neutral process, even though some subjects, endowed with lesser negotiating power, may be to some extent left out of the benefits of this process[9]. To quote but one example, let us think of what actually happens when contracts are incomplete, i.e. when their enforcement entails recourse to endogenous strategies such that the positions of power initially enjoyed by some subjects enable them to modify to their advantage the rules of the game. Actually in such cases, which are becoming more and more frequent, the market ceases to operate as a mechanism merely allocating resources, and becomes a power-regulating mechanism.

How can one imagine that a-social individuals will ever accept to conform to the rules of some kind of social order? The liberal-individualistic answer is that the market can aggregate individual preferences in an agnostic way, i.e. independently of any specific notion of common good. Yet we know this to be true only in presence of considerable homogeneity in individuals' preferential orderings, as Kenneth Arrow demonstrated long ago in his famous impossibility theorem in social choice. This is tantamount to saying that market as an institution cannot reconcile "basic conflicts"; it is not capable of leading to any kind of social order starting from the mere consideration of individual preferences (or tastes). It should be remarked that the difficulty in settling "basic conflicts" is not to be found in the market as such – this was the mistake of a large portion of Marxism that engendered the belief that the abolition

---

9. See A. SEN's important discussion *Markets and Freedoms. Achievements and Limitations of the Market Mechanism in Promoting Individual Freedoms*, in *Oxford Economic Papers* 45 (1993) 519-541. See also R. INMAN, *Markets, Governments and the New Political Economy*, in A. AUERBACH & M. FELDSTEIN (eds.), *Handbook of Public Economics,* Amsterdam, North Holland, 1987.

of the market would suffice to attain a superior social order. That difficulty instead lies in the pretension to base a co-operative decision process – like the market – simply on an aggregation of individualistic preferences through procedures and incentive schemes of an extrinsic nature.

The argument above can be summed up by saying that the individualistic version of liberalism entails a juxtaposition of what one may call libertarian individualism and institutional guarantism. On the one hand, extreme intransigence is advocated for public morality (it is not sufficient to abide by the laws of economic life, it is also required to subscribe to the principle of the supremacy of what is just over what is good, just as J. Rawls did in his celebrated *A Theory of Justice*). On the other hand, one advocates the maximum subjectivism within the private sphere, that is to say, as far as individual preferences are concerned. This is the very root of the problem of conflict at the heart of liberal individualism: how can the concept of arbitrarily individualistic preferences, which are *per se* without a relational dimension, be reconciled with the idea that society's institutional structure should offer guarantees for such preferences to be satisfied? How can one expect individualistic preferences to receive "protection" at social level?

The ultimate difficulty posed by the liberal-individualistic set-up is too narrow a concept of freedom: freedom merely as self-determination, as mere opportunity for free choice ("free to choose" is Milton Friedman's vivid expression). One cannot deny that the essence of freedom lies in the actual practice of that power represented by the act of choosing. However, as M. Botturi indicates[10], the subject does not only have the "power" to choose, it also "needs" to choose. Choosing is a function of needs not to be neglected and which must be met. Actual economic agents do not choose just for the sake of doing so, but in order to reach profitable goals. It is a fallacy to believe that flesh-and-bone persons may find satisfaction in self-determination alone. Indeed, freedom is not just an opportunity to choose, it is also the ability to do so, it is "self-realisation". This implies that self-determination is to serve the attainment of those objectives which the subject considers worthy – in one word, happiness-bringing. As A. Sen and others have recently clarified, rational choice is a function of the agent's realisation. Freedom here has a positive sense, as in Isaiah Berlin, and positive freedom is not such unless it entails the relationship to the other. Not only does freedom as self-realisation have to take into account the other's freedom (as

10. F. BOTTURI, *Fenomenologia dialettica della libertà / Dialectic Phenomenology of Freedom*, Milan, mimeo, 1998.

liberal-individualistic thought also recognises), but it has a deep, vital need for the other. It is the relation "with" the other which is crucial to freedom, not the relation "to" others *per se*. As it was well expressed by authors participating in *Controversy* about "Economy and happiness" in the 1997 issue of *Economic Journal,* happiness is the central issue in economic science, more so than utility. "Economic matters are of interest only insofar as they make people happy"[11]. But happiness is a relational concept, unlike utility which is an individualistic one. Robinson Crusoe may maximise his own utility, by himself, but for him to be happy there must be Friday.

A remarkable foretaste of the idea that there is no happiness outside of life within society is found in Antonio Genovesi. In his *Discourse about the true purpose of letters and sciences* (1754) – a true manifesto of Neapolitan Enlightenment – Genovesi wonders why Naples, albeit well inhabited, well placed for trade, well gifted with bright minds and rich talents and so on, is not so developed a nation as others in Northern Europe. Genovesi's prompt answer is that Naples lacks "love for the public good". He actually writes: "The primary support of civil society, the most important of all, is love for the public good, which can preserve these societies in the same way that it made them. Societies where private interest reigns and prevails, where none of their members is touched by love of the public good, not only cannot reach wealth and power, but also if they have already reached them, are unable to maintain this position"[12].

A final comment may not be out of place: while liberal-individualism proves its inability to embody the perspective of Catholic social thought, this does not apply to "liberal-personalism", a formulation which adopts the intrinsic value of the human person as the objective basis for the attribution of rights[13].

Civil Economy as a Way to Humanise the Market

Given today's situation, is it reasonable to expect the fulfilment of a humane model of market economy? Close observation tells us that this

11. A.J. OSWALD, *Happiness and Economic Performance*, in *Economic Journal* 107 (1997), no. 445, 1815-1831, esp. 1815.

12. Quoted in L. BRUNI & R. SUGDEN, *Moral Canals. Trust and Social Capital in the Work of Hume, Smith and Genovesi*, Norwich (UK), mimeo, 1999.

13. For a clear exposition of the personalist view of freedom and the notion of human rights, see K. WOJTYLA, *The Acting Person* (Analecta Husserliana. The Yearbook of Phenomenological Research, 10), Dordrecht, Reidel, 1979.

question involves the dimension of freedom, viewed however not simply
as self-determination, but above all as personal realisation in the sense
explained above. In this second, wider-ranging meaning, a free society
presents features quite similar to those of the decent society mentioned
by Margalit[14]. Society is decent when its institutions do not humiliate its
members, which is the case when it grants benefits and services to its
citizens but at the same time denies them their dignity, which is precisely what happens when their "preferences" are rejected or their opinions neglected. It is clear that today the most devastating humiliation,
hence hindrance to self-realisation, is economic irrelevance. Holding
down what is felt to be a useless job is even more degrading than feeling exploited, if for no other reason that awareness of exploitation
almost invariably generates some kind of reaction among the exploited,
leading perhaps to a structural change, whereas humiliation produces
resignation, thus perpetuating the status quo. This is why a free society
is one which aims at acknowledging in each person the ability to act, not
just to do. *(Agere* is altogether different from *facere,* as K. Wojtyla con-
vincingly stressed in our times in his *The Acting Person).* For this reason
it is important to recognise each person's right to act, as Aquinas noted
already in his time.

   A positive answer to the question that opens this paragraph presupposes the fulfilment of one specific condition: the creation "inside" the
market (not outside it), of an economic space composed by subjects (I
will explain what I mean in a moment) whose *modus operandi* is based
on a value system which is being nurtured by the realisation of economic
activities themselves. Since participation in these activities cannot be
severed from its originating culture, it belongs to that principle of economic behaviour which is called reciprocity. Unfortunately, the principle
of reciprocity is often mistaken for that of the exchange of equivalents,
so much so that it is opposed to the principle of gratuity or gift. Elsewhere[15], I have dwelt upon a description of the essential differences
between the principle of the exchange of equivalents underlying the
sphere of private economy, and the principle of reciprocity underlying
the sphere of civil economy. I will just highlight the main feature of

14. A. MARGALIT, *The Decent Society,* Cambridge, MA, Harvard University Press,
1996.
   15. S. ZAMAGNI, *Economia civile come forza di civilizzazione della società ital-
iana/Civil economy as civilizing force of Italian society,* in P. DONATI (ed.), *La società
civile in Italia,* Milan, Mondadori, 1997. See also S. ZAMAGNI, *Social Paradoxes of
Growth and Civil Economy,* in G. GANDOLFO & F. MARZANO (eds.), *Economic Theory
and Social Justice,* London, MacMillan, 1999, and *The Significance of Labour in a Post-
Industrial Society. Unemployment and the Role of Civil Economy,* mimeo, 1999.

reciprocity, namely the fact that the transfers it originates are inseparable from human relations. The object of transactions involves reciprocity and cannot be separated from the identity of those who originated them. Because of this, exchange ceases to be anonymous and impersonal. Literature offers evidence that in a reciprocity equilibrium it is possible to give without losing and to take without removing. This is, essentially, the meaning of the civil economy project. (The expression "civil economy" first appeared in the political economy vocabulary in 1753, when the University of Naples established the first-ever chair in economics, appointing Antonio Genovesi to hold it).

To avoid any misunderstanding, I have no intention of maintaining that human behaviour is steered solely by intrinsic reasons (such as the motives flowing from the moral constitution of agents). I simply mean that such motives "contribute" towards explaining human behaviour and, more specifically, that they are an essential item in the definition of its rational norms. Even less do I want to assert the possibility of governing a modern economy by the sole principle of reciprocity as opposed to the principle of exchange of equivalents. My belief is that a market organisation capable of stimulating pro-social behaviour instead of discouraging it, will tendentially operate more efficiently (since it will substantially reduce transaction costs), and above all in a more "feliciting" way for everybody.

Briefly, the point is: man *per se* is not basically or exclusively individualistic, as axiologic individualism has it; nor exclusively "socialising", as axiologic holism claims. Man will instead tend to develop those inclinations that are most influential in the social context in which he operates. The thesis that pro-sociality and reciprocity are "exceptions" to be explained in the light of the "natural and historical supremacy" of self-interest, appears as extreme as the opposite one. In his absolute behavioural complexity, man may be driven by a variety of motivational configurations. In a complex market society, efficiency and justice will result from the society's ability in exploiting the "best" individual motives, leaving economic agents free to strive at one time for their own and for others' maximum wellbeing. The continuing mediation between the diverse motivations which is required, obviously implies "enlightened self-interest" but is not exhausted by it. That is why I find reductionist, hence unacceptable, the stance taken by Nobel Prize George Stigler when he writes: "I arrive at the thesis that flows naturally and irresistibly from the theory of economics. Man is eternally a utility-maximise – in his home, in his office (be it public or private), in his church, in his scientific work – in short, everywhere. He can and often does err:

perhaps because the calculation is too difficult. ....what we call ethics, on this approach, is a set of rules with respect to dealings with other persons, rules which in general prohibit behaviour which is only myopically self-serving... Let me predict the outcome of the systematic and comprehensive testing of behaviour in situations where self-interest and ethical values with wide verbal allegiance are in conflict. Much of the time, most of the time in fact, the self-interested theory will ... win"[16].

How widespread is, in reality, the practice of reciprocity? Surprisingly enough, even casual observation will suggest that this is a widespread phenomenon in advanced societies. It does operate in various forms and at different levels, within the family, in small informal groups, in volunteer associations. But there is more to it: the transaction network supported by reciprocity as leading principle can be found in all undertakings, from co-operatives – in which reciprocity takes the form of mutuality – to non-profit organisations in which reciprocity flows into utter gratuitousness, to the firms making up the "Economy of Communion"[17]. Empirical evidence of the economic results achieved so far by civil economy and its practical implementation is ample and very accurate and I will not dwell on it here. As many studies on economic development have emphasised, the so-called "new competition" model requires an inclination to co-operate on the part of agents, and a close-knit network of transactions, with a structure very similar to the structure of reciprocity relations. In fact, this is the secret of so many success stories in Italian industrial districts and in emerging countries.

For all the above reasons it does not make sense, nor does it help, to raise the problem of choice between the principle of reciprocity and the principle of the exchange of equivalents. It does not make sense in that no indisputable standard is available on which to base one's choice. For sure, the criterion of Pareto efficiency cannot provide such a standard because this notion of efficiency does not apply to economic relations geared to reciprocity. It does not help – in fact, it is detrimental – because an advanced economy needs both principles to be implemented. An attempt to base successfully all kinds of transactions on the culture of the exchange of equivalents is naive. Should such a vision become predominant, individual responsibility would coincide simply with what has been agreed upon in a contract. Everybody would then take care

16. Quoted in G. BRENNAN & J. BUCHANAN, *The Normative Purpose of Economic 'Science'*, in *International Review of Law and Economics* 1 (1981) 158.

17. For evidence of results achieved so far by the practice of communion economy and for a conceptualization of this model, see L. BRUNI (ed.), *Economia di comunione*, Rome, Città Nuova, 2000.

only of what they are "in charge of", with grotesque consequences that it is easy to imagine. If the culture of the exchange of equivalents and that of reciprocity do not merge, the system's growth potential will be impaired; hence the urgent need to get the sphere of civil economy off the ground. Free competition between private economy and civil economy – both competing under equal conditions – will then decide which goods or services agents consider to be more conveniently provided according to the principle of the exchange of equivalents, and which goods or services are to be produced according to the principle of reciprocity. Without paternalism of any sort.

CONCLUDING REMARKS

The ultimate sense of the argument developed above is that the search for a way to humanise the economy contains a demand of relationality which one should carefully investigate and satisfy at best if one wants to dispel perverse effects of great magnitude. Indeed, how good the performance of an economic system is depends also on whether certain conceptions and ways of life have achieved dominance. As a growing number of economic scholars over the past couple of decades – to cite but a few: K. Arrow, A. Sen, B. Frey, R. Sugden, R. Frank, P. Dasgupta, S. Kolm – have tenaciously stressed, economic phenomena have a primary interpersonal dimension. Individual behaviours are embedded in a pre-existing network of social relations which cannot be thought of as a mere constraint, as mainstream economists continue to believe. Rather, such a social network is one of the driving factors that prompt individual goals and motivations.

It seems to me that the central problem in the current transition towards a post-Fordist society is to understand how to operate so that individuals may be at liberty to decide the procedures for the supply of the goods they demand. What is at stake here is not so much freedom to decide the overall "composition" of goods to be produced (more of private *versus* more of public goods; more merit *versus* more relational goods), but freedom to decide "how" that composition should be achieved. This is why one cannot simply advocate the efficiency principle in order to decide "what" and "how" to produce. Undiscriminating admirers of the market as a social institution seem to overlook the fact that it is the very hegemonic expansion of those relations that I called private economy, that will slowly but inexorably destroy the whole system of social norms and conventions which constitute a civil economy, thereby paving the way for new forms of statism. Today it is urgent to admit that the hypertrophic growth of both State and private market is a major explanation of the many problems that embarrass our societies. The solution cannot be found in the radicalisation of the public economy *versus* private economy alternative, or neo-statism *versus* neo-liberalism, but in a healthy flourishing of those forms of organisation that shape a modern civil economy.

The most obnoxious consequence of a narrow-minded (and obsolete) notion of market, still predominant to this day, is to lead us to believe that a behaviour inspired by values other than non-tuistic self-interest inexorably drives economy to disaster. By encouraging us to expect the worst of others, such vision eventually brings out the worst in us. Moreover, in the end it immensely hampers the exploitability of such inclinations as trust, benevolence, reciprocity, since that vision perceives these inclinations as merely inborn peculiarities of human nature, unrelated to the civilisation process in progress in our societies. As Wolfe points out with great insight referring to the sphere of the relations that shape private economy: "The problem with reliance on the [private] market as a moral code is that it fails to give moral credit to those whose sacrifices enable others to consider themselves as freely choosing agents. By concentrating on the good news that we can improve our position, rather than the not-so-good, but socially necessary, news that one might consider the welfare of others as our direct concern, the market leaves us with no way to appreciate disinterest"[18].

Since motivations sustaining the principle of reciprocity are motives whose fulfilment is at least as legitimate as the fulfilment of self-interested motives, a truly liberal society should not prevent beforehand – that is, at the level of institutional design – the growth and dissemination of the former to the detriment of the latter, as is foolishly happening today. In the absence of actual – not just virtual – competition among different subjects of supply of the various categories of goods, the citizen-consumer will be left with a reduced space of freedom. One might end up living in a more and more affluent society, more and more efficiently inundating us with commodities and services of all sorts, but more and more "indecent" and, ultimately, desperate. Indeed, the reduction of human experience to the "accountancy" dimension of utilitarian calculus is not just an act of intellectual arrogance; it is disclaimed by actual experience in the first place.

18. A. WOLFE, *Whose Keeper? Social Science and Moral Obligation*, Berkeley, CA, University of California Press, 1989, p. 102.

One final remark. To proceed solely by the rules of reason may lead to rationalisation, but rarely to inventiveness. In fact, to invent one normally needs to imagine beyond the bounds of conventional rationality. It seems to me that for this task those who experience in their lives an eschatological dimension of the sense of time are better equipped than those who live within an enlightened utilitarian dimension which is certainly capable of generating scientific certification, but much less so scientific creation. This is perhaps the most significant contribution of Catholic social thinking to the overcoming of reductionism[19] so massively present in today's economic theorising – a reductionism which is a major impediment to innovation of economic ideas and to the enlargement of the scope of economic research. It is a fact – often ignored – that the early history of the discipline was characterised by the centrality, within economic discourse, of the happiness category. Political economy was essentially seen as the "science of happiness". It was only with the marginalist revolution of the second half of the 19th Century that the category of utility completely superseded that of happiness. Since then economics has, perhaps rightly, been referred to as the "dismal science".

University of Bologna   Stefano ZAMAGNI

---

19. See my *Economic Reductionism as a Hindrance to the Analysis of Structural Change*, forthcoming in *Structural Change and Economic Dynamics*.

LA RECHERCHE DU BIEN COMMUN
JALONS POUR UNE APPROCHE POST-UTILITARISTE

Dans les sociétés modernes, l'idée de Bien commun est à la fois subsumée et niée par la domination des finalités économiques. Il se pourrait toutefois que les conditions contemporaines du développement socio-économique confèrent une nouvelle pertinence à cette notion. Nous en sommes peut-être arrivés à un point ou le futur souhaitable de l'humanité demande à être plus explicitement nommé, imaginé et construit à la lumière d'une vision normative de la vocation de l'homme. Après avoir développé ce point, je présenterai dans une seconde partie quelques concepts, théories et outils d'analyse de la société qui peuvent être mis en relation avec cette nécessaire réouverture du débat sur l'orientation du développement de la société.

LE BIEN COMMUN RÉDUIT À LA RICHESSE ÉCONOMIQUE?

La notion traditionnelle de Bien commun incorpore l'idée d'un lien fort entre le bien-être, la justice et la moralité. Par exemple, dans *Rerum novarum*, on peut lire «ce qui fait une nation prospère, ce sont des moeurs pures, des familles fondées sur des bases d'ordre et de moralité, la pratique de la religion et le respect de la justice, une imposition modérée et une répartition équitable des charges publiques, le progrès de l'industrie et des affaires, une agriculture florissante, et d'autres éléments du même genre» (*RN* 26). À travers différentes formulations, on trouve l'affirmation constante que le bien-être et la moralité se renforcent mutuellement. D'où vient la conséquence suivante: si le Bien produit le Bien, l'intérêt général et la justice doivent être recherchés consciemment pour eux-mêmes. Ils ne peuvent être que la conséquence de décisions publiques et privées induites par des choix éthiques, en relation à une attitude globale de responsabilité sociale.

Cette vision traditionnelle est en évidente contradiction avec la domination de la rationalité économique dans les sociétés modernes. Pour être précis, le principe économique doit être envisagé dans ce contexte à travers deux idées différentes, le libéralisme et l'utilitarisme. Mais la «vulgate» économique est en fait une synthèse des deux. Son paradigme central est simple à formuler: le marché libre rend possible l'existence d'une société dans laquelle la maximisation du bien-être social est non seulement compatible avec l'égoïsme individuel, mais en est le résultat quasi-mécanique. De là procède un trait singulier de la société moderne. À travers l'histoire, toutes les sociétés ont été fondées sur la répression du désir, la subordination des aspirations individuelles aux finalités et valeurs de la société, voire même une certaine valorisation du sacrifice. Notre société de marché est fondée sur la négation de la distance maintenue par toutes les traditions entre les désirs individuels et le Bien commun. La croissance économique repose de plus en plus fortement sur la consommation privée, elle-même fondée sur l'activation du désir. Quand j'agis dans le but de satisfaire un quelconque désir de nature économique, j'agis également pour la croissance économique. On voit les gouvernements agir pour encourager les gens à acheter de nouvelles voitures, etc. On pourrait définir l'économie de marché moderne comme une tentative systématique et délibérée de construire un système dans lequel des comportements orientés vers l'accomplissement personnel conduisent presque automatiquement à un accroissement du bien-être collectif. Dans ce sens, le principe économique incorpore l'idée de Bien commun et, dans le même temps, la vide de son contenu éthique.

Bien entendu, on pourrait dire que l'importance donnée à la prospérité économique était déjà en germe dans le remplacement du Bien commun par l'intérêt général comme principe régulateur fondamental du Politique. D'où la question suivante: jusqu'à quel point ce changement est-il inhérent à la démocratie moderne? Ne constitue-t-il pas un développement logique du concept traditionnel de Bien commun, si l'on interprète celui-ci comme ce qui crée les meilleures conditions matérielles et sociales pour que chaque homme exerce sa liberté morale et poursuive les buts ultimes qu'il a librement choisi? Comme l'écrit Leon XIII dans *Rerum novarum,* citant Thomas d'Aquin: «Sans nul doute, Le Bien commun (…) est principalement un bien moral. Mais dans une société bien constituée, il doit se trouver encore une certaine abondance de bien matériels et extérieurs dont l'usage est requis à l'usage de la vertu» (*RN* 27). De manière significative, Leon XIII utilise souvent l'expression «Intérêt commun» comme un équivalent de Bien commun. En d'autres termes, la notion chrétienne du Bien commun (non aristotélicienne, de ce point de vue) incorpore paradoxalement un schéma individualiste et dualiste (relié de manière évidente au paradigme augustinien des deux cités) qui ouvre la voie au libéralisme économique. Dès lors que le sens de la liberté et de la responsabilité individuelle n'est plus contrebalancé par l'idée d'une nature et d'une vocation communes à tous les hommes, et que le salut spirituel tend à s'effacer derrière des biens plus tangibles, la route est libre pour le libéralisme.

Même si nous ne sommes pas des libéraux dogmatiques, nous devons admettre la pertinence pratique du paradigme classique de la pensée économique, pour autant, du moins, qu'il est question de prospérité économique. À long terme, les pauvres eux-mêmes ont tiré avantage de la croissance économique. Ce qui ne veut pas dire, bien sûr, que la régulation marchande est totalement autosuffisante. On peut rappeler ici un argument classique mais toujours pertinent contre le paradigme de la «main invisible»: il présuppose un certain niveau de confiance entre les individus. N'importe quelle sorte d'échange économique inclut un moment d'incertitude et d'insécurité concernant le fait que l'autre partenaire va respecter ses engagements et se comporter conformément aux règles de base de la coopération. L'expression «poignée de main invisible» utilisée par Johan Verstraeten est très appropriée de ce point de vue. Le rôle crucial de la confiance en économie a été modélisé dans le fameux «dilemme du prisonnier» qui reste à la base d'un argument fort contre autosuffisance du mécanisme marchand. Pour dire les choses brièvement, le dilemme du prisonnier montre clairement qu'aucun optimum collectif ne peut résulter de conduites purement égoïste. De fait, chacun peut constater que, même dans une économie de marché, la vie économique incorpore une dimension communautaire. Les entreprises, et plus généralement les organisations productives, reposent sur des éléments de coordination non économique.

La récurrence du terme «partenariat» reflète l'importance croissante dans la sphère économique de relations non marchandes et non-hiérarchiques, que l'on pourrait qualifier de relations hybrides, fondées sur la confiance mutuelle et la sympathie autant que sur l'intérêt mutuel. Bien que leur importance dans la vie sociale ne puisse être niée, les conduites désintéressées sont *de facto* dépréciées sous l'influence envahissante de l'argent. Les comportements individuels fondés sur une stricte rationalité économique ont tendance à être officiellement approuvés, voire même encouragés, à cause de leurs conséquences bénéfiques. Les principaux objectifs de la société – non seulement le bien-être matériel et ses corollaires directs (tels que le confort et la sécurité de vie, le progrès médical, le développement des communications) mais également le plein emploi, la réduction des inégalités et plus généralement le développement et la cohésion de la société, semblent dépendre complètement de la croissance économique. Conséquence, les dimensions non économiques de la vie sociale, et même l'éthique, sont de plus en plus nettement subordonnées à l'économie. Les ressources humaines et sociales, le savoir, les compétences, la capacité à coopérer, le bon fonctionnement de la justice et des autres institutions démocratiques, etc., sont parfois considérées comme des instruments, en même temps que comme des retombées automatiques du développement économiques. Le meilleur exemple est l'Union Européenne: le développement économique a été doublement promu comme la condition pratique et la finalité ultime de son dévelop-pement institutionnel et politique.

Peut-on dire que la richesse économique est la figure moderne du Bien commun? Elle en a, de fait, quelques-uns des attributs. Dans une société démocratique et pluraliste dans laquelle l'émancipation indivi-duelle est la valeur suprême, aucune autre finalité sociale (excepté peut-être le progrès médical) ne pourrait obtenir un tel consensus. La crois-sance du Produit National Brut est l'expression condensée de ce qui est universellement désirable, par-delà les choix personnels concernant les modes de vie, la culture ou l'éthique. Encore plus que pour ses retom-bées utilitaristes directes, la croissance est aujourd'hui désirée pour ses effets sociaux (à commencer par la baisse du chômage): on ne peut donc se contenter de stigmatiser la dérive matérialiste que révèle cet aplatisse-ment des espérances collectives. La croissance nous est devenue néces-saire en tant que «solvant politique»[1], mécanisme régulateur adapté à des sociétés dans lesquelles les individus sont supposés agir librement en en fonction de leur propre intérêt.

Contrairement à la vision traditionnelle du Bien commun, le bien com-mun économique n'a pas besoin d'être reconnu comme tel par un juge-ment explicite, d'ordre éthique ou politique. Il se présente simplement comme le moyen universel par lequel toutes les variétés de buts particu-liers peuvent être poursuivies (y compris, le cas échéant, les buts éthiques). Il n'est pas nécessaire de spécifier dans quel type de société nous voulons vivre: le marché est supposé fournir la réponse. Mais en disant cela on ne dit pas tout, car nos sociétés ont également besoin d'une représentation substantielle et unifiée du bien-être social (et l'on retrouve ici le côté utilitariste de l'idéologie économique). Les choix éco-nomiques doivent être légitimés du point de vue du bien-être global de la société, et ces choix sont discutés dans la sphère publique à travers un ensemble d'indicateurs agrégés (parmi lesquels le Produit National Brut ou PNB), qui prétendent fournir une mesure objective de la richesse sociale. Mais cette mesure incorpore un ensemble de conventions qui peuvent être déconstruites et critiquées. La religion du taux de croissance

---

1. D. BELL, *The Cultural Contradictions of Capitalism*, New York, NY, Basic Books, 1995, p. 238.

est d'ailleurs l'objet de critiques récurrentes, notamment parce qu'elle ne tient pas compte de la production domestique et de toutes les productions non monétaires. Au moins en France, la non-équivalence de la richesse économique et du bien-être social est un lieu commun du débat social.

De quels arguments nouveaux peut-on nourrir cette critique déjà ancienne de l'idéologie économique? La pointe de mon argumentation est que les limites d'une conception utilitaire et matérialiste du bien-être social apparaissent plus clairement dans les sociétés d'abondance. D'après la définition qu'en donne Antony Giddens, une société d'abondance (*post-scarcity society*) est une société dans laquelle les gens sont confrontés à un «ensemble de préoccupations plus larges que celles qui relèvent du productivisme»[2]. Pour le dire de manière différente, c'est une société où les aspects «qualitatifs» de la vie deviennent plus importants.

En parlant d'aspects qualitatifs, je pense notamment à toutes les questions culturelles, sociales, écologiques ou bioéthiques qui ne peuvent trouver de solution dans un accroissement de la production économique, ni même dans une répartition plus équitable des richesses. En suivant une fois encore Giddens, nous devons reconnaître l'importance croissante des «politiques du mode de vie» (*life politics*), à savoir «les politiques dont l'objet n'est pas de créer de nouvelles opportunités mais d'agir sur les styles de vie. Des politiques qui sont ancrées dans les débats et les conflits relatifs à la manière dont nous (en tant qu'individus et en tant que communauté humaine) devons vivre dans un monde où ce qui était fixé par la nature et la tradition est maintenant livré à la décision humaine»[3].

Il nous faut certes admettre qu'aucune tradition ou vérité définitive sur la nature humaine ne peut être acceptée sans examen. Toute discussion relative à la question «comment devons-nous vivre?» doit s'inscrire dans la libre confrontation des idées qui caractérise la démocratie. Il n'en demeure pas moins que cette interrogation renvoie à des questions auxquelles le marché (c'est à dire la résultante du libre choix des individus) et/ou la rationalité économique ne peuvent fournir de réponses. Elle appelle d'autres horizons normatifs. Parce qu'elle implique une capacité collective à porter des jugements sur la manière dont nous devons vivre, la notion de «politique du mode de vie» renvoie inévitablement à la question du Bien commun.

2. A. GIDDENS, *Beyond Left and Right*, Cambridge, Polity Press, 1994, p. 182.
3. *Ibid.*, p.15

QUELQUES PROBLÉMATIQUES CONTEMPORAINES
RELIÉES À LA NOTION DE BIEN COMMUN

En complément de ces considérations générales, je vais maintenant présenter quelques enjeux, théories et débats contemporains qui peuvent être mis en relation avec la question du Bien commun (même si l'expression elle-même est rarement utilisée).

Les économistes sont de plus en plus conscients que le PNB ne peut pas mesurer d'importants aspects du développement humain, tels que l'éducation, les inégalités, la violence sociale ou la dégradation de l'environnement naturel. Qui plus est, le taux de croissance est d'autant plus biaisé que les problèmes écologiques et sociaux deviennent plus préoccupants. De nombreux experts à travers le monde cherchent à mettre au point de nouveaux instruments d'analyse et de mesure du développement social. Un exemple très connu est le système des indicateurs publiés chaque année par le Programme des Nations Unies pour le Développement. L'indicateur de développement humain (*Human Development Index*, HDI) mesure les performances globales d'un pays selon trois dimensions fondamentales du développement humain: la longévité, le savoir et un niveau de vie décent. Ces performances sont mesurées par l'espérance de vie, le niveau d'éducation (l'alphabétisation des adultes et le taux de scolarisation) et le revenu ajusté. D'autres indicateurs sont publiés dans les rapports du PNUD, parmi lesquels l'indicateur d'égalité des sexes (*Gender-related Development Index* – GDI) qui mesure les inégalités entre les femmes et les hommes pour les mêmes critères, et différents indicateurs de pauvreté. Le classement des pays selon l'indicateur HDI fait apparaître des différences sensibles. Pour ne prendre qu'un exemple, la France est en seconde position après le Canada, et les Etats-Unis en quatrième position seulement.

Cette approche est innovante, mais ses limites sont évidentes. Le choix et la pondération des critères essentiellement qualitatifs sont hautement arbitraires (aucune théorie ne peut les justifier). En fait, l'amélioration des indicateurs de développement pourrait être vue comme une tentative pour éluder l'inconsistance foncière de toute représentation synthétique et objective du Bien commun. Le rapport du PNUD lui-même est parfaitement clair à ce propos: «les Rapports sur le développement humain qui ont publié depuis leur première édition en 1990 l'indicateur de développement humain (HDI) comme une mesure du développement humain reconnaissent toutefois que le concept de développement humain est beaucoup plus large le HDI. Il est impossible de se satisfaire d'une mesure synthétique, ni même d'un ensemble complet d'indicateurs, dans la mesure où de nombreuses dimension du développement humain sont non quantifiables (…). L'indicateur HDI ne doit pas se substituer à un traitement plus complet des diverses dimensions incluses dans la perspective du développement humain» (rapport du PNUD, 1998).

C'est bien sûr un progrès d'attirer l'attention sur des éléments tels que l'éducation, l'espérance de vie ou l'égalité des sexes, qui ont tendance à être occultés par les indicateurs économiques. Mais c'est une contradiction dans les termes que de prétendre agréger toutes ces dimensions dans un indicateur synthétique débordant le champ des indicateurs économiques, dans la mesure où la comparaison et l'agrégation d'objets et de réalités hétérogènes est précisément l'objet central de la représentation économique de la réalité sociale. Le seule manière de s'opposer au réductionnisme économique est au contraire de prendre son parti du pluralisme et de l'hétérogénéité des biens. On pourrait d'ailleurs allonger indéfiniment la liste des circonstances et éléments cruciaux pour la qualité de la vie quotidienne qui ne peuvent être évalués et valorisés de manière univoque. L'un des meilleurs exemples est le temps. La régulation des temps sociaux est une condition essentielle au développement équilibré de la vie sociale. Il est vital que soient préservés un certain nombre de repères temporels collectifs (à commencer par le repos dominical) et que soit maintenue la séparation nette des temps privés et professionnels. De même, le degré de maîtrise par chacun de son propre emploi du temps est une variable essentielle de la qualité de la vie. En dépit de leur importance, cela n'aurait aucun sens de quantifier et pondérer ces différents éléments du bien-être social pour les inclure dans un indicateur de «Bonheur National Brut».

Une autre limite de la représentation économique du bien-être provient du fait qu'elle ne prend pas en compte le caractère plus ou moins durable du développement de la société, du point de vue politique, sociétal et culturel. La notion de capital, même étendue à la notion de capital humain, fait référence aux conditions de base de la production économique future. Mais si nous considérons la société comme un système incluant la culture – comme une «civilisation» au sens habituel du terme, l'économie ne nous dit rien des conditions de sa pérennisation. Il est clair que les indicateurs économiques ne fournissent aucune information sur la «durabilitè» (*sustainability)* de la culture civique et de l'organisation sociale. Dans cette ligne de pensée, il est intéressant de s'appuyer sur la notion de «capital social» introduite par un certain nombre de sociologues américains. Selon Robert Putnam, «le capital social fait référence à des caractéristiques de l'organisation sociale telles

que les réseaux, les normes et la confiance sociale, qui facilitent la coordination et la coopération en vue d'un bénéfice mutuel». Les réseaux
d'engagement civique tels que les syndicats, les clubs et les partis politiques, toutes les sortes d'association, de réseaux informels de voisinage,
les clubs sportifs et les coopératives, sont des manifestations typiques du
capital social. Plus ces réseaux sont denses, et plus il est vraisemblable
que les membres d'une communauté coopèrent en vue d'un bénéfice
mutuel. Le capital social est important pour la vie économique parce que
les réseaux, les normes et la confiance facilitent la coopération, et il
n'est pas surprenant que les sociologues américains en donnent une
interprétation utilitariste. Mais le fait le plus important de mon point de
vue est que le capital social implique un élargissement de la perspective
patrimoniale à des aspects non économiques de la vie sociale. Nous
sommes responsables de la préservation et du développement d'un capital de confiance et de convivialité, de capacité collective à vivre en paix
et à agir ensemble de manière efficace.

La croissance capitaliste telle que nous la connaissons aujourd'hui
est-elle favorable au développement du capital social? De nombreuses
observations suggèrent que ce n'est pas le cas. À l'appui de la thèse du
déclin du capital social, Putnam utilise différents indicateurs d'engagement civique ou associatif, de bon voisinage ou de confiance sociale tels
que le taux d'adhésion à un syndicat, la pratique religieuse ou la participation électorale. Il remarque par exemple que «la proportion d'Américains répondant que l'on peut faire confiance à la plupart des gens a
chuté de plus d'un tiers entre 1960 et 1993, de 58% à 37%», et la plupart des indicateurs évoluent dans le même sens. Il est intéressant pour
notre propos d'examiner les raisons possibles du déclin du capital social
mentionnées par Putnam. Deux d'entre elles paraissent de nature à nourrir une argumentation classiquement conservatrice: «le développement
du travail féminin» et les transformations de la famille (divorce, etc.).
Un bref commentaire à ce sujet s'impose: il est certes plausible que
l'importance croissante du travail professionnel dans la vie des femmes,
mais aussi des hommes, réduit d'autant le temps et l'énergie disponible
pour contribuer à l'édification du capital social à travers l'engagement
associatif et la vie de famille, mais les enjeux de l'émancipation des
femmes par le travail salarié sont bien plus complexes. Par-delà son
impact économiques, le travail féminin est loin de n'avoir que des conséquences négatives pour la famille et la vie sociale.

Les deux autres facteurs mentionnés par Putnam renvoient à des retom-
bées importantes, quoique moins fréquemment mentionnées, des tendances économiques actuelles. Ce sont d'abord la mobilité géographique

(comme le dit Putnam, «la mobilité, comme le fait de changer une plante de pot, rompt les racines, et il faut du temps pour qu'un individu déraciné développe de nouvelles racines») et la transformation des loisirs sous l'effet des nouvelles technologies. De fait, chacun peut observer que les technologies de la communication (télévision, Internet, jeux video) incitent à la privatisation et à l'individualisation du loisir. Et qu'elles sont, de ce fait, préjudiciables aux formes de loisirs plus socialisées (fêtes, carnavals, spectacles vivants, réunions de famille) qui constituent autant de circonstances propices à la formation du capital social.

L'hypothèse d'un déclin général du capital social dans les pays industrialisés doit être prise en considération et discutée longuessement, ce que l'on ne peut faire dans le cadre de cette brève présentation. En tout état de cause, il est du plus grand intérêt pour notre propos d'observer: l'évidente affinité entre les notions de capital social et de bien commun; que la thématique du capital social met en avant le rôle de la confiance, ce qui a d'évidentes implications religieuses; et que les interprétations les plus vraisemblables du déclin du capital social soulignent les effets pervers de l'évolution actuelle du capitalisme, à travers des phénomènes tels que la mobilité professionnelle excessive et la marchandisation des loisirs.

Dans une approche plus philosophique, plusieurs auteurs ont récemment mis l'accent sur la diversité des besoins personnels et communautaires, la diversité des modes de vie et le rôle spécifique des diverses ressources de la vie sociale dans le bien-être individuel et collectif. Il est clair que l'on a là une importante ligne d'argument contre le réductionnisme économique. Dans son livre *Spheres of Justice*, le philosophe américain Michael Walzer défend une conception «pluraliste» de la justice sociale opposée à la conception individualiste et contractualiste de John Rawls. Pour Walzer, l'accès à différentes catégories de ressources sociales (santé, logement, éducation…) doit être organisée en se fondant sur une compréhension partagée de la nature de ces biens, et de leur rôle spécifique comme conditions et signes d'une appartenance sociale commune. Pour ne prendre qu'un exemple, un accès égal à la justice est une condition de la démocratie. Il en résulte que la justice ne peut pas être considérée comme un bien économique ordinaire. Quand l'argent a trop d'influence sur la sphère juridique, la justice est niée et la convivialité sociale est en danger. Des considérations similaires s'appliquent à la santé, l'éducation et le logement, de telle sorte que le bien-être social repose sur la mise en oeuvre des normes spécifiques de justice sociale, adaptées à ces différents domaines. L'importance de la pensée de Walzer réside dans sa démonstration convaincante de la nécessité de prendre en considération les aspects les plus spécifiques et les plus nobles de la nature humaine et des besoins humains dans la recherche du bien-être social.

De manière complémentaire, le récent prix Nobel d'économie Amartya Sen défend l'idée que les ressources économiques prennent sens et valeur dans le cadre de «fonctionnements» propres aux individus et aux communautés. L'influence de Sen est perceptible dans la définition du développement humain proposée par le PNUD, qui utilise le même terme «fonctionnements»: «Le développement humain est un processus d'élargissement des choix des gens. Élargir les possibilités de choix des gens peut être obtenu par le développement des capacités et fonctionnements humains». Pour le PNUD, comme pour Sen et Walzer, la véritable valeur des richesses économiques réside dans leur capacité à élargir la liberté de choix des gens, ce que signifie exactement le terme anglais *empowerment*. La notion de fonctionnement est cruciale parce qu'elle souligne le fait que le bien-être est fondamentalement une question de mode de vie, d'autonomie, de capacités, d'activité et de participation sociale, même si le revenu est de toute évidence important. La véritable valeur – la valeur «existentielle» pourrait-on dire – des biens économiques, n'est pas indépendante du contexte global de la vie humaine. Comme le dit le rapport du PNUD: «parmi les domaines essentiels d'exercice d'une liberté de choix, hautement valorisés par les gens, on peut ranger les opportunités d'accomplissement de créativité et de productivité dans les registres politique, économique et social, le respect de soi, l'autonomie et le sentiment d'appartenir à une communauté».

La richesse économique contribue à l'autonomie des individus, mais elle ne doit pas être déconnectée de toutes les autres ressources sociales (y compris les ressources éthiques) qui peuvent contribuer à rendre la vie bonne. «Bonne» voulant bien sûr dire ici heureuse, mais aussi et par dessus tout sensée et digne. En fin de compte, on en revient à une conception très proche de la conception chrétienne traditionnelle du Bien commun compris comme le développement sur un plan matériel et social de la liberté et de la dignité humaine.

Cours de Compte, Paris   Bernard PERRET

PRAXIS AND POLICIES

TROCAIRE: A CATHOLIC DEVELOPMENT AGENCY
WORKING TO SUPPORT COMMUNITIES
IN THEIR EFFORTS TO OVERCOME POVERTY AND OPPRESSION

One of the aims of this collection is to generate impetus for a retrieval
of the buried tradition of non-official Catholic social thought. Underlying
this aspiration is the realisation that Catholic social thought has, in recent
decades, been dominated by reflection on and analysis of the official
social teaching of the Church, often to the detriment of non-official thinking. Of course, the focus on official teaching is in many respects both
understandable and valuable. For example, it has enabled the papacy to
play a significant political role on the international scene, as a proponent
of social justice and human rights. Moreover, this role is all the more
notable given the relentless progress of global capital and the related need
to address many social and economic issues at a transnational, global
level. Nevertheless, even though it plays an increasingly important role at
the level of international politics, this official teaching is but one dimension of the Catholic Church's rich and diverse tradition of social thought.
    This collection then highlights the importance of nurturing contempo-
rary non-official streams of social thought. In order to do this, however,
it will be necessary to reflect on the nature of non-official Catholic
social thought in our times. One of the motivating factors in this is the
recognition that the shape of non-official Catholic social thought is
changing, in fact has changed quite significantly in the past three
decades. In his background paper, Jonathan Boswell drew our attention
to this precise issue[1]. In the paper he notes the demise of certain Catholic
social movements, particularly in Europe since the 1960's. He commented that in the 1940s and '50s a variety of Catholic social movements played an important role in the development of non-official
streams of social thought. Moreover they were, in certain cases, significant sources of innovative thinking and action in the social and political
realm. The contribution of Jean-Yves Calvez to this volume attests to
this exact point. Thus one might be tempted to interpret the demise of
such movements, which undoubtedly did contribute to the development
of Catholic social thought, as an indication of a general decline in the

---

1. J. BOSWELL, *Whose Ethics? Which Priorities? Catholic Social Thought in Transi-*
tion. Unpublished preparatory paper, Cambridge, April 1999.

non-official streams of social thought. However, I would suggest that
such an interpretation fails to recognise that there has been a radical
change in the nature and orientation of what one might call Catholic
social movements and a consequent change in the idiom and character of
much of the social thought that they generate.

Although there are undoubtedly elements of continuity, many of the
contemporary "movements" are significantly different in character from
earlier non-official streams of social thought and practice. One can discern these differences, for example, in relation to the advent and growth
of Catholic development agencies world-wide. These agencies, such as
the Catholic Fund for Overseas Development (CAFOD), the Catholic
Institute for International Relations (CIIR), Caritas Internationalis and
Trocaire (to mention just a few), have become important vehicles of
social change and social thought. Most are led by lay people, are international in orientation and scope, operate with similar opportunities and
constraints to the many non-religious NGO's, work with local partners
and engage in scholarly reflection on their *praxis*. Other Catholic social
justice groups that focus on particular issues such as HIV/AIDS, home-
lessness and poverty operate with similar structures and values. Many of
these groups challenge the radical distinction made in traditional social
thought, between values and policies, between fundamentals and mutables, or between principles and their application. Instead, they operate
with an inductive, *praxis*-based and context-sensitive approach that is
uncomfortable with traditional models in which these distinctions are
unambiguously drawn. In this paper I wish to focus on one such group[2]
and, in the process, comment on its contribution to the changing shape
and character of contemporary non-official social thought. Indeed, there
are many such Catholic social justice groups world-wide, each making a
significant contribution to the development of non-official social thought
and to the Church's re-interpretation of its social role.

THE ESTABLISHMENT OF TROCAIRE

In 1973, in response to the encyclical *Populorum progressio,* the Irish
hierarchy established an organisation called Trocaire. It was set up "to
express the concern of the Irish Church for the needs and problems of

---

2. My own involvement with Trocaire has been limited to contributions to its theological education work. In that context I published an essay on human rights in its *Christian Perspectives in Development Education,* series.

the developing countries and the issues of justice involved"[3]. The name comes from the Gaelic word for "mercy"; and the intention was that it would provide an official channel through which Irish Catholics, working in harmony with other churches and development organisations, would work for the development of peoples in "the third world". A crucial aspect of this work was expressed in the pastoral letter that launched the organisation and that gave it its mandate. The bishops (echoing *Populorum progressio*) insisted that one's duties to the people of developing counties "are no longer a matter of charity but of simple justice"[4]. They enhanced this point by maintaining that not only is it one's Christian duty as an individual to share one's wealth, but that "it is equally our Christian duty to demand that the political authorities representing us always act with justice and responsibility towards less fortunate countries and be prepared to use all means necessary for this end"[5].

In the context of the Irish Catholic Church at any rate, Trocaire's mandate was certainly an innovative one. The Irish Church had long prided itself on its missionary activity world-wide, yet Trocaire marked a significant departure in terms of its understanding of its own mission. It shaped its mandate in two directions. Abroad, it would use its resources to tackle the causes as well as the effects of underdevelopment in poorer countries. At home, it would work for a better understanding of the problems which face developing countries, in particular by educating people about the causes and extent of world poverty and injustice. Inevitably, this mandate is constantly being reshaped and reinterpreted in order to respond to the dynamics of global change. One way in which one can see its mandate develop is in the growing importance of advocacy work as an aspect of Trocaire's mission. This involves working to influence the political decision-making that affects developing countries at national and international levels. Trocaire's first foray into this complex international field was in 1976 in support of Vietnam, which had been devastated by the war which had been fought on its soil. Trocaire was one of the lead agencies that, through sustained political lobbying, successfully pressured the EC to restore food aid to Vietnam, aid that had earlier been cut under pressure from the US.

The practical effect of the dual focus of Trocaire's mandate can be seen in the manner in which its financial and other resources are distributed.

3. *Trocaire Its Role and Policy,* 1973.
4. BISHOPS OF IRELAND ON DEVELOPMENT, *Pastoral Letter of the Bishops of Ireland on the Establishment of Trocaire,* Dublin, The Irish Catholic Agency for World Development, 1973, # 18.
5. *Ibid.,* # 14.

From its inception the organisation has structured its spending so that 70% of its resources are allocated to development co-operation projects and programmes in the neediest areas of the world, 20% of its funds are committed to raising awareness of social justice issues at home and 10% of its resources are reserved for responding to emergency relief, when disasters occur[6]. The allocation of resources in this manner, implying as it does a commitment to justice rather than to charity, reveals a significant change in the Church's understanding of its social mandate. Its overwhelming focus on long-term development projects and on development education (90% of its resources) means that the organisation is concerned with long-term sustainable development rather than with the short-term management of systemic problems. This complex, multi-layered response to particular instances of crisis was already discernible in the first year of Trocaire's life. In 1973 seven countries of the Sahel region of Africa (Chad, Niger, Upper Volta, Mali, Senegal, Gambia and Mauritania) were ravaged by famine and drought. Trocaire responded first at the level of emergency measures (providing food-distribution, shelter etc.). At the same time, in an attempt to raise funds for its intervention, Trocaire began the first of its development education campaigns, centered on explaining the Sahel famine and drought crisis in the context of colonialism, poverty and structural problems.

The partnering of its fundraising and development education campaigns is significant because it reinforces Trocaire's message that each particular emergency or disaster has political and historical, as well as so called natural causes. In the case of the Sahel crisis, the success of the fundraising and education campaign enabled Trocaire to initiate some development projects, beginning with the provision of seeds, transport, water, irrigation and livestock, education and training. Already then, in its first year Trocaire had articulated the central component of its innovative response to "the third world". That is, it delivered a practical emergency response, together with a sophisticated education campaign, in the context of a longer term development strategy for the region.

TROCAIRE IN RWANDA

In 1997-1998 alone Trocaire spent over IR£ 14m on more than 500 projects in over 60 countries world-wide, in collaboration with hundreds

---

6. *On the Journey Towards a Just World. Trocaire at a 25 Year Landmark,* Dublin, Trocaire, 1998, p. 4.

of international, national and local partners. As a result it would be impossible in this short essay to attempt a discussion of its work in general. What I propose to do instead is to look at its current work in one particular country, Rwanda, in order to appreciate the focus and purpose of its presence in the region. From this it will be possible to gain an insight into Trocaire's own understanding of the nature and scope of Catholic social thought as well as the manner in which this is enacted in practice.

The genocide in 1994, with over 800,000 brutally killed, brought the long-standing conflict in Rwanda to international attention. In addition to violence and murder, there was the problem of the displacement of over 2 million people, both within Rwanda and in neighbouring Zaire, Tanzania and Burundi. The combination of a culture of genocide, the radical destruction of an already fragile civil society and massive poverty, had meant that simple aid programmes to Rwanda proved to be inadequate. Yet Trocaire's response to this uniquely challenging situation was extraordinarily innovative. Its strategy was to work with local partners and to enact radical programmes for civil reconstruction, but at the parish or micro-level. It eschewed large scale grand aid projects and instead invested in local initiatives that engage directly with the systemic failures and injustices as they are experienced by different communities. So instead of bringing large numbers of volunteers from abroad in order to "rebuild the country", Trocaire now works to help individuals and communities to become the agents of their own liberation. However, because of the intricate nature of the conflict, the task of enabling individuals and communities to overcome their heritage of violence and poverty has had to be undertaken at a number of different levels. Simple economic aid would not suffice.

As a result Trocaire's profile in Rwanda, and in other developing countries world-wide, is rather different from traditional church-related interventions. This can be seen most clearly in the initiatives it funds and the programmes it has generated. It supports legal aid programmes for genocide survivors and for those accused of genocide crimes. It is involved in monitoring the genocide trials in Rwanda and in training para-legal workers as part of the rehabilitation of the justice system. It also funds a public education programme on the justice system. Other initiatives are clustered around human rights programmes. Trocaire supports training for human rights activists and for women activists specifically to promote women's and children's rights. It also gives assistance to a rural women's organisation, supports small-scale projects in training, animation, rural development and agriculture inputs and maintains revolving loan schemes and a micro-credit fund to assist with income generation. One of these initiatives, for example, involves support for local production for weaning food for children.

Trocaire also works in partnership with other developing agencies and local partners. It gives institutional aid to enable Caritas to respond more effectively to emergencies, supports the Diocesan Development Office in Gikongoro and is involved in the rehabilitation of a vocational training centre in Nyamirambo, Kigali. In addition Trocaire, with co-financing from the Irish government, the EU and other partners, is involved in the comprehensive Rwanda Operational Programme. It includes health, education and agriculture initiatives in the Gikongoro Prefecture with housing programmes for returned refugees and genocide survivors. An extensive programme of primary school rehabilitation is also running and there is a trauma counselling programme aimed specifically at women[7].

CONTRIBUTION OF TROCAIRE

Since its inception Trocaire has continued to engage in a process of self-reflection, seeking always to reinterpret its mandate in light of changing global circumstances. It is not that it is constantly re-inventing itself, but rather that it seeks to respond to the challenges of each particular instance of social injustice. This is undoubtedly an ambitious aim, both in terms of articulating the values that might guide such interventions and in relation to their practical implementation. Trocaire describes its work in terms of supporting people and communities in their efforts to overcome poverty and oppression[8]. This highlights its belief that global poverty and deprivation are the result of systemic inequality in the distribution of resources and that poverty begets social and civil violence. It also emphasises Trocaire's commitment to the empowerment of individuals and communities through education and training. Trocaire is aware that the manner in which it engages with developing countries is itself significant and that the politics of aid provision can be deeply fraught. The receipt of aid can in fact be debilitating because it can create a culture of dependency in the recipient. Furthermore, it can generate an inappropriate sense of power and superiority in the donor. Trocaire is sensitive to such risks and attempts to construct its programmes, both

---

7. *Trocaire 25 Years Working for Justice. Annual Report 1997-1998 and Consolidated Financial Statements,* Dublin, 1998, p. 26.
    8. *Ibid.,* p. 2

abroad and at home, with such concerns in mind. Nevertheless, failures in understanding and in implementation mean that the work of Trocaire, like all development work, is inevitably compromised and incomplete.

How then would one characterise the nature of Trocaire's work and the principles that guide it? Fundamentally Trocaire is committed to creating a just world in which people are free to be the instruments of their own development. This means that it attempts to attend to the uniqueness of each particular instance of conflict. It heeds the local as well as the global system of inequality and attempts to generate tailor-made responses to each local instance of poverty and injustice. Its work with local partners and grass-roots organisations both reflects and instances this commitment. Trocaire endeavours to combine this attention to the particular with an analysis of the international political and economic order. It commissions substantial academic studies of key policy matters, encourages a high degree of specialisation in its policy analysis unit and takes very seriously developments in the social and human sciences. This can be seen especially in its educational work. Since 1985 Trocaire has produced an academic journal called *Development Review*. It also publishes a well respected series called *World Topics*, that includes titles like *Bread and Freedom: Basic Human Needs and Human Rights, Poverty Amid Plenty: World and Irish Development Reconsidered* and *Third World Debt: Towards an Equitable Solution*. Recently it has commissioned another series called *Christian Perspectives on Development Education,* which includes studies on land, famine and human rights. In all of this Trocaire works in an interdisciplinary manner, drawing expertise from a diverse fund of knowledge and making strategic alliances with other NGO's, with national governments and with international bodies. Its language is that of justice, human rights and sustainable development and its guiding vision is Christian.

The short-time span of Trocaire's work means that any attempt to evaluate its significance is premature. In many respects its work to date has been impressive. Yet inevitably mistakes are likely to have been made. Interventions that at a particular stage seemed admirable may later appear to be dubious. For example, we may recognise with hindsight that strategies which were effective in reducing poverty may have undermined traditional support networks. Moreover, we may come to realise that in certain contexts the mere presence of external agencies is itself problematic. Development work is notoriously complex. It is often not evident whether or how best to intervene in situations of civil conflict. Nor is it clear whether the work of development agencies merely disguises the inequalities of the global economy, enabling developed countries to salve our consciences while maintaining unequal relations with LDC's.

The ethical, policy-related and practical problems that accompany the work of development agencies like Trocaire should form part of any evaluation of their effectiveness and importance. There is no doubt that Catholic social thought and *praxis* has gained significantly in terms of context-sensitive development strategies, personal commitment and professionalism. Yet there have also been losses. Inevitably, this kind of social engagement does have its limitations. For instance, occasionally the distinctiveness of their message and work can be lost amid the multiplicity of voices on the international stage. In addition, the kind of organised mass participation that characterised earlier social movements is not evident in this arena. So for many people social involvement may amount to no more than occasional financial contributions. There may now be more awareness of social injustice world-wide, yet for many people the commitment to working towards its elimination can be at a significant remove.

It is difficult to compare the work of Trocaire and other such agencies with earlier social movements like the Catholic Workers. In truth they are very different. The political character of Catholicism world-wide has changed in the last century and this has had a significant effect on the nature of its social involvement. Developments in social ethics and political theology have also had an impact on the character of the Church's understanding of its social role. One of the results of these and other changes has been the emergence of Catholic development agencies, of which Trocaire is one. Although each has its distinctive character and profile, many of these development agencies share a commitment to the principles already discussed here. However, although they are numerous and have an impact on the *praxis* of development world-wide, their significance as stimulators of Catholic social thought is as yet underestimated. In attempting to understand the nature of Catholic social thought at the beginning of this new century we will need to give attention to this important constituency. This is all the more necessary since it is a constituency that strives to be an exemplar of the message of Christian social justice.

Department of Theology and Religious Studies   Linda HOGAN
University of Leeds

QUELLE IDENTITÉ ET QUELLE MISSION
POUR LES INSTITUTIONS SANITAIRES ET
SOCIALES CATHOLIQUES?
UN ENJEU POUR LA VITALITÉ DE LA PENSÉE SOCIALE
DE L'ÉGLISE

INTRODUCTION

Les institutions sanitaires et sociales catholiques, qui ont été fondées par des ordres religieux (surtout des congrégations féminines) s'interrogent aujourd'hui sur le sens de leur mission et la signification de leur identité propre. Ce questionnement provient de raisons conjoncturelles, mais il est aussi suscité par des raisons de fond qui sont en relation directe avec la recherche en cours d'un renouvellement de la pensée sociale catholique.

À l'heure actuelle, parmi les quelques 700 établissements sanitaires et sociaux (hôpitaux, cliniques, maisons de convalescence, centres de soins infirmiers, maisons de retraite, maisons d'enfants handicapés, instituts médico-pédagogiques, foyers de jeunes, foyers de sans-abri, etc.), sous la responsabilité des congrégations religieuses féminines, en France, beaucoup s'interrogent sur leur avenir. Le nombre de ces établissements, qui reste considérable, a cependant beaucoup décru ces dernières années. Ce qui suscite des inquiétudes. La diminution des effectifs religieux, l'arrivée de directeurs et de cadres laïques, la pression financière, le renouvellement technique, la sécularisation de ces services et la forme de laïcité propre à la France... posent aujourd'hui la question de la nécessité, de l'identité et de la mission de ces établissements dans les prochaines années. Faut-il que l'Église et les chrétiens s'intéressent à ces établissements et cherchent à y maintenir une identité propre? Si oui, pourquoi et dans quels domaines? Si oui encore, comment transmettre à d'autres et faire perdurer le charisme de la congrégation qui a fondé ces institutions, ou du moins faire vivre l'esprit évangélique qui les a inspirées? Même si à la suite du Concile Vatican II, un débat analogue a eu lieu dans les années 60 sur la confessionnalité des écoles, des syndicats, et des institutions en général, les conditions de la réflexion actuelle sont très sensiblement différentes.

Comme on le voit, ces interrogations posent de manière très concrète la question d'une présence chrétienne institutionnelle dans une société pluraliste sécularisée. Elles obligent aussi indirectement à réfléchir non seulement à l'impact de l'Enseignement Social de l'Église (ESE) (option pour les pauvres, respect de la dignité de la personne dans toutes ses dimensions, y compris spirituelle, droit à la participation sociale de tous…) mais aussi à sa mise en pratique sous forme institutionnalisée. Elles invitent également à mettre en lumière une pensée sociale propre vécue au jour le jour dans ces institutions mais peu souvent formalisée comme telle.

Ma contribution est en partie le fruit d'une recherche en cours, réalisée à la demande de la Conférence des supérieures majeures féminines. Son objet est à la fois méthodologique et empirique. Il s'agit d'un document d'étape, qui n'a pas la prétention de faire le tour d'une question à la fois complexe et jusqu'à présent peu travaillée.

LA NOTION D'IDENTITÉ CHRÉTIENNE D'UNE INSTITUTION, SA PERTINENCE POUR L'ESE

Si l'on considère à la suite de John Rawls que la société est un système de distribution et que les institutions sont des règles de distributions sociales des rôles, des biens et des charges, des obligations et des droits, ces institutions occupent une place privilégiée dans le fonctionnement social. Elle acquièrent aussi une pertinence particulière dans le cadre de notre réflexion sur le renouvellement de l'ESE. Comme règles de distribution, les institutions sont en effet des médiateurs entre l'individu et la société, sans que l'un prenne le dessus sur l'autre. À la fois l'institution est davantage et autre chose que la somme des individus qui la composent et en même elle n'existe que par la participation active de ses membres. Ce statut particulier est donc particulièrement adapté à une pensée sociale qui évite de tomber dans des oppositions trop rigides entre un sociologisme ou un collectivisme à la Durkheim d'une part et un individualisme méthodologique à la Max Weber d'autre part. Enfin, les institutions telles que les hôpitaux, les maisons de retraite ou les maisons d'enfants en difficulté, participent du développement de ces «corps intermédiaires» dont l'ESE s'est tellement faite le champion. Je m'étonne donc que l'ESE officiel s'intéresse finalement si peu à ce niveau intermédiaire de réalité sociale, du moins dans l'époque actuelle.

En fin de compte se pose la question de ce que signifie dans le contexte contemporain l'institutionnalisation d'un charisme, ou pour le dire d'une autre manière, la mise sous forme visible et socialement stable d'une inspiration religieuse.

Le contexte pluraliste et sécularisé de nos sociétés interroge l'existence et la pertinence des institutions catholiques sanitaires et sociales. Le paradoxe d'une telle présence institutionnelle est qu'elle doit toujours chercher un chemin de crête entre l'affichage d'une spécificité et la recherche d'une pertinence sociale, entre une vision plus «sectaire» ou «communautariste» du christianisme et une vision plus sécularisée se coulant davantage dans les valeurs de la société. Si l'on se place dans une perspective d'ouverture au monde et de service rendu à la société tout entière, où donc faut-il chercher la particularité des institutions d'inspiration chrétienne? Quel est le lieu (quel sont les lieux) de leur originalité?

L'enquête réalisée en 1995 par le service santé-social de la Conference des superieures majeures (CSM – congregations feminines) sur l'identité catholique des établissements sanitaires et sociaux congréganistes a permis l'analyse des réponses de 190 établissements (soit environ 20% du total des établissements recensés en 1994). La dernière question demandait explicitement de discerner dans la vie de l'établissement où et en quoi pouvait-on retrouver les conditions d'un témoignage de foi, de quoi en somme était fait cette identité?

Des réponses très variées avaient été donné. Pour plus de détail je vous renvoie à l'analyse que j'ai faite et qui a été publiée par la CSM[1]. Certaines réponses mettaient en évidence et parfois de manière exclusive, le témoignage qui provient de la présence des religieuses et d'une communauté au sein de l'établissement. Dans le même sens, certains questionnaires insistaient sur la présence d'une chapelle, la célébration des messes, la présence d'un aumônier, ou encore sur l'existence de signes repérables comme le nom de l'établissement, ou la statue de St Joseph à l'accueil… Dans cette perspective, la disparition de la communauté religieuse est souvent ressentie comme la mort du caractère propre.

D'autres réponses mettaient davantage en avant (ou rajoutent aux réponses précédentes) l'existence d'une manière de faire propre à l'établissement, sans que celle-ci soit nécessairement liée à la présence des religieuses. On parle alors d'un «esprit», d'une «ambiance», d'une «atmosphère» particulière de la maison qui témoignent de valeurs telles que l'écoute, l'accueil chaleureux, le respect, la tolérance, le climat paisible, le souci des pauvres, etc. Cette manière d'agir si elle n'est pas spécifiquement chrétienne s'enracine dans des valeurs évangéliques

---

1. A. THOMASSET, *Identité catholique des établissements sanitaires et sociaux congréganistes. Analyse de l'enquête CSM (service santé-social) novembre 1995*, CSM, avril 1997, 60 pp.

reconnues et elle trouve à se concrétiser dans les moyens mis en place au quotidien pour le souci des personnes, la qualité de soins, l'atmosphère relationnelle.

D'autres réponses enfin ne se contentent pas de faire le constat d'un climat ou d'une histoire particulière de l'établissement mais cherchent à réfléchir aux conditions de son renouvellement et de son dynamisme. Ce sont des réponses qui manifestent davantage le souci de l'avenir, en s'interrogeant sur la participation de l'ensemble du personnel. Ces réponses insistent entre autres sur la manière dont le personnel travaille, sur la qualité du travail d'équipe, sur le fait qu'il s'agit d'une communauté soignante en cercles concentriques, sur la justice pour le personnel et les résidents. Elles relèvent l'importance d'un partenariat avec les personnels dans l'élaboration du projet d'établissement (The Religious Rule of the particular Congregation or Order), dans l'explicitation des valeurs communes vécues, dans la formation et la réflexion sur l'histoire, le charisme des institutions. Elle soulignent aussi la nécessité de lieux de réflexion éthique, de la confrontation à l'enseignement chrétien, de l'échange en réseau avec d'autres institutions du même type, etc.

La recherche en cours sur le caractère chrétien des ces institutions peut ainsi devenir un lieu privilégié d'observation sur le type de spécificité qu'induit la pensée de l'Église dans le fonctionnement social. Si la vie chrétienne induit une manière de faire propre et institue en quelque sorte un lien social spécifique, ces institutions sont de véritables laboratoires de la pensée sociale de l'Église. En même temps, on voit que le développement de cette nouvelle pensée sociale est lié à des questions d'ordre ecclésiologique qui touchent par exemple, à la collaboration entre clercs et laïcs, et aux différents visages de l'Église dans son fonctionnement concret.

QUELQUES RÉSULTATS D'UNE ENQUÊTE DE 1995
RÉALISÉE AUPRÈS DE 190 ÉTABLISSEMENTS

Au cours de celle-ci sont apparues trois types d'institutions qui varient en grande partie selon le degré de participation des laïcs et des membres du personnel dans la définition du projet de l'établissement. J'ai cherché à voir à quel degré sont présentes les conditions de la constitution d'un esprit commun fidèle aux origines de l'établissement et qui puissent être partagé avec les laïcs (voire légué à ceux-ci) et si possible avec l'ensemble du personnel. Les trois modèles correspondent donc à des phases supposées d'évolution dans le temps d'une institution qui doit se préoccuper de plus en plus de transmettre et de vivifier son «esprit» et ses manières de faire, toutes choses qu'on peut supposer enracinées dans la tradition chrétienne et une pensée sociale spécifique.

Pour déterminer les trois modèles-types, les données suivantes ont été considérées comme pertinentes, sans qu'aucune d'entre elles ne soit ni nécessaire ni suffisante pour classer un établissement dans un type donné. Ces éléments servent donc de critères:

la structure de la direction (laïque ou non);

l'existence ou non d'une association de gestion;

l'existence ou non d'un projet d'établissement;

le degré de collaboration des différents personnels à l'élaboration de ce projet;

l'existence ou non d'un réseau d'établissements ayant une réflexion régulière sur la charte, les valeurs communes;

les critères d'embauche du directeur et ses liens avec la congrégation;

la présence ou non d'un groupe de bénévoles organisés;

la place de l'aumônerie au sein de l'établissement;

les liens plus ou moins large avec l'Église locale;

les critères d'embauche et de formation du personnel;

la nature des réponses donnée à la question sur le discernement de l'identité catholique.

Une classification des établissements dans l'un ou l'autre modèle a été faite de manière intuitive, à la suite de l'analyse et de la lecture de l'ensemble du questionnaire de chaque établissement. Cette classification garde un caractère d'arbitraire mais une vérification a pu en partie être donnée en regardant la cohérence de chaque groupe par rapport aux critères précédents (voir tableaux joints en annexe).

Puisque les trois modèles s'inscrivent dans une évolution, le premier modèle correspond à une situation quasi-inchangée du point de vue du partenariat avec les laïcs, le deuxième à une situation de mutation et le troisième à une situation de partenariat vivant assurant semble-t-il les conditions les meilleures pour la pérennité du charisme fondateur même en l'absence de la congrégation. Les modèles progressent dans le sens d'une plus grande collaboration avec les laïcs et d'une plus grande ouverture vers l'extérieur, en particulier l'Église locale diocésaine et les autres établissements du même type.

Le tableau 3 et le graphique qui l'accompagne donnent une indication par modèle-type de la réalisation de plusieurs critères (type de direction, mode de gestion, existence d'un projet d'établissement, élaboration du projet d'établissement en collaboration, présence de bénévoles, existence de réseaux d'établissements).

Ces indications chiffrées ne représentent pas, à proprement parler, une démonstration de la validité des modèles puisque chaque questionnaire a été évalué en fonction d'un ensemble de critères, dont ceux qui sont indiqués dans ce tableau. Mais ce qui est plus remarquable, c'est la vérification d'une progression simultanée pour l'ensemble des critères. En d'autres termes, tous les critères indiquant une plus forte participation des laïcs augmentent ensemble. Ce résultat qui était loin d'être acquis d'avance (même avec l'évaluation synthétique qui a été pratiquée) donne ainsi une indication de la cohérence des modèles et de la pertinence des critères retenus.

Par ailleurs, dans l'ensemble les critères sont nettement discriminants. Ils marquent des différences nettes entre les modèles. Certains critères semblent plus pertinents que d'autres car les pourcentages correspondant pour chaque modèle y sont plus éloignés les uns des autres. Ainsi la présence d'un projet d'établissement (respectivement 19%, 39% et 87%) et le fait que ce projet a été élaboré ou est en train d'être élaboré avec la participation des personnels (4%, 39%, 73%) sont deux critères fortement significatifs. Ces résultats semblent confirmer que la dynamique créée autour de la rédaction d'un projet ou de son actualisation est un facteur important d'évolution des établissements. Or, au moment de l'enquête, la rédaction d'un projet d'établissement, pourtant obligatoire depuis quelques années, n'était pas accompli dans la majorité des cas (41% avaient un projet, 21% étaient en cours).

Un autre critère fortement significatif correspond à la présence ou non d'un réseau d'établissements de la même congrégation ou de la même famille spirituelle (respectivement 4%, 16%, 40%). Ceci est cohérent avec le résultat trouvé au sujet des projets d'établissement car la présence d'un réseau renforce la dynamique de participation et de réflexion au sujet des valeurs fondamentales de l'établissement et de leur mise en œuvre.

Enfin il faut signaler que les premiers résultats d'une nouvelle enquête réalisée en mai 1999 auprès des directeurs laïques de ces établissements confirment largement l'analyse précédente.

POUR UNE FÉCONDATION RÉCIPROQUE DES INSTITUTIONS CATHOLIQUES ET DE LA PENSÉE SOCIALE DE L'ÉGLISE

La recherche en cours sur l'identité et la pertinence des institutions sanitaires et sociales catholiques pose aussi la question de la pertinence et de la spécificité de l'enseignement social de l'Église, qu'il soit officiel ou non.

Au vu des résultats déjà acquis, on peut faire l'hypothèse que l'Enseignement Social de l'Église, et plus largement la vision sociale conditionnée par les symboles, les récits, évangéliques et ecclésiaux, sont «une force d'inspiration spécifique et de créativité au cœur de nos sociétés». Les institutions chrétiennes du secteur sanitaire et social sont comme des microcosmes de ce qui se joue au niveau de la société dans son ensemble, car en leur sein toutes les tensions d'une société pluraliste et sécularisée y apparaissent. On peut s'interroger, par exemple, sur la possibilité de réaliser entre les différents acteurs de ces institutions un «consensus par recoupement» sur des valeurs fondamentales qui inspirent la culture de l'établissement (dignité de la personne humaine, souci des pauvres, qualité des services...), sachant que la tradition chrétienne alimente de l'intérieur ces valeurs d'une manière spécifique. Ce «consensus par recoupement» (inspiré de la manière dont l'imagine Rawls) peut par exemple servir de modèle à la construction d'un «projet d'établissement», puisque des personnes de diverses traditions y sont présentes et y travaillent. On a vu par ailleurs, que l'élaboration d'un projet d'établissement avec la participation de l'ensemble du personnel est sans doute l'un des meilleurs moyens de construire et vivifier un esprit commun à l'intérieur d'une institution. Ce modèle de consensus suppose qu'il soit possible de se mettre d'accord sur ces points fondamentaux, même si chacun légitime cet accord pour des raisons différentes.

Mais ce consensus ne sera vivant que si des «traditions et des convictions vivantes» viennent l'alimenter (ce serait ici une différence avec la pensée de Rawls qui suppose un certain abandon des convictions dans l'élaboration du consensus). Le caractère propre d'un établissement pourrait donc se matérialiser par les structures qui cherchent à maintenir vivante dans son sein la tradition chrétienne et/ou le charisme propre de la congrégation. On peut penser à des instances de formation des cadres, de concertation, de célébration, de liens privilégiés avec l'Église locale, etc. L'existence de réseaux inter-établissements propres à une famille spirituelle, par exemple, va dans ce sens. Par ailleurs, dans certains cas, il existe déjà des structures régionales associatives qui permettent aux collaborateurs de ces établissements de vivre une expérience personnelle de renouvellement spirituel et de formation à une spiritualité propre.

Pour expliciter un peu plus cette modalité d'inspiration propre, on peut évoquer en particulier la manière dont l'appropriation des textes bibliques (ou hagiographiques) influence profondément les attitudes sociales des chrétiens. C'est ce que j'appelle, en reprenant la pensée de Paul Ricœur, une «poétique de l'existence» qui touche à la fois au rapport au temps, au rapport à l'autre, au rapport au monde et à soi-même[2]. Pour ne prendre qu'un exemple, le Sermon sur la Montagne dans l'Evangile de Matthieu ou son équivalent dans Luc, par son insistance sur les dons reçus par le croyant, par la vision de Dieu comme Père, oriente l'imagination du lien social non pas comme un intérêt réciproque mais dans le sens d'une générosité orientée vers l'autre. Une recherche pourrait être menée sur le type de récits véhiculé dans une institution donnée (récits historiques, récits biographiques, récits bibliques, autres…), sur leur impact, leur usage, et leur possible manipulation.

Enfin, ces institutions chrétiennes peuvent aussi jouer un rôle innovant, voire «prophétique», non négligeable (par exemple pour les soins palliatifs, pour la prise en charge des besoins spirituels des personnes, quelle que soit leur religion, pour la prise en charge des nouveaux besoins sociaux, dans le souci des plus pauvres, etc.). Peut-être faut-il insister sur un de ces points: s'il paraît souhaitable que les institutions de santé ou à caractère social s'émancipent d'une certaine «cléricalisation» et bénéficient d'une ouverture qui fassent d'elles une participation au service public avec des responsables laïcs, il serait en revanche désastreux que cette déconfessionnalisation aille jusqu'à une déspiritualisation des soins ou des services d'ordre social ou éducatif. Ignorer la vie spirituelle (dans ses formes variées d'expression) serait ignorer une dimension essentielle de la personne humaine. Ce serait notamment méconnaître «les images, les récits et les symboles par lesquels les êtres humains tentent de reconnaître leur dignité véritable», ou encore ignorer «ce qui dépasse l'humain dans l'humain», ce qui ouvre l'humain à la dimension transcendante de son existence.

Dans une société sécularisée et pluraliste, voilà un enjeu important où les institutions d'inspiration chrétienne peuvent montrer leur originalité et en même temps se mettre au service de tous, en montrant la voie. En intégrant la dimension spirituelle de l'existence aux services rendus à des personnes en difficultés, malades, handicapées ou en fin de vie, ces institutions répondent à une demande spirituelle réelle et me semble-t-il croissante qui est de ne pas réduire la vie à son expression physique ou matérielle, au bon fonctionnement des corps ou des intelligences. Cette spécificité des institutions d'inspiration chrétienne peut se transformer alors, en un témoignage prophétique, voire en un combat pour l'humanisation elle-même. Elle peut interroger la sécularisation de l'intérieur

2. Voir A. THOMASSET, *Paul Ricœur. Une poétique de la morale: aux fondements d'une éthique herméneutique et narrative dans une perspective chrétienne* (BETL, 124), Leuven, University Press, 1996 et aussi la contribution de J. Verstraeten, *supra*, pp. 39-50.

d'elle-même, sans animosité, ni esprit de revanche et signifier à l'ensemble de la société l'importance de la prise en compte réelle et intégrée de cette dimension de l'existence. Peut-être dans 20 ans tout organisme de soins de santé ou de service social aura-t-il dans son cahier des charges la prise en compte de l'expression de la vie spirituelle, dans sa diversité. Dans ce cas, les institutions catholiques, si elles sont fidèles à leur charisme, auront été des précurseurs. Comme bien d'autres exemples historiques le montrent, l'identité chrétienne de ces institutions aura ainsi consisté à mettre en lumière une exigence qui doit finalement s'imposer à tous et devenir un bien commun. Par son expérience propre, la vie chrétienne ne cesse d'approfondir les implications sociales du respect de toute humanité.

CONCLUSION

Le contexte présent et la réflexion qui vient d'être menée invitent à chercher un renouvellement de la pensée sociale catholique dans deux directions, à la fois théorique et empirique. Une analyse socio-culturelle du fonctionnement des institutions catholiques devrait permettre de mettre en lumière une pensée sociale propre qui est déjà implicitement à l'œuvre de la part des chrétiens, sans toujours pouvoir s'exprimer ou se formaliser sous la forme d'une doctrine. Sans doute avons-nous beaucoup à apprendre dans ce domaine. Par ailleurs une recherche plus approfondie sur les éléments imaginatifs et symboliques de la tradition chrétienne, en particulier de l'enseignement social de l'Église, officiel ou non, nous permettrait de mieux cerner sa spécificité par rapport aux visions du monde et de la société véhiculées par les courants contemporains. Il y a donc un aller et retour à mettre en œuvre entre pensée sociale et pratique sociale au sein de ces institutions.

ANNEXE

Tableau 1

	Questionnaire 95	Recensement 94	pourcentage 95/94
Secteur sanitaire	57 (dont 9 regroupés) +1 CSI	161 + 196 CSI	35% (hors CSI) ou 16%
Personnes âgées	91	510	18%
Secteur social	39 (dont 11 regroupés)	303	13%
Total	**188**	**974 + 196 CSI**	**19% (hors CSI) ou 16%**

Tableau 2

	Sanitaire	Personnes âgées	Social	Total
Modèle congréganiste (1)	7	18	1	26 (24%)
Modèle de mutation (2)	21	33	13	67 (61%)
Modèle de partenariat (3)	7	8	1	16 (15%)
Total	**35 (32%)**	**59 (54%)**	**15 (14%)**	**109**

Tableau 3

		Modèle 1	Modèle 2	Modèle 3	Total
Type de direction	Laïque	9 (35%)	41 (61%)	14 (93%)	64
	Religieuse	16	23	1	40
	La. +Rel.	1	3	-	4
Gestion	Association	14 (54%)	57 (85%)	13 (87%)	84
	Congrégation	12	10	2	24
Projet d'établissement	oui	5 (19%)	26 (39%)	13 (87%)	44
	en cours	5	15	3	23
	élaboré avec le personnel	1 (4%)	26 (39%)	11 (73%)	38
Bénévoles	oui	9 (35%)	33 (49%)	10 (67%)	52
Réseau	oui	1 (4%)	11 (16%)	6 (40%)	18

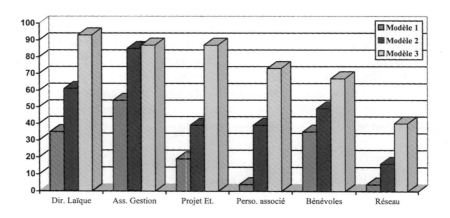

Enquête CSM novembre 1995. Analyse A. Thomasset, CERAS.

CERAS, Paris   Alain THOMASSET, S.J.

GLOBAL MARKETS AND GLOBAL JUSTICE?
CATHOLIC SOCIAL TEACHING AND FINANCE ETHICS

I. WHAT IS MISSING IN CATHOLIC SOCIAL TEACHING WITH REGARD TO FINANCIAL ETHICS?

The tradition of Catholic social teaching (CST) is, of course, older than the series of social encyclicals starting with *Rerum novarum* (1891), and it includes a broader spectrum of authors than the popes: episcopal conferences, justice and peace commissions, theologians and lay movements. Nevertheless, if we browse through *Rerum novarum* and its subsequent tradition, including some non-papal church documents on economic issues, as a possible source for a finance ethics, the results look rather meagre. We will find a number of relevant references with regard to the functioning of financial markets and institutions[1], but no systematic treatment of money, savings and investment, banking and financial markets. Why is such reflection missing, whereas the development of the financial sphere has been such an important factor in the emergence of modern economies? Why has CST been focusing on workers' rights, on property and ownership, on markets and enterprises, on the economic role of the state, on the ideological conflicts between liberalism and socialism, capitalism and Communism, on the just international order, on debt and development, while avoiding the crucial issue of money and capital markets? I see three (internally related) reasons for this defect: the pursuit of profit is viewed with deep suspicion; capital is not seen as an economic production factor in its own right; and the role of the financial sector is reduced to its distributive effects in goods and services markets.

1. *The Pursuit of Profit is viewed with Deep Suspicion*

Biblical ethics, both in the Old and New Testament, quite often treats issues of money. This discussion occurs, of course, in the context of a pre-modern economy, focused on land and bonded labour, on limited

---

1. I refer to *RN*, 35-36; *QA*, 50, 105-106, 109, 136, 143; *MM*, 104, 113, 134; *GS*, 70; *PP*, 24; *LE*, 12-13; *SRS*, 37; *CA*, 35, 43, 58. One should also include the Pastoral Letter of the NATIONAL CONFERENCE OF CATHOLIC BISHOPS, *Economic Justice for All* (United States Catholic Conference Publications, 101), Washington, DC, United States Catholic Conference, 1986, nrs. 110-118, 277, 298-306, and the document of the Pontifical Council *Justitia et Pax* on international debt (1986).

goods, and on collective ownership by families and tribes. The biblical evaluation of financial transactions is quite complex, stressing both the danger of money (i.e. of becoming an absolute value in itself, allowing for limitless accumulation of wealth) and the possibility of its fair use (i.e. of responsible stewardship, fair investment and exchange). This comprehensive vision can be retraced in the legal codes of Exodus, Leviticus and Deuteronomy (e.g. the sabbath, the sabbath year, the year of Jubilee), in prophetic literature as well as Wisdom texts.

In subsequent periods, however, during the scholastic debates of the late Middle Ages and the Modern era, Christian finance ethics became overly focused on the issue of usury. Because of a defective hermeneutics of biblical norms (and of Aristotle, and of natural law), Catholic moral theologians fought a losing battle by opposing the taking of interest for loans far into the modern era. This rearguard action on usury (which one could compare to contemporary casuistry in Islamic banking) did undoubtedly hinder the timely development of a systematic ethical appraisal of modern finance, including the role of profit. Of course, the authors of the encyclicals are right to oppose easy gain and useful investment, rejecting the former and praising the latter. But an exclusive focus on the redistribution of wealth may have led to a systematic neglect of the meaning of profit, both as an incentive and a just reward for the effective producers of wealth, and as an additional means of future production (increasing the capacity for autonomous capital investment, indicator of efficiency, source of savings, capital reserve against future risks...)[2].

2. *Capital is not seen as an Economic Factor in Its Own Right*

This limited and late recognition of the role of interest and profit is related to a larger blind spot in CST, namely its resistance to correctly estimate the role of capital (both in the sense of the pool of present savings for investment, and in the narrower meaning of available currency and monetary policy) as a specific production factor in the economic process.

---

2. A rare exception is the balanced statement on profit one finds in *QA*, 36: "Those who are engaged in producing goods, therefore, are not forbidden to increase their fortune in a just and lawful manner; for it is only fair that he who renders service to the community and makes it richer would also, through the increased wealth of the community, be made richer himself according to his position, provided that all these things be sought with due respect for a the laws of God, in accordance with faith and right reason. If these principles are observed by everyone, everywhere and always, not only the production and acquisition of wealth, but also the use of wealth, which now is seen so often to be contrary to the right order, will be brought back soon within the bounds of equity and just distribution."

Often, when the term "capital" is used, the meaning of this concept is limited to the collection of tools and machines that are needed for industrial production (e.g. *CA* 32). When discussing the factors of production, the Church's official documents will first of all refer to natural resources (land) and to human labour, secondly to industrial technology (the machine park as "capital") and, more recently, also to scientific knowledge and information. The role of capital investment in the production process, however, is only treated summarily, if mentioned at all. There is no systematic analysis of money, and of its distinctive functions as a store of value, a unit of account or a means of exchange. Also, there is no reflection on the meaning of systematically postponing present consumption by saving and investing in future goods, nor on the meaning of redistribution of risks and opportunities between different agents and time periods (generations) by the transaction of credit. Finally, there is no evaluation of the liquidity function of money, allowing for fast re-adjustments of productive forces and decisions as circumstances change. On the contrary, the liquidity of wealth is regarded with deep suspicion: the authors are prone to see the its possible abuses (speculation, fleeing responsibility for long term investments, as in *PP* 24) but not its good use (spreading of risk and uncertainty, swift response to changing economic circumstances, offering transparent information to market agents on prices).

Without denying the validity of those critiques, should CathST not be reminded of the adage: *abusus non tollit usus* (the possibility of abuse does not preclude the possibility of good use)? But it seems hard to follow this wise rule, when, as Dennis McCann has commented, "the spirit animating this tradition is that of a humane aristocrat profoundly uneasy with modernity in all its forms"[3]. The economy is regarded in a static (pre-modern) way, as an institutional framework of production, distribution and consumption, based on solid factors such as land and labour; it is not approached as a dynamic process of invention under circumstances of uncertainty, or as a continuous flow of information and expressions of (time and consumption) preferences by autonomous agents. Because of that conceptual bias, capital is not conceived correctly and systematically as a specific factor of production (of savings and investment, next to labour, natural resources, knowledge), and as a specific network of financial institutions, as it should be.

Contemporary Christians no longer hold the ancient beliefs that money is a sterile, non-fungible good, and that time cannot be sold

---

3. D. McCann, *The Church and Wall Street*, in *America* 158 (1988), no. 4, 85-94, esp. 86.

"since it is the Lord's property". But what kind of thinking about the true functions and meaning of money can replace these outdated notions in order to arrive at a systematic financial ethics for today's Christians? That question needs answering. If not, some out-dated presuppositions about money will keep lingering around, blocking the view to a correct evaluation of contemporary finance.

3. *The Role of the Financial Sector of the Economy is Reduced to Its Distributive Effects on the Markets of Goods and Services*

As a result of the above described limitations, CathST tends to limit its evaluation of financial transactions to their (negative) effects on the "real" economy: unequal distribution of access and opportunities, unequal distribution of wealth among persons and nations, resources wasted on short-term speculation, neglecting long term social benefits in investments, etc. Of course, these criticisms are important and should not be withdrawn. But the narrow focus on matters of equity is as one-sided (and detrimental to a valid ethical evaluation of economic conduct) as is the dominant contemporary tendency of modern economics to focus exclusively on efficiency. In order to restore the dialogue between CST and financial economics, something of a "paradigm shift" is needed. It is needed on both sides: modern economics would do well to include the "social acceptability of outcomes of markets" into its object of study, as CST needs to take into account the moral standing of finan-cial markets and the inner logic of its institutions.

With this notion of paradigm shift, I refer to one of the conclusions of Jonsen and Toulmin in their excellent study on casuistry: "Where a moral argument ends, depends on where it begins... We see that the choice of paradigm was most problematic in the debate about usury. This debate is still topical. Usury was first condemned in situations in which, in a subsistence economy, neighbours took advantage of misfor-tunes of the afflicted (notably, poor farmers and peasants) by charging interests on their loans and dispossessing them for non-payment. Such money-lending threatened to disrupt primitive agricultural societies and was perceived as unfair, even cruel. Taking any interest on loans thus acquired a bad name – the paradigm was "theft" – and any inclination to usuriousness came to be seen as a defect of personal character. Yet, commerce, industry and finance could never have developed if no way had been found to answer this challenge"[4].

---

4. A.R. JONSEN & S. TOULMIN, *The Abuse of Casuistry. A History of Moral Reason-ing*, Berkeley, CA, University of California Press, 1988, p. 309.

This paradigm shift occurred when the model for evaluating interest moved from "theft" to "thrift", i.e. saving and investing, and to "risk sharing" between investors and borrowers. In this perspective, with a new paradigm, a new distinction was introduced between those loans that remained and are usurious in the old sense (and they still exist, e.g. in credit lending to farmers), and those that represent a fair sharing of risks and uncertainties regarding present and future goods. We need a similar shift today when looking at the present evolution of financial markets and products.

II. DEFINING A FRAMEWORK FOR FINANCIAL ETHICS

In order to develop an applied ethics of finance, one should distinguish, first of all, between the levels of individual, institutional and systemic structuring of action[5]. This distinction is not the only possible or relevant one: one could equally start from the distinction between markets, market agents and regulating institutions (non-governmental, governments, international bodies) or from the distinction between various ethical values that are at stake (common good, justice, solidarity, truthfulness, transparency). But the chosen distinction has the advantage, a) of being common to most aspects of organisational activity and of social ethics; b) of providing a heuristic framework without immediately defining the normative outcomes of ethical reflection (except the important suggestion that one should always consider the consequences of one's actions at all levels).

Secondly, in the context of Christian ethics, it seems important equally to introduce a distinction between the positions of the professional agent and the "ordinary" person, or between the role of financial institutions and the interests of society at large. In general, this distinction refers to the fact that most financial decisions have both a reference of meaning which is internal to the institutional sphere of finance (rules and principles for professional conduct within the network of banking,

---

5. I do not enter here into the fundamental ethics of money, including the evaluation of its functions (See M. AGLIETTA, *The Future of International Monetary Relations*, in A. STEINHERR & D. WEISERBS (eds.), *Evolution of the International and Regional Monetary Systems*, New York, NY, MacMillan, 1991, pp. 141-159): such a reflection should focus on the non-neutrality of money as a means of exchange, store of value, and unit of account: money is also an expression of power, an indicator of time preference, and an expression of trust or confidence in the economy. Liquidity preferences have to be approached as a type of social value, and money can be interpreted as a form of communication, as a language.

markets, financial institutions) and another one which relates to the
larger existential frame of meaning for the agent (effects of actions on
everyday social life and well-being of agents, including non-professional
agents, or the personal life of professionals). In other words, by distinguishing (not separating) the professional and societal dimensions, I
point to the wider existential and social meanings that monetary decisions or financial transactions have outside the specific sphere of
finance. This may prove important a) to highlight in what way the common good is involved in the professional decision-making processes;
and b) what is the relevance of Christian social ethics (mostly concerned
with the extra-professional ethical dimensions of personal character
building and social well-being) for the specialised field of financial dealing and planning?

Framework for finance ethics:

	Personal & social virtues in the world of finance	Professional ethics of finance
1. Individual conduct	Detachment & stewardship in saving and borrowing; Universal destiny	impartial service: clients first; ethics of information, trust; honesty and solidarity
2. Institutional conduct management	state sovereignty stability/accountability prudence	banking ethics: risk banking rules on capital reserves hedging, credit policy, supervision
3. Systemic level	Global justice, sustainability universal destiny of all agents (and states)	fighting systemic risk: stability increasing fairness of treatment

1. *An Ethics of Stewardship as a Basic Judeo-Christian Attitude to Finance*

Money, in the biblical perspective, is most often approached with caution. This is the case because money, as a means of exchange, of valua-
tion and storage of wealth, has an in-built tendency to become estimated
as an end-in-itself. In theological terms, money tends to become perceived as an absolute, instead of being treated as an instrument to serve
the true end, namely God, and the sort of communion that He calls for.
In biblical metaphors, money tends to become an idol (e.g. the "Golden
Calf", Exodus 32; the Mammon (Luke 6), whereas it should be considered as a mere tool for service to the well-being of the person and the

community. In ethical terms, money tends to become the object of greed, of an emotional and disproportionate drive to the accumulation of wealth.

This function as a "means" or the "proportionate" use of money, implies that the use of financial instruments should not be allowed to interfere with those practices that are considered as "good in themselves", as leading to excellence in the pursuit of internal goods of a community[6], such as good governance, artistic expression, education, the pursuit of knowledge or religious vision.

This *caveat* has consequences on a personal as well as on a societal level. On the personal level, the consideration of finance as a mere means to other ends correlated with the virtues of detachment and stewardship. These two virtues should be regarded as two sides of the same coin, expressing the same basic moral attitude respectively in a negative and positive form.

Detachment means that the agent should seek the acquisition of wealth only to the degree that he/she needs these means in order to realise the goods that are good in themselves: the well-being of oneself as a responsible member of society, and the well-being of that society. In other words, the use of money is subject to the virtuous life, and to the practices that define this life[7]. The accumulation of capital should never be striven after as an end in itself but always regarded as a means towards non-monetary ends. Its use should be judged accordingly (as is the case of the use of power): to what degree do I need these means in order to serve the well-being of society, and to further my own well-being by this service? Just as enterprises are ultimately evaluated by the social value they provide through the efficient production of particular goods and services, so are financial institutions and agents to be evaluated by the social end they serve through their handling of money, be it as credit, savings, investment or the sharing of risk. This means/end relationship should always remain present as the ultimate moral measure of initiatives and decisions. If it is absent, it is likely that greed, rather than detachment and stewardship, is guiding behaviour.

This service to societal well-being is positively expressed by the virtue of stewardship. Stewardship is a biblical metaphor, but clear enough to be understood outside the religious realm of meaning. It implies that those who handle financial titles and deal in money, be it for personal

---

6. A. MacIntyre, *After Virtue. A Study in Moral Theory*, London, Duckworth, 1984.
7. J. Haughey, *The Holy Use of Money. Personal Finance in Light of Christian Faith*, Garden City, NY, Doubleday, 1986.

use or as professionals acting for clients, must always be aware of the consequences of their actions for the well-being of society: whose interests do they serve, who do they harm by their financial transactions? Each agent should be able to legitimate his conduct by pointing to the greater benefit he or she realises by his monetary transactions. This greater benefit includes a relational horizon (i.e. it is not only for my own good, or for some agents, but for society at large, as I affect its well-being through my actions) as well as a temporal one (it is not only providing a greater benefit today, but also in the future, i.e. in a sustainable and endurable manner). In classic Catholic social terms, this orientation towards the greater benefit is expressed by the principle of universal destiny of the goods of the earth: even when dealing with private property, I should always keep in mind, and take responsibility for, all foreseeable effects of my actions on the general state of welfare of the affected population or environment.

The above mentioned criterion might help us to evaluate "speculative behaviour". It seems impossible to distinguish in a material way between transactions that are estimated as speculative and those that are not, because the same action of buying or selling a financial product may be justifiable for one agent (because it provides some hedging against a risk he is exposed to, because it will offer him a chance to invest in a worthwhile product or service for society), whereas it is unjustified in another person's context (e.g. increasing the person's overall risk exposure without a proportionate reason, using insider informátion, etc.) In other words, one has to include the intention of the agent and the circumstances of his actions in order to evaluate the act in its complete consequential context.

A transaction, then, may be negatively labelled as speculative, not so much because someone is willing to buy or sell a financial title according to one's subjective estimates of the expected evolution of its price. That is what all agents do on the markets, with good or bad intentions, good or bad overall consequences.

It may come closer to the negative label once an agent actively seeks to profit from future changes in the price of an asset without actively contributing in any way to a value change of the same asset. Here we come into a grey area of speculation, where agents engage. for example, in the buying or selling of a currency without taking any interest in the effects of their actions for the economic well-being of the country whose currency they are dealing in. This type of attitude may still be justifiable in its particular context, because a) buying or selling the currency is in itself (be it minimal) a way of taking an interest in the state of the underlying asset (i.e. the country's economy) and b) because it provides a means to spread risks, or to realise a socially beneficial investment. Still, people dealing in financial titles without taking a due stake in the underlying assets (i.e. dealing in company shares without taking an active interest in the companies that brought those shares to the market, or dealing in future exchange rate changes without taking responsibility for the effect of currency devaluations on the affected population) are limiting their scope of attention and responsibility in a dangerous manner: they may be judged to fall short in stewardship.

On the other hand, a transaction will clearly be labelled as speculative when an agent is not only neglecting the secondary effects of his action on the underlying asset but is also attempting to reap some direct benefits through the market without any other motive than greed ("jumping on the wagon": no hedging rationale, no spreading of risks, no long term investment objective). Here, we have clearly passed the line of "speculation". These individual actions will add up and lead to negative cumulative effects because they tend to over-inflate the volume of financial markets (leading to herd behaviour, overreaction to fluctuations of prices) or false information (spreading rumours, trying to influence the evolution of prices without any reference to the fundamental value of underlying assets, just to create a quick and easy profit).

So, the case of speculation provides a good example of the ethic of stewardship. On the one hand, the proportionality of the means cannot be judged adequately without some reference to the consequences of the transaction for the well-being of society, including due responsibility for all the parties affected by one's transactions. On the other hand, a person may be justified in engaging in a transaction when he has some legitimate intention by doing so (e.g. spreading risk, creating the possibility of a useful investment) without actively foreseeing all the possible effects of the transaction on the underlying assets. However, one cannot permanently hide behind one's immediate good end in order to reject all responsibility for any further (involuntary) consequences of one's actions. The one who does so systematically narrows down the scope of his actions in an undue manner, and is lacking in the basic virtues of detachment and stewardship. These are important insights once we move to the ethics of professional agents, because the strength (and danger) of professional action resides precisely in this compartmentalisation of financial actions and responsibilities.

Another issue that calls for systematic ethical consideration is the basic attitude towards "saving". How do people choose between consumption and investment, or between investment now and saving for the future? Time preferences are not ethically neutral data but reflect personal and collective time preferences. These preferences include the responsibility for future generations (setting aside money for foreseeable future costs, spreading risks and welfare, e.g. in social security plans), and sustainability (saving for containing and treating nuclear waste, investing in regeneration of biotopes, etc.) Time has been an object of theological reflections in the past, some of them outdated (such as the notion that interest taking is forbidden since it puts a price on time, whereas time does not belong to men, but to God). On the other hand, ethical reflection on prevalent time preferences should not be left out of contemporary financial ethics since it affects choices on the personal level (choices between present investment *versus* present consumption *versus* future savings), the institutional (short-termism) and the collective levels of action (basic differences in savings rates of USA, Japan, and Europe, with deep effects on international financial transfers and monetary policies).

2. *Professional Financial Ethics*

Professional ethics applies whenever the ordinary agents of a society (citizens, consumers) are prohibited from intervening directly in the procurement of some valuable service or good. In matters of retribution, instead of intervening themselves to get due reparation of damages, they need to refer to policemen, to judges and barristers; in matters of health care, to physicians; in the case of money and credit services, to bankers. One could ask questions on the origin and the validity (historical, social, ethical) of the professionalisation process in different sectors of social activity, but one can hardly deny the fact that in the contemporary state of economic organisations financial agents are acting as a profession and should be judged accordingly.

In the professional context ethics is defined by a relationship between a client and a provider of services. This relationship is an unequal one involving asymmetric information and unequal competence in financial matters. Consequently, it should be governed by the requirements of confidence-building, based on the virtues of honesty and solidarity. These virtues need to accompany any contractual form in which the client/professional relationship is institutionalised.

"Service to clients" may be regarded as the first moral basis of banking. It is a form of solidarity, albeit a "weak" one, for bankers are not supposed to offer their services gratuitously; but at the same time this kind of guarantee provides a real form of solidarity treatment, since bankers are supposed not to discriminate between clients who are well-informed about markets and those who are ignorant, thus assuring similar service to all. It should be clear for all agents involved (clients, directors, executive personnel) that financial agents are first of all defending and protecting their clients' interests in their actions on the markets, and that they put these interests before their own interests or before other competing interests.

The relationship between bankers and clients is an asymmetric one as far as information is concerned, but this is true from both sides: clients may withhold information about their solvency or their future investment plans; bankers may abuse information about the financial markets to further their own interests rather their client's. That is why the scope for cheating has to be limited by the contractual commitment to render a particular service, backed up by the truthfulness of both parties.

Confidence can only be enhanced in asymmetric relations through the practice of "honesty". Honesty is a complex virtue, including at least the three dimensions of fairness, promise keeping, and trustworthiness in the information which is given or concealed. Bankers and their clients will select each other on the basis of these criteria (as well as criteria of financial profit, quality and speediness of services, etc.). The knowledge and trust built up between bankers and their long term clients provides the most important (and fixed, hard to trade) asset of a bank: its inside information about a certain segment of the population of savers and borrowers of money.

Honesty also implies that the amount of borrowing should be limited by the guaranteed ability of the borrower to pay back. This is a valid prudential rule on an individual level (screening of clients) as well as at institutional level (limiting the leverage in borrowing for banks and institutional investors on the markets).

These basic virtues are well expressed in a banker's "deontology". The principles of IOSCO (International Organisation of Securities Commissions) relate to the following topics: honesty, diligence, capability, correct handling of information for and about customers, conflicts of interest and compliance. The practice of those virtues is not a self-evident matter, as cases on insider trading, abuse of information about customers for private benefit and abuse of secrecy for the purpose of tax evasion demonstrate. Further case studies are needed, e.g. on the limits of secrecy where confidentiality of customer data needs to be balanced against the demand of public authorities to fight tax evasion, fraud and public embezzlement. On the other hand, bankers need to maintain a clear separation between financial transactions on behalf of their clients, and transactions that are executed for the direct benefit of the bank.

These separations become all the more important in a context of universal banking and of securitisation.

The ethics of information provides a sort of minimalist ethical framework, which is limited by the instrumental rationality of markets and of balancing between competing interests. Nevertheless, this framework provides a series of real ethical demands and objectives which should be taken seriously. CathST has not reflected sufficiently on the ethical requirements of finance within this professional context; it may begin with this minimal ethical framework but must take the fuller exploration of ethics beyond it. For even when the markets are functioning fairly, a number of fundamental moral questions remain to be answered about the finality of financial transactions, and about redistributive obligations to those people living outside the markets in question but affected by them.

The last *caveat* relates to the general ethics of markets, which may act as link between the individual and institutional levels of financial ethics. Markets are mechanisms of fair exchange, provided that the conditions of perfect competition are reasonably approximated (free access and exit to markets, equally available and perfect information, a large number of providers and customers of services, no fixed prices, no coercion to buy or to sell). In the model these are moral conditions, leading to maximum transparency, fairness and availability of financial services on credit and saving. Even in their best form, however, financial markets cannot deliver the following objectives: a more equitable distribution of purchasing power and benefits throughout the population; care for future generations without a discount; a correct collective estimation of non-monetary value of goods (i.e. value not reflected in price); care for public goods (i.e. which are socially provided by public authorities). Consequently, a professional deontology of bankers will provide a necessary, but not a sufficient definition of what individual agents ought to respect in their financial transactions. Here we have discovered the most fundamental reason why an ethics of stewardship precedes and is needed to complete a professional finance ethics.

3. *Institutional Setting: Regulating the Markets*

At the second or institutional level, we need to consider issues of good governance and regulation, both from the perspective of the "state" and of "financial markets". This distinction appears to be a very different one from the previous level. The distinction between non-professional and professional agents does not coincide with that between public and private institutions. Nevertheless, one can argue for a close parallelism between the distinctions. The general socio-ethical framework for financial institutions traditionally has been provided by the state and by state regulation; nation states were supposed to be the guardians of the general interest, acting as sovereign powers on behalf of their citizens. They exercised the sovereign power of issuing money, as well as controlling financial markets through direct legislation (taxes, exchange controls, chartering banking institutions, banking laws) and through financial market interventions by central banks. One can fairly say that at the institutional level citizens look to their respective state institutions to regulate financial markets and institutions in the general interest.

In the recent past this regulating role of the state has been evolving fast due to several processes (of technical innovations, leading to new financial products, globalisation and deregulation of markets and disintermediation or securitisation); consequently, the role of self-regulation by insider-institutions (non-banks as well as banks) needs to grow accordingly, in concert with the emergence of international regulators. Consequently, CST, in order to provide a more concrete ethical guidance to the contemporary world of finance, should take a balanced look at both sides of the institutional spectrum. This runs counter to traditional approaches, which showed a tendency to overestimate the role of state intervention, and to neglect the mechanisms of internal regulation by market agents.

The traditional aim of public authorities in financial markets is to strive for monetary and financial stability. Monetary stability relates, first, to the stability of internal prices (absence of inflation or deflation) within a country; secondly it may relate to the stability of the price of the currency, i.e. the exchange rates. Here a first policy choice appears: some states (such as the USA or the EU) focus on the first objective, others (with a strong import/export dependency) may have to focus on the second. Financial stability refers to the smooth functioning of financial markets (both foreign exchange and capital markets, and securities and bond markets): states will attempt to avoid excessive volatility and possible crashes (systemic risk) which may have severe negative effects on economic growth and living standards. Besides the objectives of monetary and financial stability, governments are obliged to strive after other goals which may or may not be compatible with stability: maximum employment, a stable rate of economic growth, investments in public services, social security. It is evident that some trade-off has to be made, and that stability may not always be the overriding objective of public policy. On the other hand, as the experience of governments in the seventies and eighties has demonstrated, it may be damaging to the long term interests of the country to put financial stability at risk for short-term gains which involve inflation or excessive public debt.

In the context of CathST, public authorities, especially governments, are viewed as agents of the general interest. This view has some validity, of course, because (democratically elected) public authorities have legitimacy and some of the means to intervene efficiently in the functioning of markets, correcting their above-mentioned biases in pursuit of the common good. Through the issuing of money, the imposition of taxes, reserve requirements, chartering requirements, and central bank controls and interventions, state authorities may in effect redistribute wealth or opportunities for citizens to participate in the markets. They may slow down the propensity for short termism, and stimulate savings and investment for future generations. In short, they may correct the outcomes of markets for the greater good of society.

Moreover, one should not forget that state authorities not only have a role to play in the correction of markets, but also in the promotion of the latter. If real markets are left to their own devices, it is inconceivable that anything approximating to the conditions of perfect competition will ever operate. On the contrary, markets tend to become oligopolistic, where access to valuable information is very difficult and unevenly distributed, where high transaction costs have to be paid in order to enter or exit, etc. Therefore, states have a second function, as police agents in order to guarantee fairness and transparency of the markets (this function is performed through legislation and litigation, *via* bodies like the Securities Exchange Commissions, the Central Bank, the Treasury).

In order, however, not to over-rate the moral status of national public authorities, one should keep in mind two major considerations. First, just as real-life markets may move very far from the theoretical tests of ideal markets, real states and state authorities may not be inclined to defend the general interest of their citizens. I am not only referring here to the example of dictatorships or aristocratic regimes acting on behalf of a minority of the population (or of foreign interests). That is a matter of political ethics, though the impact on financial ethics is clear. I am pointing, rather, to the fact that public authorities are not only present in financial markets as regulators, but also as customers, and often very substantial ones. A public authority which has to manage a substantial portfolio of sovereign debt or investments may easily be inclined not to act in the benefit of all agents on the market, but first of all to its own perceived advantage. Consequently, there is some argument for installing "Chinese Walls" (or "fire-walls") between the Treasury on the one hand, and other members of government on the other hand, in order to avoid this type of conflict of interest. Moreover, here is also a valid argument for delegating a substantial amount of monetary policy to an independent central bank, which is not under political pressure to surrender its impartiality in controlling the functioning of financial markets. So, a delicate separation of powers, and a true deontology of public service are needed in order to avoid the abuse of state powers in the financial realm.

Second, because financial markets (mostly so the foreign exchange markets, but also equity and bond markets) have evolved into global markets, nation states do not have the effective means anymore to control or regulate markets on their own. In the absence of an effective global public authority, they have to resort to second best solutions of close international co-operation by some of the most influential state authorities (central banks acting through the Bank for International Settlements (B.I.S.) and the Group of Ten), governments acting through the Group of Seven, the I.M.F. and the World Bank. These initiatives (especially the B.I.S.) have been rather effective in avoiding major threats of systemic crisis in financial markets since the seventies. They have even succeeded in imposing some global standards for financial institutions (e.g. the capital adequacy standards of 1988). Nevertheless, the absence of major breakdowns in international markets during the last few decades should not blind us to the fact that the present system of partial control through co-ordination by the most powerful and wealthy states has some major setbacks from an ethical perspective. It institutionalises the governance of the world financial system by the happy few, and it does not aim at a more just and sustainable distribution of wealth and opportunities for all of humanity. Rather, its rationale focuses on the national interest of the leading states, and on the negative goal of avoiding systemic risk. With this last remark, we already touch on the major issue of the systemic level of finance ethics (see later).

4. *Assessing Self-Regulation by Financial Institutions*

The social role of financial institutions involves mediation between potential savers and investors; collecting and updating qualitative information on savers and investors; transforming short term into long term debt and credit; spreading risk and uncertainty; guaranteeing the quality of financial transactions and assets as agreed upon by contract.

In the absence of adequate external regulation, more depends on internal regulation (self-regulation by financial institutions). This is also the direction in which international regulatory efforts are moving. Since major difficulties have emerged in effectively imposing a universal capital adequacy standard, regulating bodies have moved towards a combination of supervision of self-imposed safety measures by financial institutions (common credit risk calculation models, netting schemes, speedy processes of settlement and clearing, etc.). Again, this move towards supervised self-regulation can only succeed within certain limits; it forms no overall solution to an adequate moral guidance of financial markets.

One should count as lying within the ambit of self-regulation the following issues: mission, auditing, prudence, meeting adverse selection, moral hazard and combating financial crime.

Mission: Institutions, as with persons, should be evaluated ethically, first, in relation to the ends they are serving. A financial institution can be regarded as a morally responsible agent if it offers a real service to clients. Its mission statement, as well as its yearly accounts should clearly demonstrate that it favours productive investment for society and effectively spreads risks and capabilities for clients to realise those productive investments[8].

Auditing: Independent auditing practices of financial institutions should not only guarantee the conventional demands of corporate governance (correct financial reporting, transparency to shareholders, controls on management remuneration and selection) but should also demonstrate which public demands or needs the institution is serving through its clients (social utility of the bank).

Prudence, a classic virtue (of Aristotelian ethics), is highly relevant to good banking practice. Prudence implies that bankers only grant credit that is sufficiently guaranteed, that they operate within the limits of the law, that they spread their credit as much as possible, that they keep sufficient reserves, that they separate daily management of transactions and control, etc. Prudential rules are institutionalised in the banking culture, and provide "thick matter" for control by central bankers. Prudential rules should be tightened in one specific area of derivatives trading: the degree of risk exposure should be decided by competent authorities; it should take into account the possibility of market volatility (effective hedging) and it should serve the social utility which the financial institution has defined as its objective (not merely for increasing its private profit margins).

Self-regulatory proposals by themselves cannot solve the problems of "adverse selection" and "moral hazard". This means that in markets

8. J.-L. FERNANDEZ-FERNANDEZ, *The Financial System and Moral Problems. An Agenda for Ethical Reflection*, KUB Tilburg, Erasmus Program, 1994.

with widely different agents and qualities (banks and non-banks; emerging markets, derivative dealers) "bad money will tend to drive out good money", and trustworthy institutions will come under pressure from less responsible or resilient ones. This implies that there exists no alternative to an effective regulatory control backed up by public authorities, legislation and jurisdiction. This regulation should be of a trans-national nature since markets and institutions function outside the boundaries of any single state. The same point applies to issues of financial crime: self-regulation cannot solve the practices of laundering money or organising tax havens. The sheer extent of criminal finance has become a collective threat to the functioning of international markets and institutions.

Financial institutions need to balance their obligation to serve their clients' needs with their civic responsibility towards society at large, especially regarding property rights and confidentiality of financial data. The principle of respect for private property is an important element but not an absolute rule in social ethics. Therefore, banking secrecy should be limited in order to allow the supervising and juridical authorities to combat illegal transactions.

5. *Systemic Priorities: Justice implies more than guaranteeing Stability*

The needs for financial ethics at global or systemic levels have become more urgent. On the one hand, the focus on the professional side on matters of (avoidance of) systemic risk is easily understood. Priority is given to prudential measures that increase the degree of resistance to financial shocks or panics, and diminish the risk of systemic breakdowns related to lack of liquidity. Being necessarily pragmatic, these objectives are reached within the context of existing institutions, increasing the level of co-operation and co-ordination of national regulators (through B.I.S, G7, I.M.F.). When seen from the angle of justice, however, the rather narrow focus on stability and risk-avoidance is not a sufficient condition in defining the scope of ethics in the financial sector.

The present international monetary system cannot be fair because it depends on the dominance of a few nation-states and unions of states which impose their currencies and standards on the world markets (USA, and in lesser degrees Japan and the EU). These countries not only have a competitive advantage because of their wealth, but also because international dealing largely employs their currencies, diminishing their exchange costs and increasing their capacity to manipulate the value of the currency according to domestic policy-needs (as has happened with the dollar since the 1970s). The establishment of a just transnational monetary order presupposes that markets are not ruled by the national currency of some member states, but rather that they are able to refer to a neutral standard of value (i.e., one that is outside the reach of control of a single member state, such as the Special Drawing Rights of I.M.F., or the Euro within the context of EU).

The present international order cannot be effective in regulating financial markets and institutions because most often too little is done, and too late, in attempting to correct the abuses of markets (as was the case, most recently, with the Asian crisis after 1997). The I.M.F. is allowed to function like some lender of last resort, but only under the control of the most powerful nation-states, and only to the degree that systemic stability is in danger. The B.I.S. has strongly developed the possibilities of co-ordination of central bankers but only for the most wealthy nations, and not to the extent that an effective and impartial transnational central bank would require. All present data indicate that the markets have developed beyond the boundaries of nation-states, but regulation has not. This fundamental bias needs to be attacked.

In moral philosophy[9] as well as in the tradition of CathST (*PT* 80-96, 130-146) there exists a powerful argument for the construction of a just transnational order, based on a rule of law and leading to global governance and even effective world government[10]. Because of the fast increase in interdependency caused by global communications technology and trade, we urgently need to concretise this utopia of a global governance, so that it may include a truly transnational monetary and financial order. In the absence of such governance, it is difficult to see how there can be effective intervention in the already-active system of technology, trade and communications.

This transnational monetary and financial order would need to include: a transnational central bank, guarding the global standard of monetary value, and acting as a lender of last resort on the markets; a transnational court, enforcing the laws and regulations that apply to all agents acting on the markets; a transnational legislator with a balanced representation a) according to population, and b) according to wealth (i.e. effective presence and weight in the markets); a transnational executive

---

9. Immanuel KANT, in his political writings: *Zum Ewigen Frieden*, or *Idee einer Algemeinen Geschichte in Weltbuergerlichen Absicht*.

10. "Today, the common good of all nations involves problems which affect people all over the world: problems which can only be solved by a public authority which has the power, the form and the agencies competent to deal with then and whose writ covers the entire globe. We cannot therefore escape the conclusion that the moral order itself demands the establishment of some sort of world government" (*PT* 137).

which can implement the monetary and trading policies congruent with the demands of global stability, well-being and just distribution of resources; and transnational supervising bodies, co-ordinating the auditing of transnational corporations and banks.

In this context of institutional reconstruction of a global monetary order, the traditional demands of CathST for just redistribution (e.g. the debt remission debate for HIPCs) would receive a correct framework. It is necessary that we plead in favour of the poor and the excluded but we should do so within an institutional context which takes into account the internal evolution, strengths and weaknesses of the emerging transnational financial system. No sustainable solution will be found unless the demands of just redistribution of financial resources and the stable functioning of the present networks are brought together into a single vision. This is specifically relevant for treating the debt issue of the poorest countries (as is happening in the so-called HIPC initiative of I.M.F., criticised and amended by the church initiative of the Jubilee 2000). If one wants to move beyond the incremental approach of rescheduling debt service payments (and finally, writing off some amount of bad debt), a more permanent institutional reform is needed so that all countries may have a more equal access and participation in the trans-national sources of funding.

Finally, institutional measures that are meant to diminish systemic risk (such as the proposal of a Tobin Tax, increasing the transaction cost of short-term financial transactions on the markets) should also be judged by their potential for reaching a more just financial order. If the income that is collected by the Tobin tax could be used to finance international organisations such as the United Nations, the I.M.F. or the World Bank, these institutions would become less dependent on the support of (and pressure from) some dominant nation states, and more able to intervene in an impartial way in regulating global markets. In this way, one could obtain two major objectives at once: not only of fighting volatility but at also of increasing the level of participative justice in the functioning of the international financial order.

UFSIA, Antwerp University   Jef VAN GERWEN S.J.

ORDERING GLOBAL FINANCE
BACK TO BASICS

The paper aims to explore the middle-level ground between Catholic social thought (CathST) and policy analysis and prescriptions, with special reference to issues of global finance and development. The question of debt-relief for less developed countries (LDCs), which touches both ethical principles and economic and political feasibility, will also be considered. I believe that a focus by an economist on these issues provides a useful and interesting example of the relationship of ethics and economics and brings forward considerations for relationships between official Catholic social teaching (CST) Catholic non-official social thought (CNOST), and of both of these with current secular thinking on economic science.

ELEMENTARY ECONOMIC EXPERIENCE AND ITS RELATIONAL NATURE

We can easily observe that only a very limited set of economic transactions can (and maybe should) be carried out within an impersonal environment – let us call it a "perfect competitive market". It is not just that perfect competition does not exist in real life, and hence that transactions cannot be performed in such a market as a matter of fact. Studying economic transactions from first principles, even in a very general way and at a very high level of abstraction, we do not find sound economic reasons to want the large bulk of our transactions carried out in an impersonal, perfectly competitive manner. The largest part of economic transactions, because of their essential nature (either because they entail increasing returns to scale and hence produce "natural" concentration, or because of imperfect and asymmetric information, and so on) need to be carried out within a context of personalised relationships, often meant to be potentially durable and hence characterised by largely incomplete contracts.

In everyday economic experience, we notice that working, lending and borrowing, investing in human and sometimes also in physical capital, are economic decisions that almost inevitably entail personal relationships. Economic relationships among corporate agents such as firms, banks, governments are superficially anonymous. As a matter of fact the most relevant economic decisions and transactions, especially those that permanently shape the character of an economic system, are taken and realised within personal and potentially continuous relationships.

Recent advances in economic analysis are showing willingness to consider, although in a micro-economic approach, the relational nature of some economic institutions, traditionally taken as the (exogenously-given) setting in which economic decisions and transaction take place. The firm, for example, once simply regarded as a "black box" in which factors of production, say, labour and capital, are combined to produce an output, is now often studied as a network of personal relationships. Also, markets nowadays receive much more psychological attention than in the past: a "real" market for some product or service is recognised as an institution whose functioning is determined by the network of relationships that constitute it. But we are still a long way from putting micro pieces together into a sensible synthesis[1], although games theory approaches yield an impressive amount of results concerning personalised and potentially durable relations, where strategic behaviour is assumed.

Economists are traditionally good at analysing the economic behaviour of agents in isolation. It is worth noting also that, perhaps too frequently, textbook representations of "economic" behaviour in a given, unchanging environment end up being analytically indistinguishable from "mechanical" behaviour, as is the case when solving a profit maximising problem. But the mechanical nature of problem-solving can also be found in more complicated problems where economic relations are modelled, as is the case in solving a strategic interaction game, by backward induction.

But the relational nature of economic transactions goes well beyond the bounds of "mechanical" strategic interaction, requiring some sort of a priori reciprocal recognition of the partner. While the strategic approach can explain why an option is chosen among a finite number of alternatives, we miss a plausible story about how to identify all relevant alternatives. In everyday life we are often taken by surprise in interactions (even when we play chess, which is just a complicated game with a neatly defined set of alternatives). The same happens in economic interactions: when observing economic behaviour one has to describe it realistically as people acting in a substantially unpredictable environment, where the set of possible actions and reactions largely exceeds the forms

---

1. C. BERETTA, *Is Economic Theory up to the Need for Ethics?* (Quaderno, ISEIS, 9401), 1994.

of behaviour that could be "rationally" anticipated. In other words, there cannot be much mechanical behaviour in an environment characterised by "strong" uncertainty[2].

"Action", as opposed to "behaviour", is at issue when we consider personalised economic relations where both the subjective and the objective dimensions are relevant. We should also recognise that "action", as opposed to "behaviour", is the appropriate concept to use even when discussing individual economic decisions under "strong" uncertainty (non just *alea*)[3]. Action is a dynamic concept; an answer to a complex set of situations; ultimately, in a sense, an unpredictable answer.

Mainstream economists accept that they are walking on shaky ground when they have to model decisions under conditions of strong uncertainty or personalised economic relations. But everyday experience shows that there are many ways of doing business and making economic transactions, each being crucially dependent on the subjective and objective dimensions of economic decisions and transactions: who is acting, with whom and for what?

FINANCIAL TRANSACTIONS AND FINANCIAL MARKETS

Borrowing and lending is a particular form of trade (inter-temporal trade), where a personalised relation of some kind between the borrower and the lender usually exists, either directly or indirectly through financial intermediaries. Besides, choosing what sort of financial instrument to use (objective dimension of the transaction), a proper answer to the question: "Should I trust my partner?" has to be provided (subjective dimension). Borrowing and lending, as we perceive them in everyday economic experience, whether micro credit or sovereign debt, can hardly be interpreted within the standard impersonal paradigm.

The nature of financial transactions, and of financial markets especially, calls for a return to basics, i.e. assessing the fundamental nature of the transaction. From the subjective point of view, any decision about borrowing and lending occurs in a situation where each partner knows he has some relevant information that the other has not, and *vice versa* (in the economists' jargon, "asymmetric information"). From the objective

---

2. "Strong" uncertainty defines a situation in which a set of possible events is unknown, and one does not know even the consequences of a particular action for any given event. See G. DOSI, *Sources, Procedures and Microeconomic Effects of Innovation*, in *Journal of Economic Literature* 26 (1988) 1120-1171.

3. S. BERETTA, *Rischio e azione*, in *Città e società* (1998), no. 1, 23-37.

point of view, when future purchasing power is traded for present purchasing power, time and uncertainty are essential dimensions of any decision; "strong" uncertainty cannot be ruled out. Hence, giving and gaining trust should not be an option in credit transactions (think of venture capital, joint ventures and such like); and mechanical behaviour becomes unrealistic. It may be argued that we do nonetheless observe some sort of mechanical behaviour in offering and demanding credit where reciprocal trust (and reciprocal monitoring as well) are practically substituted by impersonal devices.

Mechanical behaviour may be efficient in some rare cases, in exactly the same fashion that highly competitive markets may be an efficient institutional setting for trading particular goods, since in this situation the relational dimension is not crucial (spot trade, standard quality). Consider financial markets where impersonal trading goes on for twenty-four hours a day: while some final credit relations may exist in such a situation, it is almost impossible to disentangle them from pure portfolio management, even in *ex post* circumstances; and it is impossible to do so simultaneously. Seemingly, this kind of financial market closely corresponds to the highly stylised perfectly competitive market which we find in introductory economics textbooks, where a standardised product is traded by many well informed agents operating on both the demand and the supply side and in a highly transparent environment. Much impersonal trading of this kind, and notably arbitrage operations, is machine-decided and machine-performed, in exactly the way profit maximisation problems are solved automatically in the theory of a perfectly competitive market. But again, circuit breakers are needed at times, when "strong" uncertainty patently obtains. In that situation, players suddenly regain their name and face, that is, their ability to give and gain trust in personalised relationships.

Mechanical behaviour may prevail in other situations: for example, firms are often granted credit by banking institutions after banks routinely ascertain their establishment position, while the firms' investment projects tend to be regarded as irrelevant. But this procedure is likely to produce inefficient outcomes, as the credit rationing literature and the asymmetric information literature show.

BACK TO BASICS: ETHICAL DIMENSION OF ECONOMIC ACTION

I am convinced that personalised and potentially durable relationships are the most interesting part of economic research from a theoretical point of view; and that experientially and empirically they are the most relevant part of economic life. That is, understanding economics involves understanding relations.

If this is the case, ethics has its place within economic decisions and actions; indeed, economic decisions cannot be fully analysed within the narrow boundaries of the traditional, impersonal and a-relational paradigm where ethics (or as I prefer to say, virtues) have no analytical role. In many cases virtues are needed in order to generate a realistic set of economic production or consumption possibilities. In economic relations, commitment to something and responsibility to someone are essential to any notion of adequate action. I am not suggesting that altruism does, or should, replace self interest; I would like to stress, rather, that a full specification of self-interest must include the subjective (relational) as well as the objective (material) dimension.

"Pop-versions" of ethics and economics literature often take a different perspective. On one side, economic decisions pertain to their own "closed" sphere and develop according to their own internal logic, rules and laws; on the other, the application of ethical principles represents an *ex post* corrective for some undesirable "bad" consequences of economic decisions. Such a distinction is deeply embedded in mainstream talk about economic justice, where economics is a sort of neutral field that has to do with production, while ethics has to do with distribution (of initial endowments and/or final output). In other words, "easy" economic ethics suggest that principles of justice pertain to a distinct domain connected under certain considerations to economic decisions, and that such principles ought to be superimposed on economic decisions in order to modify their consequences, for example, for individual access to income or for economic opportunities.

Again, business ethics, in its modern fashionable form, suggests that the negative externalities of business decisions should be internalised, at a cost; on the other hand, when applying ethical principles implies taking some positive actions on the part of firms, those actions are typically meant to pursue "superior" goals, where "superior" unfortunately means unintegrated core business (for example, profit taking a lower place to "superior" causes). Thus, a superficial understanding of ethics has become enshrined in daily vocabulary: some banks are described as "ethical" because they develop an alternative financial circuit, where personal savings are invested in the social economy. That is all very well, but what about ordinary banking? Is ethics only a matter of channelling part of banking profits to "superior" causes? Or is there an ethical challenge internal to ordinary banking itself?

Calls for ethics in economics and business can easily degenerate into moralistic appeals in which ethics are superimposed on economic behaviour, resulting in a sort of "code of good behaviour". Not that there is anything wrong with codes, when they are appropriate. Clearly, they can have a place in the regulation of the behavioural aspects of economic transactions. But it is more usually the case that structural realities produce situations which exceed the bounds of regular, predictable, codifiable behaviour.

CathST and Scientific Research

I perceive Catholic social thought (CathST) to be more radical and demanding than codes of ethics, since it is more concerned with action than simply with behaviour. CathST, in connection with Catholic social teaching (CST), always attends to first principles, but it deals also with the ethical implications and with action and structure. It takes no short-cuts, assessing, always, the ways in which a complete understanding of the nature of human actions opens the way for ethics.

CathST is a "tradition-constituted" discipline, and an important non-official source of the tradition of CST, which has a transcendent objective of assisting people on their path to salvation (*CA* 54). This teaching is not an ideology, or a third way, not a political or economic programme; it does not offer technical solutions (*SRS* 41). It is normative thought, a moral critique of socio-political realities. It is a foundation and motivation for action (*CA* 59), interdisciplinary and practical in its applications and stands at the intersection where Christian critique encounters the world. It is not detached and outside of history (*CA* 53), whose credibility is not meant to rest entirely on internal coherence, but is in the hands of human beings, the "millions of people" who constitute the living Church (*CA* 3). It is meant to be an instrument of human liberation. Evolving from this teaching, CathST is the initiator, experimenter, developer and applicant to policy and practice of this normative or ethical thought.

As an economist, I would see here a matter of comparative advantage. Being the Church, an "expert in humanity" (*SRS* 41), announcing Christ and revealing human beings to themselves (*CA* 54), the CathST message for economic, social and political issues is rich from an anthropological point of view, as we can see, for example, in the attention given to the development of ideas on labour, interdependence and development. The path to human liberation can be detected in CathST's vocabulary of "personal freedom", "responsibility", "solidarity", "justice", "sub-sidiarity". This is not the arid language of legal codes[4]. In CathST positive and normative issues do not propose closed answers but at least suggest an appropriate setting for posing the questions.

This is our part of the story, not to be left exclusively to specialists in CST, but the task of any actor in the socio-economic scene, who is committed to announcing the Gospel and the life of the living Church, whether in the world of finance, policy-making or academia.

A CASE STUDY: GLOBAL FINANCE AND LDC DEVELOPMENT

International finance has seen deep quantitative and qualitative changes in recent decades. The amount of gross and net financial flows of the major industrial countries increased phenomenally during the nineties, with cross border transactions reaching levels that are a multiple of national GDPs. Private sector capital flows to developing countries also exploded in the same period and peaked in 1996, only to fall again by half in 1999. The average daily turnover on exchange rate markets is about 50 times the average daily amount of international trade. Trading in derivative instruments is the fastest growing segment of international finance, growing at 40% per year. From a qualitative point of view, the information technology revolution has deeply influenced the organisation of financial markets: standardised financial transactions become cheaper and cheaper. The low costs of computing, hence of "precision" financial trading, largely explain qualitative change, i.e. market integration and de-specialisation of globalised financial institutions.

It is interesting to note that international "real" finance (finance as inter-temporal trade, or in other words net transfer of resources) was much more developed at the beginning of the 20th century[5]. At that time current purchasing power was transferred from developed economies to "new" countries (borrowers), which yielded a higher expected rate of return from investment than lenders. In the last two decades, by contrast, an enormous amount of financial transactions has ended up generating small net transfers of purchasing power, which, as it turns out, are largely directed towards large and rich countries where domestic expenditure

4. I see a sort of analogy with faith and law. As the former encompasses the latter, freedom, responsibility, solidarity and subsidiarity at once encompass and transcend ethical codes.

5. M. ARTIS & T. BAYUOMI, *Saving, Investment, Financial Integration and the Balance of Payments* (IMF Working Papers), 1989.

systematically exceeds domestic income: the US, also Italy, have been among the heaviest international beneficiaries This is a worrying indicator of the basic, "long run" functioning of financial markets; more worrying, in a sense, than short-run financial panics.

As for the relationship between international capital flows and development of LDCs, a positive role for international capital mobility is commonly acknowledged: but much attention is now focused on the instability imposed by financial liberalisation on emerging countries, where financial markets are exposed to potentially destabilising speculation[6]. A typical trade-off seems to apply to LDCs since capital flow liberalisation implies potential efficiency gains on one side but also risk of crisis induced by sudden capital outflows on the other[7].

Financial and/or currency crises have become more frequent in the nineties (EMS, Mexico, South East Asia, Russia, Brazil). A closer look at their causes and development reveals that much conventional argument on the trade-off between micro-economic efficiency and macro-economic stability in global finance should be regarded sceptically. Quite the opposite, inefficient transactions appear to be the main destabilising factor[8].

ORDERING GLOBAL FINANCE?

This "decade of financial instability" is giving way to the third millennium. Although there is currently much discussion about re-designing

---

6. It's not possible to give a detailed account of the current situation and its antecedents. We may recall that the sudden rise in the eurodollar interest rates, due to an anti-inflationary shift in US monetary policy, is at the origin of the 1982 debt crisis, after a decade of heavy borrowing from international banks, at market rates, by governments of the more dynamic LDCs. After stagnation in the eighties, capital inflows directed towards dynamic LDC regained momentum in the nineties, especially in the form of private debt issue. Recent experience indicates that euphoria in private borrowing, as in sovereign borrowing, is exposed to changes in moods of institutional investors.

7. Taxation of financial transactions may be used as "sand in the wheels" of financial markets (this is the so called Tobin Tax proposal), to reduce, it is hoped, volatility in financial markets. In addition, revenues from the Tobin tax – to be collected on a supranational basis – could be devoted to support development projects.

8. For example, the greater part of capital outflows during the Mexican crisis can be accounted for by compulsory margin calls on derivative contracts entered by Mexican institutions themselves; some interpretations of the more recent South East Asian experience point to over-investment as the fundamental cause of the crisis. These remarks may look a rather sophisticated and technical detail, but they underline the need for a serious investigation before discussing about policy options that tackle consequences (say, administrative regulation of capital flows) instead of causes.

the global financial markets[9], this largely concentrates on rules and agreements that can help to manage or, better, to prevent financial crises. Furthermore, the terms of the debate reflect, by and large, the presumption of an efficiency/stability trade-off when a country, especially a developing country, opens up to international flows of capital. Financial globalisation has gone too far, many say.

While contagion, systemic risk and exogenous instability rank high in the current debate on ordering global finance, with its focus on preventing and managing financial crises[10], this misses one basic point: what rules and agreements can help financial markets and institutions to deliver the "real" goods, i.e. inter-temporal trade, so that deserving investment projects get to be financed? Financial markets do deliver other benefits which are relevant, especially for sophisticated players: portfolio diversification, insurance, unbundling and repackaging of risk, etc. But these are substantially "derivative" benefits that still depend upon the basic trade: namely, lending for good projects.

My criticism of the current debate can be expressed as follows. There is a wealth of deserving investment projects, especially in LDCs, which are impossible to implement both because local saving is inadequate and often diverted towards alternative skewed forms of financial investment, and because the world financial markets are busy elsewhere and do not spot those investments. In other words, the missing line in the contemporary debate about financial markets is marginalisation of poor regions from the credit circuit.

This omission has a strong ethical dimension, but at this point I would prefer to stress that it is a crucial *economic* issue, economic in the received sense: a matter of convenience or of mutual interest for potential borrowers and lenders.

Debt overhang is the single most relevant cause of marginalisation because its consequences involve a self-sustaining vicious circle: potentially productive investments are delayed because of uncertainty about projected macroeconomic policies due to debt servicing. Structural reforms are also delayed since present costs must be incurred in order to increase possible future benefits; foreign would-be lenders are discouraged. A cumulative process develops leading to lower growth and progressive marginalisation.

9. For a quick summary of contemporary debate, see *Time for a Redesign? A Survey of Global Finance*, in *The Economist* 30 January 1999.

10. Although it can be argued that a patient "subsidiarity" approach would probably be more effective in preventing crises than an ambitious global redesign.

CST on Global Finance: A Prophetic Role

CST documents of different kinds have addressed the issue of external debt and LDCs[11]. The 1986 *Justitia et Pax* document, *An Ethical Approach to the International Debt Question* makes two crucial points. First, that it is urgent to identify a solution to the debt problem where the debt burden imposes an unbearable weight on the poor people living in indebted countries, imposing privations that are not compatible with personal dignity. Second, that such a solution should be found in a solidarity approach involving the poor countries, the rich countries and the international community. Solidarity requires awareness and acceptance of co-responsibility on both causes and solutions of the debt problem: sharing responsibility for causes can help in finding solidarity solutions. Different actors are explicitly identified as co-responsible: international financial institutions (official and private); governments of industrial countries and developing countries (the action of the latter is crucial if debt forgiveness is to result in increased human capital investment); citizens of rich countries, banks and industries (the agents that stand to gain most from globalisation).

Further documents on the debt issue have been published by the Episcopal Conferences of advanced countries[12] and developing countries[13]. More recently, the debt question has also been considered, with somewhat different emphases, by the Synods of African (1994) and of American Bishops (1997)[14]. The number of pontifical statements on the debt issue is also very large, especially in connection with the Jubilee. Christians have been called upon to advocate a voice for the poor people,

---

11. Before the *Justitia et Pax* document, many statements by Latin American bishops had strongly underlined the state of impoverishment of their people, due to the debt crisis. See: Consejo Episcopal Latinoamericano, *Brecha entre ricos y pobres en America Latina,* Departamento de Pastoral Social, 1985. In particular, points 2.4.4. Deuda externa; 3.2 Sugerencias frente a la deuda. After severe criticism of I.M.F. style of intervention the document proposes to "...llegar a una salida negociada que permita el pago de la deuda externa en forma tal que non se agravan aùn màs las brechas intranacionales e internacionales entre pobres y ricos", p. 33.

12. Sekretariat der Deutschen Bischofskonferenz, *The International Debt Crisis. An Ethical Challenge,* 16 May 1988; United States Catholic Conference Administrative Board, *Statement on Relieving Third World Debt,* in *Origins,* CNS Documentary Service, 12 October 1989.

13. Comision Episcopal De Pastoral Social, *La Deuda Externa del Mexico. Reflexion y Aplicacion a Mexico del Documento "Al Servicio de La Comunidad Humana: una consideracion etica de La deuda internacional",* Ciudad de Mexico, 1987.

14. *Assemblea speciale per l'Africa del sinodo dei vescovi,* Roma, 10 aprile-8 maggio 1994, in *Il Regno documenti* 11 (1994); *Special Assembly of the Synod of the Americas,* dicembre 1997, especially proposition 74 (ex76) on economic globalization.

proposing a significant reduction, if not a cancellation, of the international debt that clouds the destiny of many nations[15]. The solution of the debt problem is regarded as having a high symbolic value within the broader context of development.

It is worth drawing attention to the way in which CST took up the much-canvassed idea of under-development in the 1960s and construed it ethically as "human" development and later as "integral development"[16]. In its approach, CST made it clear that development is not the expected outcome of an *a priori* project but is a dynamic process where time and space matter and where each step is valuable in itself, since how results are obtained is as important as what they are. In terms of policy design, this concept of development as a process requires a subsidiarity approach.

Two further comments on these documents are appropriate. First, it should be noted that the ethical approach to the debt issue as it emerges in CST is not mechanical or just technical, nor is it simply "ethically correct behaviour". An essential element is the way in which its "back to basics" approach is grounded in justice *(Tertio millennio adveniente,* 13). In that document, awareness, an act of human reason, is explicitly posited as a pre-requisite for accepting the responsibility that comes from interdependence. Hence, debt cancellation for the Jubilee is at one and the same time a non-ritual religious act and a humanly reasonable deed. In other words, an ethical approach is grounded on a fundamental ontological dimension. Second, debt relief is described in CST as both an economic priority and a moral duty. It is at this point that CNOST has a role in exploring the middle ground so as to relate principles and policies. The formulation of a coherent CathST depends on this detailed and thoughtful work.

SECULAR THOUGHT VIS-À-VIS CATHST
ON DEBT RELIEF, ECONOMIC ANALYSIS AND POLICY OPTIONS

In order to bring out the prophetic role of CST I would like to underline a few points emerging from "secular" thought. The economics of financial markets include three issues which demand ethical evaluation: technology-driven behaviour and responsibility; multiple equilibria; and

15. *TMA* 51; message of Pope John Paul II, 1 January 1998; and his speech in Mexico, 1999.
16. S. BERETTA, *Globalizzazione e sviluppo. Due parole da chiarire*, in *La società. Studi, ricerche documentazione sulla dottrina sociale della Chiesa,* n. 2, 1998.

"forgiveness" as an "economic" option in routine transactions. There are two further methodological points related to debt relief as a policy option which are ethically sensitive: inertia in tackling an urgent issue; and its necessity/sufficiency for LDC development. This section may be read as naive "apologetic" or, preferably, as a sketch of a prophetic role for CathST.

The first point picks up an earlier general reference that "mechanical" behaviour in financial markets is likely to be inefficient and to generate diffuse irresponsibility. The case of international sovereign debt is clear: creditors lending on routine information, on the basis, say, of the flow of oil revenues to a potential debtor, induce borrowers and policy-makers to underestimate the probability of a change in attitude of lenders. Such a change in attitude cannot be ruled out in principle, and it is very likely to take the form of herd behaviour when lenders mechanically act as "followers" in syndicated loans. Recent experience confirms that investors do in fact quickly change their attitude, as much "contagion" literature illustrates. Mechanical formulas of interest rate indexation (LIBOR plus a fixed spread, as is most common in syndicated rollover loans) expose borrowers to potentially devastating effects of external events (for example, a severe monetary restriction in advanced countries can produce a large negative externality on borrowers in terms of higher debt service).

When externalities occur, no responsibility is taken for consequences produced by one's decisions on somebody else's situation. Hence, diffuse irresponsibility is a feature of mechanical transactions: borrowers do not account to lenders for how they use the purchasing power they receive; lenders do not respond to market events that are beyond their control; global market events can be the unintended by-product of national policy decisions where responsibility is only to domestic citizens. In terms used in CST, a "structure of sin" develops; in secular terms there has been both "a market and government failure".

Significantly, the current debate about new global financial architecture is trying to find a balance between "bailing-out" on the part of international financial institutions, acting in a sense as lenders of last resort[17], and "bailing in"[18] the private sector, since both options exhibit

17. The existence of a lender of last resort creates a "moral hazard" problem, that is, from the lending institution point of view an adverse effect on the debtor's attitude toward assuming risky positions.

18. "Bailing in" the private sector means devising contractual mechanisms for crisis prevention that can effectively pre-commit private sector participants to maintain or to provide additional net exposure, reduce debt-service burden in times of crises, while limiting moral hazard. As an example, bond contracts may include collective representation, sharing clauses, provisions for the modification of terms by qualified majorities. Further

dangerous features: excessive risk taking if institutional bailing-out prevails, marginalisation of the least resourced would-be borrowers if too much bailing-in scares away potential lenders and/or increases the price of credit.

A second feature of secular thinking relates to economics and institutions. The LDC debt issue is a good example. Within games-theory approaches to economic interdependence and repeated interactions the most common result is the existence of multiple equilibria. That is, many different configurations of the network of relationship among actors can be sustainable, each of them with identifiable consequences on the positions of individual actors and on the overall functioning of the system of relations under consideration. Multiple equilibria imply no economic "necessity", rather, many economic "possibilities"[19]. For one thing, the quality of relationships is relevant: one can say also that multiple equilibria mean that "good" or "bad" configurations of economic relations can happen, and that once they do happen they can influence the future structure of interdependence and the future set of possibilities of actions (path dependence).

At its core, a market is one configuration (among many) of economic relationships; that is, an institution whose quality depends upon the quality of the network of relations. A market can be an "institution of justice", that is, a set of agreed upon rules which can be credibly enforced in order to guarantee that (unequal) partners in an economic relation may[20] have an effective voice and working relations "as equals". But the neo-liberal inclination to accept the market as if it will deliver the best results automatically is a naïve expectation, as marginalisation or exclusion from financial markets illustrates. The human dimension of relations must be submitted for ethical judgement.

My third analytical point refers to another game theory general result, with evident application to debt relief, that is, in repeated interactions forgiveness may be "economical". Sustaining cooperation in non-cooperative games can work, provided an appropriate balance of threats and punishments is credible to the parties in question. Trigger strategies are

provisions may be needed for dealing with extreme crisis situations. See IMF MANAGING DIRECTOR, *Report to the Interim Committee on 'Progress in Strengthening the Architecture of the International Financial System'*, # 30-34, April 16 1999.

19. There is no need to stress that many mechanical trade-offs frequently proposed in "pop" ethics (the archetype of these being the efficiency – equity trade off) would be there, only provided we can identify a "necessary" efficient solution!

20. The CST idea that there are "structures of sin" finds a sociological foundation in current ideas on "structuration", as developed by Anthony Giddens and others. It is the opposite side of the coin from "structures of the common good".

important, as in the repeated prisoner's dilemma example (tit for tat).
But "forgiving" the defaulting party for past actions, after a while and
not necessarily completely, does very often improve the situation not
only of the offender but also of the offended party, yielding a higher
overall pay-off than the one associated with fully punishing the offender.
In a sense, non-myopic selfishness can be a good enough reason for
assessing ways and means to implement debt relief[21].

The present situation as regards LDC foreign debt[22] is described in the
table below:

LDC external debt and capital flows

	1980	**1985**	**1990**	**1995**
External debt (billion dollars)	615	1403	1510	2068
External debt/GNP	21.0	33.9	34.8	39.6
Total debt service/exports	13.0	20.3	18.3	17.0
Net transfers (billion dollars)	29.4	-5.1	27.2	136.3

Source: *World debt tables, Global development Finance*, Washington, selected years.

The amount of external debt has multiplied; its ratio to national production has almost doubled; the export-share devoted to debt servicing
is still well above its pre-crisis level[23]. It is striking that there is so much
debt for so little inter-temporal trade[24]! This does not make economic
sense since it is from inter-temporal trade that all parties, creditors
included, can be expected to gain. The ethical question lies at the heart
of the economic dilemma.

In the aftermath of the 1982 debt crisis the strange strategy of the
"financial vicious circle" (lending to countries which may use the
money only to service their debt, not for investing) may have been necessary as a short-run device to give time for over-exposed commercial
banks to adjust their accounts, but to continue this practice many years
after the crisis is plain nonsense. While beneficial to individual financial

21. After all, in Isle of Tortuga (arguably formed by non-myopic, selfish people) a
very sophisticated and efficient democratic system prevailed!

22. A more detailed analysis would strongly reinforce the argument.

23. See O. GARAVELLO, *Il condono del debito estero dei paesi meno avanzati alla fine
degli anni '90'*, in UNIVERSITÀ CATTOLICA DEL SACRO CUORE. FACOLTÀ DI ECONOMIA E
COMMERCIO, *Chiesa, usura e debito estero. Giornata di studio su Chiesa e prestito a
inteesse, ieri e oggi in occasione del Cinquantennio della Facoltà di Economia
(Quaderno* n. 6, supplemento), Milano, Università cattolica del Sacro Cuore. Centro di
ricerche per lo studio della dottrina sociale della Chiesa, 1998.

24. As measured by net transfers, which include also non-debt capital inflows such as
foreign direct investment.

institutions which can avoid writing off credit positions, from a global perspective round-trips freeze money in a non-productive circle instead of freeing it to finance deserving projects, which is the only way to generate gains for the entire system. Debt relief, with some agreed upon burden-sharing, is clearly economically beneficial[25] and can be designed in order to foster co-responsibility.

Despite its obvious suitability as a method of dealing with the current crises of the LDCs, we observe a tremendous inertia regarding debt relief. Once a taboo subject, discussion of debt relief is now somewhat popular among economists (although not so much among policy-makers). At an earlier stage it appeared to be in conflict with purely economic options, but is now recognised as an issue of solidarity. But in spite of this shift of opinion there is still tremendous inertia about debt relief.

With regard to official debt, in practice a significant precedent from which much can be learnt is the case of war reparations after World War I. It took World War II for it to be recognised that war reparations were not so good for the victors, and dangerous for the system. On this point the German bishops make interesting comments in their 1998 document on LDC debt.

In the private debt case, on the contrary, debt relief of some kind is more commonly observed. Financial entrepreneurs operating in relatively simple, "closed" economic systems, for example a latter-day merchant banker, typically realise that, in order to make money from their banking business they have to lend it to fresh borrowers, carefully and progressively writing off non-performing loans from their balance sheets. Cautious accounting procedures suggest that in order to keep a designated fund as a shock-absorber institutions such as bankruptcy laws and procedures can also be relied upon to find solutions to bad loans, where damages are distributed among the parties involved: that is, the costs of potential default are "internalised".

Certain developments in international private finance (that is, of financial linkages among national financial systems) open new ways for dealing with potential defaults. Domestic lenders may be in a position to try to discharge the full cost of adjusting to defaulting loans to outsiders (with the support of domestic authorities and institutions). This "beggar-my-neighbour" option is more or less what has been used in the aftermath of the 1982 LDC debt crisis: a disproportionate amount of adjustment costs has been borne by the indebted countries.

25. An indirect proof of such convenience is that, curiously enough, commercial debt relief has worked much better than official debt relief, up to now.

There is an obvious ethical challenge in finding equitable post-crisis adjustment solutions, but there are also good economic reasons for lenders to "internalise" the costs of debt default underlying the institutional design of "simple" financial systems. An unavoidable conclusion seems to be that debt relief can be defended strongly on economic grounds not as an end it itself, but as the first step in a process of "internalising" crisis adjustment costs, leading to a more appropriate global institutional design[26].

A final remark about debt relief and LDC development: although debt relief can be defended as a necessary policy to rectify past neglect, it cannot be regarded as an adequate policy. Cancelling debt overhang is not an adequate strategy for LDCs. A more complete economic strategy must be put in place: effective conditionality is practicable and must be practised. At the level of international politics, moreover, a system of global governance must be set up to secure improved outcomes and to monitor and regulate policies and projects[27].

In this context I would stress that there is a practical working hypothesis in CathST which deserves careful attention by "secular" thought about finance. I refer to the idea of subsidiarity. Conditionality, that is the top-down process by which lenders seek to ensure the proper use of resources is all very well in principle; but it is extremely hard to implement because of asymmetric information and because of the incentive structure the parties face. Subsidiarity, with its bottom-up structure, is likely to be more development-friendly: secular thinking would do well to take this idea on board

My belief is that Catholic social thought can be a catalyst for innovative thinking more widely, provided that it is not reduced to a code repeated by "loyalist" voices, or attacked by critics who have not bothered to examine its claims. It represents an intellectual challenge which is especially valuable in times of accelerating structural change, where mechanical reference to extrinsic (codified) ethical principles ends up being totally inadequate. This can be seen also in looking at the role of the official teaching and non-official thinking of the Church in historical financial controversies, as well as in contemporary issues. I find it useful and instructive to compare current financial ethics with the evolution of Catholic social teaching and non-official Catholic social thinking by

26. The current debate about "global financial architecture*" does in fact address some of the above mentioned issues. See IMF MANAGING DIRECTOR, *Report to the Interim Committee* (n. 18).

27. See WORLD BANK, *World Development Report,* 1998

exploring two profound structural transformations of European society: the commercial revolution and the industrial revolution[28].

The Ethical Challenge of Transition: A Comment on Usury

The doctrine of usury, in parallel with the commercial revolution between the twelfth and the fifteenth century, evolved from outright prohibition of receiving interest on lending (because time is God's and not our own) to a justification of an interest rate proportioned to *lucrum cessans* and *damnum emergens,* where personal conscience and the professional qualities of the merchant could make the difference between interest and usury. Subsequently, the industrial revolution prompted rethinking about the doctrine on usury because of recognition of the virtual productivity of money as capital, measured by "market" evaluations (the market interest rate as a benchmark). Today, we face the challenge of the information technology revolution, where financial transactions again assume a new character calling for fresh thinking.

The evolution of the doctrine on usury involved a fruitful tension between reason and freedom, on the one side, and authority and law on the other. Different attitudes emerged within the Church, clashing at times. Finding ways to adapt an ancient teaching (dating back to the Old Testament) was far from painless.

Significantly, at the interface between socio-economic analysis and moral teaching the doctrine evolved when moral teaching was no longer just a repetition of formal, codified moral laws but became an original synthesis of "old" and "new" in thought and in practice. In thought, the change in the analytical paradigm used both to understand finance as such and to address its ethical dimension, safeguarding the essential and the permanent in the moral teaching of the Church, emerged from original intuitions grounded on the most realistic approach to human things (business included) that we have access to: the living tradition of Revelation[29]. Teaching on moral aspects of financial transactions did in fact find a more adequate framework in response to analytical innovations in the study of economic relations and actions. In this way ethical teaching became part of a "back to basics" movement. The development of CathST, then, was not simply a matter of theory but also of practice: this

---

28. See Università Cattolica del Sacro Cuore, *Chiesa, usura e debito estero* (n. 23).

29. The innovative thought on usury documents a dynamic unity between faith and reason, along the lines of the *Fides et ratio.*

is attested to by institutional innovations in the Catholic tradition, as can be exemplified in the *Monti di pietà* during the commercial revolution and in the widespread experiment of non-profit co-operative banking in nineteenth century Northern Italy.

CONCLUSION

As interdependence and complexity are the fabric of the world economy, problems of justice in global finance are inherently complex: it is not obvious what should be deemed as "just" in a given situation, let alone as a general rule. The suspicion that business may make use of "ethically correct" principles in order to present an acceptable face and as a way of advancing their private interests cannot be easily dismissed[30]. In a complex and interdependent world no mechanical interpretation of the world economy can address change, and change is what we have to cope with. The nature of economic relations can be better understood as *action* rather than as mechanical *behaviour*.

While it may be possible to classify a given behaviour as "just" or "unjust" with reference to some extrinsic ethical principles, no such *a priori* classification can be thought to be adequate for actions, which by definition are expressions of free, personal and unpredictable responses to constantly changing realities and circumstances, although these responses are structured so that the actions are shaped at least in part (as Pope John Paul says in *SRS* 36). One vital task for social ethics is to develop the right kind of framework, with attention to its ontological foundation, so as to guide the emergence of the right questions.

Catholic social thought, always in contact with the tradition of Catholic social teaching but imaginatively probing, inspiring and interpreting, poses a continuing intellectual challenge to offer moral guidance to those who shape our economic environment, and not to be petrified as formal references to extrinsic, codified ethical principles which risk being irrelevant or inadequate.

Catholic University of Milano   Simona BERETTA[31]

---

30. S. BERETTA, M. MAGGIONI & L. SENN, *'Settimo, non rubare' nel commercio internazionale*, in *Communio: Rivista Internazionale di Teologia e Cultura* (gennaio-febbraio 1998), no. 157, 15-29.

31. The author wants to thank Carlo Beretta, Oscar Garavello, Mario Maggioni and Daniela Parisi for their insightful comments on various drafts of the paper.

ECONOMY OF COMMUNION
BETWEEN MARKET AND SOLIDARITY

The aim of this paper is to present the "Economy of Communion" (EoC) project, a particular kind of economy of sharing which developed within the Focolare movement. The "Economy of Communion" is an initiative launched by Chiara Lubich in 1991 during a visit to Brazil, stimulated by the need to respond to the extreme poverty experienced by people who are deprived of even the most basic human rights. The project proposes an original economic lifestyle based on "communion". Nowadays, the behaviour of more than two million people is influenced by this project. From the point of view of production, more than 700 firms all over the world belong to it.

Starting from this key-study the author aims to show the theoretical relevance of such a style of living, as a contribution to the current debate on Catholic social thought. Following an initial description of the EoC and the nature of the experience of those involved, the relationship between EoC and the "Civil Economy" movement will be explored. An attempt will then be made to highlight aspects which are peculiar to EoC in the context of the discussion of a Civil Economy. The essay will conclude with the examination of issues of some relevance to current theoretical debate on economics where EoC has something interesting to say.

I. THE "HUMUS" OF THE EoC EXPERIENCE

There is nothing new in the claim that every idea concerning economic activities is the fruit of a specific culture and of a precise vision of the world. As a starting point, it may be useful to explain briefly the spiritual *humus* from which the EoC arose. This account is indebted to a recent speech by Chiara Lubich, who founded the Focolare movement in 1943 in Trent, Italy[1].

The culture and style of life practised in the Focolare movement is animated by a new spirituality which is both personal and collective: the "spirituality of unity". This movement is now present in 182 nations

---

1. C. LUBICH, *L'esperienza 'economia di comunione': dalla spiritualità dell'Unità una proposta di agire economico*, in *Nuova Umanità* 21 (1999/6), no. 126, 613-619.

among people of all ages, races, languages, cultures, and faiths[2]. Although the majority of its members are Catholic there are also Christians of 300 different churches, adherents of the world's main religions, and men and women without any particular religious belief who share many values with us. The Movement also offers a new way to live the various aspects of social life, political, cultural, artistic and economic.

The Movement's vision of the world is based on God, the Father of all. Consequently, all people are called to act as his sons and daughters and as brothers and sisters, in a universal brotherhood, a bridge to a more united world. For this reason, everyone is asked to practise with determination what is called love, Christian love, or for those who belong to other faiths, benevolence, which means wanting the good of others, an attitude which can be found in all sacred books and among many men and women who do not have any particular religious affiliation. All human beings instinctively build relationships with others. In fact, every person, notwithstanding personal limitations and weaknesses, naturally possesses an ethos inclined more to giving than to having, precisely because all persons are called to love their fellow human beings.

Typical of the Focolare movement is the so-called "culture of giving" which, from the beginning, has been translated into practical terms through a communion of goods among all the members, and through social works, including some very substantial ones. In addition, if this love is lived together, it becomes mutual and gives rise to solidarity, a solidarity which can be kept alive only by silencing one's selfishness, by facing difficulties and overcoming them. And it is this solidarity, always placed at the foundation of every human activity, including that of economy, that characterises the lifestyle which some two million people seek to practice daily in the Focolare movement and which has now spread far beyond the Movement.

II. EoC: NINE YEARS OF HISTORY

The Economy of Communion is an economic and social expression of the Focolare Movement. It was launched by Chiara Lubich in 1991 during a visit to Brazil, and the Movement, present in that country since 1958, has spread to all its states, attracting people of every social category.

---

2. On the Focolare movement and Chiara Lubich's story, see G. GALLAGHER, *Woman's Work*, London, 1998.

Chiara arrived in Brazil with a vivid impression of the recently published *Centesimus annus* in her heart, and passing by Sao Paolo, was
particularly struck by the immense gap she saw between the happy few
rich and the many poor; skyscrapers surrounded by millions of *favelas*.
Her pain was deeper when she realised that in these *favelas* there were
also members of her movement. In this context Chiara had an intuition
of what was to become the Economy of Communion, as she recently
narrated: "I realised that we were unable to cover even the most urgent
needs of our members, notwithstanding the intense communion of
goods. It seemed to me, then, that God was calling our Movement to
something new. Although I am not an expert in economic problems, I
thought that our people could set up firms and business enterprises so as
to engage the capabilities and resources of all, and to produce together in
favour of those in need. They would have to be managed by competent
persons who would be capable of making them function efficiently and
derive profits from them. These profits would be put in common freely.
One part would be used for the same goals of the early Christian communities: to help those in need, to give them something to live on until
they find work. Another part, to develop structures to form 'new people'
(as the apostle Paul calls them), that is, people formed and animated by
love, suited to what we call the 'culture of giving'. Finally, one part
would certainly be used for the growth of the firm[3].

The idea was welcomed enthusiastically not only in Brazil and in the
rest of Latin America but in Europe and other parts of the world. Many
new businesses came to life and many existing ones have adhered to the
project by modifying their way of operating a business. Today there are
761 firms belonging to the *Communio* project.

Geographic distribution (data Sept. 1999)

Italy	246
Western Europe	172
Eastern Europe	60
Middle East	2
Asia	36
Africa	9
North America	45
Central America	49
Brazil	82

3. C. LUBICH, *Discourse for The Honorary Degree in Economics*, Catholic University
of Sacro Cuore, Piacenza, 29.1.1999.

Argentina	45
Australia	15
Total	**761**

Sectors of activity

Community care	327
Production	194
Commerce	161
Other activities	79
Total	**761**

III. THE PHENOMENON OF CIVIL ECONOMY

In order to understand the distinctiveness of the EoC project, it may be worth highlighting, first, a few points that the EoC has in common with similar experiences. In fact, though presenting its own elements of originality, linked with the novelty and typical characteristics of the spirituality of unity, the experience of the Economy of Communion is part of a significant recent development in the European context, that is the larger movement for the "humanisation of the economy" that has sprung up recently in Western civil society. We can call this movement "Civil Economy".

Civil economy has its roots in the Renaissance, and the "modern" economist who can be considered as its "father" is the Neapolitan Antonio Genovesi. While Adam Smith in Scotland was teaching economics based on "wealth"[4], Genovesi in Naples was also teaching economics, based, however, on the idea of "public happiness" and on the role of civic virtues: *Lectures on Civil Economy* (1765-1767) was in fact the title of his treatise[5]. And the main difference between "wealth" and "happiness" is the following: "I can be rich even alone (consuming my wealth alone, watching my television) but I cannot be happy alone; we must be at least two. Happiness is either 'public' or is not; and then it is 'solitude'."

This movement is a continuation of some alternative forms of institutional economy that have come into being in the last two centuries (for

4. *The Wealth of Nations*, 1776, is the title of his book, considered the first pillar of economic science.

5. On this see S. ZAMAGNI, *Social Paradoxes of Growth and Civil Economy*, in G. GANDOLFO & F. MARZANO (eds.), *Economic Theory and Social Justice*, London, MacMillan, 1999.

instance the so-called co-operative Movement), but at the same time it presents two characteristics which, taken together, show something new: a tendency to combine the logic and mentality of the business enterprise with an instance of solidarity; and a desire to develop also the economic side of life primarily as a "search for sense and meaning in which values play a crucial role"[6]. That is, its aim is to overcome the dichotomy of living one type of logic in business and another in the family, the group or the community, and to attempt a type of behaviour compatible with one's own values in every field of life[7].

The main novelty of this movement of civil economy can be highlighted as follows. Until recently the outlook and values on which enterprises were based (efficiency, profitability, innovation, competitiveness, etc.) were generally seen as being in contrast to the values inspiring works of solidarity such as welfare organisations, homes, charitable institutions. Enterprises were considered the realm of profit-seeking, individual gain, the iron rule of the market, while the State or private charities were the place for altruism, solidarity, compassion, values. Any relationships between these two worlds were to be delayed until the "last moment", that is the moment when the individual (or the institution, a bank for example) had to decide what to do with his/her assets, with the possibility of devoting some of them to works of solidarity. But throughout the production process there was to be no talk of solidarity within the enterprise (solidarity was considered synonymous with inefficiency and waste), while at the same time there was to be no talk of the logic of the enterprise in the realms and works of solidarity – though there were exceptions here, too, like the first savings banks or building societies.

The welfare state, where the market creates wealth and the State distributes this wealth on criteria of solidarity, represents a method of transferring money from the rich to the poorest members of society. This is usually done through progressive taxation. Today, this Welfare State system is in crisis. One of the main reasons for this is what the economist

6. The principal type of "social enterprise" in Italy is the "social co-operative".

7. The main characteristics of these experiences can be described as follows: a) They are private and "voluntary", that is they come from the voluntary decision of private individuals; b) There is to some extent a "gratuitous" element in them: the incentive behind them is not primarily and merely the profit; c) There is an element of "idealism" in them: their promoters are led by ideals that "lie outside of/ or go beyond" mere economic considerations; d) They yield a "public" benefit (which directly or indirectly increases the well-being of persons other than the promoters); e) Relations are "reciprocal": it is not easy to distinguish who is giving and who is receiving because exchanges take place in both directions.

Okun has called the theory of "the leaking bucket", that is, the State is transferring income from the richest to the poor as if it were using a "pierced bucket": almost 50% of the funds raised by taxation and destined for the poorest is eaten up yearly by the structure created in order to distribute this income. In fact, the way that the relation between market and solidarity is organised leaves out an essential: the civil society. Therefore, civil economy, the economic expression of civil society, consists of all those economic activities that are neither market nor State. Civil society is the realm of social life of people: associations, groups, movements, trade unions, families, which can be neither classified as market nor State.

This movement of civil economy is growing steadily: in Italy the so-called "non-profit sector", an important subset of this movement, is providing work for 690.000 persons (3.1% of the national work force), and voluntary activities involve some six million persons[8].

V. The EoC Form of Civil Economy

The EoC project involves firms which, although being "civil enterprises" – sharing the characteristics sketched above – have peculiar features, both at the practical and cultural level. It is a particular form of Civil Economy. Chiara Lubich in her recent speeches (Piacenza, Italy 29.1.99; Strasburg, France 31.5.99), has highlighted some points of the peculiar "personality" of the EoC. Here I would like to describe more fully some of them[9].

1. Not Merely Non-Profit

Most "civil" enterprises (in the sense I have described above) are normally "non-profit organisations". The EoC, instead, proposes modes of behaviour inspired by liberality, solidarity and care for those in need whose practice is to be applied, in the main, to "for-profit" businesses.

---

8. To discover a similar period of enthusiasm for the possibility of "humanising the economy" we have to go back to the co-operative movement at the end of the 19th century, when it was seen by many as the new type of commercial life for the future. In my opinion the co-operative movement only partly came up to expectations, and the reasons for this must be sought in the failure to rethink (perhaps because it was not possible) the basic tenets of economic theory. The concept of "mutuality" was an attempt in this direction, but nothing was done to associate theoreticians of economics with the "movement" and much more attention was paid to involving politicians and practical economists.

9. For the complete text, see *Nuova Umanità* 126 (n. 1).

As a consequence, the EoC does not present itself so much as a new form of enterprise, alternative to those already existing – as was the case at the end of 19th century with the rise of the Co-operative Movement. Rather, it intends to transform the usual business structures from within (whether they be shareholding corporations, co-operatives, or other) by striving to form all relations inside and outside the companies around a lifestyle based on communion. Thus, the EoC has a positive attitude toward the market and efficiency: the market can be an instrument of communion among people.

This aspect is particularly important for the entire trend towards "humanising economy", because it fills a gap. In fact the main critics of "civil firms" claim that their "civil" and ethical approach functions only in "marginal" sectors (community care, assistance to disadvantaged persons, etc.), but that this approach does not work when firms have to deal with the iron law of the market. The experience of the EoC, and its eight years of life, challenges this deep-rooted thesis.

2. Communio: More than Simple "Giving"

A second point which seems to me particularly interesting in the context of this paper is the relationship of the firms with the poor. Those who find themselves in economic straits, the recipients of a part of the profits of the EoC enterprises, are not persons who are "assisted" by the business. They are essential members of the project, within which they also give something: they give their needs as a gift to others. Thus they too live the culture of giving[10]. This expresses the point that in the EoC, even though there is an emphasis on giving, the accent is not put on the philanthropy of a few but rather on "communion", where each one gives and receives with equal dignity, in the ambit of a substantially reciprocal relationship.

An interesting aspect from a theoretical point of view is that the experience of communion creates a "social culture" which is fertile for the rise of new economic activities, new entrepreneurs, new economic development. Everyone knows how important the so-called "social capital" is for the economic and social growth of a particular region[11].

10. Many, as soon as they attain a minimum of economic independence, renounce the help they have been receiving, and, not rarely, they share with others less fortunate the little they do have.

11. See R. PUTNAM, *Making Democracy Work. Civic Traditions in Modern Italy*, Princeton, NY, Princeton University Press, 1993. See also, in a historical perspective, L. BRUNI & R. SUGDEN, *Moral Canals. Trust and Social Capital in the Work of Hume, Smith and Genovesi*, forthcoming in *Economics and Philosophy* (Spring 2000).

Social capital includes trust, co-operation, non-instrumental relation-ships among people, in short the informal network of civil virtues. Its role was already clear two centuries ago. For instance, Antonio Gen-ovesi in starting his professional career was asked, "Why is my state, which has a beautiful climate, is surrounded by the sea (thus making commerce easy) and has intelligent people, not rich like other countries in Europe?" Ten years later, in 1765 he gave his answer: the reason is a lack of trust among people, a lack of civil virtues.

The creation in the past eight years of three still small "industrial parks" of the EoC (in Brazil, U.S.A., Argentina), is striking sign of the "economic" role of *communio:* most of these firms would not have come into existence without the project of EoC, without the "trust" and social capital born from the experience of *communio.*

The category of "communion" is distinct but closely connected to "community", because both have their roots in "giving" (community derives from *cum-munus* or reciprocal gift). Communion is something other than mere contract: it is more demanding than reciprocity on the one hand, and altruism on the other. It is more and more becoming a the-oretical category, enabling us to grasp the reality of EoC. Moreover, as a type of community, "communion" can offer a paradigm for the vaster movement of "humanising the economy", which is in search of new the-oretical categories for expressing its experience.

V. Towards an "Economics of Communion"?

"Many people ask" – as Chiara Lubich stated in Strasburg – "how these businesses, so attentive to the needs of all the subjects they deal with and of society as a whole, can survive in a market economy. Certainly, the spirit that animates them helps to overcome many of those internal conflicts, which obstruct and in some cases paralyse all human organisa-tions. In addition, their way of operating attracts the trust and benevolence of clients, suppliers, and financiers. Nonetheless, we should not forget another essential element – Providence – which has constantly accom-panied the development of the Economy of Communion during these years ...".

If the theory of the great economist J.A. Schumpeter is true, accord-ing to which profit springs from "innovation" – where innovation means any new idea which leads to a decrease in the average cost of the firm – then perhaps we could say that the "dynamics of communion", that is the investment in non-instrumental and genuine interpersonal relation-ships, is the main innovation of EoC firms, which allows them to carry on and to grow within the market. "The quality of interpersonal relationships is our added value", as EoC entrepreneurs say often.

In the last eight years studies on a theoretical and cultural level have been emerging along with the growth of the firms. The first to study the EoC were young people: almost 100 dissertations and two PhD theses have been presented or are under way in various universities in more than twenty different countries. Furthermore, in the last two/three years the academic community is also showing a growing interest in the EoC experience, an interest which is extending outside the context of the Focolare movement where it arose. Several economists and other scholars are seriously working to develop from the "economy" of communion an "economics" of communion[12].

VI. CONCLUSION AND PROSPECT

Is there a future for the EoC project? Could it become an ordinary way of living the economic dimension of life? The answer is, of course, complex. I would like to pose just a few considerations.

First, I would say that the main reason for optimism lies in history. If we look at the history of economic and social life in a short-sighted way, keeping our horizon within the narrow boundaries of modern era, and within western societies, we must admit that an economic life based on individualistic self-interest is the rule and "communion" the exception. But if we lengthen our perspective and look at history through centuries when markets and cities came to light, the situation is completely different. Economy has been a path of encounter among people even when politics or religions were causes of conflict. The seaports of the medieval world were at once bombing warships and welcoming ships full of spices and textiles. The same is true if we look outside western society, say to Africa and China. Then we must say that "communion is the rule" of organising economic and social life, and self-interest the exception[13].

---

12. The special issue of the *Nuova Umanità* review (n. 126, 1999) is dedicated to theoretical studies on the Economy of Communion, with contributions by scholars from diverse branches of economic sciences (economics, business administration, history of economics, economic anthropology), is a sign of this new interest.

13. I cannot explore here more fully the content of this thesis. For more insights see the classical work of K. Polanyi, *The Great Transformation* (Beacon Paperbacks, 45), Boston, MA, Beacon, 1957. See also A. CAILLÉ, *Don, intérêt et désintéréssement: Bourdieu, Mauss, Platon et quelques autres* (Recherches. Série Bibliothèque du MAUSS), Paris, La Découverte, 1994.

Therefore, because the Economy of Communion has a notable past and present, it can also have a good future.

With this I come to a last consideration – the challenge beyond the EoC is an anthropological one. If we believe that the human person is fulfilled and happy in maximising his self-interest in solitude, then to be coherent we must say that the EoC and similar experiences are destined to remain an élite practice of idealistically and ethically motivated people. If, instead, we believe that the human person is a "reality of communion" who is happy only within rich and meaningful interpersonal relationships, and looking for meaning in what he or she does, then we can infer that to offer opportunities for communion even in economic life means to open to people a path towards happiness. It is therefore in this thirst for happiness, deeply present in the heart of every person, that the hope for the future of the EoC lies – the hope that it can develop and contribute towards making the economy of the third millennium a truly "civil" economy, an Economy of Communion.

University of Milan   Luigino BRUNI

OPTION FOR THE POOR RE-VISITED

I. INTRODUCTION

Catholic social thinking proposes a wide spectrum of moral values
and ideals. At one end of this spectrum there are several important moral
values which are immediately relevant to practical politics today. The
most obvious example of these is "subsidiarity" which has become such
a "buzz-word" in Europe in recent years. At this "realistic" end of the
spectrum we might also include such values as social justice, participation, respect, and human dignity. At the other end of the spectrum of
Catholic social teaching are moral values and ideals which seem less
obviously "realistic" in terms of practical politics. "Option for the
poor" is situated at the extreme end of this more idealistic part of the
spectrum.

It is useful to have a conference in which theologians sit down with
economists and other social scientists to explore some practical implications of Catholic social thinking. In such a conference it is only to be
expected that the focus would come mainly on those moral values and
ideals which are at the more "realistic" end of the spectrum. But it is
important not to lose sight of the whole range of Catholic social teaching, including values or ideals such as option for the poor which seem
less "realistic" from a political point of view. If we focus only on what
seems politically realistic at any given time, we are failing to give the
Church its prophetic role and voice. A major purpose of the Church is to
stand for, and give witness to, a different and better future which is
bound to seem unrealistic in present-day terms.

Effective prophetic witness and prophetic action can change a whole
people's attitude, bringing into the sphere of practical politics values that
previously seemed quite unrealistic. Gender equality is one obvious
example; so too is the very idea of democracy. It is salutary to recall
how Church leaders and teachers in the past allowed themselves to
become so wedded to patriarchal assumptions, and to an autocratic non-
participatory concept of state authority, that they failed to promote the
ideal of effective gender equality and dismissed the concept of democracy not only as unrealistic but even as evil. In doing so they betrayed
the prophetic dimension of the Christian vision. We must aim to avoid a
repetition of such mistakes – and that is one good reason for continuing

to hold on to the ideal of an option for the poor as an integral part of Catholic social teaching.

In the first part of this paper I intend to "look back" at the concept of option for the poor, proposing a clarification and refinement of its meaning and commenting on how the Roman authorities have reacted to it. Then, in the second part, I propose to "look forward" by suggesting a deeper understanding and some new practical applications of an option for the poor.

II. LOOKING BACK AND CLARIFYING – BIBLICAL OPTION VERSUS MARXIST OPTION

It is hardly a coincidence that the phrase "option for the poor" was adopted by liberation theologians at a time when the more adventurous of them were engaged in a serious dialogue with Marxism. But that does not mean that the theological phrase "option for the poor" should be understood as more or less the same thing as a Marxist-inspired "class option".

The liberation theologians have undoubtedly borrowed important elements from Marxism. I think there is a good case for claiming that liberation theology's emphasis on solidarity with the poor springs at least in part from a Marxist influence, and so too does its willingness to take account of the reality of the class structures of society.

On the other hand, there are major differences between the two approaches. By far the most important of these is that liberation theology draws its inspiration not from a class analysis of society but directly from Biblical sources. And what the Bible reveals is very different indeed from what Marxism teaches. The Marxist class option makes sound political sense; and that is why it was seen as such a threat by those who held power in the West. For instance it is quite easy to believe what Gramsci had to say about the so-called *intellettuale organico,* a phrase which is so misleadingly translated as "organic intellectual". As I understand it, he was suggesting that if a significant number of educated middle-class people make common cause with the poorer classes, then they could provide the masses with the analytical and organisational skills required for a successful revolution.

When we come to the Bible I think it is useful to make a distinction between an option for justice and a specific option for the poor. In much of the Bible there is an emphasis on social justice. We see the outrage of God, expressed by the prophets (and also by Jesus) about the mistreatment of the poor and the hard-heartedness and arrogance of the rich.

This is the option for justice. Option specifically for the poor is located within this wider context, but here the emphasis is different.

When I speak of option for the poor in a biblical sense I have in mind a spirituality inspired by the belief that God chooses the weak to confound the strong, chooses the foolish to show up the wisdom of the wise (1 Cor 1:27-8). Again and again in the Bible we see the weak ones, the unlikely ones, being chosen by God in order to show that what matters is not human power but trust in and reliance on divine initiative and power. We think of the letting go of most of the army of Gideon when they faced the forces of Midian (Jud 7:3-7), or of the choice of Moses who was a poor speaker (Ex 4:10-12). Similarly, the selection of Israel as God's own special people was not intended to make political sense but rather to undermine conventional political wisdom. And in the New Testament it is no accident that Jesus comes from a despised village in a despised province: "can anything good come out of Nazareth?" (Jn 1:46).

By contrast with the Marxist concept of a class option, a biblically-inspired "option for the poor" is not at all a shrewd political choice to take the side of an oppressed but potentially powerful working-class. It is rather a matter of taking the side of those who are the most marginalised and weakest people in society. There is no serious likelihood that the widows, the orphans, the "strangers" (that is, the refugees), the prostitutes or the tax-collectors will ever become major political powers in society. To opt for the poor is not to make a carefully calculated political gamble but to throw oneself on the mercy of God. It is to renounce any likelihood of political success in the conventional sense, but rather to radically re-define the very notion of success. It is a decision to find joy and fulfilment in ways that are incomprehensible in conventional terms.

1. *Relationship to Practical Politics*

Some people have been asking how "option for the poor" relates to "the Third Way" proposed by Anthony Giddens who is said to have inspired much of the "New Labour" policies in Britain. I think it is legitimate to ask to what extent "the Third Way" embodies an "option for justice"; but if one asks how it relates to an "option for the poor" (in the sense outlined above and below), this comes quite close to making a category mistake. It is rather like asking how "the Third Way" relates to the Beatitudes.

"The Third Way" is intended to be a practical political programme which can be adopted by a government. "Option for the poor", on the other hand, is an ideal which is in line with the Beatitudes and carries the same kind of moral weight. It is a serious moral invitation put before all Christians. None of us is entitled to dismiss it as not applicable to our own situation. But the manner and the degree in which each of us lives it out varies very much from person to person; and it is not for any of us to sit in judgement on the way another responds to this call, this invitation, this Christian ideal.

The institutional Church has a serious duty to promote such an option for the poor and to give witness to it in its own life and organisation. Religious Orders and Congregations have a duty to take it particularly seriously since their members take a vow of poverty. However, I do not think we can demand that the government of a country make such an option (in the strict sense), even though we can and must demand that it show particular concern for the poor and for all categories of people who have been left on the margins of society.

2. *Solidarity with the Poor and Option for the Poor*

An authentic option for the poor has two equally important aspects: a "solidarity" aspect which is about life-style, and a political or quasi-political aspect which has to do with analysis and action. The solidarity aspect involves a deliberate choice to enter in some degree into the world of those who have been left on the margins of society, to share in a significant way in their experience of being mistreated, by-passed, or left helpless. This choice of a different life-style springs from compassion, a word which means, literally, suffering with others, and it involves a choice to deepen this compassion by sharing to some extent in the suffering of the poor. By entering the world of deprived people one extends and deepens this experience of "suffering with" those on the margins. But by doing so one comes to share not only their pain and struggle but also their hopes and their joys.

Solidarity is a gift which those who are poor or marginalised may freely offer to the person who opts to share their life in some degree. It is a gift which cannot be presumed or demanded from them. They give it in their own time and in their own degree, and only to one who comes to them with no air of superiority or paternalism. Despite differences of skin colour, or accent, or background, the group may choose to accept this person as "one of us" – or at least "one with us" – one who shares their interests (in both senses of that word).

The virtue of solidarity emerges and flourishes within the matrix of experience of solidarity. This virtue is a habitual attitude and style of being and of relating which inclines one to be sensitive to the needs and feelings of others in the group and to devote oneself generously to the common welfare. In order to nurture this virtue one must be open to be challenged by other members of the group and to challenge them in turn.

It is time now to move on from solidarity, which is the first aspect of option for the poor, to the second aspect which has to do with analysis and political or quasi-political action. There are several stages in this process:

the first is a careful discernment and analysis of the situation. This is needed in order to ensure that one understands the core of the issue, that is, the fundamental reasons why this group of people have been left "on the margins", and the depth of the pain this inflicts on them. This calls not only for political insight but also for psychological insight into what it means to be marginalised;

the second stage is to ensure that one is not unconsciously colluding in this process of marginalisation. Sometimes it takes a sharp challenge from members of the group to make one aware of such unconscious collusion;

the third stage is joint action to challenge the marginalisation. It is not enough that a protest be made on behalf of those who have been marginalised; the protest must come from the group themselves. Marginalised groups who begin to stand up for themselves are profoundly changed by their action. This inner change is probably more important than any changes in behaviour and attitude in those who are being challenged;

the fourth and final stage is to search for realistic alternatives to the present state of marginalisation, a quest may involve a life-time of work with no guarantee of short-term success. What spurs one on is not a naïve optimism but a hope based on trust in the power and promises of God.

At each stage of this process those who have made an option for the poor must not assume that they know the answers or even that it is for them to set the agenda. The people who have been marginalised should be empowered to speak and act on their own behalf, so as to overcome their sense of helplessness. This means that those who have opted to be in solidarity with them often have to "hold back". And when they do intervene it should be to encourage or facilitate the disadvantaged people themselves in articulating their own experience and in planning realistic action.

3. *Ambivalence in Catholic Social Teaching/Teachers*

In the light of the account I have just given of the major components of an option for the poor, it is easy to see why there is a certain ambivalence in Catholic social teaching in relation to such an option.

On the one hand, it is very difficult to deny that it is a truly Christian thing to make a commitment to solidarity with marginalised people and to effective action for and with them. So it is not surprising that the general thinking behind this option has gradually come to be accepted more and more widely in the Church, mainly, but not exclusively, in the revised constitutions and programmes for renewal of religious congregations. The concept has gradually come to be seen as part of the mainline thrust of a renewed Church, and in this sense it has become more "respectable". In the 1980s Pope John Paul II began to include occasional references to a preferential option for the poor in some of his addresses in Latin America.

On the other hand, however, there is major resistance to the notion of an option for the poor, at least when taken in its full sense. The basic reason seems to be that many Church leaders and theologians are quite reluctant to face up to the kind of radical challenges which it involves. They are inclined to avoid it or to tone it down, without realising that they are distorting a crucial aspect of the faith they profess.

The problem gets much more serious when the institutional life of the Church comes into the question, as it usually does. As part of its evangelising mission the Church sees itself as called to insert Christian values and, perhaps, some elements of "a Christian ethos" into the community in different countries, and even into international relations. In recent centuries Church leaders have operated on the assumption that one of the most effective ways to do this is to own or control some of the major "instruments of culture" such as schools, hospitals, newspapers and other media. So the institutional Church frequently becomes quite a powerful agent in society, part of "the establishment". Consequently, Church leaders often have a certain vested interest in preserving the main structures of the society in which they live, even while they seek to bring about certain changes for the better. Church leaders and many theologians belong to a rather privileged class of people in society; and they can scarcely avoid being influenced in their opinions and values by those with whom they mix.

The new emphasis on option for the poor calls into question this whole model of Church influence and the corresponding status of the institutional Church and church leaders and theologians in society. For instance, many religious congregations in Latin America made a deliberate option to move out of most of their elite schools. They re-deployed their resources of personnel and money to serve poorer people. This angered and alienated the ruling classes who had relied on them to give a good education to their children.

By and large, the Vatican people held on to the older model. They were quite out of sympathy with the abandonment by influential Church people of their power to "mould" the future leaders of their countries. They mounted a counter-offensive at several levels. Firstly, Roman documents and teaching have included repeated warnings against Marxism and have tended to give the impression that liberation theology as a whole, including its emphasis on option for the poor, is tainted by Marxist ideas. Related to this is a consistent effort to "tone down" the language, for instance, by using the cumbersome phrase "a preferential but not exclusive option for the poor", a phrase which has irritated or infuriated some liberation theologians, e.g. Juan Luis Segundo[1]. Furthermore, the Puebla documents attempted to play down the importance of an option for the poor by putting an "option for youth" alongside it.

Another stratagem for playing down the significance of an option for the poor is a blurring of the difference between it and special care for the poor. The Church has a long and honourable tradition of providing loving care for those on the margins of society, ranging from the Lazar-houses of the Middle Ages to Jean Vanier's L'Arche communities and Mother Teresa's care for the destitute. Special care for the poor fits admirably with the older model of Church influence in society. By contrast, option for the poor presupposes a fundamentally different approach. Its basic challenge to the present structures of society does not sit easily with present Vatican policy and style.

The Vatican has also resisted the option for the poor by the way in which it has used its power and authority. Most of the bishops appointed by Rome in areas where liberation theology was influential have been very conservative; and many of them have undermined the efforts that had been made to embody the new approach in everyday Church life. Furthermore, the Vatican has intervened to exercise very tight control over CELAM (the Conference of Latin American Bishops), over CLAR (the Conference of Religious of Latin America), over religious congregations which were thought to be taking an unduly radical stance, and over the more "adventurous" seminaries in various parts of the world. There has also been an unrelenting pressure on leading liberation theologians, which has severely hindered them in their work.

Finally, the Pope has at times failed to endorse or encourage the courageous stance against injustice taken by local Church leaders. This has had a very damaging effect in countries like Kenya. It has allowed

1. J.L. Segundo, (1985) *Theology and the Church. A Response to Cardinal Ratzinger and a Warning to the Whole Church*, Minneapolis, Winston Press, 1985.

the oppressive authorities to disregard the protests of the local church
leaders on the ground that the highest church authority in Rome does not
agree with them.

It is quite evident that the outcome of all this has been a rather obvious
disparity between the official teaching and the practical action of the
Roman authorities. I have said that there are references to a preferential
option for the poor in some of the Pope's addresses in Latin America. But
they are hedged around with provisos and warnings. And, whatever may
be thought about the addresses of the Pope, it is quite clear that there is
little or no practical support from the Vatican for any really radical option,
using that term in the rather technical sense I have outlined here. Concern
for the poor, yes; "option" for the poor, not yet, and perhaps not at all...

III. LOOKING FORWARD AND GOING DEEPER

In this second part of my paper I want to propose a further development of the notion of option for the poor and suggest some practical
applications in the spheres of everyday life and of national and international politics.

1. *The Excluded in Interpersonal Relationships*

When Samuel came to Jesse's home, the youngest son of the family
was left out of the celebration because he had to look after the flocks. If
Samuel had not insisted on waiting for the young David, then Israel
would never have had its greatest king (1 Sam 16:11). Similarly, if Jesus
had gone along with the general prejudice against tax-collectors,
Matthew would not have been called, and later generations would have
had to do with only three Gospels. And what would have happened if
Mary had refused to believe that an unmarried mother from a despised
village could have a very special role to play in the plan of God?

These instances – together with the other incidents from the Bible
which I referred to early in this paper – indicate that God has special
care and concern for people who have been left on the margins of society. They even suggest that God often chooses to use such people as special instruments of divine providence, going against all the odds to make
them channels of grace. What are the practical implications of this for us
in our everyday social interactions?

It seems to me that each of us is invited to imitate God in this
approach, in so far as we can. We are called to make an act of faith that
today, just as in biblical times, the excluded and "the unlikely people"

play a vital role in human salvation, and that our task is to make space for them so that they can make their special gifts available to others. In practice, this calls for a style of relating to individuals and groups which is quite different from what normally happens. An obvious example arises when we go to a party. How do we relate to those who seem "left out" or excluded? Making an option for the poor means going out of our way to give time to the people who are being shunned, whether because they are victims of the snobbery of others, or because they are shy, or even because they are seen as uninteresting or boring. It means finding ways to draw them into the inner circle of those who feel they "belong".

We are invited to draw in these excluded ones not just out of compassion, but because we believe they have a very special gift to bring to the rest of us. This is the distinctive feature of a biblically-inspired option for the poor, the point at which it goes beyond Christian kindness and charity. It is the belief that, despite all the appearances, those who are on the margins are privileged instruments of God's providence.

2. Meetings

The same general principle applies even more sharply in relation to all kinds of community or group meetings. We usually work on the assumption that the aim of the participants as a whole – and of the chairperson or facilitator – is to achieve a group consensus on the issues before them. It is only natural that the major role in the shaping of this consensus will be played by those who are strong and articulate. It commonly happens that there are shy or quiet people who play little or no part in the dialogue; they just go along with the decision, and nobody stops to wonder what has been lost because of their silence.

If the members of the group – and perhaps especially those who have the roles of facilitator or chairperson – are really committed to an option for the poor, then they will not be satisfied with this customary way of reaching consensus. They will instead go out of their way to give a voice to the silent ones who would normally be left on the margins of the dialogue.

Such an approach is not only more Christian but also "pays off" in practical terms. In my experience there are occasions when the Spirit chooses to speak to a whole group in a powerful way through a member who has scarcely been heard up to that point, perhaps somebody who has a poor self-image and feels quite intimidated. I can recall several situations where, quite unexpectedly, the whole atmosphere of a meeting was changed by a quiet intervention from somebody who had been sitting silently on the margins of the group. This "unlikely" person offered a word of wisdom which touched the participants in their hearts. The group could see that the "word" which God was speaking to this group – that is, the fundamental truth which they most needed to hear – was coming through this person whose gifts and contribution had previously been overlooked or undervalued. In this way they came to value the patience and skill that led to the inclusion of those who had been on the margins.

3. *Intransigence*

However, a much more difficult situation arises when we have to deal with one or two "awkward" individuals whose views seem quite out of harmony with those of the rest of the group. Suppose a stubborn or "difficult" person insists on holding out against the consensus of the rest of the group. A tolerant facilitator may test the patience of the group by trying to make some space for this dissident voice. But what usually happens is that before long a great deal of subtle or not-so-subtle pressure is exerted on such "awkward" individuals by the facilitator or other members of the group to get them to go along with the prevailing view, or at least to keep quiet about their dissent.

What should we do when such people still remain intransigent and refuse to appreciate our efforts to accommodate them? It then becomes extremely difficult to believe that we should continue to make space for these awkward dissident voices which we would prefer not to have to listen to. I want to argue that it is right to "stay with them". I see this as an authentic instance of making an option for the poor, in an extended but nevertheless valid sense.

Undoubtedly, it stretches one's faith to the limit to extend option for the poor to include such truly intransigent people. It is almost impossible to believe that they may be special instruments of God for the rest of the group. We find ourselves saying: "Surely we should not give in to this kind of moral blackmail?" But this is one of those places where life is larger than logic, where as Christians – and even as human beings – we may find ourselves called to be wildly generous, to "go the extra mile", and then some more.

This kind of extravagant generosity only makes sense if we switch over to a very different model of dialogue, one which contrasts sharply with the generally accepted style. This other kind of dialogue is one in which we deliberately abandon – or at least suspend for the time being – our efforts to convince others to accept our opinions. Instead, we devote our energy to making a space *in ourselves* to really hear the dissonant voices. A little later I shall spell out in more detail what this involves;

but first I want to suggest that the notion of an option for the poor can be extended even further.

4. *Option for the Excluded in Society*

I want to put a case for applying the notion of option for the poor not merely to the awkward or excluded ones in a group or community meeting but also to finding space for those who are often seen as "the untouchables" in the *public* world, the global society in which we live out our lives. This involves extending the concept to include ways of addressing the most fundamental issues of exclusion in our world: such issues as racism, ethnic hatred, terrorism, sexism, abuse, ageism, fundamentalist extremism, and homophobia.

Of course, such issues are matters of concern for all liberal people. But the emphasis in this suggestion is on reaching out not just to the *victims* of racism, sexism, etc., but also to the perpetrators of these evils. The aim is to promote dialogue across the widest chasms which split our world today.

Needless to say, it is extremely difficult to imagine how there could be effective communication between terrorists and their victims, or between the victors and the vanquished in the bloody wars of our times, or between abused women and macho men. But why should we assume that God's grace is confined mainly to the personal and interpersonal sphere and that God's option for the excluded is itself exclusive, that it does not extend to male chauvinists, or racists, or terrorists?

Let's take the highly sensitive issue of dialogue with terrorists. The Quakers, the Mennonites, the San Egidio Community in Rome and a few priests and ministers in Northern Ireland have been involved in finding ways to initiate and promote dialogue between warring parties, even when some of those involved in the struggle are seen as terrorists.

In dialogue of this kind "the terrorists" are frequently represented for much of the time not by the "activists" themselves but by people who have a high level of credibility with them, for instance, by former paramilitary leaders who have now moved nearer to mainstream politics. The reason is that the dialogue is usually conducted in a low-key diplomatic mode where passion is muted and reason prevails. In this model of dialogue the participants have to refrain most of the time from giving immediate impassioned expression to the burning anger, pain, or hatred which they feel. So the activists allow themselves to be represented by people who have drawn back a little from "the front line" of the struggle and may have "cooler heads" and a more long-term vision. This is useful, but it also poses the danger that the negotiators may lose their credibility with the people they are representing. This is one reason for considering the possibility of a different style of dialogue, one that is less "diplomatic" and rational and that allows more room for the expression of emotion and even of passion.

5. *"Deep Democracy" and "Worldwork"*

The psycho-therapist Arnold Mindell and his associates have developed a model for dialogue of this kind. This different style of dialogue can be used for medium-sized group or community meetings of the kind I referred to in the previous section. But Mindell is particularly interested in using it in meetings of large groups of hundreds of participants. These are people who have come together with a view to facing up to really burning issues such as racism or sexism or various other issues where one group feels oppressed or excluded by another.

Mindell and his colleagues are deeply committed to the belief that all the voices in a society or group need to be heard. They use the term "deep " to express this concept. In order to foster such "deep democracy", they have developed a special kind of workshop or conference which they call "worldwork".

A typical "worldwork" conference will bring together a group of perhaps two or three hundred people. Those who convene the gatherings go out of their way to ensure that the composition of the group is very diverse. They endeavour to ensure that the group includes people who stand on the different sides of the major "burning issues" of the area. Those who take part are not asked to come as negotiators or even as formal representatives of the groups or factions from which they come; but they are people who will give voice with courage and passion to their own beliefs and values. They are not expected to be able to articulate their position with perfect clarity and compelling logic. For in this kind of dialogue personal authenticity may be more effective than cold logic.

6. *Changing the Rules*

A key element in this model of dialogue is the abandonment of the conventional norms of debate or rational discussion. The generally-accepted rules of discussion require us to put forward our case in rational terms, not to shout, not to interrupt others, and above all not to become too emotional. If we get angry or if we feel like crying, we are expected to keep these feelings well under control. But in the "worldwork" form of dialogue there is no guarantee that everybody will follow these rules. If we engage in it, we may find at times that we have to put up with people who interrupt us, or who cry, or shout, or even scream. Mindell says: "The Western world, especially, needs ... multicultural forums where feelings can be expressed, people can weep, people can rage..."[2].

One effect of this "change of rules" is to lessen the dominance of those whose forte is rational debate – and these are more likely to be the people who have had a lot of formal education. Furthermore, this alternative style is often found more congenial by people who do not belong to the dominant Western middle-class culture. Those who command attention in the new situation may well be individuals or groups who previously had little or no chance of having their voices heard or heeded. So the "new rules" can be a very effective way of giving a voice to the voiceless, and, in this sense, of making an option for "the poor".

Changing the rules of dialogue may seem like an invitation to anarchy. It is certainly true that those who are accustomed to the more conventional kind of discussion generally find this very emotional behaviour quite shocking and really difficult to put up with, at least at the beginning. However, what comes out of the alternative approach at its best is not really anarchy but a dialogue which is more inclusive and more effective. More inclusive: because there is room for alienated or disaffected people and the interaction is not weighted from the start in favour of those with a lot of formal education. More effective: because the "worldwork" dialogue leaves more room for the expression of emotions; this can lead to more profound changes than are usually attained when burning issues are discussed at a purely rational level.

7. "Inner Work" and "Eldership"

Those who facilitate this kind of dialogue need special skills over and above the facilitation skills employed in a more conventional group discussion. The facilitators are required to combine their "outer" work in the group with what is called "inner work". This involves the facilitators being aware of when and where they themselves are moved to compassion or rejection, when they find themselves becoming angry, or frustrated or sympathetic; it requires that they pay particular attention to the resistance they experience to really hearing the views of those with whom they feel out of sympathy; and this leads them on to an exploration of the roots of their resistance. Furthermore, the facilitators must be able to express their feelings authentically and "cleanly" when that is appropriate (and they need to know when it is appropriate to do so).

2. A. MINDELL, *Sitting in the Fire. Large Group Transformation using Conflicts and Diversity,* Portland, OR, Lao Tse Press, 1995, p. 165.

The facilitators must not remain aloof from the movement and struggles of the group, for the process is not one which can be steered from the outside. This applies also to those members of the group who occasionally play an informal facilitating role. On the other hand, the facilitators must not become entrenched on one side or the other of the ongoing and shifting tug-of-war within the group. They must be able to move between opposing positions and in this way to play a mediating role at times.

This mediation is not, however, a purely rational one, an effort to find a synthesis of two points of view or a compromise between them. Mindell insists that what he has in mind is quite different from the more conventional forms of negotiation, arbitration, conciliation or dispute-resolution. What have to be brought together are not primarily viewpoints but real people, people who are torn apart or brought together much more by their strong feelings than by their ideas. That is why it does not seem adequate to describe this "bringing together" role as that of a mediator. The more comprehensive term "eldership" is used by Mindell. He sees this role as akin to that of the elders in a tribal society, wise people who can resonate with the different stances that have been put forward and can find creative ways of fostering community in the group, while honouring its diversity.

I have been indicating some of the special abilities required by "worldwork" facilitators, and indeed also by those who wish to participate most fruitfully in the process. It should be evident that these abilities are not "skills" in the usual sense of strategies for managing other people. Certainly they are not "tricks of the trade" which can be quickly learned. They are more like gifts than techniques, though not the kind of gifts which come easily to many people. They have to be honed and perfected, and this is an on-going work which is never completed. In that sense these "skills" are really *virtues*, that is, fundamental spiritual attitudes which have become characteristic of a person's being.

The "worldwork" conferences are situations where the commitment to "deep democracy" is tested very severely and at times very painfully indeed. They offer participants an opportunity to develop gifts and skills and virtues of a kind which will help them to minister effectively in this wounded and broken world of ours. And in doing so they offer the possibility of empowering people to make an all-embracing and effective option for the poor.

St Patrick's, Dublin   Donal DORR

POSTSCRIPT

RETRIEVING OR RE-INVENTING SOCIAL CATHOLICISM
A TRANSATLANTIC RESPONSE

It strikes me that there are three main goals, in a symposium such as this one, in addressing once again the retrieval or reinvention of social Catholicism. The first involves an effort to help Catholics understand our own tradition of social thought and action – what it tried to do and what grounds we judge that, on balance, it was a valuable resource for Catholicism's – partially justly – ambivalent encounter with the modern world. The second objective is to attempt to bring the tradition forward in our own social and cultural settings and vastly changed sociological context – now more pluralistic (even within the Church) and more global. The third, presumably, is to bring the tradition of social Catholicism into dialogue with contemporary thought in ways which may show its relative superiority – at least in some aspects – to other competing modes of thought and praxis. I want to address, briefly, each of these three motifs as they have been raised in the chapters in this book.

I. In What Did the Tradition of Social Catholicism Consist?

Any serious assessment of the tradition of social modern Catholicism must come to grips with the following major themes. First, social Catholicism was always much more than "official Catholic Social Teaching", as found in the encyclicals. Unofficial social thought and action profoundly fed into and was spawned by the "high" tradition as its originating charter. The tradition's major purchase on contemporary thought was also always more through the unofficial vehicles of independent social thought (e.g. Maritain, Mounier, Barbara Ward, John Courtney Murray) and the social movements (labour unions; journals of opinion; political parties; spiritual social justice movements, such as *Pax Christi*) which it generated than through the official teaching itself which got, at best, a respectful nod and then lay largely dormant. Secondly, for much of the period 1891-1965 official Catholic social thought was an essentially Euro-centered project with some ideological misuses. Yet it espoused an underlying distinctive anthropology which can be described as communitarian liberalism, and it allowed for alternative carriers in non-European settings. Thirdly, the tradition was never really a purely "secular" modern project, untouched by motifs which came from the Bible and religious thought. Nor was the tradition ever fully a self-enclosed system. It engaged in a continuous subterranean dialogue with Marxist and liberal thought – both of which left their imprint on social Catholicism.

1. *Always More than "Official Catholic Teaching" as found in the Encyclicals*

My first encounter with social Catholicism came not from encyclicals but from my father (a labour union official). My father's admiration for labour priests and his enthusiastic approval of courses at American Catholic universities aimed at training labor leaders found a visible epiphany in a yearly Palm Sunday trek from our neighbouring parish to the grave of Father Peter Yorke, a notable and beloved San Francisco labor priest and pastor[1]. Encyclicals only came later to my ken. At Yorke's graveside, the oratory, if it rhetorically evoked or echoed Leo XIII's *Rerum novarum* and Pius XI's *Quadragesimo anno*, remained much more intent on eliciting on-going Church support for post World War II San Francisco stevedores on strike or argued the justice of health care and pension schemes for workers.

In my high school years, I made contact with a Catholic Worker House where we students helped feed a soup line. There I discovered the personalist communitarianism (influenced by Emmanuel Mounier and Eric Gill) of Dorothy Day and her confrere Peter Maurin (himself a latter day *detritus*, thrown up on American shores, from the *Le Sillon* movement in France which emerged as a French Catholic social movement in response to *Rerum novarum*)[2].

When later, as a Jesuit seminarian, I finally read and studied the papal social encyclicals, I tended, at first, to regard them as a kind of "background music", spiritual reading essentially, to evoke sufficient motivation and ecclesial justification to become involved in the Catholic Inter-Racial Councils, the Civil Rights movement, the farm workers' movement for unionisation and the anti-war movement during the period of the Viet Nam War. Much more than the encyclicals with their bloated Latinate ecclesiology-speak, I found the writings of unofficial thinkers

1. P. YORKE, *Sermons*, San Francisco, CA, The Text Book Publishing Company, 1931.

2. D. DAY, *The Long Loneliness. The Autobiography of Dorothy Day*, San Francisco, CA, Harper and Row, 1981; P. MAURIN, *Easy Essays*, West Hamlin, WV, The Green Revolution, 1971.

within the tradition of social Catholicism cogent and capable. Jacques Maritain's classic treatise, *Man and the State,* John Courtney Murray's *We Hold These Truths,* Barbara's Ward's *The Rich Nations and the Poor Nations*, and the writings of Josef Pieper became for me, more than the encyclicals, the founding documents for a vision of social Catholicism in action[3]. These writers, akin to what Jean-Yves Calvez claims to have tried to do with his own magisterial *The Church and Social Justice*, attempted to unlock a hitherto missed – or frequently hidden – unity in Catholic social thought[4]. They connected together and showed the contemporary relevance, in a way more compelling and coherent than the encyclicals ever achieved, such key Catholic concepts as human dignity, solidarity, subsidiarity, the common good, distributive justice. They turned the often sprawling or merely evocative concepts of the encyclicals into a system of social thought.

I have much sympathy, then, with this Cambridge symposium's emphasis on what it calls "Catholic non-official social thought". *The New Catholic Encyclopaedia* states that *Rerum novarum*, "the first of the great social encyclicals", "marked the bestowal of significant papal approval on the then emergent Catholic social movement"[5]. As Gordon Zahn has noted, this "opened the way to the further emergence and development of a wide range of other new Catholic social movements on a scale almost certainly beyond its eminent author's expectations", including the aforementioned *Le Sillon*[6]. Zahn insists further that "the importance of that 'bestowal' should not be minimised. Whatever else the encyclical achieved or did not achieve, it represents a distinct, though not yet dramatic, breakthrough that opened the way to that proliferation of social activity by predominantly lay-staffed and directed organisations that characterises so much of Catholic social action today"[7].

Zahn privileges what he calls "Catholic social thought from below". He suggests that we read "official teaching" as primarily a response to

3. J. MARITAIN, *Man and the State*, Chicago, IL, University of Chicago Press, 1951; J.C. MURRAY, *We Hold These Truths. Catholic Reflections on the American Proposition*, New York, NY, Sheed and Ward, 1960; B. WARD, *The Rich Nations and the Poor Nations*, New York, NY, Norton, 1962; J. PIEPER, *Justice*, New York, NY, Pantheon Books, 1955.

4. J.-Y. CALVEZ, *The Church and Social Justice. The Social Teaching of the Popes from Leo XIII to Pius XII, 1878-1958*, Chicago, IL, Henry Regnery Company, 1961.

5. *The New Catholic Encyclopedia*, New York, NY, Publishers Guild, 1967, vol. 12, p. 386.

6. G. ZAHN, *Social Movements and Catholic Social Thought*, in J.A. COLEMAN S.J. (ed.) *One Hundred Years of Catholic Social Thought. Celebration and Challenge*, Maryknoll, NY, Orbis, 1991, p. 44.

7. *Ibid.*, p. 48.

earlier emergent Catholic social movements for reform, justice and
social betterment, and then see the official encyclical documents as, substantively, charter documents for subsequent Catholic-based social
action:

> The more significant contributions made by or in the name of the church –
> in supporting programs for economic justice; in opposing the evils of
> racism and anti-semitism; in denouncing the weapons and strategies of
> modern war and depending on the priority of conscience – all of these orig-
> inated from 'below', from individuals and movements which, at first, were
> denied official recognition and support and obliged to overcome official
> suspicion and outright opposition. Later, often much later, these would
> become formally proclaimed policies of the Church[8].

If we take Zahn's principle as a hermeneutic lens to read even high
"official" Catholic thought, we might indeed read the encyclicals in a
very different light. Behind and ante-dating *Rerum novarum* lay the
developed economic conceptual thought of the Fribourg circle around
Cardinal Gaspard Mermillod; the working-class pilgrimages to Rome
of Leon Harmel; pressure for support for the labouring classes from the
Opera dei Congressi; Cardinal Manning's championing of the London
Dock strikers; Baltimore's Cardinal Gibbons' interventions in Rome to
prevent a condemnation of the American Knights of Labor as a secret
society. Between the paragraphs of the document one finds a careful
balancing act, adjudicating between Catholic movements in Austria of
romantic medievalists who rejected capitalism as immoral and
espoused a Catholic variant of the labor theory of value (following
Joseph Goeres and Karl von Vogelsang), and the meliorists in Germany (such as the Solidarist School of economics and Bishop von Ketteler) who sought reform within the capitalist framework. "Official"
teaching did not spring, as some virgin birth, unrelated to the real
Catholic social movements to which it responded[9]. Again, *Quadragesimo anno* hides, under its relatively unhistorical and trans-cultural conceptual language, much of its deep indebtedness to the close collaboration of its author, Oswald von Nell-Breuning S.J., with German
Catholic labor unions and the Center Party. Behind the encyclical also
lies the thinking of the remarkable network of economists, historians
and ethicists of the inter-disciplinary seminar, the Königswinter Circle,

8. *Ibid.*, p. 53. For confirmation of Zahn's theory in work for justice on race-relations
where the unofficial Catholic movements predated episcopal authoritative teaching, see J.
LA FARGE S.J., *The Catholic Viewpoint on Race Relations*, Garden City, NY, Hanover
House, 1956.

9. For much of this history, see P. MISNER, *Social Catholicism in Europe*, New York,
NY, Crossroad, 1991.

and, more largely, the social-economic thought of the München-Glad-bach school[10].

Sections of this encyclical, especially the part devoted to the question of Catholics voting for labor parties, are quite specific to Germany. The remarks about socialism in *Quadragesimo anno* that "no one can be at the same time a sincere Catholic and a true socialist ", even a mitigated democratic, non-Marxist socialist who, in Pius XI's own words, has come gradually to hold tenets of mitigated socialism "no longer different from the program of those who seek to reform human society according to Christian principles", were largely aimed at a small group of religious socialists in Germany. These had urged collaboration between Catholics and socialists and threatened to siphon off some Catholic votes from the Center Party. Cardinal Bourne had to gain an exemption from this stricture in the English-speaking world. To understand another section of *Quadragesimo anno* – one that seems patient of a Fascist interpretation of corporatism – the reader has to go behind the text to delicate relations between the Vatican and Mussolini's government[11].

Later papal teaching also shows sensitivity to Catholic social movements from below, especially in Germany, Italy and France. Pius XII, in response to a *Katholikentag* in Bochum in Germany in 1949, showed a decided coolness toward workers' co-determination schemes in industry decisions. John XXIII in *Mater et Magistra* reversed Pius's decision. The idea for "socialisation" in *Mater et Magistra* seems to have originated in a *Semaine Sociale* held in Grenoble in 1960. Clearly, John XXIII's famous opening to the left and socialism in *Pacem in terris* was closely articulated with moves by the Italian Christian Democratic Party to find new support from Italian socialist and Marxist groupings.

Nor is the social teaching of John Paul II unrelated to unofficial Catholic social movements. His long and often tortuous move toward the embrace of "a preferential but not exclusive love for the poor" (found in *Sollicitudo rei socialis*) makes no sense without a prior knowledge of the rise of liberation theology and the base community movements in the Latin American church. Again, as Peter Hebblethwaite has shown, portions of *Laborem exercens* (especially the sections which

10. See the references to von Nell-Breuning and to *Quadragesimo Anno* in J.A. DWYER (ed.), *The New Dictionary of Catholic Social Thought*, Collegeville, MN, Liturgical Press, 1994, pp. 676-678 and 802-813.

11. O. VON NELL-BREUNING, *The Drafting of Quadragesimo Anno*, in C.E. CURRAN & R.A. MCCORMICK (eds.), *Official Catholic Social Teaching* (Readings in Moral Theology, 5), New York, NY, Paulist, 1986, pp. 60-68.

insist that labor unions "do not have the character of political parties struggling for power; they should not be subjected to the decision of political parties or have too close links with them") only make sense in a Polish context of the rise of solidarity as a struggle to de-link the Communist Party's monopoly over the labor movement. It made little sense, however, (certainly as a major tenet of Catholic social thinking) in the American, British or Continental contexts[12]. Even in the American context, a former official of the AFL-CIO, speaking in Rome after the publication of *Laborem exercens*, could only expostulate: "it is only our involvement in politics that enables us to work for a government which will 'act against unemployment' and plan for providing work for all"[13].

Clearly, no robust exegesis of "official" encyclical teaching is possible which cuts it off from broader social movements to which it responds or which it evokes. Hence, we need a more encompassing term to enfold both "official" encyclical teaching (which cannot be simply privileged in ways which totally cut it off from unofficial thought and action) and "unofficial" thought and movements. I am, thus, very sympathetic to Verstraeten's formulation which refers to Catholicism as a social tradition of both *praxis* and reflection. My own usage has always been to refer, more generally, to what I term, "social Catholicism". The aim in either phraseology is to postulate a much broader unity between official encyclical traditions and unofficial action and thought. And, naturally, this broader unity should show up in syllabi and curricular material on social Catholicism. I could not conceive of teaching a course on social Catholicism without reference to historical works covering unofficial Catholic movements for justice and democracy, such as Paul Misner's *Social Catholicism in Europe* or Thomas Bokenkotter's *Church and Revolution: Catholics in the Struggle for Democracy and Social Justice*[14]. In such a course, especially for the more recent post-Vatican II period, papal encyclicals would be read as crystallisations of the wider social struggle and, moreover, be juxtaposed to episcopal social teaching in countries such as Chile, the United States, Canada and the Philippines.

12. P. HEBBLETHWAITE, *The Popes and Politics. Shifting Patterns in Catholic Social Doctrine*, in CURRAN & McCORMICK, *Official Catholic Social Teaching* (n. 11), pp. 264-283.

13. T.R. DONAHUE, *From Rerum Novarum to Laborem Exercens: A United States Labor Perspective*, in CURRAN & McCORMICK, *Official Catholic Social Teaching* (n. 11), pp. 384-410, esp. 404.

14. T.S. BOKENKOTTER, *The Church and Revolution. Catholics and the Struggle for Democracy and Social Justice*, New York, NY, Doubleday, 1998.

2. A Euro-Centred Project with Ideological Misuses

An eminent commentator on these issues, Peter Hebblethwaite, tends to dismiss the "official" encyclical tradition as simply ideological. His sympathies lie entirely with Chenu's ground-breaking study, La "doctrine sociale" de l'Église comme idéologie. "By placing doctrine sociale in quotes, Chenu is suggesting that it is a figment; by calling it an ideology, he is saying it is unacceptable"[15]:

> Catholic social doctrine (CSD) as conceived in the 1930's lectured the world from the outside. It stated abstract, a-temporal principles that ignored the diversity of situations. It was nostalgic for a vanishing rural and peasant world. It ignored the fact of class conflict, which it tried to gloss over with the concept of *interclassismo* – the harmonious collaboration of all social classes – which brought comfort only to dictators like Franco in Spain and Salazar in Portugal, both of whom claimed to be implementing CSD.
> The difficulty of CSD was this: it could fly so high in the stratosphere of principles that, from above, the whole landscape was flattened out and no details could be perceived; or – more rarely – it could hew so close to the ground, that its particular statement was too localised to be applicable elsewhere[16].

There is no question in my mind that much, if not most of official Catholic social thought, as found in the encyclical tradition, was tied to an essentially Euro-centered project and involved, at times, ideological misuse. Both Lesch and Verstraeten in this volume allude to the ideological misuses to which high encyclical teaching has been put. Clearly, Anglo-Saxons could never quite understand an emphasis on confessional unions and political parties. They also never felt the same pincer movement from frequently rabid, anti-clerical, organised political constellations of liberals and socialists. It may well be, as Chenu claims, that the hiving-off of Catholics into movements of their own was wrong-headed: "To divide the labor movement in order to evangelise it was to make an error about the Gospel. For the real task was not to create a separate Catholic workers' group but to bring the Church to birth within the workers' movements as it actually existed"[17]. In historical context, the Church's option seems more understandable.

Yet some severe cautions are called for before we issue blanket dismissals of even official Catholic thought and action as simply ideological,

15. HEBBLETHWAITE, *The Popes and Politics* (n. 12), p. 265.
16. HEBBLETHWAITE, *The Popes and Politics* (n. 12), p. 268.
17. M.-D. CHENU, *La "doctrine sociale" de l'Église comme idéologie* (Essais), Paris, Cerf, 1979, p. 22.

hopelessly abstract and totally Euro-centered. As Chantal Delsol notes in
her essay, it was social Catholics – and not socialists – who first introduced legislation in Germany and France regulating work hours, controlling the labor of minors, supporting government subventions for the
unemployed and aged. Nor were the Christian Democratic Parties in
Europe – on balance – less helpful for forging a humane and democratic
modern welfare state than their socialist counterparts. I, for one, retain a
relatively benign judgement over-all of post-war Christian Democratic
Parties in Europe, at least through and into the decade of the 1980's[18].
I also found the Chilean Christian Democratic Party of Eduardo Frei a
credible vehicle for ordered justice[19].

Nor did the largely Euro-centered official Catholic teaching neglect
some larger global issues of world peace, disarmament, de-colonialism,
trade, debt and aid and development concerns, as found in the series of
remarkable encyclicals from *Pacem in terris* through *Populorum proges-
sio* down to *Solicitudo rei socialis*. Surely, only some more balanced
judgement that social Catholicism, whatever its ambiguities, contributed
to a more just and peaceful and democratic world – with a conspicuous
concern for human rights, social participation and human dignity –
would lead us, in the first place, to our questions about bringing the tradition forward in new settings. Moreover, whatever a retrospective view
on confessionally separate organisations may now yield, the Catholic
unions, welfare institutions and parties did serve as relatively effective
social carriers for injecting the ideas and strategies of social Catholicism
into the modern European setting. Not from nowhere (nor for ill!) did
the European community simply fall upon the twin, decidedly Catholic
slogans of the "common good" and "subsidiarity" as key catch phrases
for conceiving of the European Community as a true community and not
just a trading bloc. It would be near unthinkable, for example, that those
two would serve as equally conspicuous slogans for social thought in the
North American context.

Thus the bite in Verstraeten's wise remarks that social Catholicism, as
we have known it, "cannot survive without both a fundamental reinterpretation of its theoretical content and the discovery or creation of a new
bearer of that tradition. In other terms, when the social context in which

---

18. D. HANLEY, *Christian Democracy in Europe. A Comparative Perspective*, London, Pinter, 1994.
    19. M. FLEET, *The Rise and Fall of Chilean Christian Democracy* (Princeton Paper-
backs. Political Science), Princeton, NJ, Princeton University Press, 1985; B.H. SMITH,
The Church and Politics in Chile. Challenges to Modern Catholocism, Princeton, NJ,
Princeton University Press, 1982.

Catholic social tradition concretises itself becomes radically different from the past, when the classic forms of Catholic social movements disappear or become secularised, Catholic social thought would become meaningless, if it would maintain its original form and content without fundamental reinterpretations and adaptations".

Several of the contributors to this symposium, most eloquently and persuasively, Boswell, turn to the anthropological core of the tradition, what I like to call its communitarian liberalism, with its distinctive categories. Perhaps there is overlap with other traditions on any given conceptual element but the constellation and inter-penetration of concepts is distinct: of human dignity, solidarity, subsidiarity, social justice, the option for the poor, the common good, justice as participation etc. Verstraeten speaks of this anthropological tradition as "a particular set of shared understandings about the human person, social goods and their distributive arrangements". Delsol refers to "an anthropology which points to finitude, the social nature of the human, human autonomy and concomitant responsibility, linked to the human being who is the product of original sin". Boswell insists, persuasively for me, that even notions of freedom in social Catholicism get tightly linked to a deep metaphor of human solidarity so that, as Michael J. Schuck has insisted, "Catholic social thinkers as a whole have retained a distinct understanding of freedom, equality, rights and justice in the modern world"[20]. As McHugh and Boswell rightly insist, "distributive justice and the notions of "solidarity", "subsidiarity" and "a preferential option for the poor", the four marks of sound Catholic social thought, are ultimately connected and indeed cannot be understood independently of each other".

Whether we see this unique Catholic constellation as the historic product of a determined social location in modern European history which wedged the practising Catholics between the natural social and political constituencies of classic liberalism and Marxism, as I once tried to argue, or you locate the uniqueness in a theological anthropology (and, perhaps, we do not have to choose totally between these two alternatives), I have no doubt of the unique constellation of Catholic anthropological assumptions[21]. I was convinced of this uniqueness once again by an excellent recent American book by Brian Stiltner, *Religion and the*

20. M.J. SCHUCK, *Modern Catholic Social Thought* in DWYER, *The New Dictionary of Catholic Social Thought* (n. 10), pp. 611-632, esp. 631.

21. J.A. COLEMAN S.J., *Neither Liberal Nor Socialist. The Originality of Catholic Social Teaching*, in J.A. COLEMAN (ed.), *One Hundred Years of Catholic Social Thought* (n. 6), pp. 25-42.

Common Good: Catholic Contributions to Building Community in a Liberal Society[22].

Stiltner engages in a wide-ranging conversation with the thought of John Locke, Ronald Dworkin, John Rawls, Michael Walzer, Michael Sandel, Alasdair MacIntyre and Charles Taylor. He characterises social Catholicism's core notion of the common good as a theory of "communal liberalism". It is a liberalism inasmuch as modern Catholicism espouses procedures and norms for the protection of human rights and champions freedom and pluralism as positive social goods in their own right. It is a *communal* liberalism "because it suggests a political theory that justifies policies of freedom, tolerance and pluralism by reference to the good of the political community and its sub-communities, not only by reference to the rights of individuals"[23]. Drawing on the work of Jacques Maritain in his classic treatise, *The Person and the Common Good,* Stiltner argues that we exist in and for communities [which are not, as some strands of liberal theory often have it, merely *instrumental* for personal autonomies]. The very human capacity for the engagement with community is itself a positive perfection of personality. But if the dignity of persons can be realised only in community, genuine community, in its turn, can only exist where the substantial freedom and the dignity of the human person is secured. Hence, Catholic notions of the dignity of the human person, based both on human needs and human moral agency, get linked to the common good. But these concepts of dignity and freedom protect against any one-sided smothering of human agency by the traditions. They are the reason Stiltner denominates the Catholic theory of the common good a "communal *liberalism*". I will be returning to this notion of the common good later, but let me round out the evocation of Stiltner's remarkable work by his formulation of the Catholic notion of the common good, which, insists Stiltner, is both a procedural and a substantive good:

> The ideal vision of the common good in the modern Catholic conception is the mutually beneficent relation of social actors, oriented toward protecting and enhancing the dignity of persons and toward supporting the nourishing of diverse and good institutions. What is required to approach the ideal are procedures for cooperation and dialogue within a pluralistic, democratic framework and substantive norms such as defending human dignity through rights and providing for opportunity for participation in society's common life through its public and voluntary institutions. The

---

22. B. STILTNER, *Religion and the Common Good. Catholic Contributions to Building Community in a Liberal Society*, Lantham, MD, Rowman and Littlefield Publishers, 1999.
    23. *Ibid.*, p. 47.

broad definition of the common good in modern Catholic writings is beneficial because it is flexible enough to accommodate developments in moral
sensibilities and to be applied to various socio-political contexts. It is also
specific enough to guide political and social choices within a pluralistic,
liberal society[24].

A characteristic modern liberal complaint about any notion of the
common good can be found in Rawls' throw-away line in his book,
Political Liberalism: that "a public and workable agreement on a conception of the good can be maintained only by the oppressive use of
state power"[25]. Here, Catholic notions of subsidiarity guarantee a pluralism in any deliberative democratic discourse about public goods and
shared interests. For subsidiarity is, fundamentally, a plea for pluralism.
As Stiltner reminds us, "The plurality of associations is a consequence
of human finitude and a guard against *hubris*. In sum, pluralism is central to the common good because different communities centre on the
pursuit of different components of the complex human good; because
institutional diversity facilitates extensive participation in social life
[a strong element of the Catholic component of the good is, after all, justice as participation]; and because no one association [one presumes
Stiltner includes here the Church] can claim to be the perfect community"[26]. In sum, in the Catholic understanding the search for the common
good takes place *within* and not *against* the experience of plurality.
Questions about the common good can only be ruled out, as Rawls tries
to do, if a firmer notion of a deliberative, as opposed to a mere interest-
balancing adversarial democracy is also ruled out[27].

But those who see a distinctive and valuable Catholic anthropological
constellation around a notion of communal liberalism (or, if you prefer,
personalism) cannot rest content, as it strikes me Delsol does in her
essay, with this splendid legacy taken alone. For Verstraeten forces us to
face head on the Weberian point: ideas have impact in history and on
society only through a distinctive institutionalisation and carrier units. If
older forms of these have been lost, there is no way that a mere evocation of the superior Catholic anthropology will have much contemporary
impact on politics or social policy. Only through a set of institutions will
Catholicism generate the middle axioms to guide social policy which

24. *Ibid.*, p. 10.
25. J. RAWLS, *Political Liberalism* (The John Dewey Essays in Philosophy, 4) New
York, NY, Columbia University Press, 1993.
26. STILTNER, *Religion and the Common Good* (n. 22), p. 178.
27. J. MANSBRIDGE, *Beyond Adversary Democracy*, Chicago, IL, University of
Chicago Press, 1980.

flow from its anthropological unique legacy. Moreover, without belabouring the point, it would be illuminating to see how social Catholicism gained some purchase on social thought in non-European settings such as Australia, Canada and the United States where its institutional vehicles were quite different than those of the Continent. I will return to this point but it is relevant here as a reminder that the anthropological presuppositions of the tradition were not totally Euro-centered. Nor did it lack alternative social carriers in non-European settings.

3. *Complex Ambivalent Relationships with Secular Thought*

There is a strong division among the essays in this symposium, perhaps most starkly seen between Verstraeten and Lesch, but also implicit in some of the remarks in McHugh's splendid and, in my estimation, quite original contribution on natural law, about just how "secular" Catholic social thought has been or can be. Verstraeten does not share Lesch's Enlightenment project of a "Christian social ethics as a deontological, procedural, universalistic and cognitive type of theory in close contact with secular moral philosophy". Lesch evinces a certain "sceptical tendency concerning the plausibility of a theology-based social doctrine" and he bluntly dismisses "the strange paternalistic side and burden of natural law". I detect a certain inconsistency between these claims and a later remark of Lesch's: "We have to organise our research in the hermeneutical triangle of the biblical narrative, the doctrine of Christian community and the claims of secular reason". Just how appeal to the biblical narrative and some doctrine of Christian community mesh with secular moral philosophy (and cease making that correlation, in some sense, a *theology*-based social doctrine) eludes me in Lesch's essay.

My own sympathies lie closer to Verstraeten and McHugh's projects. Verstraeten would appeal, to overcome the crisis in contemporary social Catholicism, for inspiration not only "from other traditions of interpretation and inquiry but from a living relation to the text of the Bible". He suggests that Catholic social teaching contains powerful, biblically inspired "root metaphors which change our pre-reflective fundamental understanding of social reality". Surely, solidarity (rooted in both God's covenant in creation and God's universal salvific will for redemption, as well as in our common solidarity in the sordidness of sin) and the preferential option for the poor (treated extensively in Dorr's essay where Dorr reminds us that the option is surely not a distillate of reason alone but flows from the biblical God's option for the poor) serve as two such biblically and metaphorically soaked, rich root images in the imagination of social Catholicism.

McHugh also suggests that lurking, even in the high modern tradition of a Catholic reliance on natural law, with its emphasis on rational method, clarity and certainty, a residual appeal remains to biblical foundations. He asserts (rightly, I think) of *Rerum novarum,* what Thomas Gilby said of Aquinas' ethical teaching in the *Summa:* "That it is integrated in *sacra doctrina,* the teaching of the Gospel revelation and its full import can be appreciated only when it is read as a living part of this organic whole". To be sure, when less guarded, social Catholicism veered, on the surface at least, toward a tendency to overstress the philosophical aspect.

These divisions among the contributors again raise two large issues, namely the role of Scripture in Christian social ethics and the retrievability of a distinctively Catholic notion of natural law, which would take, each of them, a entire separate essay to explore in full. I am much informed in my response to these two issues, however, by Jean Porter's recent study, *Natural and Divine Law: Reclaiming the Tradition for Christian Ethics* and her as yet unpublished paper, "Catholic Social Thought and the Natural Law Tradition"[28].

Porter is quite dubious about the modern project (from Pufendorf in the seventeenth century to modern attempts by John Finnis and others), whether secular or Catholic, of finding a purely autonomous natural law which is said to generate a universally valid morality which would be recognised, as such, by all rational persons[29]. She shares, with Alasdair MacIntyre, a sense that all reason is tradition-dependent and historically specific[30]. "I am not persuaded by those who claim to isolate a 'tradition-independent' core of the natural law tradition because every such account that I have seen appears to me to be either philosophically implausible or so abstract as to be without much theoretical force. Secondly, and more fundamentally, this claim simply does not seem to me to do justice to what we know about the evolution of the natural law tradition". Yet Porter is no more enamoured of the currently popular idea of a purely Christian morality (perhaps most strongly associated in this symposium with the work of John Milbank). "A purely Christian morality which is

28. J. PORTER, *Natural and Divine Law. Reclaiming the Tradition for Christian Ethics* (Saint Paul University Series in Ethics), Grand Rapids, Mich., William Eerdmans, 1999; *Catholic Social Thought and the Natural Law Tradition,* unpublished paper presented at the *Commonweal* magazine colloquium, "American Catholics and the Public Square", New York City, May 12-14, 2000. My citations are from this paper.

29. J. FINNIS, *Natural Law and Natural Rights,* New York, NY, Oxford University Press, 1980.

30. A. MACINTYRE, *Whose Justice? Which Rationality?,* Notre Dame, IN, University of Notre Dame Press, 1988.

self-contained, self-justifying and unintelligible to everyone else seems
to me to be as unrealistic as the Enlightenment ideal of a universal
morality, which is its mirror image".

Medieval theology (in both its theologians and in canonists, such as
Gratian) took up a tradition, largely pre-Christian in its origins, of the
Stoic natural law. Yet the medieval scholastics expressed their distinctive
concept of the natural law in terms derived from both patristics and classical sources (principally Cicero). The scholastics said of the natural law
that it was a product of reason. "Yet, at the same time, they interpreted
reason itself in theological, and ultimately scriptural, terms. That is why
they did not hesitate to draw on Scripture as well as rational arguments
in order to determine the concrete content of the natural law, and it is
also why they did not attempt to derive a system of natural law thinking
out of purely natural data or rationally self-evident intuitions". It is only
the modern exponents of natural law who attempt to do this – and their
project seems to have failed. It is the theologically informed medieval
notion of natural law, rather than its modern, semi-autonomous, rational
variant in Catholicism, which Porter wants to revive. She sees the
medieval natural law tradition (and the residues of that tradition which
passed over to social Catholicism in the nineteenth century) as less
"secular", "modern" or purely "natural" than appears. In her argument,
"while the scholastics do ground their account of the natural law in naturally given aspects of human existence, these natural givens are interpreted within a framework of theological convictions. The scholastics
appeal to scriptural and theological concepts to determine which aspects
of human nature should be given greatest weight morally and to guide
their formulation of specific moral judgements. This process of theologically guided interpretation, in turn, led to the emergence of a social doctrine which still provides the basis for Catholic social teachings".

The truth of Porter's account becomes readily apparent in two central
Catholic natural law propositions: human dignity and private property.
Catholic notions of a radical moral equality, inherent in its appeals to
human dignity, imply the theological notion of the human as an *imago
dei*. It may be, as the legal scholar Michael J. Perry has recently argued,
very difficult, if not impossible, to ground a concept of the sacred invio-
lability of the human conscience and will (despite Kantian and neo-
Kantian efforts to try to do so) on purely rational appeals to autonomous
moral agency[31]. Similarly, the Catholic natural law account for private

    31. M.J. PERRY, *The Idea of Human Rights. Four Inquiries*, Oxford, Oxford Univer-
sity Press, 1998.

property becomes inextricably enmeshed with the patristic *dictum* that the earth is intended, in God's providence, for the sustenance of all persons, which puts a mortgage on any purely private concept of property. Only if we engage in totally tendentious dichotomous thinking which assumes that: 1) *either* there is a morality grounded in human nature/the product of practical reasoning or we have nothing but purely contingent and culturally bound moral codes; and that 2) *either* we can establish a purely Christian morality derived from biblical narrative or we must fall back on some variant of a universally valid morality derived from the Enlightenment–only with such dichotomies do we land in some hopeless *aporia*. But an alternative exists. Rather sensibly, Porter suggests that:

> Matters are more complex than these dichotomies would suggest. The tradition of the natural law is not a distinctively Christian tradition, if only because it is clearly pre- Christian in its origins. Yet it is adopted by early Christian thinkers for specifically theological reasons, and transformed by this appropriation into a distinctively Christian doctrine... While this tradition cannot be said to generate a universally valid morality which would be recognised as such by all rational persons, neither is it so fundamentally tradition-bound as to be unintelligible to those in other traditions. Because it is grounded in a construal of our shared humanity, and shaped by genuine, albeit contextualised moral reasoning, we have every reason to expect it to be intelligible even to those whose religious and cultural traditions are quite different from our own.
>
> Even though the natural law is a historically specific tradition of enquiry, it does offer points of entree into public discourse, both in our own society and in the wider forum of the world community. It does not offer us a universally valid morality, or even a systematic program for moral enquiry. Nonetheless, it does offer us starting points for dialogue, together with a set of moral ideals to which we [Catholics] are committed, and which we can offer to others as attractive and persuasive ideals.

It would be difficult to talk about a *retrieval* of classic social Catholicism which rejected the notion of natural law altogether or reinterpreted it in such general terms that it becomes the equivalent to moral reason as such. This would be tantamount not to some retrieval of a tradition but the start of an entirely new tradition. In so doing, we would run the risk of cutting ourselves off from a tradition of moral reflection which has played a central role in Catholic social thought. To be sure, the distinctively modern conception of the natural law, which dominated in Catholic moral theology until Vatican II, stands in need of some fundamental revisions. It needs to deal much more with the Council's call for a renewed attention to the scriptural roots of theology (which a retrieval of the more medieval sophisticated use of natural law addresses) and to the very historicity ingredient in the notion of human nature. A totally unchanging human nature seems difficult to accept. Yet, as Porter argues, "In my view, this (i.e. "by and large, Catholic theologians have gone beyond critical revision to reject the idea of natural law altogether or to reinterpret it in very general terms equivalent to moral reason, *tout court*") is an unfortunate development; all the more so since new developments in medical technology and family relations have led to a wide-spread reconsideration of the moral status of human nature in the wider society. The time has come for a Catholic retrieval of the natural law tradition".

The time has also come for such a retrieval because of the limits, as Frank McHugh shows in his essay, of virtue theory, taken alone, to engage in a critique of institutions. I have always felt that the reduction of either Aristotle or Aquinas to a simple version of virtue theory does an injustice to both of them. The treatment of justice in Book V of the *Nicomachean Ethics* makes it a virtue rather different from all the other virtues, and one which calls for a set of principles and norms and not only the narrower version of virtues as inclinations and habits. Aristotle, after all, does refer to a variant of justice he calls "natural" and thus does not himself rely entirely on tradition-bound virtue theory. Aquinas clearly felt the need to wed together both virtue theory and the treatise on the law in his *Summa* (largely derived from natural law forms of thought) in order to do justice to a rounded social ethics.

4. *Encounters with Marxism and Liberalism*

In his essay in this volume, Jean-Yves Calvez speaks of his early and enriching encounter with Marxism. It has always struck me how many seminal voices in social Catholicism – von Ketteler with the socialist Lasalle; Maritain, Chesterton and Dorothy Day who brought socialist back-grounds to their conversions; von Nell-Breuning and Mounier who also poured over their Marx – diligently studied the classic Marxist texts. Nor was their intent simple refutation. They emulated aspects of their adversary. Moreover, even in a context mainly of polemics, extensive engagement in dialogue with an alternative mode of thinking begins to seep into one's own categories.

On the other side, an extensive dialogue – again, not only polemical – with liberal thought lies behind the work of Maritain and Murray. Clearly, the post-war Catholic human rights strategy – first enunciated in the encyclical tradition by John XXIII but long anticipated by unofficial Catholic participation in post-war debates in UNESCO and the discussions over the UN Charter of Rights – owes much to this dialogue with liberalism (as Julie Clague indicates in her essay). Selectively, social Catholicism has incorporated elements from these two competing modern ideologies even if, generally, basing them on distinctively Catholic philosophical and theological grounds. All the liberal liberties are there even if they get supplemented in ways not usually found in liberalism, by a corresponding positive notion of social rights to subsistence more akin to the Marxist tradition[32].

This inner dialogue within the tradition of social Catholicism with liberalism and socialism and its own renewal through this dialogue means that social Catholicism does not lack for interesting secular interlocutors sympathetic to the Catholic constellation. Others, besides Catholics, see themselves as communitarian liberals. They can and do provide allies with social Catholics on policy issues[33]. Moreover, the long, two-sided, sometimes polemical, sometimes sympathetic dialogue of social Catholicism with both liberal and Marxist social thought and social Catholicism's subsequent refining of its own thought as a result of this dialogue, puts a brake on any too robust claims for an utter uniqueness to the conceptual apparatus of the tradition. Sometimes an overly aggressive emphasis on Catholic distinctiveness can actually feed into making social Catholicism more peripheral to contemporary discourse than it needs to be.

II. NEW CONTEXTS FOR BRINGING THE TRADITION FORWARD

Three issues in particular force the discussions about a retrieval or re-invention of social Catholicism: 1) the changed economic and political context of a more inter-dependent world (especially after the Cold War) and globalisation; 2) the changed ecclesial climate for understanding and enacting social Catholicism since Vatican II; and 3) the collapse or inner secularisation of older social carriers of the tradition which forces us to imagine new forms of institutionalisation and social carriers for the tradition. I will now address each of these briefly.

The classic corpus of social Catholicism assumed the sovereign nation-state, although from John XXIII onwards it pressed for inter-national and

32. Catholic human rights development is treated in D. HOLLENBACH, *Claims in Conflict. Retrieving and Renewing the Catholic Human Rights Tradition* (Woodstock Studies, 4), New York, NY, Paulist, 1979.

33. Some representative communitarian liberal allies for Catholics would be P. SELZNICK, *The Moral Commonwealth. Social Theory and the Promise of Community* (Centennial Books), Berkeley, CA, University of California Press, 1992; W. GALSTON, *Liberal Purposes. Goods, Virtues and Diversity in the Liberal State* (Cambridge Studies in Philosophy and Public Policy), Cambridge, Cambridge University Press, 1991; A. ETZIONI, *The Spirit of Community. Rights, Responsibilities and the Communitarian Agenda*, New York, NY, Simon and Schuster, 1994.

regional institutions to anchor a more global common good, and it dealt with issues of inter-class conflict and cooperation and distributive justice largely within the context of national, relatively self-contained economies. Clearly, the end of the Cold-War and the new globalisation forces social Catholicism – as it does the whole world – to re-think its economic categories. Luckily, the new economic phenomena of trans-national capital and global finance allow social Catholicism to address these changed realities with fresh energies, relatively unencumbered by polemical freights.

This new economic and political context of globalisation adequately justifies the inclusion, as indispensable, in this volume of the essays by Van Gerwen, Bruni and Beretta. It also justifies McHugh's notice of unusual vocabulary (quite congenial to Catholicism) in the recent World Bank Group document, *The World Development Report on Poverty*: empowerment, opportunity, voice and participation, vulnerability and safety nets, global forces and the poor. Similarly, it highlights Bernard Perret's treatment of post-utilitarian thought about development as found in the emergence of the Human Development Index, in new notions of social capital and in Amartya Sen's insistence on developing human social capability. Perret shows overlap between these concepts and social Catholicism's concept of the common good. Finding such allied voices and forging strategic alliances with them may be essential to remove some of the (perhaps partially unjust) stigma of "Catholic" from social Catholicism's proposals. I have in mind here Delsol's comment that a built-in bias and deep suspicion against Catholic sponsorship greet her attempts to discuss the social anthropology of Catholicism. Here again, we find a *motif* which argues to the need for unofficial – true yet un-authoritarian or triumphalist – Catholic voices and presence in the new debates about globalisation.

Gaudium et spes made clear that official social teaching could not be privileged over unofficial forms of social Catholicism: "With the help of the Holy Spirit, it is the task *of the entire* people of God, especially pastors and theologians, to hear, distinguish and interpret the many voices of our age, and to judge them in the light of the divine word". Vatican II also changed the metaphors of the Church. No longer "over against the world" or representing a fortress besieged by a fundamentally hostile world, the Church joins all men and women of good will in seeking for justice and the common good. Cooperative efforts and not just distinctively Catholic struggles are called for. Nor could the "signs of the times" (Vatican II tended to define the social task, as Paul VI put it in his encyclical *Populorum progressio*, as "throwing the light of the

Gospel on the social questions of our age") any longer be discerned universally. They had to be studied on the local level. Finally, in his remarkable Apostolic Constitution, *Octogesima adveniens*, Paul VI declared:

> In the face of such widely varying situations, it is difficult for us to utter a unified message and to put forward a solution which has universal validity. Such is not our ambition, nor is it our mission. It is up to the Christian communities to analyse with objectivity the situation which is proper to their own country, to shed on it the light of the Gospel's unalterable words and to draw principles of reflection, norms of judgement and directives for action from the social teaching of the Church. It is up to these Christian communities, with the help of the Holy Spirit, in communion with the bishops who hold responsibility and in dialogue with other Christian brethren and all men of good will, to discern the options and commitments which are called for in order to bring about the social, political, and economic changes seen in many cases to be urgently needed.

Many thought that Paul VI's words here spelt the death-knell for international social Catholicism. I do not agree. The Vatican still has a useful role to play to help elucidate and propagate the more generalised principles of reflection, norms of judgement and directives for action (as John Paul II did in his encyclicals on work and on the market). Clearly, Paul VI's call for ecumenical and even wider solidarities in investigating and addressing social questions does justify a wide swathe indeed for unofficial Catholic action. It suggests limits, by subsidiarity, on any overly intrusive Vatican interference in local discernments of the signs of the times and the public policies to address them. Palpably, the United States bishops saw these words as a mandate for their very particular treatments of U.S. nuclear policy and of the American economy in the 1980's. Yet larger global issues (frequently lost to the purview of more local efforts or too caught up in perduring national self-interests) still justify a more international approach to global economic issues such as one finds in *Sollicitudo rei socialis*.

I was quite intrigued by Thomasset's study of the impact of a renewal of Catholic identity – on new bases – in the welfare and social service institutions of French religious orders. It dovetails nicely with some recent research I have been doing on Catholic Charities, U.S.A. where I have been focusing on this organisation's approach to the question of Catholic identity in a pluralistic setting and its attempts at advocacy and public policy[34]. It also provides a link to McHugh and Boswell's concerns about

---

34. For a history of Catholic Charities USA. which treats of its policy advocacy, see D. Brown & E. McKeown, *The Poor Belong to Us. Catholic Charities and American Welfare*, Cambridge, MA, Harvard University Press, 1997.

middle-level axioms drawn from social Catholicism which might inform policy studies and advocacy.

Briefly stated, policy generation usually stems from institutions which have both a legitimate interested stake in the outcomes of, and an expertise and experience to bring to, questions of social policy and national legislation. I cannot speak for Europe, but in the contemporary United States the Catholic vehicles to translate social Catholicism into middle-level policy are, essentially, rooted in the following four institutional realities:

The United States Catholic Conference (USCC) acts as the service and advocacy bureaucracy for the U.S. bishops. It maintains close liaison with and on occasion seeks to correlate closely with the nationwide networks of Catholic institutions. The USCC maintains an active lobbying arm which testifies before Congress at every level of a legislative bill's career; suggests specifically worded amendments to legislation and enters into alliances with other lobby groups to affect policy. Many of these lobbying efforts are addressed to protecting the self-interest of Catholic institutions or highly salient Catholic moral issues such as abortion and the protection of marriage. But the USCC has also widely engaged in debates on foreign policy, immigration, penal law, foreign aid and welfare and health care reforms To justify episcopal support for their middle-level yet often quite specific policy advocacy, the USCC lobbyists need to show close connections to anthropological presuppositions of social Catholicism. Outside observers of Washington lobby groups give the USCC relatively high marks for its serious research, access, impact and effectiveness, at least among American religious lobbies[35].

Twenty-eight of the separate state units maintain a State Catholic Conference, serving the conference of bishops for that state, which also lobbies state legislatures and the amending of bills on education, health, welfare and penal policy. In Maine and Maryland the State Catholic Conferences drafted the welfare reform bills which were adopted by the state legislatures.

The large national networks of Catholic social institutions (schools, hospitals, Charities) wield considerable clout during debates about public

---

35. The lobbying efforts of the U.S. Catholic Conference are treated in T.S. REESE, *A Flock of Shepherds. The National Conference of Catholic Bishops*, Kansas City, MO, Sheed and Ward, 1992. An outside look at the effectiveness of the Conference's lobbying efforts can be found in A. HERTZKE, *Representing God in Washington. The Role of Religious Lobbies in the American Polity*, Knoxville, TN, University of Tennessee Press, 1988.

policy. Catholic schools represent the largest private school system in the country. Catholic hospitals similarly represent over ten percent of all hospitals. Catholic Charities, USA (with an annual budget of over 2.5 billion dollars) is the largest non-governmental dispenser of social welfare services in the United States. Each of these national networks of Catholic institutions has engaged, in the last decade or so, in serious on-going reflection on the Catholic identity of the institutions in a pluralistic setting of service. Their staffs, clienteles (70 percent of those served by Catholic Charities are non-Catholic) and funding sources are quite pluralistic. Each, but especially Catholic Charities USA, has tended to link its Catholic identity rather closely to the Catholic tradition of social thought as it touches issues of service, the common good, pluralism, human dignity. Catholic Charities USA, arguably, has wielded a seminal policy voice on the issue of welfare reform. In a recent book on social Catholicism and public policy in the United States, focused on the welfare reform debates, Thomas Massaro shows how the anthropology of social Catholicism gets translated into middle-level policy axioms by the USCC, State Catholic Conferences and, especially, Catholic Charities USA[36]. Similar studies would show much the same for the Catholic engagement on issues of immigration reform and housing and health care.

Other groups, such as diocesan peace and justice offices, autonomous organisations such as Pax Christi, Network (an autonomous Catholic lobbying group, founded by religious sisters for the issues of the poor), The Catholic League for Civil Rights also enter this institutional mix as social carriers of social Catholicism. I remember clearly during the debates among the bishops which led up to their adoption of their pastoral on peace, how Pax Christi members, meeting in a group, carefully monitored the advance text and pressed the bishops, in some cases with success, for emendations in the text more favourable to their pacifist stands. Again, we see in this example ways in which unofficial social Catholicism and more official forms mesh. As another example, the Los Angeles archdiocese's peace and justice commission played a key role in construing a public debate/discussion with the President of the World Bank about the Jubilee Justice Debt relief program for the poorest debtor nations.

The four major national networks of Church-based community organising groups (all four of Catholic origin) work to empower local citizens

---

36. T. MASARRO, *Catholic Social Teaching and United States Welfare Reform*, Collegeville, MN, Liturgical Press, 1998.

to hold their elected officials accountable for the deliverance of social services (e.g., garbage collection), police protection, public safety and democratic participative access. Most of the Church-based national community-organising networks (despite their inter-denominational and inter-faith constituencies) appeal to elements of social Catholicism, human dignity, subsidiarity and local control, the common good, to make their case in public. While mainly local in scope, in places the Church-based community organising groups have effectively moved state or municipal governments to enact living-wage statutes, reform access to low-cost housing or enable charter-schools under parental control[37].

In sum, something of the institutional clout of Catholicism which Thomasset talks about, when wedded to a clear commitment to the tenets of social Catholicism, can serve as effective vehicles – with allies – to turn Catholic social thought into the search for middle-axioms which drive social policy. They have the legitimate institutional interest and expertise to gain voice to public discussions about health, welfare, family policy and immigration.

III. CATHOLIC SOCIAL THOUGHT IN DIALOGUE WITH CONTEMPORARY THOUGHT

A final goal of a symposium such as this one is to evince the relative superiority – in some aspects and without, God help us, any triumphalism – of social Catholicism to other competing modes of thought and *praxis*. In what has already been a longer essay than I initially anticipated, I will be more evocative (and, perhaps, controversial by being so) than discursive in offering brief comments on three concepts which call for more such dialogue and development: 1) Catholic personalism; 2) exclusionary norms which set the rules for public discourse as necessarily neutral as to any determinative conception of the good and also, necessarily, secular; and 3) the concept of the common good.

Over time, our public discourse in the liberal democracies has come increasingly to rest on an expansive and un-nuanced account of personal autonomy which often de-couples rights and responsibilities or denies any shared or public goods. The Catholic insistence on a communitarian or solidaristic content ingredient in the very notion of the person helps to correct the imbalance in the increasing "possessive individualism" of

---

37. I treat of one national church-based community organizing group in my essay, *Under the Cross and the Flag. Reflections on Discipleship and Citizenship in America*, in *America* 174 (May 11, 1996), no. 16, 6-14.

modern market economies, driven by a reductionist notion of rational choice theory (on which see Zamagni's essay in this collection). This one-sided emphasis on personal autonomy almost always lets choice trump over commitment. It is inherently tradition eroding. Moreover, an atomistic and individualistic notion of rational choice theory, perhaps inadequate to explain even the markets which served as its original focus, has moved aggressively into the arenas of jurisprudence, social policy and as an explanatory theory for understanding the social sciences.

By contrast, I do not think it is chance that the most forceful exponents of a more communitarian understanding of the self among contemporary political philosophers have included the prominent Catholic voices of Alasdair MacIntyre and Charles Taylor[38]. Social Catholicism has something unique and definite to offer to contemporary liberalism to help it move into a more communitarian set of correctives for its notion of a dis-embedded, autonomous self. It needs to press this issue in dialogue precisely because the policy implications of a one-sided sense of personal autonomy may be eroding any robust set of community in modern society[39].

A set of political philosophers, especially in the Anglo-Saxon world, notably Richard Rorty, John Rawls and Ronald Dworkin, have been promulgating norms of "public reason" which demand that this be *totally* secular, construed entirely in procedural terms and divorced from any substantive sense of the good or of human flourishing[40]. It strikes me that this notion of public reason, put forth by the "procedural liberals", stacks the deck against those who would speak from their comprehensive doctrines, constraining them before they speak with the condition that their arguments should be "reasonable" (i.e., construed according to the Rawlsian or some equivalent method). The opponents of this putatively "neutral" secular reasoning in public are correct, it seems to me, in seeing that it is neither quite as neutral nor as purely procedural as it claims. The neutralists smuggle in their highly particular conception of the good of unencumbered agents, privileging choice over commitments or tradition[41].

---

38. C. TAYLOR, *Sources of the Self. The Making of Modern Identity*, Cambridge, MA, Harvard University Press, 1989.
39. This is the complaint lodged by R.N. BELLAH e.a., in their study of expressive individualism in America, *Habits of the Heart. Individualism and Commitment in American Life*, Berkeley, CA, University of California Press, 1985.
40. Cf. R. DWORKIN, *A Matter of Principle*, Cambridge, MA, Harvard University Press, 1985.
41. M. SANDEL, *Liberalism and the Limits of Justice*, New York, NY, Cambridge University Press, 1998.

Social Catholicism should make common cause with adherents of other religious groups and with those many if not legion liberals who think that a genuine deliberative democracy should not impose gag rules on voices in public. Nor should it dictate in advance what kind of reorientation non-public reasons might be permitted to effect on "public" (i.e., explicitly secular) reason and the content of justice. Many of the now "secular" concepts of the West, after all, came originally from a religious provenance. Even today some people have been evoking some notion of "societal forgiveness" – whose origin is undoubtedly religious – as a "secular" concept for the healthy or good society. If Rawls's rules for exclusively secular reason in public obtained, such a transfer from particular religious discourse to a more general secular usage would never be warranted–perhaps with some real social loss. Just because "the preferential option for the poor" is ineradicably religious does not preclude its being urged in policy discussion, nor its adoption (perhaps for secular resonances) by those who do not share the biblical source.

Clearly, Catholic social thought should be well poised to claim the right of religious language to a legitimate access to open public discourse. The Vatican II document on religious liberty insisted that it belongs to the very notion of religious freedom that religious bodies should be able to expound policy proposals *in public* which show the implications of their beliefs for social action and policy. It is possible, as Jose Casanova has argued, for there to be a *public religion* (which follows the rules of a deliberative democracy and helps to anchor the institutions of civil society) in the modern world[42]. Even many liberals see the moves of the procedural liberals to ban all religious discourse from the public arena as a betrayal of the deepest liberal principles, related to freedom of speech. People should speak in public deliberations from their deepest motives and insights. Naturally, in order to persuade, they need to translate their religious concepts into terms which are meaningful and intelligible (which is not the same as *per se* persuasive). But they do not need, as the procedural liberals are increasingly insisting, to put gag rules on their biblical metaphors or to excise what evangelicals in America–facing this stricture–refer to as "Christianese". If all reason is tradition-dependent, then religious thinkers – so long as they construe an ideal of true reason which remains, at least procedurally, public and open to debate and genuinely intends to reach beyond the circle of

---

42. J. CASANOVA, *Public Religions in the Modern World*, Chicago, IL, University of Chicago Press, 1994.

fellow believers–need not and should not abandon their tradition as the very price of public discourse.

The retrieval of the concept of the common good in contemporary society (of which Perret speaks in his essay) is more fraught with peril than Catholics usually acknowledge. The common good may be interpreted as those societal and economic conditions which a) guarantee access to any goods which are, as such, public goods; b) enable true social participation in the goods of society; and c) establish the possibility for human (at least minimal) flourishing both as individuals and in one's own fated or chosen groups. The common good is seen as an ensemble of enabling conditions for the societal flourishing of human potential. But our contemporaries are often wary of appeals to the common good either because the definition of public goods is always contested and contestable; or because power is unequal in society so that alleged "common good" arrangements are, often, class-privileged institutional settings; or pluralism and freedom are viewed as values in themselves. Jane Mansbridge speaks to these dangers inherent in the concept of a common good:

> The public good is a dangerous concept. Asking people to act in the public good and not in their self-interest asks them to leave a terrain in which their everyday experience gives them relatively reliable messages on what is good for them and to enter a terrain in which, because uncertainty is far greater, authoritative others play a far greater role in suggesting what the public good should be. In the continuing conflict over meaning, two sources of influence have greater weight than they should: individuals and groups who appeal to the exclusivity and hatred that may be part of group loyalty and individuals and groups whose privileged social positions allow them to use force and the threat of sanction as well as unequal deliberative resources to promote their opinions and interests. Yet neither the dangers nor the necessity of ongoing contest over the very meaning of the words should lead us to discard appeals to the public good... In an extraordinarily large number of contexts, human beings need, in order to cooperate, some concept of a public good. We must learn to live with, even welcome, a concept that remains continually in contest[43].

Many contemporary liberals have been persuaded by Isaiah Berlin's argument in *Two Concepts of Liberty* that goods are plural, non-hierarchical and often in tragic conflict. They do not see how we can construe a notion of *a* or *the* common good. Goods are simply plural, perhaps radically antagonistic and cannot be aggregated, let alone conjoined in some larger sense of public purpose and good.

43. J. MANSBRIDGE, *On the Contested Nature of the Public Good*, in W.W. POWELL & E.S. CLEMENS (eds.), *Private Action and the Public Good*, New Haven, CT, Yale University Press, 1998, esp. p. 17.

It strikes me that some common ground can be found between the modern Catholic notion of the common good and some modern liberal virtue theorists who do accept, albeit in a thin way, some notion of human flourishing. Brian Stiltner's treatment of the common good insists that the common good "is not the province of any particular group [presumably he includes the Church] but of the whole political society"[44]. Catholic treatments of the common good typically vacillate between thicker notions of human flourishing and more modest insistence that it refers to the goods *we* (as common citizens) determine together as those which will serve as our public goods and institutional arrangements for the flourishing of a common citizenry. The common good looks to both some objectivity of the good and a concomitant societal consensus. A putative blueprint for the common good which seriously divides the society and ceases to be common may not continue to be a genuine *societal* good. Consensus remains a constitutive part of any notion of the common good. Hence, we may need to appeal to a thinner notion of a common good which reaches less to total human flourishing than, precisely and restrictively, to the virtues necessary to flourish in our common life together as citizens, whatever our own tradition's more thick account of human flourishing[45].

In any event, much work will be needed to re-appropriate in contemporary settings the Catholic notion of the common good. Catholics may have to confront a more robust pluralism of the good than they have hitherto entertained to engage those liberals who a) accept an *objective* sense of the good; b) refuse to always privilege the right over the good; and yet c) accept a radically plural, non-hierarchical and not easily harmonisable notion of the good. If, in the first two dialogues I suggest, I think the learning curve goes primarily from social Catholicism toward liberalism, in this last dialogue, I still think Catholics may have to learn more about a robust pluralism of the good from the liberals. Yet there are liberals who can join us in a discussion of a substantive common good. I have in mind, for example, Philip Selznick's idea of the common good as profoundly systemic, "not reducible to individual interests or attributes yet testable by its contribution to personal well-being":

---

44. STILTNER, *Religion and the Common Good* (n. 22), p. 75. GALSTON, *Liberal Purposes* (n. 33) is a major exponent of virtue theory among the liberal thinkers.

45. M. WALZER, *Thick and Thin. Moral Argument at Home and Abroad* (Loyola Lecture Series in Political Analysis), Notre Dame, IN, University of Notre Dame Press, 1994 argues that we need to use thinner notions of the good when we are dealing with pluralistic attempts to achieve consensus and cooperation. Just how thin they have to be remains still a matter of debate.

> The common good is served…by institutions that provide collective goods, such as education or public safety. The strength or weakness of these institutions is a communal attribute, not an individual one. Furthermore, it is not necessarily in every individual's interest to support such institutions. They may be better off, as individuals, if they can avoid paying taxes for school or other services they do not use but which are important for society as a whole.
>
> Similarly, a major collective good is social integration. When social integration is measured, the measure will take account, at least indirectly, of individual attitudes, behaviours, opportunities and affiliations. And a connection is likely between personal and social integration. People can live more coherent lives and have more coherent personalities when they belong to coherent social worlds[46].

Catholics may need to learn from liberals a greater hermeneutic of suspicion about misuses of appeals to the common good, a deeper appreciation of the perduring, legitimate and conflicting pluralism about the nature of the good in modern societies, a better recognition that the pursuit of the common good is not a panacea. Catholics may also need to add a crucial word to their lexicon when discussing the common good, one quite unusual in Catholic discourse: interest (self and group interests). Although the common good may not, as Selznick notes, be in the self-interest of all individuals, any appeal to the common good, unless it be hopelessly moralistic and abstract, must take the legitimate role of self-interest into account. Catholic social thought typically remains overly sanguine that, at the end of the day, doctrines and conflicts (and goods) can be harmonised. But in reality opinion is divided and these divisions will show up in conflicts over moral, religious and political issues. No theory can eliminate the conflictual elements from life. Nor should Catholic proponents of a common good expect to do so. Those who urge a commitment to the common good merely do not despair, in advance, of the possibilities (as Mansbridge urges) of achieving some real, if limited, consensus about what we will consider public goods and which goods (and institutional arrangements) we will pursue in common as fellow citizens. The language evokes consensus on some issues and institutions and operates as a bridging between self-interest and the interests of others (what Alexis de Tocqueville once referred to as "self-interest rightly understood", i.e. a marriage of my interests with more common ones.) At the end of the day, I do not think the Catholic notion of a common good can be much more robust than this. Stiltner helps us see, at any rate, the issues we may need to address, with liberals and others, if we want to talk about a common good:

46. SELZNICK, *The Moral Commonwealth* (n. 33), p. 422.

Different interpretations perdure, so different people can mean quite different things in appealing to the common good. It matters greatly to know whether an appeal to the common good is an appeal to the good of every member of society, including oneself, or to a social good that transcends and supersedes individuals' goods. It matters whether each sub-community within a society has its own common good and whether these can conflict with the common good of the whole society – and, if so, how the conflicts can be settled. It matters whether a democratic society can have a common good only in a procedural sense, by making the political process open to all on an equal basis, or whether it can share a substantive common good wherein citizens experience unity around shared moral, or even religious, values[47].

Jesuit Residence   John A. COLEMAN, S.J.
Los Angeles, CA

---

47. STILTNER, *Religion and the Common Good* (n. 22), p. 180. I treat of the question of the common good at greater length in my, as yet unpublished paper, *Pluralism and the Retrieval of a Catholic Sense of the Common Good* presented to the *Commonweal* magazine colloquium on "American Catholics and the Public Square", New York City, May 12-14, 2000.

LIST OF CONTRIBUTORS

Simona Beretta, studied at Catholic University of Milano and London School of Economics and Political Science. Associate Professor of Monetary Economics and of International Economic Institutions at the Faculty of Political Science, CU Milan since 1991. Recent publication: (with Mario Maggione & Lanfranco Senn) *"Settimo, non rubare" nel commercio internazionale* in *Communio,* No.157, gen-feb 1998; (co-author Carlo Beretta) *Footpaths in Trade Theory. Standard Tools of Analysis and Results from General Equilibrium Theory,* ISEIS, April 1998.

Jonathan Boswell, modern historian and political economist, earlier work in industry, politics, business schools. Senior Research Associate, Von Hügel Institute. John Fisher Scholar in Catholic Social Thought 1998-1999. Publications include *Community and the Economy* 1990/94; (with J. Peters) *Capitalism in Contention, Business Leaders and Political Economy in Modern Britain* 1997; and writings on CathST.

Luigino Bruni, post-doctoral researcher at University of Padua on 'Economic Analysis of Interpersonal Relations'. Also currently working on Economy of Communion of the International Focolare movement. Academic work and publications related to history of economic thought, Paretian economics, theory of choice, economics and ethics.

Alois Joh. Buch, professor of Moral Theology at Lantershofen (major seminary, diocese of Trier). Director of Clementia Foundation, Düsseldorf. Editor-in-Chief, *Zeitschrift für Medizinische Ethik.* Interests include business ethics, bio-ethics, critical theory. Recent articles on "conscience" and on *Values in Modern Societies* (forthcoming).

Jean-Yves Calvez, Jesuit, philosopher, social ethicist and theologian at the Centre Sèvres, Paris; leading international authority on CathST. Long succession of books from *La pensée de Karl Marx,* to (with Perrin) *The Church and Social Justice,* 1959 (Engl. trans. 1961), to recent works on ecology, work, socialisms and Marxism; and (1999) *Les silences de la doctrine sociale catholique.*

Julie Clague, lecturer in Roman Catholic Theology, Glasgow University. First degree in Chemistry. Postgraduate studies in theology, University of London. Currently completing a doctorate on Catholic moral theology in the twentieth-century at Cambridge University. Publications include articles on Evangelium vitae; Veritatis splendor; and "The human genome project".

John A. Coleman, Jesuit; Casassa Professor of Social Values at Loyola Marymount University, Los Angeles, USA. Sociologist, social ethicist and expert on Catholic social thought. Author of *The Evolution of Dutch Catholicism 1958-74*; *Development of Church Social Teaching* (1986); (ed.) (1991) *One Hundred Years of Catholic Social Thought: Celebration and Challenge* (including his own important article "Neither liberal nor socialist: the originality of Catholic social thought"); *Under the Cross and the Flag. Reflections on Discipleship and Citizenship in America* (1996); *Pluralism and the Retrieval of a Catholic Sence of the Common Good* (2000).

Chantal Delsol, professor of Political Philosophy, University of Marne-la-Vallée. Books include *Le pouvoir occidentale,*1985; *L'État subsidiaire, ingérance et non-ingérance,*1992; *Le souci contemporain,* 1996. Currently writing book on hope in modern society.

Donal Dorr, author of *Option for the Poor. 100 Years of Vatican Social Teaching*, 1991; and further publications in areas of spirituality and social teaching. Currently developing networks for Christian responsibility and action, particularly vis-à-vis forms of social exclusion and deprivation.

Staf Hellemans, professor of Sociology of Religion, Catholic University, Utrecht. Has researched history of Catholic and socialist sub-cultures in Europe. Currently working on a theory of religious (particularly Catholic) modernisation. Publications include *Strijd om de Moderniteit*, 1990; (jointly) *Beyond the European Left* 1990; *Nieuwe sociale bewegingen in België 1965-1995*, 1995, and other writings on these issues.

Linda Hogan, lecturer in Gender, Ethics and Religion, University of Leeds. Recent publications, *From Women's Experience to Feminist Theology*, 1995; *Christian Perspectives on Development Issues: Human Rights*, 1998; forthcoming: *Confronting the Truth. Conscience in the Catholic Tradition*. Research: cross-cultural engagement and the ethics of difference.

Walter Lesch, studied in Münster, Fribourg, Jerusalem, Tübingen. At University of Fribourg worked on theological issues. Currently professor in social ethics at Université Catholique de Louvain, lecturing in the Faculty of Theology and at the Institut Supérieur de Philosophie. Research interests: foundations of moral philosophy and theology; bioethics; media ethics. Publications: (with A. Bandolfo) (eds) *Theologische Ethik in Diskurs. Eine Einführung,* 1995, and other writings on these issues.

Frank McHugh, priest, ethicist, political economist. Director of Von Hügel Institute. University and seminary teaching in sociology, Marxist studies, Christian and social thought. Publications include *Ethics. Keyguide to Information Sources*, 1988; *Things Old and New. Catholic Social Teaching Revisited*, 1992; (ed) *Financial Decision-Making and Moral Responsibility*, 1996. Articles on financial ethics, debt, social exclusion, aspects of CathST.

Bernard Perret, in charge of policies evaluation at the Ministry of Equipment, Paris. Social economist. Comité de Redaction, *Ésprit,* previously on *La Croix.* Publications include *Les nouvelles frontières de l'argent,* 1999; & (jointly) *L'économie contre la société,* 1993; *L'avenir du travail,* 1995; *Vers un nouveau contrat social,* 1996.

Alain Thomasset, Jesuit, theologian, ethicist. Teaches in Centre Sèvres, Paris and member of Centre de Recherche et de l'Action, Paris. Published *Paul Ricœur. Une Poétique de la Morale,* 1995. Currently working on cultural analysis of (Christian or secular) institutions. Joint editor, *Projet.*

Jef Van Gerwen, Jesuit, professor at the University of Antwerp, where he teaches Social and Religious Ethics, Business Ethics, Ecological Ethics. Recent research in political issues and financial ethics. Present research: a project on the relationship between ethics and tragedy. Recent publications: (with J. Sweeney) *More Europe? A Critical Christian Enquiry into the Process of European Integration,* 1997; (with L. Van Liedekerke & D. Cassiman) *Explorations in Financial Ethics,* 2000.

Johan Verstraeten, Professor of Theology, KU Leuven. Director of the Centre for Catholic Social Thought. Chairman of the board of directors of the European Ethics Network. Teaches business ethics, peace ethics, engineering ethics, Catholic social thought. Research and writing on professional ethics, Catholic social thought, issues of narrative and imagination in Christian ethics. Recent publications: (with G. de Stexhe) (eds.) *Matter of Breath. Foundations for Professional Ethics,* 2000; (ed.) *Business Ethics. Broadening the Perspectives,* 2000.

Stefano Zamagni, Professor of Economics and Chairman, Department of Economics, University of Bologna. Executive Committee, International Economic Association. Member of Pontifical Council for Justice and Peace. Recent publications include *The Economics of Altruism,* 1995; *Living the Global Society,* 1997; *Non-Profit as Civil Economy,* 1998. Current research on the economics of reciprocity, economics and ethics, the economics of the welfare state.

INDEX OF NAMES

The asterisk refers to footnotes.

INDEX OF SUBJECTS

BIBLIOTHECA EPHEMERIDUM THEOLOGICARUM LOVANIENSIUM

SERIES I

* = Out of print

*1. *Miscellanea dogmatica in honorem Eximii Domini J. Bittremieux*, 1947.
*2-3. *Miscellanea moralia in honorem Eximii Domini A. Janssen*, 1948.
*4. G. Philips, *La grâce des justes de l'Ancien Testament*, 1948.
*5. G. Philips, *De ratione instituendi tractatum de gratia nostrae sanctificationis*, 1953.
6-7. *Recueil Lucien Cerfaux. Études d'exégèse et d'histoire religieuse*, 1954. 504 et 577 p. FB 1000 par tome. Cf. *infra*, n°s 18 et 71 (t. III).
8. G. Thils, *Histoire doctrinale du mouvement œcuménique*, 1955. Nouvelle édition, 1963. 338 p. FB 135.
*9. *Études sur l'Immaculée Conception*, 1955.
*10. J.A. O'Donohoe, *Tridentine Seminary Legislation*, 1957.
*11. G. Thils, *Orientations de la théologie*, 1958.
*12-13. J. Coppens, A. Descamps, É. Massaux (ed.), *Sacra Pagina. Miscellanea Biblica Congressus Internationalis Catholici de Re Biblica*, 1959.
*14. *Adrien VI, le premier Pape de la contre-réforme*, 1959.
*15. F. Claeys Bouuaert, *Les déclarations et serments imposés par la loi civile aux membres du clergé belge sous le Directoire (1795-1801)*, 1960.
*16. G. Thils, *La «Théologie œcuménique». Notion-Formes-Démarches*, 1960.
17. G. Thils, *Primauté pontificale et prérogatives épiscopales. «Potestas ordinaria» au Concile du Vatican*, 1961. 103 p. FB 50.
*18. *Recueil Lucien Cerfaux*, t. III, 1962. Cf. *infra*, n° 71.
*19. *Foi et réflexion philosophique. Mélanges F. Grégoire*, 1961.
*20. *Mélanges G. Ryckmans*, 1963.
21. G. Thils, *L'infaillibilité du peuple chrétien «in credendo»*, 1963. 67 p. FB 50.
*22. J. Férin & L. Janssens, *Progestogènes et morale conjugale*, 1963.
*23. *Collectanea Moralia in honorem Eximii Domini A. Janssen*, 1964.
24. H. Cazelles (ed.), *De Mari à Qumrân. L'Ancien Testament. Son milieu. Ses écrits. Ses relectures juives* (Hommage J. Coppens, I), 1969. 158*-370 p. FB 900.
*25. I. de la Potterie (ed.), *De Jésus aux évangiles. Tradition et rédaction dans les évangiles synoptiques* (Hommage J. Coppens, II), 1967.
26. G. Thils & R.E. Brown (ed.), *Exégèse et théologie* (Hommage J. Coppens, III), 1968. 328 p. FB 700.
27. J. Coppens (ed.), *Ecclesia a Spiritu sancto edocta. Hommage à Mgr G. Philips*, 1970. 640 p. FB 1000.
28. J. Coppens (ed.), *Sacerdoce et célibat. Études historiques et théologiques*, 1971. 740 p. FB 700.

29. M. DIDIER (ed.), *L'évangile selon Matthieu. Rédaction et théologie*, 1972. 432 p. FB 1000.
*30. J. KEMPENEERS, *Le Cardinal van Roey en son temps*, 1971.

SERIES II

31. F. NEIRYNCK, *Duality in Mark. Contributions to the Study of the Markan Redaction*, 1972. Revised edition with Supplementary Notes, 1988. 252 p. FB 1200.
32. F. NEIRYNCK (ed.), *L'évangile de Luc. Problèmes littéraires et théologiques*, 1973. *L'évangile de Luc – The Gospel of Luke.* Revised and enlarged edition, 1989. x-590 p. FB 2200.
33. C. BREKELMANS (ed.), *Questions disputées d'Ancien Testament. Méthode et théologie*, 1974. *Continuing Questions in Old Testament Method and Theology.* Revised and enlarged edition by M. VERVENNE, 1989. 245 p. FB 1200.
34. M. SABBE (ed.), *L'évangile selon Marc. Tradition et rédaction*, 1974. Nouvelle édition augmentée, 1988. 601 p. FB 2400.
35. B. WILLAERT (ed.), *Philosophie de la religion – Godsdienstfilosofie. Miscellanea Albert Dondeyne*, 1974. Nouvelle édition, 1987. 458 p. FB 1600.
36. G. PHILIPS, *L'union personnelle avec le Dieu vivant. Essai sur l'origine et le sens de la grâce créée*, 1974. Édition révisée, 1989. 299 p. FB 1000.
37. F. NEIRYNCK, in collaboration with T. HANSEN and F. VAN SEGBROECK, *The Minor Agreements of Matthew and Luke against Mark with a Cumulative List*, 1974. 330 p. FB 900.
38. J. COPPENS, *Le messianisme et sa relève prophétique. Les anticipations vétérotestamentaires. Leur accomplissement en Jésus*, 1974. Édition révisée, 1989. XIII-265 p. FB 1000.
39. D. SENIOR, *The Passion Narrative according to Matthew. A Redactional Study*, 1975. New impression, 1982. 440 p. FB 1000.
40. J. DUPONT (ed.), *Jésus aux origines de la christologie*, 1975. Nouvelle édition augmentée, 1989. 458 p. FB 1500.
41. J. COPPENS (ed.), *La notion biblique de Dieu*, 1976. Réimpression, 1985. 519 p. FB 1600.
42. J. LINDEMANS & H. DEMEESTER (ed.), *Liber Amicorum Monseigneur W. Onclin*, 1976. XXII-396 p. FB 1000.
43. R.E. HOECKMAN (ed.), *Pluralisme et œcuménisme en recherches théologiques. Mélanges offerts au R.P. Dockx, O.P.*, 1976. 316 p. FB 1000.
44. M. DE JONGE (ed.), *L'évangile de Jean. Sources, rédaction, théologie*, 1977. Réimpression, 1987. 416 p. FB 1500.
45. E.J.M. VAN EIJL (ed.), *Facultas S. Theologiae Lovaniensis 1432-1797. Bijdragen tot haar geschiedenis. Contributions to its History. Contributions à son histoire*, 1977. 570 p. FB 1700.
46. M. DELCOR (ed.), *Qumrân. Sa piété, sa théologie et son milieu*, 1978. 432 p. FB 1700.
47. M. CAUDRON (ed.), *Faith and Society. Foi et société. Geloof en maatschappij. Acta Congressus Internationalis Theologici Lovaniensis 1976*, 1978. 304 p. FB 1150.

48. J. KREMER (ed.), *Les Actes des Apôtres. Traditions, rédaction, théologie,* 1979. 590 p. FB 1700.

49. F. NEIRYNCK, avec la collaboration de J. DELOBEL, T. SNOY, G. VAN BELLE, F. VAN SEGBROECK, *Jean et les Synoptiques. Examen critique de l'exégèse de M.-É. Boismard,* 1979. XII-428 p. FB 1000.

50. J. COPPENS, *La relève apocalyptique du messianisme royal. I. La royauté – Le règne – Le royaume de Dieu. Cadre de la relève apocalyptique,* 1979. 325 p. FB 1000.

51. M. GILBERT (ed.), *La Sagesse de l'Ancien Testament,* 1979. Nouvelle édition mise à jour, 1990. 455 p. FB 1500.

52. B. DEHANDSCHUTTER, *Martyrium Polycarpi. Een literair-kritische studie,* 1979. 296 p. FB 1000.

53. J. LAMBRECHT (ed.), *L'Apocalypse johannique et l'Apocalyptique dans le Nouveau Testament,* 1980. 458 p. FB 1400.

54. P.-M. BOGAERT (ed.), *Le livre de Jérémie. Le prophète et son milieu. Les oracles et leur transmission,* 1981. *Nouvelle édition mise à jour,* 1997. 448 p. FB 1800.

55. J. COPPENS, *La relève apocalyptique du messianisme royal. III. Le Fils de l'homme néotestamentaire.* Édition posthume par F. NEIRYNCK, 1981. XIV-192 p. FB 800.

56. J. VAN BAVEL & M. SCHRAMA (ed.), *Jansénius et le Jansénisme dans les Pays-Bas. Mélanges Lucien Ceyssens,* 1982. 247 p. FB 1000.

57. J.H. WALGRAVE, *Selected Writings – Thematische geschriften. Thomas Aquinas, J.H. Newman, Theologia Fundamentalis.* Edited by G. DE SCHRIJVER & J.J. KELLY, 1982. XLIII-425 p. FB 1000.

58. F. NEIRYNCK & F. VAN SEGBROECK, avec la collaboration de E. MANNING, *Ephemerides Theologicae Lovanienses 1924-1981. Tables générales. (Bibliotheca Ephemeridum Theologicarum Lovaniensium 1947-1981),* 1982. 400 p. FB 1600.

59. J. DELOBEL (ed.), *Logia. Les paroles de Jésus – The Sayings of Jesus. Mémorial Joseph Coppens,* 1982. 647 p. FB 2000.

60. F. NEIRYNCK, *Evangelica. Gospel Studies – Études d'évangile. Collected Essays.* Edited by F. VAN SEGBROECK, 1982. XIX-1036 p. FB 2000.

61. J. COPPENS, *La relève apocalyptique du messianisme royal. II. Le Fils d'homme vétéro- et intertestamentaire.* Édition posthume par J. LUST, 1983. XVII-272 p. FB 1000.

62. J.J. KELLY, *Baron Friedrich von Hügel's Philosophy of Religion,* 1983. 232 p. FB 1500.

63. G. DE SCHRIJVER, *Le merveilleux accord de l'homme et de Dieu. Étude de l'analogie de l'être chez Hans Urs von Balthasar,* 1983. 344 p. FB 1500.

64. J. GROOTAERS & J.A. SELLING, *The 1980 Synod of Bishops: «On the Role of the Family». An Exposition of the Event and an Analysis of its Texts.* Preface by Prof. emeritus L. JANSSENS, 1983. 375 p. FB 1500.

65. F. NEIRYNCK & F. VAN SEGBROECK, *New Testament Vocabulary. A Companion Volume to the Concordance,* 1984. XVI-494 p. FB 2000.

66. R.F. COLLINS, *Studies on the First Letter to the Thessalonians,* 1984. XI-415 p. FB 1500.

67. A. PLUMMER, *Conversations with Dr. Döllinger 1870-1890.* Edited with Introduction and Notes by R. BOUDENS, with the collaboration of L. KENIS, 1985. LIV-360 p. FB 1800.

68. N. LOHFINK (ed.), *Das Deuteronomium. Entstehung, Gestalt und Botschaft / Deuteronomy: Origin, Form and Message*, 1985. XI-382 p. FB 2000.
69. P.F. FRANSEN, *Hermeneutics of the Councils and Other Studies*. Collected by H.E. MERTENS & F. DE GRAEVE, 1985. 543 p. FB 1800.
70. J. DUPONT, *Études sur les Évangiles synoptiques*. Présentées par F. NEIRYNCK, 1985. 2 tomes, XXI-IX-1210 p. FB 2800.
71. *Recueil Lucien Cerfaux*, t. III, 1962. Nouvelle édition revue et complétée, 1985. LXXX-458 p. FB 1600.
72. J. GROOTAERS, *Primauté et collégialité. Le dossier de Gérard Philips sur la Nota Explicativa Praevia (Lumen gentium, Chap. III)*. Présenté avec introduction historique, annotations et annexes. Préface de G. THILS, 1986. 222 p. FB 1000.
73. A. VANHOYE (ed.), *L'apôtre Paul. Personnalité, style et conception du ministère*, 1986. XIII-470 p. FB 2600.
74. J. LUST (ed.), *Ezekiel and His Book. Textual and Literary Criticism and their Interrelation*, 1986. X-387 p. FB 2700.
75. É. MASSAUX, *Influence de l'Évangile de saint Matthieu sur la littérature chrétienne avant saint Irénée*. Réimpression anastatique présentée par F. NEIRYNCK. *Supplément: Bibliographie 1950-1985*, par B. DEHANDSCHUTTER, 1986. XXVII-850 p. FB 2500.
76. L. CEYSSENS & J.A.G. TANS, *Autour de l'Unigenitus. Recherches sur la genèse de la Constitution*, 1987. XXVI-845 p. FB 2500.
77. A. DESCAMPS, *Jésus et l'Église. Études d'exégèse et de théologie*. Préface de Mgr A. HOUSSIAU, 1987. XLV-641 p. FB 2500.
78. J. DUPLACY, *Études de critique textuelle du Nouveau Testament*. Présentées par J. DELOBEL, 1987. XXVII-431 p. FB 1800.
79. E.J.M. VAN EIJL (ed.), *L'image de C. Jansénius jusqu'à la fin du XVIIIe siècle*, 1987. 258 p. FB 1250.
80. E. BRITO, *La Création selon Schelling. Universum*, 1987. XXXV-646 p. FB 2980.
81. J. VERMEYLEN (ed.), *The Book of Isaiah – Le livre d'Isaïe. Les oracles et leurs relectures. Unité et complexité de l'ouvrage*, 1989. X-472 p. FB 2700.
82. G. VAN BELLE, *Johannine Bibliography 1966-1985. A Cumulative Bibliography on the Fourth Gospel*, 1988. XVII-563 p. FB 2700.
83. J.A. SELLING (ed.), *Personalist Morals. Essays in Honor of Professor Louis Janssens*, 1988. VIII-344 p. FB 1200.
84. M.-É. BOISMARD, *Moïse ou Jésus. Essai de christologie johannique*, 1988. XVI-241 p. FB 1000.
84A. M.-É. BOISMARD, *Moses or Jesus: An Essay in Johannine Christology*. Translated by B.T. VIVIANO, 1993, XVI-144 p. FB 1000.
85. J.A. DICK, *The Malines Conversations Revisited*, 1989. 278 p. FB 1500.
86. J.-M. SEVRIN (ed.), *The New Testament in Early Christianity – La réception des écrits néotestamentaires dans le christianisme primitif*, 1989. XVI-406 p. FB 2500.
87. R.F. COLLINS (ed.), *The Thessalonian Correspondence*, 1990. XV-546 p. FB 3000.
88. F. VAN SEGBROECK, *The Gospel of Luke. A Cumulative Bibliography 1973-1988*, 1989. 241 p. FB 1200.

89. G. THILS, *Primauté et infaillibilité du Pontife Romain à Vatican I et autres études d'ecclésiologie,* 1989. XI-422 p. FB 1850.
90. A. VERGOTE, *Explorations de l'espace théologique. Études de théologie et de philosophie de la religion,* 1990. XVI-709 p. FB 2000.
91. J.C. DE MOOR, *The Rise of Yahwism: The Roots of Israelite Monotheism,* 1990. *Revised and Enlarged Edition,* 1997. XV-445 p. FB 1400.
92. B. BRUNING, M. LAMBERIGTS & J. VAN HOUTEM (eds.), *Collectanea Augustiniana. Mélanges T.J. van Bavel,* 1990. 2 tomes, XXXVIII-VIII-1074 p. FB 3000.
93. A. DE HALLEUX, *Patrologie et œcuménisme. Recueil d'études,* 1990. XVI-887 p. FB 3000.
94. C. BREKELMANS & J. LUST (eds.), *Pentateuchal and Deuteronomistic Studies: Papers Read at the XIIIth IOSOT Congress Leuven 1989,* 1990. 307 p. FB 1500.
95. D.L. DUNGAN (ed.), *The Interrelations of the Gospels. A Symposium Led by M.-É. Boismard – W.R. Farmer – F. Neirynck, Jerusalem 1984,* 1990. XXXI-672 p. FB 3000.
96. G.D. KILPATRICK, *The Principles and Practice of New Testament Textual Criticism. Collected Essays.* Edited by J.K. ELLIOTT, 1990. XXXVIII-489 p. FB 3000.
97. G. ALBERIGO (ed.), *Christian Unity. The Council of Ferrara-Florence: 1438/39 – 1989,* 1991. X-681 p. FB 3000.
98. M. SABBE, *Studia Neotestamentica. Collected Essays,* 1991. XVI-573 p. FB 2000.
99. F. NEIRYNCK, *Evangelica II: 1982-1991. Collected Essays.* Edited by F. VAN SEGBROECK, 1991. XIX-874 p. FB 2800.
100. F. VAN SEGBROECK, C.M. TUCKETT, G. VAN BELLE & J. VERHEYDEN (eds.), *The Four Gospels 1992. Festschrift Frans Neirynck,* 1992. 3 volumes, XVII-X-X-2668 p. FB 5000.

SERIES III

101. A. DENAUX (ed.), *John and the Synoptics,* 1992. XXII-696 p. FB 3000.
102. F. NEIRYNCK, J. VERHEYDEN, F. VAN SEGBROECK, G. VAN OYEN & R. CORSTJENS, *The Gospel of Mark. A Cumulative Bibliography: 1950-1990,* 1992. XII-717 p. FB 2700.
103. M. SIMON, *Un catéchisme universel pour l'Église catholique. Du Concile de Trente à nos jours,* 1992. XIV-461 p. FB 2200.
104. L. CEYSSENS, *Le sort de la bulle Unigenitus. Recueil d'études offert à Lucien Ceyssens à l'occasion de son 90e anniversaire.* Présenté par M. LAMBERIGTS, 1992. XXVI-641 p. FB 2000.
105. R.J. DALY (ed.), *Origeniana Quinta. Papers of the 5th International Origen Congress, Boston College, 14-18 August 1989,* 1992. XVII-635 p. FB 2700.
106. A.S. VAN DER WOUDE (ed.), *The Book of Daniel in the Light of New Findings,* 1993. XVIII-574 p. FB 3000.
107. J. FAMERÉE, *L'ecclésiologie d'Yves Congar avant Vatican II: Histoire et Église. Analyse et reprise critique,* 1992. 497 p. FB 2600.

108. C. BEGG, *Josephus' Account of the Early Divided Monarchy (AJ 8, 212-420). Rewriting the Bible*, 1993. IX-377 p. FB 2400.
109. J. BULCKENS & H. LOMBAERTS (eds.), *L'enseignement de la religion catholique à l'école secondaire. Enjeux pour la nouvelle Europe*, 1993. XII-264 p. FB 1250.
110. C. FOCANT (ed.), *The Synoptic Gospels. Source Criticism and the New Literary Criticism*, 1993. XXXIX-670 p. FB 3000.
111. M. LAMBERIGTS (ed.), avec la collaboration de L. KENIS, *L'augustinisme à l'ancienne Faculté de théologie de Louvain*, 1994. VII-455 p. FB 2400.
112. R. BIERINGER & J. LAMBRECHT, *Studies on 2 Corinthians*, 1994. XX-632 p. FB 3000.
113. E. BRITO, *La pneumatologie de Schleiermacher*, 1994. XII-649 p. FB 3000.
114. W.A.M. BEUKEN (ed.), *The Book of Job*, 1994. X-462 p. FB 2400.
115. J. LAMBRECHT, *Pauline Studies: Collected Essays*, 1994. XIV-465 p. FB 2500.
116. G. VAN BELLE, *The Signs Source in the Fourth Gospel: Historical Survey and Critical Evaluation of the Semeia Hypothesis*, 1994. XIV-503 p. FB 2500.
117. M. LAMBERIGTS & P. VAN DEUN (eds.), *Martyrium in Multidisciplinary Perspective. Memorial L. Reekmans*, 1995. X-435 p. FB 3000.
118. G. DORIVAL & A. LE BOULLUEC (eds.), *Origeniana Sexta. Origène et la Bible/Origen and the Bible. Actes du Colloquium Origenianum Sextum, Chantilly, 30 août – 3 septembre 1993*, 1995. XII-865 p. FB 3900.
119. É. GAZIAUX, *Morale de la foi et morale autonome. Confrontation entre P. Delhaye et J. Fuchs*, 1995. XXII-545 p. FB 2700.
120. T.A. SALZMAN, *Deontology and Teleology: An Investigation of the Normative Debate in Roman Catholic Moral Theology*, 1995. XVII-555 p. FB 2700.
121. G.R. EVANS & M. GOURGUES (eds.), *Communion et Réunion. Mélanges Jean-Marie Roger Tillard*, 1995. XI-431 p. FB 2400.
122. H.T. FLEDDERMANN, *Mark and Q: A Study of the Overlap Texts*. With an *Assessment* by F. NEIRYNCK, 1995. XI-307 p. FB 1800.
123. R. BOUDENS, *Two Cardinals: John Henry Newman, Désiré-Joseph Mercier*. Edited by L. GEVERS with the collaboration of B. DOYLE, 1995. 362 p. FB 1800.
124. A. THOMASSET, *Paul Ricœur. Une poétique de la morale. Aux fondements d'une éthique herméneutique et narrative dans une perspective chrétienne*, 1996. XVI-706 p. FB 3000.
125. R. BIERINGER (ed.), *The Corinthian Correspondence*, 1996. XXVII-793 p. FB 2400.
126. M. VERVENNE (ed.), *Studies in the Book of Exodus: Redaction – Reception – Interpretation*, 1996. XI-660 p. FB 2400.
127. A. VANNESTE, *Nature et grâce dans la théologie occidentale. Dialogue avec H. de Lubac*, 1996. 312 p. FB 1800.
128. A. CURTIS & T. RÖMER (eds.), *The Book of Jeremiah and its Reception – Le livre de Jérémie et sa réception*, 1997. 332 p. FB 2400.
129. E. LANNE, *Tradition et Communion des Églises. Recueil d'études*, 1997. XXV-703 p. FB 3000.

130. A. DENAUX & J.A. DICK (eds.), *From Malines to ARCIC. The Malines Conversations Commemorated*, 1997. IX-317 p. FB 1800.
131. C.M. TUCKETT (ed.), *The Scriptures in the Gospels*, 1997. XXIV-721 p. FB 2400.
132. J. VAN RUITEN & M. VERVENNE (eds.), *Studies in the Book of Isaiah. Festschrift Willem A.M. Beuken*, 1997. XX-540 p. FB 3000.
133. M. VERVENNE & J. LUST (eds.), *Deuteronomy and Deuteronomic Literature. Festschrift C.H.W. Brekelmans*, 1997. XI-637 p. FB 3000.
134. G. VAN BELLE (ed.), *Index Generalis ETL / BETL 1982-1997*, 1999. IX-337 p. FB 1600.
135. G. DE SCHRIJVER, *Liberation Theologies on Shifting Grounds. A Clash of Socio-Economic and Cultural Paradigms*, 1998. XI-453 p. FB 2100.
136. A. SCHOORS (ed.), *Qohelet in the Context of Wisdom*, 1998. XI-528 p. FB 2400.
137. W.A. BIENERT & U. KÜHNEWEG (eds.), *Origeniana Septima. Origenes in den Auseinandersetzungen des 4. Jahrhunderts*, 1999. XXV-848 p. FB 3800.
138. É. GAZIAUX, *L'autonomie en morale: au croisement de la philosophie et de la théologie*, 1998. XVI-739 p. FB 3000.
139. J. GROOTAERS, *Actes et acteurs à Vatican II*, 1998. XXIV-602 p. FB 3000.
140. F. NEIRYNCK, J. VERHEYDEN & R. CORSTJENS, *The Gospel of Matthew and the Sayings Source Q: A Cumulative Bibliography 1950-1995*, 1998. 2 vols., VII-1000-420* p. FB 3800.
141. E. BRITO, *Heidegger et l'hymne du sacré*, 1999. XV-800 p. FB 3600.
142. J. VERHEYDEN (ed.), *The Unity of Luke-Acts*, 1999. XXV-828 p. FB 2400.
143. N. CALDUCH-BENAGES & J. VERMEYLEN (eds.), *Treasures of Wisdom. Studies in Ben Sira and the Book of Wisdom. Festschrift M. Gilbert*, 1999. XXVII-463 p. FB 3000.
144. J.-M. AUWERS & A. WÉNIN (eds.), *Lectures et relectures de la Bible. Festschrift P.-M. Bogaert*, 1999. XLII-482 p. FB 2400.
145. C. BEGG, *Josephus' Story of the Later Monarchy (AJ 9,1–10,185)*, 2000. X-650 p. FB 3000.
146. J.M. ASGEIRSSON, K. DE TROYER & M.W. MEYER (eds.), *From Quest to Q. Festschrift James M. Robinson*, 2000. XLIV-346 p. FB 2400.
147. T. RÖMER (ed.), *The Future of the Deuteronomistic History*, 2000. XII-265 p. FB 3000.
148. F.D. VANSINA, *Paul Ricœur: Bibliographie primaire et secondaire - Primary and Secondary Bibliography 1935-2000*, 2000. XXVI-544 p. FB 3000.
149. G.J. BROOKE & J.D. KAESTLI (eds.), *Narrativity in Biblical and Related Texts*, 2000. XXII-307 p. FB 3000.
150. F. NEIRYNCK, *Evangelica III: 1992-2000. Collected Essays*. Forthcoming.
151. B. DOYLE, *The Apocalypse of Isaiah Metaphorically Speaking. A Study of the Use, Function and Significance of Metaphors in Isaiah 24-27*, 2000. XII-453 p. FB 3000.
152. T. MERRIGAN & J. HAERS (eds.), *The Myriad Christ. Plurality and the Quest for Unity in Contemporary Christology*, 2000. XIV-593 p. FB 3000.
153. M. SIMON, *Le catéchisme de Jean-Paul II. Genèse et évaluation de son commentaire du Symbole des apôtres*, 2000. XVI-688 p. FB 3000.
154. J. VERMEYLEN, *La loi du plus fort. Histoire de la rédaction des récits davidiques de 1 Samuel 8 à 1 Rois 2*, 2000. XII-746 p.

155. A. WÉNIN, *Studies in the Book of Genesis. Literature, Redaction and History*. Forthcoming.
156. F. LEDEGANG, *Mysterium Ecclesiae. Images of the Church and its Members in Origen*. Forthcoming.
157. J.S. BOSWELL, F.P. McHUGH & J. VERSTRAETEN, *Catholic Social Thought: Twilight of Renaissance?*, 2000. XXII-307 p.

PRINTED ON PERMANENT PAPER • IMPRIME SUR PAPIER PERMANENT • GEDRUKT OP DUURZAAM PAPIER - ISO 9706

ORIENTALISTE, KLEIN DALENSTRAAT 42, B-3020 HERENT